The State And Social Welfare

The State and Social Welfare

The objectives of policy

Edited by Thomas and Dorothy Wilson

Routledge
Taylor & Francis Group

LONDON AND NEW YORK

First published 1991 by LONGMAN GROUP UK LIMITED

Published in the United States of America
by Longman Inc.

Published 2014 by Routledge
2 Park Square, Milton Park, Abingdon, Oxon OX14 4RN
711 Third Avenue, New York, NY 10017 USA

Routledge is an imprint of the Taylor & Francis Group, an informa business

ISBN: 978-1-315-84502-9 (eISBN)

© Taylor & Francis 1991

British Library Cataloguing in Publication Data
The state and social welfare: The objectives of policy.
 I. Wilson, Thomas II. Wilson, Dorothy
 361.60941
 ISBN 0–582–08513–6

Library of Congress Cataloging in Publication Data
The State and social welfare : the objectives of policy / edited by
 Thomas and Dorothy Wilson.
        p. cm.
 Chiefly papers presented at a workshop, held Jan. 1989, University
College, Oxford.
 Includes bibliographical references and index.
 ISBN 0–582–08513–6 (paper) : £14.99
 1. Social policy—Congresses. 2. Welfare state—Congresses.
3. Public welfare—Congresses. I. Wilson, Thomas, 1916–
II. Wilson, Dorothy.
 HV8.S73 1991
 361.6'1—dc20

Set in 9/10 Linotron Bembo

                                                                91–11335
                                                                CIP

Contents

Contributors

A.B. Atkinson, FBA, Professor of Economic Science and Statistics,
London School of Economics

Peter Barclay CBE, Chairman, Social Security Advisory Committee

Nicholas Barr, Reader in Economics, London School of Economics

Sir Charles Carter, FBA, Chairman, Policy Studies Institute

Frank Field, Labour Member of Parliament

Alastair McAuley, Professor of Economics, University of Essex

Steen Mangen, Lecturer in Social Policy and Administration, London
School of Economics

Sir Alan Peacock, FBA, FRSE, Director, David Hume Institute, Edinburgh

Raymond Plant, Professor of Politics, University of Southampton

Robert Pinker, Professor Emeritus of Social Work, London School
of Economics

Alan Ryan, FBA, Fellow of New College, Oxford, and Professor of Politics,
Princeton University

The Rt. Hon. Timothy Raison, Conservative Member of Parliament

Ann-Charlotte Ståhlberg, Professor, Swedish Institute for Social Research,
University of Stockholm

Dorothy Wilson MVO, formerly Lecturer in Social Administration,
University of Glasgow

Thomas Wilson, FBA, FRSE, Professor Emeritus of Political Economy,
University of Glasgow

Jack Wiseman, Professor Emeritus of Economics, University of York

Introduction

The purpose of this book is to review the issues raised by the state provision of social benefits in cash and in kind and, in particular, to examine the principles on which their provision may be deemed to rest. The cash benefits are those provided to pensioners, to the sick and the unemployed and to families, especially those with children. The benefits in kind are the health service, the personal social services, and the assistance given to poor families with the costs of housing. Much of what is said in general terms about these benefits in kind would also apply to education, which is not, however, taken as a case study. The book is concerned, that is to say, with those services that are commonly regarded in Britain as the central core of the 'welfare state'. That term is, of course, a colloquial one, long sanctioned by common usage but lacking in precision. Taken at face value and out of context, strange inferences might be drawn. Thus the term might be taken to imply that the state is the only source of 'welfare' or that the state's activities, even if not the sole source of welfare, do nevertheless always contribute to the well-being of its citizens. Even if such absurd interpretations are avoided, there is still plenty of scope for disagreement about what should be included. Thus if the medical services are brought in, can we logically exclude measures to prevent illness and to protect the public's health? Clean air and clean water as well as pills and hospital beds? Or, if the welfare services which provide for the unemployed are included, should we not also include measures to increase employment? Clearly there is no firmly delineated boundary, and what is in fact covered in an investigation of this kind must be substantially determined by practical feasibility. It should, nevertheless, be observed that the benefits in kind with which we shall be concerned are benefits provided to identifiable individuals and therefore differ from national defence against aggression, the preservation of law and order and much of the public expenditure on the environment. This difference is of practical importance because benefits such as those provided by the national health service can also be privately produced and sold through the market, and the choice of methods thus available opens up a lively topic for debate. Benefits in cash permit wider scope for the expression of individual preferences in expenditure but differ from normal market transactions in that there is no close correspondence between payments and what is received. Most people will have contributed in the past through social insurance contributions or taxation, or will do so in the future, but the benefits received need not depend at all closely upon contributions, even on an actuarial basis. For these are pay-as-you-go transfers, similar to the unilateral transfers made by private charity, but financed by contributions that are compulsorily levied by the state. Compulsion always requires explanation and defence, and these must be sought in the objectives of policy and the means required for their achievement.

What, then, is the purpose of this vast area of public activity which accounts for some three-fifths of public expenditure in Britain? What are these elaborate social services meant to achieve? By what criteria are they to be judged? By what authority have the objectives been adopted and the criteria applied? The answers to questions such as these will obviously reflect both differences in basic value judgements and differences in appraising the facts of any social situation. But the objectives effectively pursued may be of a less disinterested kind and may rather be those of different interest groups, each determined to better its own particular position with little regard for any conception of the common good. In so far as the outcome is determined by the interaction of these forces, it may not correspond to anything clearly envisaged or intended by any of those concerned and will, to this extent, be similar to the outcome of market activity. It has long been demonstrated that, in the case of the market, a reasonably coherent, although not necessarily an ideal, outcome will emerge, as though, in the figurative language of the eighteenth century, an 'invisible hand' were at work. Whether there is also an invisible hand which brings order when the play of competing interests is in the public sector is, of course, a different matter!

In the first chapter, the editors review the principal policy issues, analyse some of the responses made and offer suggestions about the scope for change. The question 'whose objectives?' must be asked as well as 'what objectives?' and 'interests' must be distinguished from 'ideas'. There is then a discussion of 'ideas' based on altruism and of 'ideas' reflecting a regard for fairness. Neither the welfare state nor the general rise in affluence caused by economic growth appear to have brought an end to 'poverty'. The various senses of that ambiguous term are examined, including the definitional link with inequality. The reasons for providing some benefits in kind (notably the health service) are then considered with social solidarity as well as cost-effectiveness as a declared objective. The chapter ends with an assessment of the scope for a better targeting of resources towards those in need, whether by means of a negative income tax or some less radical changes. This brings out the difficulties to be met when account has to be taken of different and sometimes conflicting social objectives.

The second part of the book takes up, in more detail, some of the questions of principle raised in Chapter 1. These are controversial issues and it is obviously desirable that different points of view should be presented. That of the first two authors – *Alan Peacock* and *Jack Wiseman* – can be broadly described as libertarian. Peacock, however, sets out not so much to urge the libertarian case as to explain how it differs from others, conveniently grouped as 'social market' and 'collectivist'. The conflict of opinion thus described is partly explained as a reflection of differences in value judgements which cannot, he believes, be usefully debated. Although the influence of 'ideas' in the shaping of policy is fully recognised, he also stresses the often decisive force of special 'interests'. It is this force, he suggests, which largely explains why, even in affluent societies where most people could make provision for their own needs, the welfare state has not withered away but has rather grown to vast dimensions and still continues to expand.

In the following chapter, Wiseman explains that the libertarian emphasis on personal freedom of choice is not based on some doubtful assumption of universal egoism. On the contrary the principal concern in his chapter is with 'caring', and the 'welfare state' is identified with the set of policies appropriate to a free society whose members want to have their caring sentiments translated into effective action. Thus his public choice approach leads to a theory of social contract that legitimises compulsion. There is no single uniquely efficient welfare state but only arrangements better or worse adapted to reflect the caring feelings of citizens in a particular situation.

It seems to be generally agreed that there should be a minimum income provided by the state to those who cannot, currently, look after themselves, but also much disagreement about the level to be provided and the conditions to be attached. As Peacock observes, libertarians could be expected to recommend a basic level of subsistence which would not change greatly over time. In Chapters 4 and 5 respectively, *Raymond Plant* and *Alan Ryan* would go much further and stress the social solidarity implied by 'citizenship'. Plant refuses to accept Hayek's contention that 'social justice' is a meaningless concept and maintains that all have a right, as citizens, to incomes sufficient to permit them to participate in the life of the society in which they live. 'Poverty' is defined as the inability to do so, and is further described as a lack of the 'positive freedom' needed to complement the 'negative freedom' with which the New Right is exclusively concerned. The old debate about the appropriate use of language has now been given a new edge. Behind the semantic debate, there is of course deep disagreement about the proper extent and scale of public policy.

Ryan, for his part, takes an approach that is broadly similar to Plant's but he directs particular attention to the question why some social benefits are provided in kind rather than in cash. He sympathises with the individualistic case against paternalistic interference by the state but suggests that, for certain goods, paternalism may be justified. The provision of these 'enabling' goods which go well beyond what would be needed for mere subsistence will ensure that everyone is better able to cope with modern social conditions. Thus a limited resort to paternalism may enhance and enlarge the scope for exercising, in a much wider field of activity, the negative freedom that means absence from constraint. Much objection has sometimes been taken to the 'minimalist' view that the welfare services are primarily concerned with protection against poverty, but 'poverty' can be interpreted in such a way as to suggest that the word 'minimalist' may not be altogether appropriate.

The third part of the book moves on to the practical implementation of policy. It begins with a chapter by *Charles Carter* in which he sets the economic context within which decisions have to be made. In the 1990s the claims on the gross national product will be heavy, even with a reasonable allowance for future growth. His statistics show that the welfare services – even if restricted to social security transfer payments together with the health service, the personal social services and education – account for much the larger part of public expenditure. When the remaining part of expenditure is examined in detail, it becomes apparent that there will be resistance to robbing other programmes in order to give a further boost to the welfare services. Even the 'peace dividend' is likely to be small. All governments of whatever complexion will be obliged to set firm limits to the growth of 'welfare' expenditure, and thus the conclusion is reached that the various claims to additional resources put forward on behalf of these different services are likely to be in sharp competition with one another.

The objective of securing a national minimum has long been a central aim in the provision of social benefits in Britain. How, from time to time, has the minimum been determined? This is the topic taken up and developed by *Tony Atkinson* in Chapter 7. He suggests that, in addition to the information given in official pronouncements, inferences about government intentions can be drawn from the choices actually made. He reviews these choices from 1908 onwards and shows how much ambiguity there has been in presenting the objectives to be pursued. This is attributable in part to a fudging of the issues raised by the need to balance different claims on resources, in part to differences in the degree of responsibility accepted by different governments for meeting a minimum considered to be appropriate and in part to the different approaches taken to the definition of the minimum – a bare subsistence level or one that would allow the beneficiaries to take part in the normal life of society. He draws attention to the importance of the methods by which real benefits have been raised over time and carries the discussion forward into the twenty-first century.

The next chapter (8) is a case study in relating the various complex features of pension schemes to possible social objectives. *Nicholas Barr* provides a historical review of state pensions in Britain and describes the present basic flat-rate pension and the State Earnings Related Pensions Scheme (SERPS) with each feature systematically related to the objectives it might be deemed to serve. In this process, the salient issues in pensions policy come under examination: the redistributive effects, the extent to which compulsory participation should be enforced; the place, if any, of actuarial principles; the respective merits from the point of view of the pensioner of funded and pay-as-you-go financing, and their possible respective effects on saving, investment and growth.

In the fourth section of the book, lessons are sought from the experience of some other European countries. *Steen Mangen* (9) offers a comparative study of objectives and policies in three EC countries – the Federal Republic of Germany, France, and Spain – written from the point of view of a political scientist with a detailed knowledge of European affairs. Although it is generally known in Britain that some benefits are provided at higher levels elsewhere in the EC, it may be less well appreciated that 'social solidarity' in these European contexts means joint action to preserve status, especially in retirement, rather than joint action to secure a national minimum. The importance of 'interests' as well as 'ideas' may be inferred.

What is the significance of these wide differences in social policy between different members of the European Community? It has not been suggested that the coming of a Single Market after 1992 would require uniformity – which may be thought reassuring in view of the complexity of the schemes and the appalling obstacles that would be encountered if uniformity were to be attempted. The fact remains that comparisons will be made and pressures for change stimulated – usually in an upward direction. Account must also be taken of the wide differences between countries in the rates of payroll tax, by which cash transfers are largely financed. These differences will already be reflected in price levels and rates of exchange between currencies but, with exchange rates fixed, or with monetary union, subsequent changes would bear directly upon competitiveness. The scope for subsequent relative changes in benefits, if financed by payroll taxes, must therefore be limited.

What did the welfare state mean in Russia under communism and, with the fall of communism, what changes now seem appropriate? *Alastair McAuley* analyses the objectives of the Soviet welfare state and the way these evolved after the revolution. He draws attention to changing Soviet attitudes towards the satisfaction of 'merit' wants, the reduction in inequality and the alleviation of poverty. The main programmes for income maintenance, health and child support are described and discussed. The whole scene has been changed by *perestroika*. What developments can now be expected to take place?

Sweden has long been regarded as a model welfare state. The critical tone of *Ann-Charlotte Stählberg's* case study of the Swedish pension system may, therefore, come as a surprise. She uses the results of her research into the earnings and pension profiles of a random sample of 6,000 individuals to demonstrate the very generous benefit/contribution ratios the system provides. Stählberg expresses doubts, however, as to the willingness of future generations of workers to accept constraints on current expenditure on the scale that would be required to finance the increasing rates of pension contributions. Her concern is not only with demographic trends but, even more, with certain features of the pension system itself: pension rights based on the 15 best earnings years; a short contribution period of 30 years for full pension; and above all, in her view, the short-sightedness that pay-as-you-go arrangements so easily encourage.

Part 5 begins with two chapters which discuss the difficulties involved in translating principles – whatever these may be – into practice. Attention is once more directed primarily to conditions in Britain although what is said may, with appropriate modifications, have a wider application. In the first chapter, *Albert Weale* states his reasons for believing that the traditional style of public administration in Britain is ill-adapted to making rational choices between various objectives. 'The preference is for the particular over the general, the concrete over the abstract, the commonsensical over principles.' For the objectives are not presented with sufficient clarity and precision and when conflicts occur these are likely to be settled less by open confrontation and debate than by bureaucratic compromise. The meaning of 'a right to health care' is taken as one example. Another is the control of air pollution. He then goes on to make a number of suggestions for improvements in the British administrative style.

The chapter that follows is written by *Peter Barclay*, who is actively engaged in the policy-making process in an advisory capacity as Chairman of the Social Security Advisory Committee. Whereas in an academic assessment of different policies, it may be permissible to assume that all options are open, a less orderly procedure is followed in practice with decisions usually taken 'on the hoof'. On administrative grounds alone, he is cautious about the scope for any radical reconstruction of the social services in Britain until well into the next century. Time is still required in order to cope with the changes already made in the 1980s, limited though they were, apart from any new departures that might now be recommended.

In the next chapter, two members of Parliament, *Frank Field* (Labour) and *Timothy Raison* (Conservative) express their personal views about issues in welfare policy to which they attach particular importance. For Field, a central issue is the creation, largely by the welfare state itself, of a demoralised underclass, seemingly unable to raise itself out of a state of dependency. Another is tax reform. For Raison, the future viability of the institutions of marriage and the family, which he sees threatened by forces from within and without the welfare services, is a cause of deep concern. Both politicians have their own personal suggestions to offer which reveal what may seem to be a surprising degree of convergence.

The final chapter is a wide-ranging review of the whole field by *Robert Pinker*. He refers back to the previous chapters and to the extensive literature on the subject as he expounds his views about 'the middle way in the pursuit of welfare objectives'. Given the commitment to a free society, compromises have to be made between the plurality of value judgements and interests underlying welfare objectives, with different degrees of emphasis placed on protection from poverty, redistribution and the fostering of social solidarity. The middle way must also allow for the various responsibilities of central government and of local government, and of a variety of voluntary agencies and individuals. He goes on to consider whether the 'convergence theories' may nevertheless be vindicated. Membership of the European Community is an additional factor which will further extend welfare pluralism, with marked differences in systems between different member countries. The economic pressures which have impeded radical changes, as Mangen has described, may prove to be the decisive factor in the 1990s.

We record with sorrow the death of Professor Jack Wiseman on 20th January 1991. This is not the place to attempt any assessment of his contribution to economic thought over so many years, and it must suffice to observe that the intellectual vigour with which he approached every subject is well displayed in his contribution to the present volume.

ACKNOWLEDGEMENTS

We are grateful to the Halley-Stewart Trust, which has provided the financial support needed for the preparation of this work. We are also indebted to the University of Bristol, which administered the grant, and to Professor Phyllida Parsloe, who maintained our lines of communication with both the Trust and the University. We must also express our thanks both to the authors and to a number of distinguished social scientists and retired senior civil servants who participated in a workshop, held at University College, Oxford in January 1989, at which most of the papers in this book were discussed so vigorously and helpfully. Finally, we would like to acknowledge our debt to Carol Marks, who worked so diligently and efficiently on the final typing of the book for publication.

Dorothy J. Wilson
Thomas Wilson
Bristol November 1990

The publishers are grateful to Her Majesty's Stationery Office for permission to reproduce the following copyright material:

Tables 1.1, 6.1, 14.1 and 14.2.

The Debate about Social Policy

1 Social Policy: Issues and Objectives
Thomas and Dorothy Wilson

1.1 THE NEED FOR AN INQUIRY

'To be blunt the British social security system has lost its way'.[1] This opening observation in an official Green Paper on the need for reform echoes the sense of disillusionment often expressed in Britain, as in other developed countries with lengthy experience of the social security and other policies loosely comprehended by the term 'the welfare state'. Although various reforms have been carried out, dissatisfaction remains. Welfare expenditure is immense. If attention is confined to cash benefits, which constitute the social security system, to the health service and to the personal social services, Britain's annual public expenditure corresponds to over a fifth of gross national product. One person in two at any one time is in receipt of a cash benefit of some kind. Yet this vast outlay does not seem sufficient. Even the protection against want seems inadequate with large numbers still living 'in poverty', in some sense of that admittedly ambiguous term. There has been a similar disappointment in the failure to meet the full 'need' for health services, education and housing. These various failures have often been explained by saying that, although much has been spent, still more is required. Or it may be held that the means adopted for implementing welfare policies have been seriously defective and vulnerable to manipulation by special interest groups. It is also possible that the disillusionment may reflect obscurity and ambiguity in the objectives themselves and thus in the criteria by which success or failure have been determined. Or – a very likely explanation – there may be a conflict between objectives which has resulted in unsatisfactory compromises. Whatever the explanation, the difficulties and the dissatisfaction are not to be regarded as peculiarly British, for this is the common experience throughout the developed world. A striking example is the Swedish social security system – often held up as a model of its kind – where serious problems are being encountered in sustaining its towering edifice of pensions (Ch.11). In other European countries, and in North America, there are similar problems.

The need for a fresh assessment had already become increasingly clear after the oil crises of the 1970s had marked the end of a period of well-sustained and reasonably steady economic expansion. During that earlier period

support for the welfare services seemed so widespread in Britain and elsewhere as to come close to a consensus, even if the 'rediscovery of poverty'
in Britain in the 1960s – or its redefinition – had the effect of damping an
earlier pride in the achievements. The moral widely drawn was not that a
false start had been made but that faster progress along the same path was
socially desirable. This was the period of 'incrementalism' which was
brought to an end by the change in economic conditions and prospects.
The central emphasis placed on inflation was then bound to be echoed in
concern about the growth of public expenditure. Although the rise in output was subsequently resumed and unemployment reduced from the high
levels of the early 1980s, the confidence of previous decades had not been
fully restored before the troubles of the 1990s began. It might be over-dra-
matic to talk of a crisis in the welfare state but the prospects for the new
decade must be viewed with caution.

Admittedly the previous consensus was not so complete as to exclude
differences of opinion about the scope and scale of the various benefits and
services. Thus within government there was an unsuccessful attempt to
achieve economies in public expenditure on the social services in 1955-57.[2]
Although the need for a fresh look at objectives was then incidentally acknowledged by some of the participants, this did not take place. Subsequently, the divergence of opinion has widened and deepened, and the
future of social policy has become a party political issue in Britain to an
extent not previously experienced since the end of the Second World War.
The fact remains that expenditure in real terms rose substantially under
Conservative governments – by almost a third on health and personal social
services between 1979/80 and 1989/90, by almost a third on social security
and by over a tenth on education and science. The widespread belief that
the welfare state has been hacked away may be at least as much a reflection
of the hostile rhetoric directed against 'welfarism' as it is a reflection of
apparently hostile action. For the measures actually adopted since 1979 have,
in fact, been mainly concerned to contain the *rate of growth* of expenditure
in real terms rather than to reduce it absolutely. Even so, some acute shortages have been felt because rising demand has outstripped the constrained
rise in supply. This has been notably the case in the health service, where
advances in medical science and increases in the number of elderly people
have laid heavy claims upon it in addition to large increases in the pay of its
staff. The persistence of waiting lists for operations, together with the very
visible closing of hospital wards, has been partly a consequence of the
greater rise in costs relative to output than in the economy as a whole – the
'relative price effect'. In the case of cash benefits, the growth in the number
of pensioners, the unemployed and single-parent families accounted for
much of the increase in real expenditure, for there was no increase in real
benefits per head after 1982. The severe cut by two-thirds in public expenditure on housing did, indeed, reflect a large-scale change in policy. Not

least important, the introduction of the poll tax in 1990 was widely taken to indicate insensitivity to social welfare. For reasons such as these, another shift of emphasis seems to have taken place in British opinion with the stress increasingly laid on the need for a more 'caring' society.

However, more 'caring' may mean higher taxes or some cutting back of other claims on public resources. These other claims are large and some have become increasingly urgent – including the demand for greater effort to protect the environment. Unfortunately the growing pressure for more public expenditure of all kinds has come at a time when the weaknesses of the British economy have once more become painfully clear. The constraints are likely to be disagreeably tight. Apart from competition between claims made for the welfare state and those made for other public measures, there is also competition between the various services loosely grouped together as 'the welfare state'. Moreover, if so much expenditure has apparently produced such disappointing results can it be sensible simply to spend more? What objectives is all the effort designed to achieve?

1.2 SOCIAL IDEALS AND SOCIAL PRESSURES

A factual account of the objectives behind the welfare services would seek to explain *how* the various services were introduced and *how* their subsequent development took place. The objectives thus investigated would be those of the politicians, administrators, pressure groups and public-spirited persons or organisations by whose combined, though sometimes conflicting, efforts the outcome had been determined.[3] Their aims will have been diverse, and this diversity will be reflected in the various social measures that have emerged. The task of the social historian is then to identify the various pressures, to trace their effects and to assess their importance. A different path may, however, be taken. For an inquiry can be made into the consequences to be expected from certain basic behavioural assumptions that are themselves believed to be firmly based on fact. This is the deductive method of the economic theory of politics or the theory of public choice.[4] Politicians pursue votes, officials seek to advance their self-interest by defending and expanding their bureaucratic empires, powerful interest groups are at work. And so on. It is an old theme freshly presented.

By contrast, in the 'normative' approach, well-informed but disinterested persons seek to prescribe the measures that are, in their view, most likely to contribute to social welfare. These investigators may disentangle moral value judgements from more technical scientific propositions with varying degrees of punctiliousness and success, and a variety of different recommendations for the promotion of social welfare will emerge. But although a philosopher king – or a William Beveridge – may design a scheme with a coherent conception of social welfare in mind, his creation will be subjected to the force of the vote motive and something substantially different may then emerge. 'Ideas' may succumb to 'interests'.

A particularly strong expression of scepticism about the outcome for social welfare is contained in the assertion that the 'welfare state' has been hijacked by the middle class, with the result that it is they, not the workers, who benefit. The Far Left and the Far Right have joined forces in this attack – the former because they wish to discredit 'reformist capitalism', the latter because they fear that such reforms will destroy capitalism. That there is some substance in this assessment may be conceded at once but it is exaggerated. Although attempts to calculate the net redistributive effects must be hedged with reservations – not least about the elusive incidence of taxation – the official statistical estimates do not support the view that it is the lower income group that benefits least from the tax/benefit system in Britain (see Table 1.1).

1.3   THE OBJECTIVES OF POLICY – AN INTERIM STATEMENT

The objectives of social security in Britain were presented with particular clarity by Beveridge in 1942. He surveyed a range of circumstances – such as old age and unemployment – in which benefits seemed appropriate and then put forward a comprehensive scheme which would apply consistent principles throughout. This unified structure, broadly adopted by government in 1948, became a special feature of the British arrangements which contrasted with those in other countries where different benefits – such as pensions and unemployment pay – have been financed in different ways and provided at different rates by different agencies. The central objective of the British system was protection against poverty on a scale to be uniformly applied. It is true that Beveridge did not deal adequately with the situation of the *working* poor, and it is also true that his proposals were not fully implemented. Moreover, various changes have subsequently been made over the years which have introduced additional complications. When therefore the new official review of social security was carried out in 1985, it differed in coverage and detail from the old Beveridge Report. The fact remains that the central emphasis was still placed on protection against poverty. This continues to be so to a greater extent than in other European countries or in the USA.

The provision of a minimum income as a safety net – sometimes opprobiously described as the 'minimalist principle' – may have the appearance of at least being simple and straightforward. This appearance is deceptive. The ambiguity of the term 'poverty' is a warning of the difficulties ahead. Thus as the poverty level is raised, in an increasingly affluent society, the emphasis shifts from 'subsistence' to 'social solidarity' and 'the ability to participate in

Table 1.1: Redistribution of income in the UK through taxes and benefits, 1986

	Households ranked by original income in £ per year					All households
	bottom fifth	next fifth	middle fifth	next fifth	top fifth	
Average per household (£ per year)						
Earnings of main earner	10	1,420	5,980	9,400	16,050	6,570
Earnings of others in the household	–	80	710	2,760	6,720	2,050
Occupational pensions, annuities	50	770	720	480	620	530
Investment income	50	400	480	430	1,180	510
Other income	10	130	130	110	220	120
Total original income	130	2,800	8,030	13,180	24,790	9,790
+Benefits in cash						
Contributory	1,750	1,880	740	380	270	1,000
Non-contributory	1,620	840	510	490	410	780
Gross income	3,500	5,520	9,280	14,060	25,470	11,570
- Income tax* and NIC†	– 10§	330	1,490	2,880	5,650	2,070
Disposable income	3,510	5,200	7,790	11,170	19,820	9,500
- Indirect taxes	880	1,540	2,280	2,900	4,250	2,370
+Benefits in kind						
Education	370	450	650	850	850	630
National Health Service	910	870	730	710	720	790
Travel subsidies	50	60	50	50	100	60
Housing subsidy	130	80	50	30	20	60
Welfare foods	50	40	30	20	20	30
Final income	4,130	5,150	7,020	9,940	17,260	8,700
Average per household (numbers)						
Adults	1.4	1.7	1.9	2.2	2.6	2.0
Children	0.4	0.4	0.7	0.8	0.7	0.6
Economically active people‡	–	0.6	1.2	1.8	2.2	1.2
Retired people	0.8	0.8	0.3	0.1	0.1	0.4
Number of households in sample	1,435	1,436	1,436	1,435	1,436	7,178

(Source: Central Statistical Office, from Family Expenditure Survey)

* After tax relief on mortgage interest and life assurance premiums

† Employees' national insurance contributions

‡ Comprising employees, the self-employed and others not in employment but who were seeking or intending to seek work, but excluding those away from work for more than one year

§ Negative average tax payments result largely from imputed tax relief on life assurance premiums paid by those with nil or negligible tax liabilities

the life of the community'. In effect, the aim of providing protection against poverty may be gradually merged with the aim of reducing inequality. It may indeed be pointed out that some measure of redistribution has always been an obvious feature of any scheme in which benefits are provided to the retired, the unemployed and the sick at the expense of those who are currently at work. But these beneficiaries will themselves have contributed in their active years and it cannot be simply taken for granted that, in the longer run, a vertical life-time transfer between rich and poor has taken place.

A social security system that is designed to provide protection against poverty can appeal to altruism or to a regard for fairness, but it is more difficult to find a satisfactory moral basis for graduated pensions related to previous income when at work. The aim is said to be 'income-maintenance' and it is, of course, only natural that retired people should wish to have incomes that are some tolerable proportion of what they received in their working years. But it is not immediately apparent that a state scheme, backed by compulsion, is required. Yet income-related pensions have been common throughout the developed world with Britain and Australia as the main exceptions, until Britain too fell into line for reasons to be investigated in a later section.

The egalitarian theme is resumed in a consideration of benefits in kind – such as the health service. These benefits may seem to lie outside the scope of social security systems concerned with cash transfers, but it would clearly be impossible to consider the adequacy of these transfers without taking into account the free or heavily subsidised provision of benefits in kind. (For example, if this is not done, misleading conclusions may be drawn from comparisons of cash transfers in Britain with those in some other countries.) Moreover, it is highly relevant to ask why some benefits should be in kind, for this imposes a restraint on the citizen's freedom of choice. Thus the paternalism which is a feature of the welfare state as a whole is more marked in the case of benefits in kind.

It is not only the nature and scale of the social benefits that must be viewed in the light of social objectives but also the manner in which these benefits are delivered. Here too value judgements conflict. Whereas liberals may insist that the paternalism behind benefits in kind requires special explanation and defence, collectivists may insist that the social uniformity thus imposed is an appropriate and desirable expression of social solidarity. Hence the insistence that the same health service should be available to everyone in the same way and, furthermore, that the service should be not only fully financed by the state but also supplied by an agency of the state. For the market is held to be the domain where self-interest prevails, and that domain should be, if not abolished, at least restricted in scope by the communal provision of social benefits. Moreover, where a 'gift relationship' is possible it should be preferred to a 'cash relationship'. The most usual example is that of blood which, Titmuss held, should be donated free to hospitals, not put up for sale.[5]

A great deal has also been said about the effect on personal dignity and self-reliance of the way in which cash benefits are provided. Selectivity by means test has long been criticised, but means tests have the offsetting merit of targeting benefits towards those in need. We are touching here on one of the most difficult policy dilemmas in this field.

Even these preliminary observations suggest that conflicts between different objectives are bound to arise and it may well be that the disillusionment sometimes expressed about the welfare state is a consequence of confining attention to one or other of these aims to the neglect of others. Thus, as well as the possible conflicts already implied in what has been said above, there is a further conflict between simplicity in administration and sensitivity in meeting diverse individual requirements. Yet another social objective that may, perhaps, receive too little attention from the advocates of radical change is the obligation to respect public commitments – such as commitments to pensioners – on which people have planned their personal affairs. But, as we shall see below, this respect for commitments may be a barrier to changes in the system that might otherwise be thought desirable.

These objectives, and the measures taken to achieve them, must be set in a wider economic and social context. The financing of the welfare services may affect national output by affecting the willingness to work and to save and by influencing wage demands. According to the post-war consensus, social security and full employment were complementary, for the former would provide a substantial amount of steady expenditure in both good times and bad, and the short-term variations that took place – mainly in social security contributions and in unemployment pay – would be counter-cyclical. According to the modern neo-classical school, unemployment pay is itself one of the main causes of unemployment. The gain from working, though positive in the vast majority of cases, may sometimes be so small as to be unattractive, and those in such a position will be caught in the 'unemployment trap'. A constraint is therefore imposed on raising the effective poverty level in the benefit structure for this level must be related to the disposable incomes of the low paid workers – that is to say, wages *less* taxation *plus* whatever cash benefits are available to those in employment. Or – to make the same point with a shift of emphasis – means may need to be sought to increase disposable income from work at the lower levels if an otherwise tolerable poverty level is to be established. These means might, for example, include training schemes to raise gross incomes and fiscal adjustments to raise disposable incomes.

With any given level of output, the cost of supplying benefits in cash or in kind will be the diversion of resources from other uses – a painfully obvious point, perhaps, but one that social scientists must constantly repeat in order to counteract the apparently widespread tendency to assume that government has resources of its own. How, then, is the decision to incur a particular cost to be made? To be borne by whom? These questions raise value judgements and no unanimity can be expected. There may be disagreement as to what benefits should be available but still more disagreement about their amount and the conditions for their provision. For example, although there is widespread agreement in Britain that the National Health Service should be maintained, there is much less agreement about the additional resources that should be devoted to it. A public benefit, like a privately supplied good, cannot be valued without regard to its amount. *Valuation must always be at the margin.* If economic theory does nothing else, at least it provides a warning that confusion will follow if 'first priority' is assigned to any particular policy or benefit, be it health, education, the environment or whatever. The question should be 'how much', and the answer will depend upon a scale of preferences. Whose scale? How ascertained? With what claim to legitimacy?

1.4   PROTECTION AGAINST POVERTY: ALTRUISM AND JUSTICE

Common humanity requires that no one, irrespective of personal merit, should die from hunger and exposure when resources are available to prevent it, and, in a modern industrialised society, the final responsibility rests with the state. So much is all but universally agreed. Need anything more be said? In fact a great deal more needs to be said, for protection against destitution is far too narrow an objective to explain the scale, duration and range of the benefits actually supplied. In 1942 when Beveridge was making his recommendations, the minimum income he prescribed was thought, by him, to be sufficient for an austere but bearable standard of living. Subsequently, benefits have been greatly increased in real terms. As the standard rises, the moral imperative to provide benefits up to the higher level may be felt by many people to lose some of its force. There would be a wide difference between attitudes towards emergency assistance to those in desperate need and the provision of benefits for extended periods to those who could make shift to provide for themselves. In particular assistance to the able-bodied below retirement age would be widely thought unjustified if it were unconditional. If no jobs are available, the unemployed are expected to show that they are willing to work or go on training schemes if required. There would probably be widespread support for the view that anyone who refused to comply with such reasonable conditions would forfeit a claim to assistance. A different view appears, however, to be taken by the proponents of a Social Dividend. For they have maintained that, irrespective of income from other sources, *everyone* has an unconditional right to a basic payment from the state with no conditions attached which, in Samuel Brittan's words, would 'enable people who are content to live at a modest subsistence scale to do so. For a rich society can afford to have some people "opting out" '.[6] In fact, the difference of opinion with regard to the wilfully unemployed may be less than at first appears, for even those who recommend a tough line might also accept the view we have expressed above that no one, irrespective of merit, must be allowed to fall into total destitution. The real question then is the level at which unconditional assistance should be provided, and Brittan, for his part, insists that it should be only at a subsistence level with 'a distinct and growing gap between national income per head and the target minimum'. The position in Britain is that a person who refuses reasonable employment can have his or her claim to means-tested assistance reduced by 40 per cent but will retain the normal benefits for dependants. For householders housing costs will also be met.

There has been a great deal of nonsense talked about people living in comfortable idleness on the dole, but there has also been a great deal of nonsense talked about people being hounded out of benefit by official investigators when the objective has been to induce them to accept work or training – or to ascertain whether they are in fact already employed and are 'doing the double'.

The willingness to provide assistance may derive not from altruism or some sense of social solidarity so much as from a desire to prevent social unrest. Desperate need could lead to desperate action and it is prudent, therefore, to meet that need. This, of course, was the historical reason quite explicitly given for some modest public provision of relief. In modern times a good deal has been said about 'managing the poor' in capitalist economies – sometimes with the unconvincing implicit suggestion that there would be no poor to manage in communist societies. The point can be better made by saying that the provision of social benefits does much to preserve social harmony. It is also true that, if the defence of capitalism is the reason, the cost imposed is high, for the benefits exceed distributed profits – or 'distributed surplus value' – even in the USA. But, after all, 'capitalists' are not alone in seeking to avert social conflict. In any case it may again be pointed out – perhaps a little caustically – that what may be decisive is neither the generosity nor the nervousness of the 'haves' but the voting power of the 'have-nots'. Is the welfare state not the child of the universal franchise?

The combination of altruistic and self-regarding motives that underlies the welfare services can be expressed as a desire for the *fair* provision of mutual aid between citizens. The emphasis can then shift towards conceptions of justice and this may be welcomed, for an exclusive emphasis on charity, whether public or private, can become distasteful. 'Caring', or altruistic giving, may make those who give feel too good, and those who receive feel too dependent. An emphasis on fairness is also required and may be more consistent with the preservation of a sense of self-respect. To say this is not to exclude those claims on altruism that may go well beyond what a strict regard for 'just deserts' might seem to require.

A large field of enquiry, and one of some antiquity, is thus opened up. The starting point must, rather obviously, be a conscious effort to make impartial disinterested assessments, and to this end various devices of the imagination have been employed. Thus we might suppose the matter to be referred to an 'Impartial Spectator' who, though not omniscient, is well-informed and disinterested.[7] Rawls, for his part, has preferred to suggest that we should suppose our own future positions to be concealed from us by a 'veil of ignorance'.[8] We shall then be obliged to recognise the importance of *chance* in determining the distribution of income and wealth – heredity, upbringing and education, the inheritance of capital, the luck of being in the right place at the right time, and so on. Even the capacity for hard work depends upon physical inheritance as well as moral motivation. How far should this determinism be carried? We are in danger here of becoming ensnared in an age-old philosophical controversy, but we can at least plead for consistency. It would be inconsistent to talk about personal dignity and self-respect as many do in the context of the welfare state, and, at the same time, to claim that we are all the helpless victims of circumstances. But we can also reject the assumption that a special legitimacy attaches to the distribution of income and wealth that would emerge from market transactions based on some initial endowment if no steps were taken to alter it. The expression, 'finders are keepers', as applied to any and every endowment of human or physical capital, lacks decisive moral force. In this controversy, Wiseman begins with the assumption that any change in the distribution of income and wealth requires unanimous support and can, therefore, be vetoed. But people have caring feelings which will lead them, not only to make personal gifts to charity, but also to accept a political system which imposes compulsory transfers. The distributional change whether large or small will have been made legitimate by a social contract. Is it, however, the case that the initial distribution is being accorded a special legitimacy? For finders will still be keepers unless they choose not to be.

What, then, would be regarded as fair and just protection against the danger of finding oneself among the least advantaged in an unequal society? What conclusions can be drawn from Rawls's theory of justice that are particularly applicable to the welfare state? If, as he assumes, everyone is intensely averse to risk, complete equality would be regarded as the most prudent and, in a sense, the most fair outcome. He goes on to say, however, that inequality should be sanctioned in so far as it provides a stimulus to efficiency and thus leads to a rise in output from which the least advantaged income group would benefit. Inequality has long been regarded as the price to be paid for growth from which all will benefit, but Rawls carries this contention a stage further. *Relative poverty* is the acceptable price for reducing *absolute poverty*.

It has frequently been observed that this extreme assumption of a universal aversion to risk cannot easily be reconciled with the obvious fact that many people do take avoidable risks in the hope of obtaining a better outcome. From this it has been inferred that they would therefore be more likely to choose a social contract based on the assumption that they would find themselves near the middle of the pile rather than at the bottom. The desire for a safeguard against the worst contingencies would, however, remain, and a regard for justice would at least require the provision of a *social minimum*. This is surely the more convincing conclusion to which the whole analysis leads. Given that a safety net was in place, everyone would be more ready to accept the risky chance of reaching a level of personal income above that minimum.

Two other inferences of some importance can be derived from the Rawlsian analysis:

(i)   A regard for fairness, in his sense, would make it seem right to fix the minimum, in a developed economy, at a level higher than that required for bare subsistence – perhaps well above.

(ii) We should expect the contracting parties to opt for subsequent real increases in this minimum as income per head was raised in a growing economy. But how should such increases be determined? The theory points us in certain directions but does not – and obviously cannot – say how far we should go. As Lessnoff has pointed out, the answer here, as with (i), will depend partly upon attitudes to risk.[9]

What marks are to be given, by these criteria, to the policies of the governments led by Mrs Thatcher? Has Mrs Thatcher been a Rawlsian? Our thumb-nail sketch of the theory may be illustrated by considering a question which is less bizarre than it may at first appear! For government policy during the 1980s was frequently explained and defended on the ground that, by lowering rates of direct taxation, the reward for effort and risk-bearing would be strengthened and the higher growth of output that would follow would bring benefit to everyone on a scale not otherwise attainable. Those who were worst off would share in this gain, although there was, of course, no special Rawlsian emphasis on their position. In the event, the lowest tenth did benefit, but with a rise in income of only 2.5 per cent over the decade, or less than half the average increase. Furthermore the whole of the lower half of income recipients had increases appreciably below the average percentage increase.[10] Was it, however, the case that, but for the rewards that went to the relatively rich, incentives would have been blunted and national output would have risen less to an extent that would have left everyone worse off? Many people would find that proposition unconvincing. Some might accept it eagerly enough. What is uncomfortably apparent is the difficulty of establishing firm causal links. Thus it is hard to make the

Rawlsian theory operational – and also to test the validity of the claims made on behalf of government policy.

The increase in inequality in the 1980s has presumably fostered the opinion that, in a market economy, the most that can be expected by people with low incomes, and indeed by the working class as a whole, is a slow and niggardly 'trickling down' of the gains from growth. But this is scarcely fair. First, the distribution that emerges from market transactions will vary with variations in the distribution of capital. Secondly, the market is responsible only for the distribution of gross income. In some periods, this gross distribution becomes more favourable to capital, in others more favourable to labour. (In the early 1990s, profits may lose much of their relative gain of the 1980s, which was itself a correction after a still earlier profits squeeze.) Thirdly, the figures quoted above substantially reflected changes in the tax–benefit mix – reflected, that is to say, government policy rather than market forces. Nothing that has been said alters the fact that, over the long run, economic growth has been incomparably the most important factor in raising the standard of living of all income groups. But for some, the gain in disposable income may indeed be reduced, for many years, to a modest trickle.

1.5   EARNING THE RIGHT TO BENEFITS

No ground as yet has been advanced for benefits provided without test of means to all who fall within particular categories such as the old, the unemployed and the sick. How can such 'universal' benefits be justified? This question was prompted by the proposals put forward by Beveridge himself. In Crosland's words:

> If the object of the social services is the abolition of want, then an income test to establish the existence of want is a logical corollary. If, on the other hand, payment of benefit regardless of means is elaborated into a principle, then the object cannot simply be the elimination of want. Evidently some new and different aim has crept in; but it was never made clear, either in the [Beveridge] Report or in the debates which followed, just what this was.[11]

There are in fact certain practical considerations in favour of selecting beneficiaries by category rather than individually by means test, in particular a substantially lower cost of administration and little danger that beneficiaries, through ignorance, infirmity or a sense of stigma, will fail to claim their due. But there are also other considerations that were of great importance in Beveridge's view and are stressed throughout his Report. If no one was to be denied support, no one should be allowed to escape the obligation to help in supporting others. 'Free-riding' must be prevented by making contributions compulsory. But this was not all. Self-respect and personal dignity would be protected and fostered by the contributory principle. What was implied was in large part a 'better distribution of purchasing power . . . among wage-earners themselves as between times of earning and not earning, and between times of heavy or light or no family responsibilities.'[12] Vertical redistribution between different cohorts in the income scale was given less attention. The important point, and one which in his view accorded best with the sentiments of the British people, was that '. . . each individual should stand in on the same terms . . . and stand together with their fellows.'[13] Solidarity would be strengthened and a sense of common citizenship fortified by means of flat-rate contributions for flat-rate benefits. Justice, rather than altruism, appears to be at the centre of the Beveridge proposals, although not in the sense given it by Rawls. Benefits were justly deserved by those who had made the appropriate contributions. Charity need extend only to those who could not do so.

Have subsequent developments entailed a sacrifice of these principles? The belief that this has been so was expressed in the Meade Report of 1978,[14] which contained proposals for a 'New Beveridge'. Selectivity by test of means, far from being reduced to a few special cases, had persisted on a large scale, and social stigma had thus been perpetuated. Universal benefits should therefore be raised to the 'poverty level'. There was, however, a shift of emphasis between the original Beveridge and the New Beveridge. Although he had not devoted much space to them in his report, Beveridge undoubtedly disliked means tests, which, in any form, discourage self-reliance.[15] Hence his advocacy of the contributory principle in the *financing of benefits* as a means of preserving a sense of responsibility. The modern emphasis has rather been on the weakening of self-respect caused when benefits are *distributed* by means tests.

Should this contributory principle be retained? That is to say, should national (or social) insurance be retained, or abandoned in favour of financing from the general government budget? Even under the Beveridge plan, potential beneficiaries were not expected to pay fully for what they might receive. The scheme was not actuarial and could not have been made so unless unemployment benefit had been treated separately – for unemployment is not an actuarial risk. Moreover, costs were to be shared by employees, employers and the state. But the employers' contribution, unless passed back to employees in the form of lower pay, is passed forward as an indirect tax. A large part of the cost was therefore to be met, in effect, from taxation. Why not the whole? Is there really a case for earmarking a particular tax for a particular purpose?

From Beveridge's point of view, even a partial contribution from future beneficiaries was better than none. From a quite different point of view, a social insurance scheme could be expected to provide more security against cuts than general budget financing, when benefits could be more readily changed as some minister of finance might find convenient. This last consideration would surely weigh heavily in the USA and in the continental EC in favour of retaining earmarked social security contributions.

1.6   THE 'SCANDAL' OF THE WELFARE STATE

Although welfare expenditure has increased so much, 'poverty' has not been abolished. This seems a scandalous outcome. Is the explanation to be found in a benefit system so distorted by politicians, bureaucrats and pressure groups, that its primary objective has not been fulfilled? Or can the failure be substantially, if not fully, accounted for by changes in what is meant by 'poverty'? Another source of confusion is the occasional failure to make clear whether the numbers in poverty have been calculated before or after the receipt of benefit. If the former, then it may appear that the welfare state is not to blame, but this favourable verdict must be qualified by the extent to which the anticipation of benefits weakens the incentive to make private provision, while the capacity to do so is reduced by having to pay compulsory contributions when at work. To an uncertain and much debated extent, the welfare state creates the dependency it seeks to relieve.[16] The fact remains that some poverty persists even after benefits have been provided because their scope is incomplete or administration faulty, or because some people fail to claim what they are entitled to receive. A further cause of confusion in Britain is the practice, sometimes followed, of measuring poverty after the receipt of national insurance benefits but before the receipt of means-tested benefits. Even a substantial rise in the former will not then reduce 'poverty' if the means-tested benefits are also raised in line – the practice deplored by Frank Field (p266 below.). For all these reasons, it is unfortunate that the media should so often refer to the number 'in poverty' as though it could be calculated in only one way. Moreover the term 'poverty level' is itself ambiguous, rivalled only by 'need' in its capacity to confound and confuse.

Even at one time and in one place, the 'destitution' level cannot be given a wholly unequivocal and objective meaning. As Adam Smith put it: 'By necessaries I mean not only commodities which are indispensable for the support of life, but whatever the custom of the country renders it indecent for creditable people, even of the lowest order, to be without'.[17] When it is recognised that the necessaries deemed to constitute the social minimum have also changed over time, it becomes much less surprising – and much less of a scandal – that the welfare state has not succeeded in eliminating 'poverty'. When the 'socially acceptable minimum' is expressed as a fraction of average income, the scope for disagreement becomes clear. For example, the European Commission has now suggested a half of average disposable income for a single person, as Mangen explains in Chapter 9. Some may favour more, some less.

In recent years, particular attention has been directed to 'poverty' as a barrier to adequate participation in the life of the community, with the conclusion that citizenship conveys – or should convey – a 'right' to have this barrier removed. Citizenship does indeed convey certain legal rights to which non-citizens, even if resident in the territory, cannot lay claim. Presumably, however, the term is not really being used in its legal sense, but rather as a synonym for 'social solidarity' or 'social responsibility'. Thus we are led back to those issues previously discussed with reference to altruism and social justice.

If the social minimum is now to be described as the minimum resources required to participate in the life of the community, what is to be the scale of participation? How can it be calculated? Townsend made a valiant attempt to answer that question by estimating how much would be required for various items of consumption and various forms of activity.[18] But a large element of subjective judgement must inevitably remain. So much seems undeniable.

In Britain the level of means-tested income support is often taken to be 'the poverty level', though not officially so described. Sometimes it is used as a convenient bench-mark from which a preferred minimum is derived, as when 140 per cent of this level has been taken to be appropriate. This cash benefit is roughly the same as the social insurance benefits provided without means tests. Its basis is to be found in the estimates made in the distant past by Rowntree and later by Beveridge, as modified by the Labour government in 1948. By 1982 the real value of the minimum had been raised, in a succession of stages, by 85 per cent above the 1948 level in the case of short-term benefits for the sick and the unemployed, and by 135 per cent for the larger, long-term benefit for pensioners. These new levels were the cumulative outcome of successive increases reflecting current views about social welfare, political expediency and financial feasibility. After 1982 however, the poverty level in Britain – as measured by basic means-tested cash benefits – was not raised in real terms. Nor were the national insurance benefits.

There is a second part to the minimum benefit in Britain, that is help with housing costs. Actual rents – a large item and one that varies greatly between different households – are fully met, subject to means tests, in virtually every case for those receiving social insurance benefits or means-tested cash benefits now termed 'income support' (see Appendix). For these reasons there is not one 'social minimum' or one 'poverty level' at any given time but, implicitly, a very large number reflecting the differences in rents. Beveridge, for his part, had recommended the inclusion in cash social insurance benefits of an allowance for *average* rent. As rents varied greatly the residue for food, clothing and so on would also have varied greatly. We have thought it appropriate to go into some detail for it appears to be widely and uncritically believed that national insurance has failed to reduce poverty to vestigial numbers because Beveridge's proposals were not fully accepted. In fact the cash benefits for national insurance initially provided by the post-war Labour government were slightly above means-tested cash benefits and – the crucial point – actual rents were also covered on a means-tested basis for the recipients of insurance benefits as well as means-tested cash benefits. This is not the place to identify and assess the various changes in the housing market that would be required before a uniform allowance for rents would be socially or politically acceptable, but it is safe to predict that it all lies some distance ahead! As a first step in that direction, it would be right to consider the case for uniform allowances within different regions or areas – as has long been the practice in Sweden.

Housing benefit is the joker in the pack. So long as the diversity of rents is reflected in benefit, means tests will be required. Furthermore, if poverty is *identified* as eligibility for means-tested assistance, including assistance with housing costs, the national insurance cash benefits must lie below the 'poverty level'. Even if the latter were simply raised by an allowance for 'average rent', there would remain a large number with higher rents who could still apply for selective assistance.

1.7   POVERTY LEVELS OVER TIME

The 'poverty level' can be determined in different ways with different implications for policy.[19]

(i)   *A static poverty level* held constant in real terms. This new label seems wiser than the old expression 'absolute' poverty level. The static level might be the amount needed to provide protection against 'destitution' but, realistically, would be much higher. The definition simply requires that the minimum should not change over time.

(ii) *A fully relative poverty level* expressed as some percentage of average earnings which will be maintained over time, so that the poverty level rises with rising real earnings. A reduction in the number in poverty will then require a reduction in inequality.

(iii) *A qualified relative poverty level* which rises less than current average earnings but permits some gradual adjustment to increasing affluence.[20]

There would be a general inclination in Britain to regard (i) as the minimum level that would be socially desirable. Admittedly, extreme circumstances can be envisaged in which the real value of benefits might be reduced. For example a sharp deterioration in the terms of trade could lower incomes from work so much in real terms as to make some lowering of real benefits seem appropriate. (So much was recognised in Sweden when, in the oil crisis of the 1970s, energy prices were excluded from the operational price index.)

It is interesting to recall in passing that both Beveridge and Keynes had expressed strong opposition to the indexation of benefits; in their view it was the function of the state to keep inflation under control. Speaking in the House of Lords in 1958 with reference to a Labour Party proposal to increase pensions in the event of price rises, Beveridge was firm: 'That is as good as saying, "Do not heed inflation, you will be all right". That is a further incentive to inflation.'[21]

There is a case for calculating a poverty level that is static in real terms as a bench-mark even if it is not used in the determination of benefits. Otherwise historical improvements in the standard of living of the bottom income group might be overlooked, and, with attention concentrated on relative poverty − (ii) above − it might seem that neither the welfare state nor economic growth had done anything to raise the standard of living of the less well-off. That would be an absurd conclusion.

In Britain, as we have observed, means-tested benefits have risen substantially over the trend and so have national insurance benefits. In 1975 a Labour government decided in favour of statutory rules for indexation, with long-term benefits, both national insurance and means-tested, to be raised every year in line with rising prices or with rising earnings, whichever went up more. By comparison with this generous provision for pensioners, the benefits paid to the sick and the unemployed would be adjusted only for prices. The poverty level was to be static for one group but relative for another, with, however, the further proviso that, in the case of pensioners, their benefits would never be reduced in real terms if real wages fell. The Conservative government which came into power in 1979 swept away these arrangements and replaced them by price indexation alone. Since 1982 Britain has had static poverty levels and static real benefits. This has been so in principle at least, although the quirks of price indexation have caused a marginal decline in real benefits since 1982.

Child benefit has not been protected against inflation as consistently as other benefits. The combined effect of changes in tax allowances and cash benefits, as illustrated for a two-child family on average earnings, was an increase in real terms of just under three-fifths between 1948 and 1989. This is a much smaller increase than that for pensions and somewhat below that for unemployment benefit. The peak, in real terms, was reached in 1984 and this was followed by a fall in its real value of 17 per cent by 1989. The drop naturally gave rise to the suspicion that this particular benefit was being phased out, which, as Timothy Raison stresses in a subsequent chapter, would seem a perverse development in view of the gradual shift of emphasis towards the needs of working families with children. The Budget of March 1991, however, provided for full price adjustment in future.

The third procedure – (iii) above – could be made operational by ruling that real benefits would be raised each year by some fraction of the lagged increase in real earnings. For example, a 4 per cent rise in real wages might be accompanied by a 2 per cent rise in real benefits. This would reflect the opinion that people should share in economic growth but should also make some provision for themselves. In much of the modern literature on social benefits there has been a tendency to exclude the latter possibility.

1.8   THE DUBIOUS CASE FOR EARNINGS-RELATED BENEFITS

It is not altogether easy to find a convincing case in social ethics for compulsory pension schemes with pension rights related in some state-determined way to previous earnings. These schemes cannot be defended as a form of forced savings helpful to economic growth because nearly all the official earnings-related pension schemes throughout the world are *unfunded* – unlike most private occupational schemes. The contributions are not paid into an accumulating fund from which benefits will subsequently be paid. Apart from small reserves against unforeseen contingencies, there *are* no funds. Current pensions, both flat-rate and graduated, are financed by current contributions on a pay-as-you-go basis.

It is true that a person will normally wish to maintain in retirement a standard of living related to that of working life, but this might be regarded as a private objective for which private provision can be made. It is one thing to maintain that there should be compulsory contributions in order to ensure that no one falls below some minimum level of income, for the provision of that minimum is a social obligation and free-riders must be prevented. But it is a different matter to compel people to submit to official arrangements that will prevent them from determining their own chosen patterns of lifetime expenditure. Why should people be *compelled* to opt for a high level of income replacement in retirement if the cost is hardship in working life when there may be a family to be supported? That is the objection from a liberal point of view, and it is not merely an academic objection as can be seen by considering the complaints now made in Sweden (Ch. 11). Moreover, from an egalitarian point of view, why should the state be at pains to preserve in retirement some of the inequality of working life?

Private occupational pensions schemes also usually require the individual employee to fall into line as part of a contract of employment. Anyone who wished to do so, would usually find it hard to opt out, but would be foolish to try in view of the large tax concessions. Thus state support for occupational pensions has long been available, although indirectly so in the form of 'tax expenditures' – that is to say, tax allowances and exemptions. But this support has not been universal in coverage because occupational pensions were not universal and, when available, were provided on very different terms, until the State Earnings Related Pension Scheme (SERPS), introduced by a Labour government in 1975, at least established a minimum supplementary pension for all. If, then, the need to curb the growth of public expenditure sets a limit to rises in state pensions, it can properly be asked why these tax expenditures should escape attention. It is true that occupational pensions can be treated as deferred pay and the employers' contributions can, therefore, be properly deductible from tax liabilities and treated as a cost like current wages and salaries. But the exemption of the employees' contributions is a different matter. Moreover pension funds are exempted from income tax and from capital gains tax. The cost to the Exchequer is a huge £7 billion a year (excluding exemptions on the employers' contributions). Admittedly occupational pensions will be taxed when payable as will state pensions, and it may also be argued that these pensions are usually funded, as state pensions are not, and thus make a much-needed contribution to investible funds in a country, such as Britain, which saves so little. If, however, saving really deserves to be heavily subsidised – a contentious issue – the subsidy should not be denied to private persons who save from taxed income and then pay both income tax and capital gains tax on these savings. This point has now been officially accepted in principle, although applied only on a still restricted scale.

In Chapter 8, Nick Barr explains the main features of SERPS – the State Earnings Related Pension Scheme. The primary objective was to provide retired people with sufficient income to make it unnecessary for them to seek further cash assistance subject to means tests. It may be suggested that this aim could have been better achieved by raising the basic flat-rate pension, but this basic increase would have been paid to everyone, including those who already had occupational pensions that carried them well above the poverty level, and would therefore have been more costly. However, for the poorer pensioners to have been helped, SERPS pensions should have been made fully available immediately on a PAYE basis. This was not done. Full pensions were not to be paid for twenty years. Contributions were however levied immediately and used for other purposes, for there was no attempt to build up a fund against future liabilities. Ironically one of the reasons given for having compulsory earnings-related pension schemes is that ordinary people may take too short a view of their own requirements. They are said to be myopic, whereas a government will take a long view – undeflected apparently from the path of duty by any short-term regard for the effect of their actions on election prospects. A somewhat unconvincing assumption! If a Labour government had been elected in 1979, the current surplus from SERPS might have been used to raise the real value of other benefits. Under the Conservatives, there was, in fact, an increase in real pensions in 1982 but thereafter the SERPS surplus has been used to eliminate the Exchequer contribution to the cost of national insurance benefits.

We may conclude this section by noting a somewhat odd feature of the benefit system. The flat-rate pension – still regarded as the basis of the pension structure – is adjusted for *prices* only. The second-tier SERPS pensions are however *earnings-related* and *new* SERPS pensions will therefore reflect a lagged rise in earnings although, once in payment, the subsequent adjustment will be for prices only.[22] For this reason, as well as because of the gradual maturing of the scheme, SERPS will grow relative to the basic pension. (See also Chapter 11 on the Swedish pension.)

1.9   WHY SHOULD THERE BE BENEFITS IN KIND AS WELL AS IN CASH?

A minimum income, or poverty level, is usually expressed as the cash made available for the purchase of goods and services, but its generosity – or lack of it – will also depend on the benefits supplied in kind. The benefits in kind provided without charge or heavily subsidised may naturally vary, but the most important items in Britain constitute a familiar list: the health service, the personal social services, education and housing for poor families. Public expenditure on these items comes to roughly as much as expenditure on pensions and other cash benefits and is equivalent to a tenth of GDP. In other developed countries there is a similar list of benefits in kind, but with some important differences in scale and method of provision.

These are the 'merit goods' of the Musgraves' terminology.[23] A merit good, of which medical treatment is an important example, is one that private persons could be left to buy, according to their preferences, on the market, and it thus differs from a true public good such as defence against foreign aggressors or an environmental health service such as the maintenance of clean air. The distinction is important because, in the case of merit goods, there is the choice between private purchase and financing through taxation. The expression is somewhat question-begging, however, for it may suggest that only merit goods have merit! Alan Ryan finds it more illuminating for his purpose to refer to 'enabling goods' – goods that will enable a citizen to take part in an 'appropriate' way in the life of the community (Ch. 5). In Plant's terminology, these are part of the 'liberating' package a citizen requires in order to enjoy 'positive liberty' (Ch. 4).

As an alternative, the state could raise cash benefits and thus allow people to spend as their preferences dictated, with more or less 'merit' accorded to 'merit' goods. Does the provision of benefits in kind, financed by compulsory taxation, entail an unwarranted interference with personal choice? To say that these merit goods are 'important' is no answer. So is food. So are clothes – and many other things. Special reasons are then required for using the tax system in order to provide a free or heavily subsidised supply of these particular goods.

These reasons may be grouped under three headings: (i) externalities, (ii) paternalism, (iii) 'specific egalitarianism' – a particular presentation of the paternalistic case, as explained below.

(i)   *Externalities*: Education is a familiar example of social investment for which private support may be inadequate because private people, however rational and far-sighted, cannot reasonably be expected to take full account of possible gains to society as a whole. Adam Smith himself believed that public support was therefore desirable, and this has been generally acknowledged to be the case. Admittedly, it is easy to multiply the examples, for many forms of personal expenditure affect other people, for good or ill. The selection of merit goods for special treatment may therefore be taken to reflect both the importance of the externality and the administrative feasibility of coping with it.

(ii)   *Paternalism*: The second explanation is that, externalities apart, ordinary people cannot determine what they themselves really 'need', and guidance or even compulsion is required. It is unfortunate, however, that the word 'need' should be commonly used as though it had a clear and objective meaning. This is far from being the case. Who can be relied upon to identify a 'need' – and to do so more accurately than the person who is said to have that 'need'? What is meant by 'need' in education, medical treatment or housing? And when different needs compete for scarce resources, who is to determine the weight to be attached, *at the margin*, to each? Traditionally economists have thought it prudent to avoid such a question-begging word and to confine themselves to the more neutral term 'wants'. Wants can then be simply accepted as data on the ground that the economist's concern is strictly empirical, not normative. Or a somewhat stronger position can be adopted by assuming that, empirically, individuals appear to be better satisfied, by and large, if free to determine their own wants in whatever ways they prefer.

Medical services exemplify the difficulties that arise. Obviously, private people will allow their medical wants to be shaped by professional advice, whether or not there is a state health service. Suppose, however, that if left to make their own choices, they would spend 'too little' on health as judged by professional standards. To a liberal such as John Stuart Mill, there would still be no case for interference. Responsible adults should be treated as adults. Unless others are affected – the 'externality' argument – they should be left to choose. The provision of merit goods does, however, entail interference in that, for example, people are compelled, as taxpayers, to contribute to a public health service. This policy may rest on the assumption that the professional recommendations will be more widely sought and better implemented when medical services are free or heavily subsidised. But the scale of provision will not, even then, be the aggregate of what thousands of doctors would prescribe as professionally ideal in the millions of cases with which they have to deal. For any government must weigh the many rival claims on the nation's resources and, in doing so, will be well aware that the provision of medical services is not always a matter of life and death. The doctors themselves may well feel it unrealistic to prescribe everything they might wish to prescribe from a purely professional point of view, especially new forms of treatment that are both expensive and speculative. There is, then, no unambiguous professional assessment of 'need' that any government could fully underwrite, even if it wished to do so. So much must be conceded – conceded a little impatiently, perhaps, as being rather obvious.

Will the proportion of national income devoted to the health service really be larger if provided free than would be the case if paid for directly by those who use it? The income from which it would then be paid would be relieved of the tax burden of the NHS – about £500 per head each year. As it happens, total expenditure on health, public and private combined, is relatively *lower* in Britain than in a number of other countries, including the USA, where there is no comparable health service. But various adjustments ought to be made in order to allow, for example, for differences in age structure – and even in proneness to hypochondria. Moreover, when doctors are paid directly for what they do, they may behave like 'economic men' and try to do more. At all events there are, for example, three times as many tonsillectomies and hysterectomies performed per hundred thousand of the relevant populations per year in the USA as in Britain. Another possible explanation is that the NHS is after all relatively efficient, notwithstanding the many familiar complaints. Unfortunately it is not easy to define 'medical efficiency' or to measure it.

(iii)   *'Specific egalitarianism'* has been described as follows by Tobin. 'Our society,' he says, with reference to the USA, 'accepts and approves a large measure of inequality, even of inherited inequality. . . . But willingness to accept inequality in general is, I detect, tempered by a persistent and durable strain of what I shall call specific egalitarianism.'[24] There is much greater equality in the consumption of some goods and services than in the distribution of income as a whole. Bread is an obvious example. Such differences come about quite naturally without any interference with market choice. If, then, some items of personal consumption are said to require special treatment outside the market, special reasons must be given. One reason may be the irregular way in which the demand for them arises, but provision can then be made against such contingencies by private insurance. Admittedly some people would be deemed to be bad risks, perhaps quite unacceptably bad, and unsubsidised health insurance would also impose a heavy strain on families with low incomes, even when good risks. Specific egalitarianism would thus require public supply or public subsidies for private supply.

Just as no one must be allowed to fall into total destitution, so no one must be denied the medical services required in the case of serious illness, without regard to current ability to pay. Much more than this minimum may indeed be publicly provided, but this is the core. When a life is at immediate risk or suffering is acute, medical assistance must then be based on 'need' in a fairly clear sense of the term. Presumably there would be little disagreement about this, but there is disagreement about how the service should be organised and its costs defrayed.

The egalitarian case can be presented in much stronger terms for it can be held that the objective should be complete equality of treatment even in cases that are not acute and that this treatment should be socially provided. Why should anyone deserve better treatment than his or her fellows? If this is accepted as a basic moral principle, no one should be allowed to jump *any* medical queue by paying – and no decent person should wish to do so. Common humanity requires common treatment, which, it is held, should come from the same public source. Social solidarity in this particular area is then an objective *in itself*, for which other objectives may, if necessary, be sacrificed at the margin, but the question is how far that sacrifice should be carried. If there were convincing reasons to believe that larger and better equipped hospitals would be made possible by encouraging more private medicine, but with the needs of the poorer patients fully respected, would this improved health service be worth the loss in 'solidarity'?

Support for the National Health Service in Britain remains sufficiently strong to ensure its survival. So much seems clear. The real choices lie between the various forms that state assistance may take, and between the various combinations of public and private medicine. Much of what was done or proposed during the Thatcher years was directed towards greater efficiency in production by contracting out some of the ancillary work, such as laundering and also, much more ambitiously, by proposing to create a competitive internal market within the health service itself. The resistance – when it has not come simply from interested parties, such as the unions and some sections of the medical profession – reflects the fear that the whole egalitarian ethos of the NHS will be placed at risk by the introduction, even to this extent, of commercial criteria.

Unfortunately the distinction between who pays and who supplies has too often been neglected. For the state may finance a service that is privately provided. Thus a free health service could have been established in 1948 without nationalising the the municipal and charity hospitals. The case for one source of supply is a question of technical efficiency rather than egalitarianism.

The government's attempts to push more of the cost of health care on to the private market have been surprisingly limited. Whatever the reason, little has been done either to make private insurance more attractive or to raise more money from charges, two methods tried and tested in many European countries as well as in the US (see Ch. 9). Thus *tax allowances* for health premiums were long delayed and when introduced applied only to retired people. If extended to the whole population, this would represent a much greater change, and private medicine – which accounted in the late 1980s for only 2 per cent of national health expenditure – might increase substantially. The objective would presumably be to remove the unfairness of requiring that those who elect to pay for private medicine must also continue to contribute as taxpayers towards the cost of the NHS. If, however, more scarce resources – such as the services of orthopaedic surgeons – were then to be drawn away from the public sector, the human cost of the change would be unfairness of a different kind, as poorer patients found the waiting time for, say, their hip operations further extended. In the longer run, supply could be expected to expand substantially. In this connection conditions in some other EC countries, as described by Mangen in Chapter 9, deserve attention.

Charges for any form of medical treatment obviously conflict with the vision of specific egalitarianism on which the NHS was initially based. The case for charges today, as when they were first introduced by a Labour government in 1950, rests on two grounds: to bring in revenue and to discourage wasteful demands. However, the revenue thus collected has never accounted for more than 3 per cent of NHS annual revenue, and generally for substantially less. The reasons lie in the modesty of the charges relative to cost, their restriction to a few areas of medical expenditure, and the exemption from charges of broad categories of the population, such as the elderly and children under school-leaving age, irrespective of means. If it were considered desirable to increase income from charges, different courses would be open: to raise existing charges, to introduce new ones for, say, hospital boarding costs or for visits to GPs, or to replace the blanket exemptions by narrower categories such as elderly patients, or children in families, sufficiently poor to be entitled to some means-tested benefit (that is, income support, housing benefit or family credit). If there are to be charges, there is no reason, in fairness, why elderly people, whatever their income, should receive preferential treatment over younger people at lower income levels. The same applies to families with children. This rationalisation of the present system of charges might well be the first step towards a wider extension of charging. The gains would obviously have to outweigh the administrative cost and the political hassle entailed.

Julian Le Grand has presented evidence in support of the view that the middle class makes better use of the health service than does the working class. (See Table 1.1 above, where the figures also reflect the fact that, in old age, when incomes are lower, the claims on the health service are also larger.) He then suggests that charges might reasonably be imposed.[25] Even with charges, however, he does not believe that the NHS would be an effective instrument for reducing inequality in *total* income – mentioned above as one of the possible aims of the welfare state. It might be objected that in the case of benefits in kind the primary aim is *specific* egalitarianism. Even if the middle class does better from the NHS than the working class, the medical care is presumably more equally shared than if we had no health service nor even, as an alternative, an arrangement for subsidising the health insurance of the less well off. As for the effect on the distribution of total income, this cannot be determined without allowing for the progressiveness of the taxes used to finance expenditure. Although Le Grand's final inferences may therefore be open to some question, the view that charges would be appropriate may be sustained.

1.10 A MORE EFFICIENT WELFARE STATE

In the opening paragraphs of this chapter we referred to the apparently widespread dissatisfaction with the welfare state. Although the cost of the various services has grown to such a formidable size, some of the basic objectives still appear to be inadequately met, in particular protection against poverty. We observed that one response has been to recommend still more expenditure in total and even relative to gross national output. But the constraints are severe, as Carter demonstrates (Ch. 6) and the demands on the taxpayer so many and so large. It would admittedly be wrong to emphasise the constraints in such a way as to exclude, by implication, the possibility that more expenditure on the NHS might be preferred to cuts in income tax, as the results of various opinion polls suggest.[26] For a paternalistic policy need not, as is usually supposed, mean a higher level of public expenditure with higher taxation than people would prefer if they could make their preferences fully effective. The opposite may sometimes be the case, with people required by a paternalistic government to have lower taxes rather than, say, shorter waiting lists for hospitals. The need remains, however, to consider whether social expenditure, at any given volume, might not be more effectively spent. A proper assessment of the possibilities would entail lengthy and detailed treatment on a scale far beyond the scope of the present volume, but we would venture the opinion that any savings from improvements in NHS efficiency would be substantially offset by the growing pressure caused by the ageing of the population and the continuing advances in medical science. Other countries are, of course, in a similar situation. It is interesting to observe how, as Mangen records, the pressure to economise has become a dominant consideration in France, Germany and Spain (Ch. 9).

Let us now turn again to cash benefits, long criticised on the ground that large sums are paid to well-off people, although many others fall below a poverty level which is itself too low. If, as some have suggested, selectivity were to be further reduced in favour of universally available benefits, expenditure would be further swollen. The proponents of a Social Dividend are nevertheless in favour of a new universal benefit to be paid to everyone, whether at work or not at work, whether rich or poor. No one would then forfeit any benefit by taking a job, and it is rightly claimed that the 'unemployment trap' would therefore be closed. It is also claimed that benefits would be more fully taken up than is the case with existing means-tested benefits, especially family credit for low-wage working families – although the importance of this point can be easily exaggerated.[27] The cost would be enormous. Thus it has been estimated that one version of the scheme, even when pared down, would cost £30 billion – or substantially more than the total cost of the National Health Service. This would be equivalent to a rise in income tax from 25 per cent to 40 per cent.[28]

The opposite view that what is really desirable is a closer targeting of benefit on those in need has been frequently expressed, notably in official pronouncements on policy objectives in Britain. Some marginal improvements were, in fact, achieved in the 1980s but there has been no inclination to make the really radical change of integrating the tax and social security systems by substituting a negative income tax (NIT) for the whole existing range of cash benefits. The failure of successive governments to do so has been viewed by proponents of the scheme as evidence of a dull conservatism or of moral weakness in the face of 'interests' that would be threatened by better targeting. Whatever the real reasons, Britain is not alone in its conservatism. No other country has replaced the whole range of cash payments with a negative income tax although, as Stephanie Holmans has reported,[29] there has been a partial substitution of 'benefit credits', given through the tax system, for more traditional forms of family assistance in Canada and Germany.

The first step is to see how much of the expenditure on existing social benefits could, in fact, be regarded as ill-directed if the sole aim were to relieve poverty. The figures show that a very substantial part of expenditure on cash benefits *is*, after all, directed to the poor. In the late 1980s, 60 per cent of *all* benefit expenditure went to the 30 per cent of households with the lowest incomes. By contrast, households above median incomes received less than one-fifth of the total. There were marked differences between benefits. Almost nine-tenths of housing benefit went to households in the bottom three deciles but little over a fifth of child benefit went to those groups, whereas the largest amount – almost two-thirds – went to households in the middle-income groups (fourth to eighth deciles).[30] Figures such as these suggest that, although the existing arrangements are less unselective than their critics sometimes imply, a substantial saving might be made.[31]

The demands on the taxpayer, at any given level of expenditure for other purposes, could therefore be reduced and this should offset, at least partially, the harm done to incentives by the adoption of a fully selective system.

With a negative income tax (NIT), a minimum income would be provided through the tax authorities, but only to those whose incomes would otherwise fall below a prescribed minimum – or rather minima, with allowance made for the number of dependants. Various terms have been applied to the payments thus made, the most convenient of which is probably 'benefit-credit'. For persons with other sources of income, this benefit–credit would be gradually withdrawn and would finally disappear at a break-even point above which positive tax would have to be paid. This break-even income would, in effect, be the 'poverty level', and what has been said about the determination of this level and about changes in it over time would still apply. There would be no question of providing assistance to persons with incomes from other sources above this minimum.

The incentive to save – and the incentive to earn the incomes from which savings can be made – would be discouraged by the knowledge that any income from accumulated savings would reduce the claim to a negative income tax. Moreover, NIT could be regarded as a form of public charity. As we have seen, the old case for social insurance rested partly on the contention that beneficiaries would themselves have contributed to what they received and had therefore earned the right to benefits. This relationship between benefits and contributions has subsequently been clouded by the practice of collecting contributions together with income tax through PAYE but it may not have been wholly obscured. The employers' contributions must also be considered. With social security fully financed from the general budget this payroll tax would presumably be abandoned with the loss of revenue perhaps made good by a rise in VAT. The change might be welcomed on the ground that the payroll tax discourages labour-intensive means of production but it must be recognised that VAT is also largely a tax on labour. There would be some effect but it might be small.

If NIT is compared not with the present universal benefits but with the present selective benefits, a slightly more favourable verdict on the effect on the incentives to save may be possible. In both cases incentives would be blunted but there is this difference: NIT, as normally expounded, would impose an *income* test, whereas the current system of income support imposes a *means* test which applies to both income and capital. Under NIT it would not be necessary to dispose of capital in order to claim benefit (as is the case in Britain above a small amount) and the capital could be held in a form that yielded little income. The same result could be obtained however, without introducing NIT, by simply changing the present system from means test to income test. (Australian experience would be relevant.)

How would NIT pass the test of simplicity in administration? The case for greater simplicity has been urged repeatedly – but has scarcely been achieved under the existing social security arrangements! NIT would have the great merit of bringing the tax system and the benefit system together in a way which should, in principle, permit a more coherent and consistent pursuit of objectives. Unfortunately a revenue department could not really be expected to provide and to withdraw unemployment benefit with the speed required (see Barclay, Ch.13). The same applies to sickness benefit. This objection does not, however, hold in the same way in the case of old-age pensions, disability pensions or child benefit. It would seem realistic, therefore, to regard NIT as a possible substitute for long-term rather than short-term benefits.

Unfortunately it is particularly in the case of long-term benefits that a switch to NIT would encounter another important objection. For the expectation of receiving a pension on which personal plans had been reasonably based would be disrupted by the abandonment of this universal benefit in favour of a selective one, payable only to those whose incomes would otherwise fall below the break-even level, or poverty line. This would be regarded as a breach of faith and the political opposition might well be insuperable. It may be asked whether it would not be possible to make the change more acceptable by introducing it gradually. Thus persons already middle-aged might have their existing pension rights guaranteed but younger people would be told they would have to rely on NIT although, meanwhile, they would have to finance the unselective pay-as-you-go pensions of the retired. It would be a long time before any significant economy in expenditure could be made and, meanwhile, the younger people would perceive that any savings they managed to accumulate would reduce their own ultimate claims to assistance from NIT. (We may note in passing that a switch from a PAYG to a funded pension system – as often recommended by the New Right – would mean that a transitional generation would have to pay twice, both for currently unfunded pensions and for those to be derived from an accumulating fund.)

The abolition of universal unselective benefits would therefore encounter the dual obstacles of 'interests' and 'ideas'. The obstacle from 'interests' would be those of persons excluded from benefit, notably those already on pension and those already middle-aged who would soon retire. No government could afford to disregard the political strength of this opposition. The obstacle from 'ideas' would be the need to respect previous undertakings and to fulfil reasonable expectations. This latter objection on moral grounds might not, however, be regarded as decisive, for the harm so done might be outweighed by the benefit in other respects. Thus we are brought back once more to the basic objectives of policy and the value judgements they embody.

If the complete replacement of existing cash benefits by a negative income tax were considered too radical, the existing administrative machinery could be used more selectively and effectively. Pensioners provide an example. Although the situation of the average pensioner has been greatly improved over the years, there is much dispersion around the average, with some elderly pensioners – often single or widowed women without occupational pensions – still facing serious hardship. Although the basic state pension might be raised, it would be costly to do so on the scale required to provide additional assistance to these very poor elderly people. But the 'special premiums' attached to income support, which were introduced in 1988 to meet the needs of particular groups, might be used more fully to provide selective help. Another example may be some groups of the disabled. Again there are the problems of families with children. Special assistance is given to single-parent families but more attention may need to be paid to two-parent families on income support whose benefit is raised by the family premium by less than a tenth even when there are two children. There may also be a case for giving more support to working families by more generous provision of family credit (see Appendix). In the case of child benefit, payable to all families, the obvious way of 'clawing back' benefit from the relatively well-off would be by use of the income tax system, and this could be done without going so far as to replace cash benefits by a negative income tax. The difficulty in this case is that, with the benefit paid to the mother, the effectiveness of the clawback would be reduced. This particular difficulty would also arise with a full-scale negative income tax.

There is another area where the scope for action may be less impeded by either 'interests' or 'ideas'. This is the area of indexation discussed in Section 1.7 above. As we have seen, benefits are indexed only for changes in prices, which means a freezing of their real value and therefore, in a growing economy, a relative decline as compared with incomes from employment. There has already been some pressure to allow pensioners 'to share in growth' and the Labour Party is committed to a policy of raising benefits in line with rising earnings or rising prices, whichever should rise the more. But a further burden would then be imposed on the working population – and one which, by its nature, could not be eased by economic growth. As it happens, the 'interests' are less formidable here than those considered above, partly because the gain from wage indexation would be slow and gradual – and partly, perhaps, because 'indexation' is a more abstruse policy measure. Nor would there be the same affront to 'ideas' – which means in this case the principle of keeping faith – for there seems to be no generally accepted understanding that wage indexation will supersede price indexation. We have, however, proposed in Section 1.7 that the 'poverty level', or 'levels', should indeed be raised over time with rising earnings but at a lower rate. This formula would be applied to the flat-rate social security benifits as well as to selective benefits. Moreover it would apply to short-term benefits for the sick and the unemployed as well as to pensioners. The latter would, however, continue to benefit from sustained increases in the second–tier pensions – SERPS. A Labour Party proposal for the full wage-indexation of the basic pension as well as more generous terms for SERPS would, in our view, be over-generous at the expense of other social benefits or of the working population. But we have suggested increases in the special selective premiums paid in addition to income support to certain groups in particular need of more assistance, including some of the pensioners. Moreover, a selective and more generous form of assistance to families, provided through the tax system, may yet be devised.

With the value judgements falling thick and fast, no universal agreement about the 'right' approach is to be anticipated, but action may be needlessly hampered, and even paralysed, by confusion that reflects rather an inadequate assessment of the objectives of the welfare state and of the weights that are being accorded to each of them when conflicts arise and choices have to be made. This, at least, is something we should seek to avoid.

NOTES

1. HMSO (1985).
2. Lowe (1989).
3. See, for example, Ashford (1981), Heclo (1974), Thane (1982).
4. See, for example, Buchanan and Tullock (1977), Downs (1957), Mueller (1979), McLean (1987).
5. Titmuss (1970).
6. Brittan and Webb (1990) p 3. See also Rhys-Williams (1942), H Parker (1989). It might be supposed that the main proponents of a Social Dividend would be socialists but this has not been the case.
7. By introducing the notion of an 'Impartial Spectator', Adam Smith could bring in disinterested assessments without turning people into abstractions, as Rawls has done with his 'veil of ignorance'. See Smith (1976b) and Raphael (1975).
8. Rawls (1972). There is a sharp contrast between Rawls's abstract analysis and the more empirical approach followed by Beveridge, the administrator, who devoted little attention to finding a basis for his proposals in social ethics. 'The aim of the Plan for Social Security is to abolish want' he said, and probably felt that was enough (Beveridge 1942). His biographer records that '... at no stage did Beveridge discuss with his committee the general scope of the inquiry and the goals to be attained'. Harris (1977) p 385.
9. Lessnoff (1986) ch 7.
10. HMSO (1990a).
11. Crosland (1956) p 120.
12. HMSO (1942) p 167.
13. HMSO (1942) p 13.
14. Meade (1978).
15. HL Debates (1953).
16. For a particularly strong statement of this point of view see Novak (1987).
17. Adam Smith (1976a) p 869–870.
18. Townsend (1979); Piachaud (1981).

19. In considering the British case it must again be kept in mind that means-tested benefits are virtually the same as the basic flat-rate insurance benefits.
20. For a more extended discussion see T and D J Wilson (1982) Ch 5.
21. HL Debates (1958); Keynes (1980).
22. In a number of continental European countries earnings-related pensions in payment were originally indexed for changes in current earnings – 'double indexation'. See Wilson (1975). This practice was largely abandoned after the oil crises of the seventies.
23. Musgrave and Musgrave (1975).
24. Tobin (1970) p 448.
25. Le Grand (1982).
26. Taylor-Gooby (1985) p 76.
27. It is estimated that about half of those entitled to family credit fail to take up the benefit. But the number is small – less than 1 per cent of all family units. Moreover, a common explanation is that family incomes are so close to the upper limit at which claims will be accepted that the small sum to be obtained is not thought worth the trouble of submitting a claim.
28. Brittan and Webb (1990) p 45.
29. Holmans (1984).
30. HMSO (1990b).
31. Dilnot, Kay and Morris (1984) p 89.

REFERENCES

Ashford D E (1981) *Policy and Politics in Britain*, Temple University Press, Philadelphia, USA.

Ashford D E (1986) *The Emergence of the Welfare State*, Blackwell, Oxford.

Brittan S and Webb S (1990) *Beyond the Welfare State*, Aberdeen University Press for the David Hume Institute, Edinburgh.

Buchanan J and Tullock G (1977) *The Calculus of Consent*, University of Michigan Press, Ann Arbor, USA.

Crosland C A R (1956) *The Future of Socialism*, Jonathan Cape, London.

Dilnot, A W, Kay J A and Morris C N (1984) *The Reform of Social Security*, Oxford University Press, Oxford.

Downs A (1957) *The Economic Theory of Democracy*, Harper and Row, New York, USA.

Harris J (1977) *William Beveridge: A Biography*, Oxford University Press, Oxford.

Heclo H (1974) *Modern Social Politics In Britain and Sweden*, Yale University Press, New Haven, USA.

Hill M and Bramley G (1986) *Analysing Social Policy*, Blackwell, Oxford.

HL Debates (1953) 20 May.

HL Debates (1958) 8 December.

HMSO (1942) *Social Insurance and Allied Services* Cmd 6404, London (Beveridge Report).

HMSO (1985) *The Reform of Social Security* Cmnd 9517, London.

HMSO (1990a) *Low Income Statistics*, Social Services Committee, Fourth Report, London 25 April.

HMSO (1990b) *Government Expenditure Plans: Department of Social Security* Cm 1014, London.

Holmans S K (1984) *Social Security Systems in Selected Countries and their Integration with Tax Systems*, HM Treasury, London.

Keynes J M (1980) *Collected Writings of John Maynard Keynes*, Activities 1900-6: Shaping the Post-War World: Employment and Commodities, vol XXVI, Macmillan, London.

Le Grand J (1982) *The Strategy of Equality*, George Allen and Unwin, London.

Lessnoff M (1986) *Social Contract*, Macmillan, London.

Lowe R (1989) Resignation at the Treasury: The Social Services Committee and the Failure to Reform the Welfare State, 1955-57, *Journal of Social Policy*, **18**(4): 505-26, Cambridge.

McLean I (1987) *Public Choice: An Introduction*, Blackwell, Oxford.

Meade J E (1978) *The Structure and Reform of Direct Taxation*, Allen and Unwin, London.

Mueller D (1979) *Public Choice*, Cambridge University Press, Cambridge.

Musgrave R A and Musgrave P (1975) *Public Finance in Theory and Practice*, 3rd edn, McGraw Hill, New York, USA.

Novak R (1987) *The New Consensus on Family and Welfare*, American Enterprise Institute, Washington DC, USA.

Parker H (1989) *Instead of the Dole*, Routledge, London.

Phelps-Brown H (1988) *Egalitarianism and the Generation of Inequality*, Oxford University Press, Oxford.

Piachaud D (1981) Peter Townsend and the Holy Grail, *New Society*, **57**: 417-21.

Raphael D D (1975) The Impartial Spectator in Skinner A S and Wilson T (eds) *Essays on Adam Smith*, Oxford University Press, Oxford.

Rawls J (1972) *A Theory of Justice*, Oxford University Press, Oxford.

Rhys-Williams B (1942) *Something to Look Forward to*, Macdonald, London.

Smith A (1976a) *The Wealth of Nations*, ed Campbell R H, Skinner A S and Todd W B, Oxford University Press, Oxford.

Smith A (1976b) *The Theory of Moral Sentiments*, ed Raphael D D and Macfie A L, Oxford University Press, Oxford.

Taylor-Gooby P (1985) The Politics of Welfare: Public Attitudes and Behaviour, in Klein R and O'Higgins M (eds) *The Future of Welfare*, Blackwell, Oxford.

Thane P (1982) *The Foundations of the Welfare State*, Longmans, London.

Titmuss R M (1970) *The Gift Relationship*, Allen and Unwin, London.

Tobin J (1970) On Limiting the Domain of Inequality, *Journal of Law and Economics*, **13**, reprinted in *Economic Justice*, ed Phelps E S, Penguin 1973.

Townsend P (1979) *Poverty in the United Kingdom*, Allen Lane, London.

Wilson T (ed) (1975) *Pensions, Inflation and Growth*, Heinemann Educational Books, London.

Wilson T and D J Wilson (1982) *The Political Economy of the Welfare state*, Allen and Unwin, London.

Part Two

Questions of Principle

2 Welfare Philosophies and Welfare Finance
Alan Peacock

2.1 INTRODUCTION

This chapter concerns the choices open to governments in devising financial arrangements which are designed to fulfil the objectives of the 'welfare state', or, more particularly, of the social security element in it. I distinguish between four choices:

(i) The choice between an absolute or relative poverty line.
(ii) The choice between universality or selectivity in the provision of social benefits.
(iii) The choice between types of benefit provision – tax allowances, money transfers and communal consumption.
(iv) The choice between general taxation and earmarked contributions as a method for financing benefits.

It is as well to begin with the realisation that the most that we can expect from an analysis of the financial arrangements is to see how these categories of choices can be made consistent with one another. There are many ways in which this consistency can be achieved, depending on the initial value judgements chosen to govern the aims of the 'welfare state'. There is therefore no point in following the conventional pattern of classifying the 'pros' and 'cons' of any combination of choices. The ranking of the choices is derived solely from the particular value system chosen as the point of departure of the discussion. It follows that it is fruitless to attempt to derive a logic of choice solely from the conditions for economic efficiency in Paretian welfare analysis buttressed by some view of equity objectives. There need therefore be no consensus amongst economists about the 'proper' choices.[1]

These propositions suggest a procedure for developing the exposition which follows in this contribution. First, categorise the more influential political philosophies from which 'operational' value judgements may be derived in order to specify the objectives of the welfare state. This will make clear the initial disagreements about aims. Secondly, translate these 'operational' judgements into policy prescriptions regarding financing arrangements. Thirdly, consider how far differences between the various philosophies are derived from (i) the philosophy itself, (ii) the models of human behaviour and their reflection in economic modelling, and (iii) differing judgements about the practicality of financial arrangements designed to fulfil the policy aims.

This typology of welfare state philosophies may then be used in order to review recent government attempts to change the thrust of welfare policy.

2.2   THE LIBERTARIAN POSITION

It is absurd, of course, to talk about 'the' libertarian position but there are sufficient common elements in libertarian writing for us to be able to construct a view about society's obligations which involve transfer of resources between individuals.

A useful starting point is Nozick's view on 'entitlement'[2]. The only claim we have on resources is that based on our own efforts and abilities. Our entitlement is to be able to exert effort and to use our abilities in any way we choose provided this does not limit any other individual's entitlement to do the same. It follows that no one has a prior right to a particular standard of living, such as a minimum level of subsistence. This does not carry the implication that people will be left to starve, as it would be wholly consistent with a society in which people could use their own resources as they think fit, for a large proportion of them do, in fact, wish to see poverty eradicated. The motives, as always, may be mixed. Some may wish to see poverty eradicated because they would suffer from feelings of guilt and repugnance or because they are empathic; others may be worried about possible social unrest and attacks on their own perceived entitlements. In short, the relief of poverty would reflect some contractual relationship between members of the community and would not be legitimised by an appeal to some principle of distributive justice.

The translation of this philosophical position into the designing of institutions to give effect to any wish to relieve poverty seems to be regarded as a rather secondary matter by social philosophers; or perhaps they realise that the translation is far from easy. The only general guidance given is that one must minimise the intervention of the state as much as possible and, by implication, the degree of compulsory income distribution. All that an economist can do is to identify the kind of institutional arrangements which would appear to be compatible with the 'minimalist' position.

So far as the poverty line is concerned, it is doubtful if libertarians could accept the concept at all, for poverty is not capable of exact measurement. They are usually the first to complain about the false precision given to the term by poverty action groups. Nevertheless, there is a clear commitment in the libertarian literature to a community responsibility to prevent starvation, however caused. Thus Hayek,[3] after referring to the brilliant success of the capitalist countries in creating the means to eradicate poverty, quotes with approval the words of the famous Poor Law Commissioner and economist, Nassau Senior:

> to proclaim that no man, whatever his vices or even his crimes, shall die of hunger and cold, is a promise that in the state of civilisation of England, or of France, can be performed not merely with safety, but with advantage, because the gift of mere subsistence may be subjected to conditions which no one will voluntarily accept.[4]

The commitment clearly only extends to the relief of absolute poverty. Hayek's view is probably representative of this position:

> poverty in the relative sense must of course continue to exist outside of any completely egalitarian society; so long as there exists inequality, somebody must be at the bottom of the scale. But the abolition of absolute poverty is not helped by the endeavour to achieve 'social justice'; in fact, in many of the countries in which absolute poverty is still an acute problem, the concern for 'social justice' has become one of the greatest obstacles in the elimination of poverty.

and again:

> Misfortune, however, cannot create a claim for protection against risks which all have had to run in order to attain the position they occupy. The very language in current use which at once labels as a 'social problem' anything which causes dissatisfaction of any group, and suggests that it is the duty of the legislature to do something about such 'social injustice', has turned the conception of 'social justice' into a mere pretext for claims for privileges by special interests.[5]

In order to understand the libertarian attitude to universality versus selectivity of benefits, it is necessary to consider the 'minimalist' position about the responsibility of the individual to make provision for himself or herself against the possibility of becoming poor. The initial presumption is that individuals might be able to insure against various calamitous events or predictable conditions (e.g. old age) which would destroy or at least reduce their income earning power. If individuals cannot be relied upon voluntarily to take out such insurance this does not make a case for some compulsory state scheme, but it does suggest some form of government regulation which would make a minimum level of provision through private sector insurance compulsory. However, even assuming that such a regulation would be enforceable, this would not guarantee the eradication of absolute poverty. First it is quite probable that a fair proportion of insurees would have to pay annual premia which would leave them with an annual disposable income below the poverty standard and there will be a residuum of persons who cannot provide for themselves anyway. (It is often claimed that poorer people are worse health risks than richer persons so that compulsory insurance premia could be regressive.) Secondly, loss of earnings resulting from unemployment is uninsurable. (Now it is true that some form of insurance against temporary unemployment is provided indirectly through extension of credit under hire purchase agreements and temporary suspension of mortgage payments, but lenders will expect some form of security, e.g. other physical assets and investment in skills, which can only be supplied by the relatively well-off.) Unemployment is virtually uninsurable because of (a) the adverse selection problem – the insuree can control the incidence of unemployment; and (b) the risks are not separate and independent – unemployment can hit a large number of persons at once.

The minimalist position, therefore, recognises that inducing or compelling individuals by regulation to re-allocate their income through time would not eliminate poverty, and that some form of payment from public funds would be required – the form of which is yet to be discussed. Clearly, however, given the overriding requirement that compulsory redistribution of income must be minimised, such payment must be targeted to those who are not able to cover the risks of poverty for themselves and targeting must be related to the particular cause of poverty, such as sickness, old age, housing conditions or unemployment. The inevitable concomitant to targeted benefits must be means testing.

So far as the form of benefits is concerned, there must be a presumption that the libertarian position would entail a preference for money transfers. Individuals who receive some form of subsidised income would be paid in money in order to cover their minimum needs during periods of sickness, unemployment or old age. Such devices as food subsidies, and health provision at zero cost rather than by payment through compulsory health insurance would be frowned upon, because these would interfere with market forces.[6] It would also be emphasised by libertarians that transfers-in-kind would inhibit the preservation and development of basic household management skills which would enable poorer persons to make the most of scarce resources. At the very most, libertarians might tolerate the issue of vouchers designed to effect payments for particular services, particularly those which protect the interest of minors, such as housing and education. This would still enable a free market to operate in the provision of 'social services' through rent allowances, education vouchers and the like paid directly to recipients of income support and redeemable by private suppliers and targeted to the 'desired' components of a minimum standard of living.

There is, finally, the question of financing the various elements in the

provision of income support. The principle in operation which comple-
ments the minimising of compulsory transfers is that of relating benefit to
cost so far as possible. Therefore, in an ideal libertarian world, individuals, as
we have seen, insure against the incidence of poverty. Taking a longer view,
the incidence of poverty might be reduced by investment in human capital,
which suggests that somehow a market in educational and training investment should be created with the offer of loan finance. If the absolute minimum payments simply make it impossible for all individuals to pay the
premia or amortise the loans, then the next step would be to subsidise the
premia and loans on a means-tested basis. The important point to note is
that while insurance would have to be compulsory, there is no argument
deployed in support of a state monopoly in insurance provision. The one
important exception would be unemployment, which cannot be insured
against, though it is sometimes claimed that any state provision might be
financed primarily from a payment by each industry in proportion to the
incidence of unemployment 'generated' in it.[7]

Controversy must obviously surround the feasibility of such a system of
income and its very compatibility with other principles dear to the heart of
minimalists. The onus of proof of entitlement to support would presumably
rest with the individual or the head of the family, and it seems impossible to
avoid major difficulties in deciding on levels of support and in carrying out
detailed enquiries into means. This presents policy makers with a dilemma.
On the one hand, if information is to be supplied solely by those demanding support, claimants may exaggerate their needs – the adverse selection
problem. On the other hand, obtaining accurate information might entail
rigorous methods of enquiry and heavy penalties for non-compliance which
might appear incompatible with a libertarian disposition.

There has been some recent discussion about the prospects for devising
an administrative system which would enable a government to differentiate
between 'self-provision' requirements and the residuum of financial support
which would be targeted towards those who cannot meet the minimum
standard of individual and family provision. One such scheme[8] is derived
from the principle of taxation according to benefit developed by Wicksell.
Each individual is given a social security account by the public authorities.
Premia payments are recorded on the credit side on evidence supplied by
the individual, who may claim partial or complete exemption depending on
evidence of means. Social security payments are recorded on the debit side,
with some such payments (e.g. education vouchers, family allowances) also
recorded as loans. A separate loan account records loans taken up and records interest and amortisation payments. The account is normally 'closed'
when the individual reaches pensionable age with provision made for 'early
closing' in the event of death before retirement or emigration. Depending
on the individual's circumstances, any deficit on the account may be written
off, the resultant loss being covered by taxation. Of course, such a scheme

does not rule out strategic behaviour by individuals, who may work less and save less, in contemplation of the likelihood that the government will always provide for them. However, if they have a deficit against their name, then they will have to pay up, though they would always be left with a subsistence level of pension.

This kind of scheme raises a basic question about the operation of any social security system, even if it is confined to minimum income support. Unless there is some compelling reason for operating a separate compulsory social insurance scheme run by the government, it would seem logical to integrate the social security account with the individual's 'account' with the tax authorities. Only then would it be possible to have full information on the impact of government transfers and taxes on the disposable income of the individual. Full consideration of proposals to amalgamate social security and income tax administration will be given when proposals for tax credit or negative income tax schemes are examined in Part 3 below.

2.3   THE SOCIAL MARKET ECONOMISTS

The 'social market economy' (*Soziale Marktwirtschaft*) was a term invented by the German economist and senior government adviser Alfred Muller-Armack to denote a reconciliation of the free market economy with the demands of distributive justice.[9] It is a useful term to describe the attitudes of a regiment of economic and social thinkers who have extended the concept of 'entitlement' to cover the right of every individual to a 'basic' standard of living and also to access to resources in order to develop their latent talents, for example through investment in their education and social environment (health and housing). At the same time, the choice of means for giving effect to these 'rights' should recognise the importance of developing individuals' capacity to choose for themselves and of expressing these choices through an efficiently operating market economy.

Space does not allow a discussion of the different approaches leading to the delineation of this extension of the concept of entitlement. It is sufficient to say that whether these entitlements are derived from a utilitarian view of economic welfare, based on the assumption that marginal utility falls as income rises, or from a Rawlsian view of social justice, based on maximising the welfare of the least advantaged person (which does not require interpersonal comparisons of utility), the constraint of minimising income redistribution no longer applies. This follows directly from the more positive commitment both to a basic standard of living and also to the funding of services designed to promote investment in human capital.

If there is any distinction to be made between the various social market economists, it lies in their view of the organisation of production; and this is germane to the choice of practical measures matching their value judgements. One group does not specify in any detail how production should be organised, except to state that competition must be preserved within the market economy – how this is to be done is a separate question. There is another group, following John Stuart Mill, which would argue strongly in favour of much more equality in the ownership of capital. In Mill's case, this extended to the proposition that the future of the market economy depended on the growth in labour-managed firms – 'an association of the labourers themselves on terms of equality, collectively owning the capital with which they carry on their operations and working under managers, selected and removable by themselves'.[10] The most distinguished contemporary exponent of attempts to reconcile conflicts between capital and labour is James Meade,[11] who has developed a scheme based on joint holdings of risk capital in a company by both 'capitalists' and workers. However, the sharing of risks by labour and capital presupposes, according to Meade, an automatic entitlement by all individuals to 'a certain and reliable tax-free Social Dividend'.[12] Social security income becomes the essential source of stable income alongside the fluctuating capital and wage income received by the worker.

As before, an attempt will be made to trace the connection between the philosophy of the welfare state and the level of benefits. The removal of the constraint on compulsory redistribution immediately suggests that social market economists (SMEs) would be more sympathetic to a minimum level of subsistence which depends on the growth in real GDP; in other words the 'poverty line' is a relative concept. (This is a logical necessity in the case of the utilitarian theory of income redistribution, provided that pre-tax/transfer income distribution remains unequal.) A more difficult question is how far SMEs are committed to a much more radical requirement, namely some proportional relation between income levels and benefits, as in the case of earnings-related pension schemes. The usual argument supporting the claim that such benefits should be earnings-related rests on the supposed 'consensus' between political parties in several European countries which lies behind the 'dynamic' pension schemes operating in such countries as Germany, Italy and the UK. 'Consensus' does not however imply that there is any logical connection between the SME position and what happens to be agreed, if in fact it is, between different political factions. A more likely explanation of consensus is that offered by Barry,[13] namely that, with no constitutional limitations, public expenditure decisions are taken which commit future generations. Earnings-related pensions become an 'electoral bribe' on a large scale and one which works because of the opportunities open to governments to disguise the long-run economic costs of pensions provision.

A more obvious difference between libertarians and SMEs lies in the firmer commitment of the latter to 'access' by poorer persons to education, health and housing facilities, which can, of course, be justified on the grounds that, in the long run, investment in human capital may reduce the incidence of poverty. This extension of 'entitlement' must be important in the devising of appropriate government measures to give effect to the objectives of policy, but it is difficult to give any precision to terms such as 'access' or 'entitlement' in trying to translate them into resource requirements. On such matters there is room for considerable variations in points of view amongst SMEs.

Turning to the choice between universality or selectivity of benefits, we observe again no logical necessity why SMEs should vote for one or the other, as a matter of principle. Indeed, much of the discussion concerns the danger that selectivity may defeat its own purpose by offering no incentive to beneficiaries to acquire the skills or make the effort to be able to fend for themselves; and this must be an empirical matter which can only be resolved, if at all, by scientific investigation. However, the more explicit commitment of SMEs to income redistribution removes a major objection to the use of universal income provision, e.g. some form of 'Social Dividend' for all, as a major means for eliminating poverty. Therefore, apart from the argument advanced above for a Social Dividend based on the need for a 'certain and reliable' component of income, the claims of the Social Dividend are extended as a way of remedying the perceived deficiencies of selective benefits.

It might be thought that the extension of the definition of welfare provision and the more relaxed attitude to income redistribution would point towards major differences between libertarians and SMEs over the types of benefit provision, but this is not so. Tax allowances (or expenditures) were not specifically mentioned in Section 2.2 above, though it is conceivable that the libertarian position would support tax relief granted to charities directed at helping poorer persons. However, such relief becomes of some importance in the SMEs' scenario. This applies particularly to earnings- related pensions. Given the SMEs' interest in combining their views on social justice with an efficient market economy, there is no necessity for such a pension scheme to be nationalised. A pensions standard must be laid down, which could be either contribution-based or final-salary-based, and the employee could be a member of either an occupational or personal pension scheme. It is an open question how much tax relief should be given alongside the compulsory requirement to meet the pension standard, and it must be borne in mind that such tax relief has to be given at the cost of either raising taxes elsewhere, given the level of public expenditure, or reducing the level of public expenditure, unless the government wishes to face the consequences of a growing public debt. There are three arguments in favour of tax allowances. The first is that SMEs are likely, as a matter of general philosophy, to wish to encourage private saving even at the cost of a reduction in government saving. Second, encouraging competition in the provision of pensions would fit with the SMEs' disposition to support the market economy. (This, of course, would suggest, in strict logic, preference for 'portable' personal rather than occupational pensions, which may be specifically designed to reduce occupational mobility.) Third, although this point is the subject of much argument, a state monopoly of pension provision runs the risk of being highly bureaucratic and therefore slow-moving and costly, because not subject to market pressures.

Clearly, money transfers are a major instrument of SME social policy, particularly one wedded to a Social Dividend approach. The more interesting area of discourse on benefits concerns access to educational, health and housing services. The difference between libertarians and SMEs is more one of degree than of kind. For SMEs there is no reason why these services should have to be provided at zero cost by government institutions. Even if it is believed that some form of consumer protection is necessary because of the perceived inability of citizens to make sensible choices regarding education, health and housing, there is no case for turning them over to the government. Consumer protection can be afforded by regulation and by advisory services, with the latter if need be receiving public subsidy. The difference with libertarians will arise over the *degree* of 'entitlement' to such services, and is likely to be reflected not in the form of provision but in the method of financing. We should therefore expect SMEs to be in favour both of money transfers and also of educational, health and housing voucher systems, with the production of the associated services being left partly if not wholly in private hands, and perhaps with a bias towards co-operatives and non-profit-making institutions as suppliers.

Whereas the libertarian position takes 'the insurance principle' as the starting point and modifies it only to the extent necessary to prevent absolute poverty, the SME's positive emphasis on distributive justice severs the nexus between contribution and payment, at least in any strict way. SMEs may support the proposition that, as a matter of principle, every citizen should pay something towards the provision of public services, but there is no presumption that such payment should be earmarked for the payment of social security and associated services. At most, labelling finance of social security as 'contributions' or 'premiums' is only a sales pitch, and may contain the danger of deluding contributors that they are paying in full for the benefits received.[14] It therefore comes as no surprise to find that SMEs have been closely concerned with attempts to amalgamate the personal tax and social security systems, particularly if some form of Social Dividend scheme is to become the cornerstone of the social security system. As is well known, if they are not amalgamated or at least not closely co-ordinated, those who move out of entitlement to benefits because they have become fit or have found jobs may be faced with such high marginal tax rates that they are worse off than if not working.[15]

To sum up this section, there is some consonance between the libertarian and SME's position, as found, for instance, in the wish to channel income support through the individual or family and to avoid collectivising the services designed to alleviate poverty. However, the kind of 'life-cycle accounting' suggested above (pp 41-2) as a logical consequence of libertarian financing arrangements would presumably be regarded by SMEs as neither desirable nor necessary. Individuals suffering from poverty are not considered as being 'in debt to society' as a result of being in this condition. Furthermore, in so far as individuals move from being poor to being better off, they acknowledge any 'debt to society' by the payment of a greater proportion of their incomes in taxes as they move up the income scale. This argument is only subject to dispute amongst SMEs if we adopt such a broad definition of social policy as to include access to higher education. Some would continue to argue that those undergoing higher education should not have to bear the cost, even if as a result their income prospects are enhanced – if that were the result then the fortunate graduates would pay higher taxes anyway. Others recognise a problem of horizontal equity between those obtaining free access to capital if they invest in themselves and those who have to borrow the capital if they invest in a business and initially are at the same income level. Here, the 'life-cycle accounting' concept seems to make sense, with students paying off loans used to finance their studies, though repayment might take into account the economic circumstances of the graduate.[16]

2.4   THE COLLECTIVIST POSITION

The common characteristic of the two previous positions has been the emphasis on public financing as distinct from public provision of welfare services. Redistribution is regarded as a means by which poorer persons are enabled, as far as possible, to help themselves. In the last analysis, if there were no poverty, then the 'welfare state' would disappear. Hence my previous prescription that: 'the proper function of the welfare state . . . is to teach people how to do without it', and the associated conditional projection that, if it were so desired, in the long run the welfare state could wither away.[17] This position, however, is not acceptable to a wide range of influential writers on welfare state problems, though few economists appear to occupy their ranks.

The modern debate out of which the general differences between individualistic and collectivist positions emerge has centred in medical care. Let us assume that A fulfils his obligations to government under a libertarian regime and insures against illness, as he is required to do, whereas B evades his obligations. If they both fall ill with a similar complaint, A receives better treatment than B because the insurance company will pay up. This is unjust, it is claimed, because such an important service as medical care should be allocated according to people's needs and not according to their means. The fact that B chose to evade his obligations does not alter the situation. The general point being made is that equal access to consumption of 'priority' goods such as medical care fosters the ideal of fraternity and emphasises interests held in common rather than the diversity of interests and viewpoints which libertarians believe to be the important characteristic of individuals in society. Diversity of interests, so it is held, particularly if matched by income inequality, make for a divided society. This idealist point of view is associated in recent times, of course, with Richard Titmuss.[18] In his view, there was at least a minimum of priority goods and services which must be enjoyed in common, such as health and education. Ryan puts it thus:

> the market can be left to give beer to beer drinkers and champagne to champagne drinkers but not to give blood to those who need transfusions. Both sorts of appeal rely on the belief that there are morally valuable side effects from communality of consumption; the Spartans thought they got extra loyalty and comradeship, Green . . . and Titmuss . . . thought they got extra altruism on the one side, and gratitude and a sense of belonging on the other.[19]

Even a brief résumé of the 'communality of consumption' position makes it clear that concentration on the concept of a 'poverty line' is misplaced. However, our previous distinction between social security provision in the narrow sense and social services may still be useful. In the collectivist position, the emphasis shifts from 'entitlement' to some minimum standard of living to the fact of inequality of income distribution. Recalling the utilitarian argument, if in one situation every income receiver was at the margin of subsistence and then the situation changed and half of the income receivers increased their incomes twofold and the rest remained at the margin of subsistence, this would represent an improvement in welfare, though it would almost certainly not represent an *optimal* position to utilitarians. However, the fact that inequality had increased might warn the collectivist that a divisive element had been introduced into society. In short, instead of meeting a poverty standard subject to minimising income redistribution, it must be shown why any income equality is necessary in the first place – something like the position taken by Rawls. However, this only takes us to the position of requiring positive income redistribution from rich to poor, which, other things being equal, need only mean a redistribution of purchasing power as between individual citizens who would then be responsible for their own welfare. An essential element in the collectivist position is that the redistribution must take a form which furthers the aim of equal access to 'priority' goods such as health, housing and education. While redistribution must be reflected to some extent in government transfers, the main impact on the national accounts will appear in an increase, not in individual disposable income, but in a rise in expenditure on consumption goods and services by government.

It follows that the issue of universality versus selectivity of benefits is hardly an issue to collectivists, at least in its traditional context. The categorising of the different causes of poverty may seem necessary, if only to determine the differing 'needs' in each condition, with benefit payments fixed by reference to these needs for each category as perceived by, say, social administrators. At the same time, a 'Social Dividend' payable in cash may be thought too insensitive an instrument to take account of the differing needs of the ill-off, and one which in any case could be overshadowed by payments in kind, which must now be considered in more detail.

Sufficient has been said so far to explain why collectivists would favour benefits in kind, but it is worth considering further the philosophical basis of this change of emphasis away from the simple provision of cash to the ill-off. First of all, the question of the form of redistribution must be discussed before its provision and extent are considered. The libertarian and, to some extent, the SME's position emphasises the important 'negative freedom' valued by individuals in the sense of freedom from outside interference in their exploitation of their preferences. It has been argued, however, that 'social justice' involves a 'natural right' to certain commodities such as food, shelter and medical care. It is interesting that this argument has been deployed by Dasgupta[20] as consonant with the pursuit of the idea of freedom – not simply freedom from want but a right which would guarantee individuals' access to particular forms of consumption. A familiar argument is the paternalist one – the ability of individuals to make choices that will 'better their condition', as Adam Smith might have put it, diminishes with the degree of poverty. Even if choice is constrained by a voucher system, the ill-off may have neither the courage nor the skill to make the right choices among competing suppliers. There is a touch of this in Dasgupta's argument, but its main thrust is that the variability in needs is difficult to ascertain by the government and that if it polls individuals on what their needs are, it faces the prospect of non-truthful disclosure. The best that the government can do is to assume that individuals have equal needs. Then he adds his bull point. If incomes are more-or-less equally distributed, the deviation from the mean 'demand' for such needs would be negligible and a voucher system would achieve the aim of 'positive freedom'. If incomes are unequally distributed, then the rich would top up their vouchers and receive more than their 'natural rights'; only a state rationing system would achieve the desired aim of equal access.

The term 'equal needs' is clearly ambiguous, but what Dasgupta is concerned to emphasise is that for certain social services the collectivist is not demanding *minimum* but *uniform* standards of provision. This view is fully consonant with Titmuss's precept that there should be communality of consumption, for the most efficient way for the state to provide uniform standards of provision is to set aside the price mechanism and itself to provide the services in kind.

It follows from this argument that, whereas social security transfers would still remain an integral part of the welfare state, tax allowances would be frowned upon. Encouraging individuals to 'contract out' of state provision of health and education services by offering them tax relief on payments made to private suppliers would undermine the moral foundations of the welfare state. Not only would such individuals be denying that they had something in common with others, but they might prefer to be 'more equal than others' by purchasing more of these services than would otherwise be available to them through state provision. The real test of the pure collectivist argument, however, is whether it entails prohibition of any private provision of such services, whatever the tax régime. The logic of the Dasgupta position suggests that the answer is 'yes', in which case another look has to be directed at the definition of freedom. Are people to be prevented from travelling abroad in order to seek some preferred private provision of health and education services?

With the collectivist position, we move even further away from the 'insurance' principle in which there is some close relation between benefits and contributions. In the case of state-provided social services at zero cost, there is clearly no need for any form of earmarked taxation. The amount and composition of expenditure must be decided on 'scientific' lines without reference to any form of hypothecated revenue. So far as transfers, such as pensions, are concerned, collectivists might support the idea of the payment of a minimum contribution as a kind of 'badge of citizenship'. However, why have so many collectivists supported an entirely state-run pension scheme with benefits related to final salary or wage when this would provide a different standard of pension provision according to income? Various explanations are possible, but none of them can be derived from the logic of 'communality' in social provisions, which would appear to support only uniform pensions for all. I hazard the view that collectivists are not generally in favour of draconian methods for creating income equality and consequently would have to be prepared to accept that diversity of preferences and incomes would produce diversity in the pattern of saving for the future, for example through private pension schemes. The damage that this creates for 'communality of purpose' in the welfare state can be limited by making it compulsory for individuals to join a *state* pension scheme with earnings-related benefits. A variant of this explanation would add the cynical observation that such a scheme would offer the opportunity for the state to build up reserves which could be used as a powerful control by the government over the capital market[21] – what Hugh Dalton once called 'a gun to shoot bears'.

One major institutional difference between the collectivist position and the others is clearly the large proportion of the production of services which is under the direct control and operation of the public sector. Teachers, doctors, dentists and nurses, construction workers (in the case of publicly produced housing) and housing administrators are no longer subject to the pressure of the market. The challenge that this affords to the practical implementation of their ideals is clearly formidable. For writers such as Titmuss[22] expected that the professional classes, not subject to the pressures of the market, would be better infused with the spirit of 'communality' and better able to devote themselves single-mindedly to public service. For those who are aware of the economic analysis of non-profit-making institutions and their propensity to be designed to maximise the interests of the producers but which nevertheless support public provision of social services, the challenge consists in devising substitutes for market forces in order to promote efficiency, such as controls over performance.

2.5   IDEOLOGIES, INTERESTS AND IMPLEMENTATION OF CHANGE

There is clearly a close correspondence between Labour Party ideology and the collectivist position and between the libertarian wing of the Conservative Party and the 'minimalist' position. This correspondence is not, however, reflected in the composition and structure of the welfare services within the periods when both parties have held office for more than one full term. There is a striking contrast between the 'build-up' of the welfare state in the immediate post-war period during the Labour period of office, and the failure to 'prune' the welfare state during the ten years of Conservative government from 1979. Indeed, as Dilnot (Dilnot *et al* 1984) has calculated, in 1978–88 more than 25 million out of 56 million persons in the UK at any one time were receiving one or more social security benefits. The numbers, in descending order, were 12 million recipients of child benefit, 9.6 million pensioners, 7 million recipients of means-tested housing benefit, and 3 million recipients of unemployment benefit or supplementary benefit. It is interesting to speculate on this contrast.

One obvious source of explanation must lie in the firmness of commitment to ideology, following the familiar adage of Keynes that ideas and not vested interests are the mainspring of political change. There could be something in this argument. Ideological dispute on the broad dimensions of the welfare state within the Labour Party has been minimal. The most effective challenge from within the party in Labour's political heyday came from Crosland's *Future of Socialism* (1956), which questioned the necessity for perpetuation of benefits in kind, such as food subsidies, but certainly did not call for major changes in the provision of health and education services. In contrast, prominent Conservative ideologists have expressed strong doubts about the privatisation of education and health services and the destruction of an income-related pension scheme[23] as steps towards the perceived improvements associated with the 'Thatcherite' position. However, this division of opinion is not reflected in the range of proposals discussed at Cabinet level and which have reached at least the Green Paper stage, and even in government measures which have reached the statute book. The difference in commitment seems, therefore, to offer at best a small part of the explanation.

The influence of ideology on political events has been strongly challenged in recent years by public choice theorists as at most a necessary but not a sufficient condition for political change.[24] Put very briefly, and inevitably superficially, public choice analysts emphasise the constraints governing the implementation of policy, which are reflected in the way different interest groups view the effect of policy changes on their economic position. When these changes conflict with the interests of a particular group, they will use alternative instruments of political participation – voting strength, lobbying, negotiation with officials and so on – to protect their position. The 'easy way out' for governments is to buy off political opposition by expansion of government services which improve the welfare of organised interest groups and to rely on some form of 'tax illusion' effect to diminish the perceived costs of expansion. This expansion will itself increase the immunity of relevant interest groups from the rigours of the market. When expansion of public services meets increasing taxpayer resistance, expressed in avoidance and evasion, then a government may still be able to retain interest group support by recourse to exemptions from the application of the law or by some comparable form of legal privilege.

The public choice explanation accordingly would emphasise that a postwar Labour government would face little resistance from trade union, consumer and professional interest groups to a social policy which appeared to offer prizes for practically everyone. The atmosphere of a positive-sum game was also maintained by exploiting the prevalent under-consumptionist, left-wing, Keynesian view of economic prospects which claimed that expansion of government expenditure through provision of social services was a particularly appropriate way of maintaining the economy on a full employment growth path. The social opportunity cost of the growth of the public sector could be presented as zero. By the time the welfare costs of expansion of the public sector became apparent, professional groups such as doctors, nurses, teachers and administrators had been able to unionise and to obtain recognition of their bargaining rights with government. Therefore, any government trying to reduce the relative size as well as alter the composition and funding of welfare services is in a 'game' probably perceived by the players as 'zero-sum' rather than 'positive-sum'. In such a game each interest group will try, either individually or by forming coalitions, to throw the costs of change onto others.

It may also be a game of considerable uncertainty if, as is the case with health and education services, the benefits may be broadly assignable, but the financing of them is a quite separate operation. Thus if it is decided to charge for health and education services and to offset charging by a reduction in taxes, individuals' welfare loss from having to pay for the services can be clearly perceived by them, but the benefits from tax reduction may be widely diffused and hardly perceptible. In short, 'players' enjoined to enter a game of this kind perceived as zero-sum (possibly negative-sum), non-co-operative and beset by uncertain outcomes, will have a strong incentive to use political action designed to destroy the game itself.

2.6   CONCLUDING REFLECTIONS

It is ironic that the predictions derived from public choice theory, which draws its inspiration from both the philosophical and technical analysis of classical libertarianism, should come to the conclusion that currently influential liberal ideas have such a slim chance of practical implementation in the case of welfare policy. For those such as the present author, who are broadly sympathetic to the 'minimalist' position (save on questions of wealth distribution), such a pessimistic conclusion presents a challenge rather than an admission of defeat. As Norman Barry has put it: 'ideas about economics and politics must, in some ultimate sense, influence politicians and legislators irrespective of group pressure. Otherwise, how would change occur (except by revolution)?'[25] There is no lack of ideas floating around about the adaptation of government institutions to further ultimate goals. In practice also, perhaps something has been achieved in Britain in the partial dismantling of the state pension system. The severing of the iron link between compulsory pension provision and final salary and the move towards personal pensions, combined with a growth in many alternative private sector sources of supply, go some way towards a reduction in the collectivist element in the British welfare state.[26] Public choice analysis would probably account for this by the fact that there was a discernible link between changes in benefits and in their financing. No prizes are offered for an answer to the 'riddle of the voucher'[27] and why the long and sustained campaign to introduce choice and competition in schooling failed to be regarded as anything more than an attractive idea.

NOTES

1. Charles Rowley and I deal with this matter *in extenso* in Rowley and Peacock (1975). For economists' varying attitudes on welfare state questions, see Ricketts and Shoesmith (1990).
2. Nozick (1974) has been followed by a considerable number of (predominantly) US writers, as in the representative collection of writers in Letwin (1983).

3. See Hayek (1976) for one of his several statements on this issue.
4. Hayek (1976) p 190.
5. Hayek (1976) p 140.
6. As we shall observe later, the libertarian position on this issue is widely accepted by economists.
7. This issue has been fully investigated, and, not surprisingly, is found to be a very complex and difficult one, as examined for example by Diamond (1977).
8. See Soderstrom (1989).
9. See Muller-Armack (1989).
10. See Mill (1871). I have examined Mill's views in more detail in Peacock (1979).
11. See Meade (1989), which is an extended statement of his long-standing commitment to this position.
12. See Meade (1989) app B.
13. See also Meade's 'public choice' analysis of pensions, in Peacock and Barry (1986).
14. One recalls the quip by Lewis Meriam (Meriam *et al* 1950) that 'adoption of the term "insurance" by the proponents of social security was a stroke of promotional genius' p.21.
15. For demonstration of this effect, see Barr (1987) ch 11.
16. See Peacock and Wiseman (1964). For a detailed working out of a scheme closely related to the present-day debate see Barr (1989).
17. See Peacock (1961). For a detailed criticism of my position see Wilson (1985).
18. See Titmuss (1976).
19. The reference is to T H Green and not to David Green! See Ryan (1989) p 59 for a penetrating analysis of Titmuss's position.
20. See his controversial essay, Dasgupta (1989).
21. For a detailed examination of the scheme, see Peacock (1957).
22. See Titmuss (1970).
23. A good example is David Howell (1986) ch 15.
24. For a useful examination of the debate see Barry (1984).
25. Barry (1984) p 64.
26. The author was a member of the Fowler Committee on Pensions but recommended the total abolition of SERPS. For a criticism of the government's final position, see Peacock and Barry (1986).
27. The rejection, after considerable government discussion, of the educational voucher system was one of the great disappointments of liberal economic thinkers. For a full account of the argument between the academics and the Department of Education and Science see Seldon (1986).

REFERENCES

Barr N (1987) *The Economics of the Welfare State*, Weidenfeld and Nicolson, London.

Barr N (1989) *Student Loans: The Next Steps*, David Hume Paper no 15, Aberdeen University Press for the David Hume Institute, Edinburgh.

Barry N (1984) Ideas versus Interests: The Classical Liberal Dilemma, in Hayek F A (ed) *'Serfdom' Revisited*, Hobart Paperback no 18, Institute of Economic Affairs, London.

Crosland A R C (1956) *The Future of Socialism*, Jonathan Cape, London.

Dasgupta P (1989) Positive Freedom, Markets and the Welfare State, in Helm D (ed) *The Economic Borders of the State* ch 5, Oxford University Press, Oxford.

Diamond P (1977) Insurance Theoretic Aspects of Workers' Compensation, in Blinder A S and Friedman P (eds) *Natural Resources, Uncertainty and General Equilibrium Systems*, Academic Press, New York, USA.

Dilnot A W, Kay J A and Morris C N (1984) *The Reform of Social Security*, Oxford University Press, Oxford.

Hayek F A (1976) *Law, Legislation and Liberty* vol 2, The Mirage of Social Justice, Routledge and Kegan Paul, London.

Howell D (1986) *Blind Victory*, Hamish Hamilton, London.

Letwin W (ed) (1983) *Against Equality*, The Macmillan Press, London.

Meade J E (1989) *Agathotopia: the Economics of Partnership*, Hume Paper no 16, Aberdeen University Press for the David Hume Institute, Edinburgh.

Meriam L et al (1950) *The Cost of Financing Social Security*, Brookings Institute, Washington DC, USA.

Mill J S (1871) *Principles of Political Economy*, University of Toronto Press Edition, 1965.

Muller-Armack A (1989) The Meaning of the Social Market Economy, in Peacock A and Willgerodt H (eds) *Germany's Social Market Economy: Origins and Evolution*, Macmillan, London.

Nozick R (1974) *Anarchy, State and Utopia*, Blackwell, Oxford.

Peacock A (1957) The Economics of National Superannuation, *Three Banks Review*, September.

Peacock A (1961) *The Welfare Society*, Unservile State Paper no 2, Liberal Party Publications, London.

Peacock A (1979) *The Economic Analysis of Government*, Martin Robertson, Oxford, ch 5.

Peacock A and Barry N (1986) *The Political Economy of Pension Provision*, Hume Occasional Paper no 2, The David Hume Institute, Edinburgh.

Peacock A and Wiseman, J (1964) *Education for Democrats*, Institute of Economic Affairs, London.

Ricketts M and Shoesmith E (1990) *British Economic Opinion*, Institute of Economic Affairs, London.

Rowley C and Peacock A (1975) *Welfare Economics: A Liberal Restatement*, Martin Robertson, Oxford and London.

Ryan A (1989) Value Judgements and Welfare, in Helm D (ed) *The Economic Borders of the State*, Oxford University Press, Oxford.

Seldon A (1986) *The Riddle of the Voucher*, Hobart Paperback 21, Institute of Economic Affairs, London.

Soderstrom L (1989) Almost Genuine Insurance Schemes as an Alternative to Tax-financed Pensions and other Social Security Benefits, in Chiancone A and Messere K (eds) *Changes in Revenue Structures*, Wayne University Press, Detroit, USA, for International Institute of Public Finance.

Titmuss R M (1970) *The Gift Relationship*, Allen and Unwin, London.

Titmuss R M (1976) *Essays on the 'Welfare State'*, 2nd edn, Allen and Unwin, London.

Wilson T (1985) The Unwithered Welfare State, in Greenaway D and Shaw G K (eds) *Public Choice, Public Finance and Public Policy*, Blackwell, Oxford.

3   The Welfare State: A Public Choice Perspective
Jack Wiseman

3.1   A SPECIFICATION

A 'shopping list' identification of the 'welfare state' is poorly suited to the discussion of general principles. Conceptually, it obscures the character of the problem to be examined. Practically, it precludes consideration of the fact that the diversity of welfare arrangements to be found in different countries, which encourages definition-by-extension, is itself a significant phenomenon which requires explanation.

I shall identify 'welfare' with the *existence of caring feelings*. Such feelings exist in any situation in which individual citizens believe that a reduction in their own material well-being is desirable if accompanied by particular improvements in the well-being of other citizens. Where such caring feelings exist (and in some form they are clearly widespread), and citizens do not believe that they can be satisfied by normal market transactions, they will wish their government to pursue policies which reflect them. I shall use the term 'welfare state' to describe the set of policies which such a government should adopt. Our concern, therefore, is with how the appropriate policies for a society characterised by caring are to be identified and implemented.

This approach stands in contrast to one which attempts to identify the welfare state with some particular bundle of policies. This formulation is unhelpful in identifying underlying principles, and encourages comparative assertions ('Switzerland does not have a welfare state') which contribute nothing to understanding. The formulation I propose implies that there is no point in seeking to discover 'the' policy characteristics of 'the' welfare state. In general, the structure of public policy in any country will reflect the actual nature of the caring feelings of its citizens, on the one hand, and the willingness and ability of the government to translate those feelings into effective public policies, on the other. 'Welfare efficiency' is to be appraised, not by reference to some universal abstract general standard, but by the consonance of welfare policies with the wishes of citizens. There is no reason to believe that the diversity of welfare policies to be observed between countries is incompatible with 'welfare efficiency' in this sense.

The form and extent of the caring feelings of individuals is not a given, any more than is their taste for apples. Observation supports the belief that individuals care about the specific consumption of others as well as their general well-being. But beyond this, there is little ground for generalisation. Equally important, caring feelings about the forms of consumption concerned ('welfare services' such as health care) often appear to relate not only to the act of consumption itself, but also to the means by which that consumption is delivered. Policy thus has to be concerned not only with the use of, e.g., health resources, but also with the procedures (delivery system) through which that use is obtained. The fact that citizens attach value to the means of delivery as well as to the good being delivered is essentially no different from the attachment of value to, for example, the package in which a perfume is provided. Simply, the value of consumption incorporates the packaging (delivery procedure) as well as the basic product. But this can become an issue of great practical importance in the case of welfare services. The historical record suggests that the confusion of what might appear to be means with ends in the provision of welfare services, and the influence of existent systems of delivery upon the judgements of citizens about alternative policies, may be a powerful influence upon individual perceptions of the relation between caring and policy.

3.2   THE NEED FOR WELFARE POLICIES

The existence of caring does not of itself provide a rationale for the involvement of government in the delivery of a good or service. Consider a society in which the accepted objective of productive activity is the satisfaction of consumers' wishes, given their money incomes. This goal will be achieved if consumers are obliged to bid against each other for goods, and suppliers to compete one against another in providing them. In such a society, the government needs to become involved only in providing the legal infrastructure of property rights, in preventing the erosion of competition, and in the facilitation of the provision of those goods and services whose technical characteristics make competitive provision through private markets difficult to organise.[1]

These technical problems may of course affect goods and services which are also the subject of caring feelings (health care is a case in point). But, it will be helpful to keep the two possible causes of government action distinct for present purposes.

The immediate point is that caring does not in principle change the nature of the policy problem. Conceptually, citizens can give expression to their caring feelings simply by entering into contractual relationships with others, whether their concern be with the alleviation of poverty by the transfer of income, the improvement of health by the facilitation of access to health care facilities, or whatever. Market imperfections apart, government intervention will be needed only if there is reason to believe that caring feelings cannot be given adequate expression solely by means of market transactions. The reasons why this may be so fall into two broad groups, concerned respectively with the nature of caring feelings and with the difficulties of reconciling the 'caring preferences' of individuals.

3.3   SOME CHARACTERISTICS OF CARING

COMPLEX AND CONDITIONAL CARING

It has been implicit in the discussion so far that the concern of A for B's welfare is related solely to B's condition, and not at all to B's own behaviour. This may not be the case. It is equally possible that A will be willing to transfer resources to B only if B agrees to behave in some specified fashion.[2] Such a situation is not incompatible with a market solution; the carer–donor need only attach appropriate contractual obligations to the transfer. But clearly, the more complex the conditions, and the greater the number of caring transactions concerned, the more individuals may think it worth considering the substitution of general rules (including government intervention) for individual transactions.

This kind of conditional caring may be reinforced by another. A's willingness to transfer to B may be influenced by the behaviour of C. For example, if A believes that C should participate in the sacrifice needed to increase B's relevant consumption, then A will be willing to transfer resources to B only if C also undertakes to do so. Once again, a market-oriented contractual solution is conceptually possible, but the possibilities of other transactional relationships need to be considered.

DIFFERENCES IN CARING PREFERENCES

Caring preferences differ from one individual to another. A may care about B's poverty, C about the education of B's children. Even if they care about the same characteristic of B's condition, they may do so to different degrees and in different ways. They may also attach different values to delivery arrangements. With large numbers of potential carers and categories of recipient, the scope for diversity and conflict of objectives is obvious. Consider a simplified illustration. Let A and C both care about the same characteristic of B's condition (such as B's health state). In terms of some arbitrary numeraire, A would like to improve B's access to health care by 150 units, C by 100 units. If A and C are unaware of each other, B will get 250 units – more than either wishes. If they are aware of each other, but are not in a bargaining relationship, B may get anything from zero to 250 units, depending upon the prediction each makes about the behaviour of the other. If they do bargain, neither has an incentive to reveal his or her own caring preferences. The actual outcome remains arbitrary, and there is no reason to expect that the change in B's situation will be the one desired by either of the carers. The outcome of this simple situation becomes even more uncertain as the number of donors and recipients is increased, or if we take into account the (not unrealistic) possibility that A or C cares, not simply about B's final condition, but also about their own contribution to that condition. These are archetypical 'free-loading' situations, in which carers can seek to achieve their caring goals at less personal sacrifice than they would, if necessary, be willing to accept. Caring individuals will then have an interest in the use of procedures, including government policy, that constrain or reduce uncertainty about the caring behaviour of others.

GROUP PARTICIPATION

Nothing in the argument suggests that voluntary, market-related arrangements cannot still resolve, or at least contribute to the resolution, of the problems involved. Both logic and evidence suggest otherwise. An individual may find it possible to give expression to caring feelings simply by seeking out suitable recipients and making the appropriate transfers to them. But if this search requires the use of time or resources, or if caring preferences are complex in the fashions just explained, then some form of cooperative behaviour may be a preferable alternative. I have examined the characteristics of group-participative behaviour elsewhere (Wiseman 1978, 1989). In the present context, it involves the individual in giving expression to caring feelings indirectly, by contributing to the activities of an organised group of individuals with similar caring preferences.

In deciding between direct action and participation in voluntary organised charitable behaviour, the caring individual will be influenced by conflicting considerations. The potential benefits of such participation consist in the greater efficiency of giving, through scale economies in making the relevant caring transfers, and in resolution through the group of some of the problems of complex giving. An example of the first kind of benefit would be a reduction in the costs of search. In respect of the second, the individual carer can acquire information about the caring feelings of others by way of participation in the group, and can seek to bind or channel those activities by influencing the rules and policies of the group. The disadvantages of participation relate to the subordination of different individual preferences to the rules of the group. Members will seek to influence the rules and policies of the group toward consonance with their own caring preferences, and individual carers will have to accept a compromise.

Thus, the existence of an 'organised market' in caring presents the individual with a choice: whether to make transfers directly and accept the disadvantages, or whether to accept the constraints imposed by group participation in order to avoid them. There is no 'technical' solution to this opportunity–cost problem: individual carers will choose that pattern of direct action and group participation which best reflects their caring feelings and their assessment of the available possibilities for giving them expression.

However, it is unlikely that participation in voluntary groups will solve all the problems we have identified. Specifically, there may be difficulties in respect of reciprocity and free-loading. Since membership of the groups concerned is voluntary, individual carers cannot use membership to ensure the participation of others in welfare provision. More, the ability of individual members of a group to dictate the detailed character of the participation of others is constrained by the ease with which membership can be terminated. Individuals who find the conditions attaching to membership too onerous can simply withdraw, and, depending on their view of the situation, either act independently or simply free-load.

A potential role for government now begins to emerge. In the immediate context, the government is simply the executive organ of 'the state', which is a group with the special characteristics that initial membership is involuntary and exit is not easy (so that the government of the state enjoys coercive powers). These characteristics make the government a potentially useful instrument for the implementation of welfare policy if the transfers concerned are believed to reflect caring feelings embracing the population at large, and if citizens accept that non-carers can properly be coerced. But this is a statement of the problem rather than a solution. The government is no more able than any other group to identify and deal with free-loading. (If, for example, welfare services are financed from general taxation, this implies the implausible assumption that caring feelings can be inferred from tax liability!) Recognition of the ability to coerce is simply an invitation to consider the ways in which that ability may properly be used. Our outstanding task is to identify guiding principles by which the caring feelings of citizens, whatever they might be, can properly be translated into public policy.

3.4.   THE POLICY CONTENT

THE NEO-CLASSICAL ECONOMIC MODEL

The standard model used by economists to elucidate issues of economic policy (the 'welfare economics' model) is essentially a logic of choice-through-markets whose normative content is concerned with the satisfaction of consumers' wants, the touchstone of efficiency being the allocation of resources in the fashion that best satisfies consumer preferences. The implications are apt to be confusing to the non-economist, and indeed generate difficulty for economists interested in problems of social welfare policy. For example, the non-economist might reasonably expect income distribution to be a question of importance to welfare policy. But it is a question that creates serious problems for this construct. The essential reason is the difficulty of making propositions about income distribution which can be supported as 'scientific' conclusions rather than statements of personal value judgement. The efficiency criterion can rank alternative situations by reference to their ability to satisfy the preferences of consumers, *given* their money incomes, but produces no agreed method for deciding what relative incomes should be. There may be some general belief that the transfer of income from a millionaire to a starving man will 'increase welfare' (though even that requires that the millionaire should care about the welfare of the other if the transfer is not to be coercive). But there is no reason to expect agreement about less extreme or more complex situations.

Perhaps the most interesting attempt to deal with the problem is the development of theories of 'voluntary redistribution' (Hochman and Rogers 1969). Caring feelings can be treated as an extension of other consumer preferences: A may improve his own 'welfare' by transferring income to B rather than by spending on direct consumption. The equity problem thus becomes a matter simply of the voluntary transfer of income from carers to those whose poverty they wish to relieve. The optimal pattern of redistribution in such a society will in this context be decided by the *donors*, subject only to the right of potential recipients to refuse what is offered. But this is not a formulation which has gained widespread acceptance among economists interested in 'welfare state' type activities. In preference to the 'voluntary solution', economists commonly choose simply to exclude distributional considerations from the scope of the model. The status of the equity concept is thus curious. Frequently, it represents no more than a statement of the personal value judgement of the writer. Or it may represent a belief about the nature of the caring feelings of citizens. What is important is that equity propositions are often simple assumptions which are not seen to require extended discussion or even explanation, and are in this sense authoritarian. These underlying assumptions about equity may be of major importance for recommendations for welfare service policy; they account in large part for the seeming paradox that economists apparently using broadly the same intellectual construct can reach widely different conclusions about welfare policy. Equally, proposals ostensibly concerned to implement the preferences of citizens may in fact be much more influenced by the personal preferences (value judgements) of the writer; the citizen is free to choose only within the constraints predetermined by those judgements.

The explanation of this situation lies in the fact that, although it purports to be a generalised logic of choice, this welfare thesis is essentially concerned with choice-through-markets. But in fact, the market operates in the context of a set of institutions and constraints which are themselves in one way or another also the outcome of the choices of citizens. The relationships between such institutions (constitutions, governments, legal systems) and markets is intimate and complex, and there is no obvious reason to evaluate the efficiency of social arrangements by reference to the operation of only one of them. For the satisfactory examination of the kind of questions raised in earlier sections of this chapter, we need to replace the model of choice-through-markets, extended by essentially arbitrary personal value judgements, by a more satisfactory treatment of 'equity' in a comprehensive model of choice-in-society.

LIBERTARIAN PUBLIC CHOICE

In place of the specification of an efficient situation as one in which no one can be made better off without someone else being made worse off, an approach derived from Wicksell may be held to require that no policy should be implemented to which any citizen objects. Important general characteristics of this formulation are:

(i)   In contrast with the identification of efficiency with the way resources are used, Wicksellian efficiency is concerned with *rights*, that is the ability of the citizen to veto policies that he believes would make him 'worse off'. Thus, while it is possible to argue that the two models can be made formally consistent by the reasonable assumption that citizens will object to any policy that would make them worse off, the *conception* of efficiency is essentially different (as will be seen below when the implications of the right of veto are further developed).

(ii)   The argument at (i) is reinforced by the fact that the welfare model is concerned essentially with choice-through-markets, while the Wicksellian construct enhances all choice-activities to which citizens themselves wish to attach significance.

(iii)   The interpretation of 'equity' becomes quite different in a Wicksellian world. What is considered 'equitable' is itself something to be decided by citizens. Economists and other 'scientific observers' may offer observations concerning the implications of particular views of equity, but can have no 'scientific' standing in championing any one set of equity value judgements over another.

Historically, interest in the Wicksellian approach has emerged from dissatisfaction with an economic model which claimed to throw up policy recommendations by way of a study of the market behaviour of individuals, although the nature, activities and competence of the governments responsible for policy implementation lay outside the analysis. The *locus classicus* is *The Calculus of Consent* (Buchanan and Tullock 1962), the fundamental contribution of which lay in its insistence that the political process and its institutions are themselves an integral part of the process of choice-in-society, at least in part substitutable for or complementary to the choice-through-markets which dominates the welfare approach. A considerable literature has developed out of this initial insight. It is this Wicksellian political economy, in the form of the *libertarian public choice model*, which will be argued below to provide the most satisfactory explanatory tool for our present purpose.

3.5   PUBLIC CHOICE AND POLITICAL ECONOMY

THE NATURE OF EFFICIENCY

Efficiency concerns the achievement of goals. The goal specified by Paretian welfare economics is the fulfilment of individual choices. The Wicksellian goal, in contrast, concerns the achievement of social arrangements that generate no policies to which any citizen objects.

The use of either concept of efficiency to prescribe or evaluate public policy requires a value judgement; in the case of welfare efficiency, that the purpose of policy is the satisfaction of individual preferences; in respect of Wicksellian efficiency, that the values of all citizens must be equally respected, in the sense that the right of veto is equally available to all. This latter would not appear to be a value judgement which enjoys universal acceptance, since probably a majority of the world's population lives in states which are not libertarian in this sense. But there are strong arguments for its use. Any other proposition must weigh the values of some citizens more highly than those of others, and there are no convincing arguments for this differential treatment. The value judgement would seem to be particularly appropriate to the consideration of caring preferences. Finally, it is a useful starting generalisation even for the examination of other (non-libertarian) states, since departures from 'libertarian efficiency' can be explained either by the need for institutional change or by some form of rejection of the underlying value judgement.

There are some further general problems in the interpretation of the right of veto. As indicated earlier, the Wicksellian value judgement has the implication that no policy should be implemented to which any citizen objects. This invites doubt as to the operational plausibility of the construct. It can be argued that this proposition, narrowly interpreted, would render government impossible, since there are few policies that would pass the test. (A single vegetarian, on this view, could use the rule to prevent anyone eating meat.) But this interpretation effectively isolates a specific choice-situation from the ongoing process of choice-in-society; the citizen is perceived to evaluate particular policy proposals solely in terms of their direct personal implications. The problem looks very different if we begin from the more realistic assumption that the citizen sees the decision concerning any one policy as part of a continuum of such decisions emerging through time in the society of which all citizens are members. In this situation, the exercise of a veto will be perceived to have much more far-reaching implications. The citizen will be concerned, not just about the expected consequences of a proposed policy for his personal well-being, but also about the predicted consequences of a veto for the reciprocal behaviour of other citizens – for example by their veto of other policies that would have improved his situation. This more plausible interpretation envisages the individual as willing to constrain his own use of veto in the expectation of reciprocal behaviour from others. The rules, procedures and institutions of a society reflect these mutual constraints, and 'unacceptable coercion' comes to mean any situation in which citizens find the rules unacceptable, and 'efficient' (rule-using) veto is displaced by other action, such as refusal to obey the law, illegal emigration, or armed insurrection. This more realistic interpretation of the libertarian criterion opens up some complex and fascinating issues which I cannot pursue here. For our immediate purpose, it is enough to observe that it makes the notion of the veto much less constraining than the naive interpretation would suggest, but also makes it unlikely that libertarian efficiency will be easy to translate into operational concepts. The interpretation of the unanimity rule in relation to the *ongoing opportunity-costs of social participation* makes it more practically relevant. But in practice, the development of procedural rules to deal with particular situations of improper coercion cannot be expected to be an easy matter.

There is a further set of problems which cannot be ignored. 'Libertarian efficiency' is compatible with particular citizens enjoying special rights only in so far as those rights are freely granted by, and able to be withdrawn by, citizens generally – by means that those citizens accept to be appropriate (that is, not improperly coercive). For example, there is clearly nothing anti-libertarian in principle in the licensure of physicians. The exercise of some other special rights would be excluded in principle. This is a matter of considerable practical importance, especially in the area of our interest. In so far as citizens believe they know better than others what is 'good' for those others (have 'meddlesome preferences'), or see the propagation of particular caring policies as means to their personal advantage ('rent-seeking'), the institutions of the libertarian society will need to distinguish coercive behaviour resulting from these causes from that resulting from 'acceptable' causes.

Citizens are seen, in this present context, to be in a contractual relationship with others through the medium of a government which they can elect and dismiss (which is why the formulation of the problem is labelled contractarian liberalism). The rules, procedures and institutions of the society, and through these the actual policies adopted, emerge from this contractual relationship. Any system of social rules is by nature coercive, in the sense that such rules constrain (and are intended to constrain) individual freedom of action. But for the reasons just explained, citizens are willing to be coerced, in so far as they value the loss of personal freedom of action less highly than the gain resulting from the reciprocal acceptance of constraint by other citizens. Conceptually, that is, the efficient libertarian society is not one from which coercion is absent (since that is incompatible with the existence of social rules), but rather one in which citizens do not believe themselves to be *improperly* coerced, and in which meddlesome preferences and rent-seeking are adequately controlled.

There are two implications which should be noted. First, there is no simple sense in which freedom from coercion can be identified with freedom to choose. The need to choose is an unavoidable implication of scarcity, so that the fact that individuals can be observed to choose does not of itself differentiate any one system of social organisation from another. What is of importance is the nature of the constraints upon choice, and the ability of the citizen to change or influence these. Second, and as a corollary of this, coercion is concerned with the perception by individuals of their own situation. That is, the judgement as to whether the rules, institutions and policies of a society are acceptable or improperly coercive is one that citizens themselves must make by reference to their own values. The role of the economist or other technical specialist can only be to inform these judgements, whether by improving understanding of the implications of policies or proposals, or by elucidating the possibilities of alternative institutional arrangements. I suspect that this is a proposition that most economists would find acceptable in principle; but I have pointed out earlier that the neo-classical construct facilitates the introduction of personal value judgements which then assume an unmerited 'scientific' status. It follows that, if the values or perceptions of citizens differ, then so may their conception of the institutions and policies of the 'good society'. There is no one 'right' system of delivery of any particular good or service waiting to be discovered, and there is nothing surprising or disturbing in the observation that different countries adopt different arrangements for the provision of such services as health care.

It is one thing to identify social efficiency with the absence of improper coercion, quite another to find means to identify such efficiency (or its absence) in practice. It is to this question that we must now turn.

3.6 CHARACTERISTICS OF THE EFFICIENT LIBERTARIAN SOCIETY

TWO PREREQUISITES

Governments consist of particular individuals with their own goals and their own values. In the libertarian society, the government and its members will be elected by the members of the society, by way of rules and procedures that give those same citizens the right to remove them from office. The public choice literature interprets the power relationship between citizens and government in a variety of ways, from the extreme version of the median voter model, which sees the government once elected as obligated to carry out the policy agenda of the median voter, through other variants that leave the government with greater freedom of action. The most plausible model for our purposes is that proposed by Buchanan (1975) and Brennan and Buchanan (1980), of Government-as-Leviathan. This envisages the government pursuing its own goals, which may depart from those of citizens.

An efficient society will thus be one whose rules and procedures successfully constrain the ability of Government-as-Leviathan improperly to coerce the citizens. It should be emphasised that the Leviathan formulation does not in any way imply that government is wholly malignant. It is simply an extension of the proposition that individuals have different values to incorporate the further proposition that individuals as members of a government face a different goal-situation and have different powers from other citizens. For example, the Leviathan situation might be one in which the government wished to pursue caring policies more extensive than those wanted by most citizens. At the same time it is clearly the most realistic model for any society, embracing 'rent-seeking' or 'meddlesome' citizens. Participation in government or bureaucracies is the obvious means for such citizens to pursue their own ends, and the institutions and organisations of society need to be robust in the protection of other citizens against them.

Second, we need to take account of the fact, usually ignored by economists, that the future is not only unknown, but is unknowable in the fundamental sense that the actual future may take a form different from anything conceived by individuals in the present. This has serious consequences for economics generally. Here, its prime importance lies in the implication that citizens will not only be unsurprised if the outcome of their plans should be different from their predictions, but will actually make and implement their plans on the expectation that this will happen. Thus, citizens may agree to rules, procedures and policies which do not appear to them to be improperly coercive at the time of agreement, but yet wish to protect themselves from the possibility that this judgement may be falsified by future events. It follows that a general rule of the libertarian society should be: *there should be no rule which does not embody a rule/procedure for its own peaceful change.*

THE APPRAISAL OF EFFICIENCY
In this general context, the efficiency of social arrangements is evaluated by citizens themselves; improper coercion is what is so regarded by the individual members of society. Following the earlier argument, the citizen can be seen as concerned with an ongoing process of opportunity-cost evaluation: how easily (at what cost) can undesired proposals or situations be avoided or changed? Following Hirschman (1970), it is useful to think of the answer to this question along two dimensions, those of 'voice' and 'exit'. Voice relates to the ability of citizens to affect the procedures or policies of their society by direct action, for example by voting about policies proposed within the existing rules, or by using available procedures to change those rules. The more satisfactory these arrangements are perceived to be, the less citizens will regard themselves as able to be improperly coerced, and the more efficient the society in our sense. Exit concerns the ease with which citizens can escape the jurisdiction of a society whose behaviour they come to re-

gard as intolerably coercive. For example, citizens of a federal country may regard the ability to move from one province to another as a valuable protection against coercion by their own provincial government, but attach less weight (impute higher cost) to the possibility of migration to another country. Considerations of both voice and exit enter the individual opportunity-cost appraisal of the efficiency of their society's institutions.

A HIERARCHY OF JUDGEMENTS

We have identified efficiency with the existence of rules which citizens accept because, although coercive by their essential nature, their existence is seen as on balance beneficial. It remains to enlarge this perception to take account of the hierarchical nature of rules. The characteristics of choices can be studied within whatever rules are extant, and the notion of efficiency clearly applies to such situations. But these present rules must themselves be the product of other rules, and of the same criterion of efficiency within a set of extant rules which are not themselves efficient. Following Brennan and Buchanan (1980) we need to distinguish the 'within-period' characteristics of any situation or proposal (its efficiency within, say, the life of an elected government), and its 'between-period' efficiency (concerning perhaps the procedures by which governments are dismissed or elected). Appraisal in terms of opportunity-cost, voice and exit needs to be brought to bear in relation to each relevant 'level' of decision.

3.7 THE WELFARE STATE IN CONTRACTARIAN PERSPECTIVE

The translation of general principles into operating rules applicable to the present circumstances of a particular society can never be a straightforward matter. Problems of this kind are commonly resolved by ignoring them; an understanding and acceptance of the philosophical underpinnings of the policy argument is taken for granted. This causes problems only if this assumption is ill-founded, or if the intellectual construct used is inappropriate or inadequate for its purpose. But I have argued that this is indeed the case in respect of much of the discussion of the so-called welfare state; an understanding of the caring society requires a better intellectual construct than that provided by neo-classical economics. To complete this paper, I must consider the implications of the libertarian public choice model for the form and character of actual welfare (caring) policies. It is an implication of the model that there can be no objectively identifiable 'best' welfare policies, since efficient policy must be responsive to the caring wishes of citizens, whatever these might be. At best, we can hope only to develop policy proposals relevant to a particular time and place.

Further, I can do no more than provide *guidelines for policy development*.

Gratifying though it would be to conclude this paper with a set of firm policy recommendations for the UK (the 'new welfare state'), it would be foolish to suggest that I can do so. The application of public choice ideas to concrete policy situations is still relatively new. The most I can hope to do here is to suggest directions of development, by attempting to identify some of the interesting new questions to which the proposed approach directs attention. Also, the argument underscores the essentially *conditional* nature of 'expert' advice on welfare (or other) policy. As technical experts, we are in no position to prescribe the goals which policy 'should' serve; our contribution is limited to the provision of advice and information about the implications of pursuing certain ends, or about the relation between identified ends and the means available for their attainment.

I am also constrained by space. Even if I had the confidence to try, I could not hope to provide a comprehensive exposition of the application of the concepts and principles I have suggested to actual policy situations. I shall confine myself to a single example, chosen for its illustrative potential (though the policies concerned are not practically trivial).

THE CASE OF RENT CONTROL

Rent control provides a useful 'test bed', for a number of reasons. Housing is a policy area that would commonly appear on the 'shopping list' of welfare state policies, or, in my formulation, is a form of consumption which appears to attract caring feelings. Rent control is a not uncommon characteristic of housing policies (in recent history, at least ten jurisdictions around the world have pursued policies of rent control). Finally, it is an area in which there has been increasing dissatisfaction with the orthodox economic evaluation of policy, and growing interest in the relevance and application of public choice ideas.[3]

Neo-classical analysis of rent control interprets the policy as the control of a competitive market price, with predicted consequences (such as deterioration of the housing capital stock, excess demand and long-term decline in the supply of rented housing, and inhibition of the mobility of labour), confirmed by the available evidence. The consequent redistribution of income, from landlords to tenants, corresponds only coincidentally and approximately with redistribution between income groups. In fact, little good is found in the policy, the closest available approach to a defence being the value judgement that the achieved income redistribution is 'probably on balance in a desirable direction'. That authors frequently recommend gradual or piecemeal reform rather than outright abolition can be explained only by their pragmatic recognition that governments would be unlikely to listen to more drastic advice.

For a policy with such adverse consequences, rent control has demonstrated a remarkable capacity for survival; once in place, the policies seem to persist for a very long time. For example, some form of rent control has existed in the UK for seventy-four years, and even a government as antipathetic as the present UK one to policies of this kind has spent a decade evolving policies to get rid of it, and is still not completely assured of success. An intellectual construct that cannot explain this is clearly deficient. Recognition of this is to be found in attempts to supplement the argument by a property-rights interpretation of the effects of rent control policies. Once implemented, it is argued, the policy confers valuable rights on tenants, which they will protect at the polls. Since there are more tenants than landlords, any government proposing to abolish rent control will lose electoral support. The argument has some merit, but is not completely convincing or supported by comparative evidence. The same arguments could be applied to many other commodities whose prices governments and citizens do not seek to control (though it could be argued on the other side that housing differs from many of these in its significance in the typical household budget). Landlords are arguably more powerful than tenants in their ability to influence policy through means other than voting (e.g. through pressure group behaviour or capture of the regulatory authority).

A public choice model incorporating caring provides a more satisfactory explanation. Citizens generally exhibit concern about the nature and extent of the consumption of housing by others, and this is reflected in notions of security of tenure and a 'fair rent' (with 'fairness' perhaps being related not just to the level of rent but also to its justification – cost-related rent increases being acceptable, but demand-related ones 'improper') (Knetsch, Kahneman and Thaler, 1984). The public choice/caring model also helps explain the observed differences in rent control policies in different countries (McCormick and Tollison 1980; Fallis 1988). Indeed, it might be deemed an efficient policy, in terms of the criteria enunciated earlier, if citizens believe themselves to have adequate powers to change or abolish the controls, but choose not to do so because they believe these adverse consequences are less important than the 'caring benefits' they derive from it. As policy advisers, we need to find means to distinguish between this possibility, and the alternative explanation that the policy persists for two reasons: first, because it encourages vested interests and attracts political support accordingly; and second because of misunderstanding or lack of information, whether about the constitutional rules, or about the consequences of the policy and its available alternatives. Citizens may conceivably be willing to pay the price of houses falling down in order to give expression to their caring feelings; but we can try to ensure that they understand the implications of their choice!

The general normative question to be answered is: What kind of policies are compatible with the rules of a contractarian-liberal state, and how do policies of rent control chime with these? The discussion by Buchanan (1986) of the constitutional rules of a libertarian society provides a valuable general insight and point of departure. He argues that the extent to which an acceptable set of arrangements would incorporate powers to change the distribution of income and wealth generated by the market would depend crucially upon the inequality of the initial endowments and capacities of the individual citizens. The greater the initial inequality, the more likely it is that such powers will be acceptable. But the essential purpose of the constitutional arrangements (and of the right of veto) is to safeguard essentially self-interested individuals from unacceptable coercion. In the absence of quite significant inequality, then, the redistributive powers of the state will be severely restricted; Buchanan does not envisage them extending much beyond such things as the public finance of education and inter-generational transfers of income and wealth.

A common objection to the Buchanan position is that it provides no role for altruism. The objection is frequently rooted in misunderstanding. The interpretation of Government-as-Leviathan rests, not on the *irrelevance* of other motives, but on the *prevalence* of self-interested purposes. Buchanan (1986) himself argues that economists have improperly neglected the moral and ethical aspects of human behaviour, and need to seek a better understanding of 'how morals impact on choice'. We can accept the general Buchanan position, and ask how his conclusion might be modified to take account of more sophisticated caring preferences, and in particular preferences bearing upon the market for housing.

If individuals have strong and complex caring preferences, they may wish their government to concern itself with such problems as reciprocity and free-loading, whether by direct action or by policies impacting on the creation and behaviour of other 'clubs' (such as private charities), or of individuals. The constitutional arrangements would not be considered by citizens to be improperly coercive. If housing is a relevant form of caring consumption, then the rules and procedures concerned would embrace policies affecting the housing market.

The distribution of caring burdens and benefits should reflect the actual character of caring preferences. Rent control would appear to perform badly by this criterion. The policy reduces the income of landlords, whatever it might be, and provides cheap housing to tenants, whatever their income may be. It seems unlikely that this is consonant with the nature of caring preferences concerning either access to housing or redistribution of income. For might we not expect citizens also to advocate (e.g.) the provision of health care or education by reducing the incomes of the suppliers of these products! The central principle which rent control violates is the principle of equal treatment before the law (Fallis 1988). Related policies, such as protection of tenure, are subject to a similar interpretation.

So far as the effects of rent control policies on the behaviour of the housing market are concerned, the orthodox economic analysis successfully identifies the adverse consequences, but the limited impact made by this information can be explained in several ways. First, because the policy model does not encompass caring preferences concerning the consumption of housing, it can provide no plausible intellectual justification for any policies other than outright abolition. Governments consequently tend to react to this argument not by abolition, but by the introduction of further ancillary policies (e.g. on demolitions and maintenance, conversions, security of tenure), which attempt to preserve caring goals but further damage the operation of the market. Second, and related to this, the effect of control is obscured for the citizen–voter by the simultaneous impact of such other housing market policies as mortgage tax-relief and municipally owned rental housing. Third, the difficulty in understanding these issues is compounded by the fact that, simultaneously with the successive adaptations of policy just described, the apparent benefits of rent control are often also eroded through time (for example, by the long-term shrinkage of supply at controlled rents).

The public choice model does support some general suggestions about the general approach to policy in this area.

(i)   There are strong arguments for reform, in that a more thorough understanding of the issues would be likely to cause citizens to prefer other means of giving expression to their caring feelings.

(ii)   Of great importance is the provision of adequate policy-relevant information which comes to terms with the fact that citizens do have special caring preferences concerning the consumption of housing.

(iii)   It follows that the information provided must be concerned with the housing market as a whole, and needs to be accompanied by some serious effort to inform, and obtain better information about, the actual caring preferences of citizens. It is noteworthy that most survey material is seriously deficient in this regard, in that the questions asked do not pose realistic opportunity–cost situations.

(iv)   It is characteristic of specific forms of intervention such as rent control that they both emerge from the undesired 'meddlesome preferences' of politicians and, once in place, encourage further meddlesome and rent-seeking behaviour. (This is reflected for example in the mounting complexity of rent control legislation.) The caring preferences of citizens would be less vulnerable to such influences if housing policy were more general in nature.

(v)   The arguments above suggest two avenues along which progress might be sought. First, while many of the societies with rent control policies have constitutional arrangements which are in general 'efficient' by our criteria, it is worth considering whether the 'rules' might not fruitfully be strengthened to make this type of specific intervention more difficult. Second, the policy argument needs to be better informed, by relating the present situation more explicitly to the considerations identified at (iii). It cannot be an easy task; the issues are complex. Our own recognition of the need for a fresh approach will be a valuable beginning.

NOTES

1. This latter category is often cited as a major reason for government activity: it embraces a set of problems variously referred to as 'market failure', 'externality', or 'public goods'. This is an important topic, but too large and complex for me to pursue here. There are two points of special relevance to my immediate context:
    (i) First, and contrary to much that has been written in this field, public goods are not an objective category capable of identification simply by their technical characteristics. The decision as to which goods 'should' be treated as public is itself a product of the political process (which *inter alia* decides the nature of individual property rights).
    (ii) Second, public goods are specially susceptible to free-loading. In so far as I · shall argue that free-loading is also likely to be characteristic of the caring relationship. the policy relevance of this phenomenon must be enhanced.
2. I have elsewhere named this the 'principle of reciprocity' (Wiseman 1985). The present paper is a generalisation of the idea first presented there.
3. See for example *Journal of Real Estate Finance and Economics* (1988), especially papers by Fallis and Arnott, and further references cited therein.

REFERENCES

Arnott R (ed) (1988) Rent Control: The International Experience, special issue of *Journal of Real Estate Finance and Economics* **3**: 203–15.

Brennan G and Buchanan J M (1980) *The Power to Tax: Analytical Foundations of a Fiscal Constitution*, Cambridge University Press, Cambridge.

Brennan G and Buchanan J M (1985) *The Reason of Rules: Constitutional Political Economy*, Cambridge University Press, Cambridge.

Buchanan J M (1975) *The Limits of Liberty: Between Anarchy and Leviathan*, University of Chicago Press, Chicago, USA.

Buchanan J M (1986) *Liberty, Market and State*, Wheatsheaf Press, Brighton.

Buchanan J M and Tullock G (1962) *The Calculus of Consent*, University of Michigan Press, Ann Arbor, USA.

Fallis G (1988) Rent Control: The Citizen, The Market and The State, *Journal of Real Estate Finance and Economics* **3**: 309–20.

Hirschman A O (1970) *Exit, Voice, and Loyalty*, Harvard University Press, Cambridge Mass., USA.

Hochman H M and Rogers J A (1969) Pareto-optimal Redistribution, *American Economic Review* **59**: 542–7.

Knetsch J, Kahneman D and Thaler R (1984) *Residential Tenancies: Losses, Fairness and Regulations*, Commission of Inquiry into Residential Tenancies, Toronto, Canada.

McCormick R F and Tollison R D (1980) Wealth Transfers in a Residential

Democracy, in Buchanan J, Tollison R and Tullock G (eds) *Towards a Theory of the Rent-Seeking Society*, College Station, Texas A & M University Press, Texas, USA.

Wiseman J (1978) Some Reflections on the Economics of Group Behaviour, in Caroni P, Dafflon P and Enderle G (eds) *Nur Oekonomie ist keine Oekonomie*, Paul Haupt Verlag, Berne, Switzerland.

Wiseman J (1985) Genesis, Aims and Goals of Social Policy, in Terney G and Culyer A J (eds) *Public Finance and Social Policy*, Wayne State University Press (for International Institute of Public Finance), Detroit, USA.

Wiseman J (1989) *Cost, Choice and Political Economy*, Edward Elgar, Aldershot and Vermont, USA.

4   Welfare and the Enterprise Society
Raymond Plant

Since the mid 1970s the New Right in its neo-liberal form[1] has dominated the debate about welfare and social policy. It is natural that this should have been so in that the creation of an enterprise culture was bound to have some bearing on the future of the welfare state and was always going to involve a rethink of its aims and values. When properly presented, neo-liberal arguments strike at the heart of the normative assumptions of the post-war welfare state, and only if they are answered with the same rigour is it likely that the alternative view will recover the ground it has lost. The aim of this chapter is to consider the theoretical basis of New Right arguments in the sphere of values and principles, rather than the empirical case deployed against the welfare state, in order to subject these arguments to some critical analysis. I shall be concerned with a number of issues: with the relationship between welfare and freedom; social justice; the public choice critique of public sector interest groups; the status of welfare rights; the nature of poverty and dependency; and the role of the state in social policy. First of all, however, I will outline some of the common normative assumptions about the nature of the welfare state which the neo-liberals reject.

The first argument has been common since the end of the nineteenth century,[2] namely that welfare in terms of the possession of resources and opportunities is closely linked to liberty. The claim here is that free markets would deprive the worst-off of resources without which they could not act as free citizens. The state as the guarantor of equal liberty had to be concerned not just with civil and political liberties, but also with the resources and opportunities which individuals had to have if they were to be able to act as citizens and make a reality of the formal liberties which they possessed in terms of civil and political rights. In this sense the link between freedom and welfare became central to the citizenship view of the welfare state; a fairer distribution of resources is necessary to secure more equal freedom between citizens.

The link however was not just with freedom but also with the idea of social justice and with welfare rights. As this way of thinking developed, it was argued that welfare policy had to be governed by social justice, a just distribution of social resources so that the worst-off could exercise to some degree the range of choice available to the better-placed. It brought in the idea of welfare rights, that individuals had a right to resources without which they would not be really free and would not be fully citizens. This idea in turn assumed a doctrine about basic needs that had to be satisfied if individuals were to live as autonomous citizens. In this sense, needs underpinned the claim to social and economic rights. These ideas taken together also implied an idea of a modern form of community. The welfare state embodies the idea that individuals have responsibilities to one another. The political recognition of these responsibilities and the collective action to meet the needs of all members of society embodies a viable idea of community in the modern world. These interrelated ideas are rejected by the neo-liberal critics of the welfare state.

4.1   FREEDOM AND WELFARE

A central issue, as I have suggested, is that of the nature of freedom in relation to citizenship. The point at stake here can be stated in two rather different ways. The first is to argue that freedom actually implies the possession of powers, resources and opportunities as well as the absence of intentional coercion. On this view liberty is positive as well as negative. The second argument is rather different and implies an acceptance of the notion of negative liberty combined with the claim that the value of negative freedom, which is seen as freedom from the intentional interference of others, varies depending on the nature of the resources that one has. Freedom in the negative sense is worth more to the rich than to the poor; they are able to do more things with the 'space' that is secured to them by negative liberty. This latter view does not entail a dispute with the neo-liberal about the nature of liberty, but rather about the social conditions which make negative liberty a worthwhile feature of human life.

The neo-liberals decisively reject both of these claims. First of all they reject the positive account of liberty, and they also reject, at least in its most straightforward sense, that securing a fairer distribution of the resources necessary for the exercise of negative liberty requires the state to use welfare as a redistributive mechanism. This double rejection is nowhere put more starkly than in Keith Joseph's book on equality, where he argues that 'Poverty is not unfreedom'.[3]

There are two arguments used by neo-liberals against the assimilation of freedom to act with ability to act, that is to say positive freedom.[4] The first is that if freedom is assimilated to ability, then we are only fully free if we are omnipotent, that is to say if we are able to do all that we are free to do. This is absurd. It links freedom too closely with desire and means that individuals are differentially free depending on whether they can fulfil the desires which they happen to have. This leads to paradoxical results. The person with extravagant desires, but few resources, is less free than the individual with limited desires but with the resources to satisfy them. If we link freedom and desire in this way then the idea of freedom loses its objectivity. If however we argue that freedom is diminished if we cannot fulfil our most important desires, or perhaps needs, then we have to assume a moral consensus about what are the important desires or needs, and this assumption is rejected by the neo-liberals. Increasing resources to the worst-off does not mean increasing their freedom.

It is therefore important in the neo-liberals' view to resist positive liberty, or liberty as power or capacity, in favour of negative liberty. This is important because it allows the critic to block a further argument in favour of welfare and to clarify the role of the market in relation to liberty. The welfare case against the market in the context of liberty is that the distribution of resources which the free market will produce is in fact likely to restrict the freedom of the worst-off. However, in the view of the critic, the market cannot restrict liberty if we understand liberty correctly as the absence of coercion because the outcomes of markets – the distribution of income and wealth – is not intended or foreseen by anyone. In a market, people buy and sell for all the particular reasons which they may have. The outcome of all this buying and selling is that some get more and some get less, but this outcome is not itself intended. Given that liberty can only be restricted by intentional action, it follows that the unintended outcome of free market exchanges cannot infringe liberty.

The argument about the value or worth of negative liberty is also rejected by the neo-liberals for two reasons. The first is that if we accept that there has to be a redistribution of resources to secure a fairer value of liberty among citizens, then first of all we have no clear view of where this will stop.[5] But because we do not share a consensus either about what are the essential conditions for the exercise of negative liberty or about the extent of redistribution which has to take place to secure this fairer value for liberty, then we are committed to an unprincipled extension of the welfare state and its institutions, and thus to the interference which this will involve both with the economy and with individual choice. In the view of critics this will actually then pose a threat to the very existence of negative liberty as freedom from coercion. This response is then linked to an empirical claim, namely that the free market will in fact secure resources and opportunities to individuals through the 'trickle-down effect', more effectively than state distribution of resources through the welfare state, and in a way that does not require us to solve deep moral differences about what we mean by fairness and the just distribution of resources.

4.2 SOCIAL JUSTICE

If freedom is to be understood as ability or power, and the associated resources required to secure this capacity to individuals, as many welfare theorists believe, it follows that we need a criterion for the distribution of resources, and this will be provided by an appeal to social justice. However, in the view of the critic, this appeal is purely rhetorical and illusory. The appeal to social justice is rhetorical because we cannot specify its meaning with sufficient precision to enable it to act as a guide to public policy, and in any case the moral status of the appeal to social justice is misconceived.

Let us take this second point first because the argument here mirrors the argument about freedom and intentionality which I discussed earlier. Injustice can only be caused by intentional action, according to the neo-liberal view.[6] If something happens to me as the result of an impersonal force, for example the weather, or as caused by the genetic lottery, for example if I lose my crops as the result of a drought or if I am born with spina bifida, these things are caused by an impersonal unintended process. I therefore do not suffer an injustice so much as a misfortune or bad luck. If I do suffer from injustice then there is at least a *prima facie* case for arguing that the state should seek to rectify, or compensate me for, my condition. However, if I simply have bad luck then the question is much more one of an appeal to generosity, charity, benevolence or humanity. These are discretionary and private virtues which it is not the duty of the state to coerce. If we now return to the characterisation of markets offered by the neo-liberal, we can see that they are determined to say that poverty or the lack of resources cannot be seen as injustice so much as misfortune. The outcomes of markets are like the weather in the sense that they are unintended and unforeseen and cannot therefore produce injustice. The moral demands of social justice therefore evaporate.

Secondly, the critic will argue that there are many possible criteria for social justice. We can distribute resources according to need, merit, desert, entitlement, property rights and so on. In order to appeal to social justice as a guide to policy we need to specify the principle of distribution involved. In a free and morally pluralistic society this cannot be done. We have no consensus about the priority of one criterion of distribution over others. Even if we could agree, let us say, that some needs should have precedence over others, the open-endedness of the idea of needs, and the incommensurability of different needs, make distribution according to need a very poor guide to public policy, with two very unfortunate political results.

In the first place public policy charged with the duty to distribute resources according to socially just criteria will have to be arbitrary and discretionary because we lack a clearly specified criterion of distribution. This will mean that at the very heart of the public policy of a welfare state will lie the arbitrary and discretionary power of welfare bureaucrats and experts charged with the impossible task of distributing resources according to intrinsically unspecific criteria.[7] The idea of the rule of law is at the heart of liberal democracy, but there is no way in which the distribution of resources can follow any clear rule of law just because of the lack of specificity about the nature of human needs, which is the obvious criterion of distribution in a welfare state.

The second political consequence is that if government seeks to distribute resources in the context of an ethical vacuum about the distributive principles involved, then it will follow that there will be a destructive competition for social resources between interest groups. In such a situation social justice will turn into a camouflage for the rent-seeking behaviour of the most powerful interest groups in society.

4.3   WELFARE RIGHTS

This argument is followed through in an attack on the idea of the welfare state as necessary to secure social and economic rights, an idea which received its classical articulation in T H Marshall's *Citizenship and Social Class*, a book which has exercised a great deal of influence upon our thinking about the nature of the welfare state. In the view of the neo-liberals there is a clear and categorical distinction between genuine rights, which are essentially traditional civil and political rights, and post-war ideas of social and economic rights, which are essentially dubious.

The argument against welfare rights depends crucially upon the issue of scarcity, given that welfare rights are necessarily rights to resources. It is argued that traditional civil and political rights imply little or nothing in the way of the commitment of resources. A right, such as the freedom of expression for example, is respected by other citizens and the government forbearing from action: that is to say not interfering with my exercise of that right. Other civil rights are in the same category, they imply negative duties of forbearance, rather than the commitment of resources. Scarcity implies a limit on the right, which means that welfare rights cannot be considered as categorical and absolute in the way that it is possible to treat civil and political rights, given that the latter only imply duties of forbearance. A right implies the existence of a rule under which the right is secured. However, it is not possible to write a rule of law securing to individuals scarce resources. Resources such as health care and education have to be subject to a large degree of discretion in their allocation just because of scarcity.

The political consequences of assuming that there can be rights to welfare mirror the same political consequences as arise from the pursuit of social justice. Welfare rights would presumably be based upon a conception of needs: that certain needs are so basic that they should be seen as implying rights to those resources necessary to satisfy them. Such needs would involve education, health, social security. However neo-liberals take the view that such needs are intrinsically open-ended and thus the range of rights postulated on the basis of such needs could grow inexorably. With the idea of a right go assumptions and expectations about the extent to which society will seek to protect that right. The facts of scarcity make this impossible and the failure to fulfil these dubious rights will lead to frustration and resentment.

In the neo–liberal view, the concern with poverty on which these various welfare strategies are based is a misplaced concern. They tend to reject a relative view of poverty, which interprets poverty as a failure to attain some standard of living which is regarded as a norm in the society, and which is sometimes linked with the idea of citizenship; that citizenship requires the possession of a range of resources which will enable each individual citizen to act effectively in the society. This is rejected in favour of a more absolut-ist idea, which means that what matters to the poor is not their position relative to other groups in society so much as whether their standard of living is improving year by year, whatever the degree of inequality involved. In the view of the government the market and the trickle-down effect of increasing real weekly earnings are the keys to tackling the problems of poverty and deprivation, and this mechanism will work far more effectively than any set of regulations in terms of rights and greater equality. The mar-ket rather than the state is the main instrument of empowerment, even though it leads to greater inequality.

4.4   WELFARE AND OBLIGATIONS

The other facet of the critique of the welfare state which is currently receiv-ing quite a lot of attention under the pressure of the thinking that is being done in the USA, particularly by Charles Murray,[8] Lawrence Mead[9] and Michael Novak,[10] is the claim that an extensive welfare state creates moral hazard because it reinforces the very dependency which it aims to eradicate. The claim here is that the possession of resources, while a necessary, is not a sufficient, condition for eradicating poverty. The poor become dependent on the state and upon welfare bureaucracies, they are not independent and do not take responsibility for their own lives. The welfare state has to be modified in order to deal with this, although New Right thinkers disagree quite markedly on how this is to be done. Two strategies have been sug-gested. The first by Charles Murray in *Losing Ground*, in which he argues that in order to create greater independence, benefits should be cut. People will then be thrown more upon their own devices and their own wits if they cannot calculate how to survive on state benefits.

The second alternative, developed by Mead and Novak, is in favour of workfare and learnfare. That is to say, for the able-bodied, benefits should only be given conditionally, the condition being a willingness to undertake work or training. Citizenship is a matter of duties as well as rights and entitlements. The obligations in question, to undertake work or training, will, it is argued, break the cycle of dependence, and link the recipient of benefits much more to the disciplines and obligations of work, which the employed have to accept and which form a dominant part of the values of society.

All of this adds up to quite a formidable, systematic critique of the post-1945 welfare state. Obviously in a short paper I cannot hope to provide a fully developed critical response to the New Right approach, nor would I wish to do so in all respects. Some of the arguments are powerful at both a moral and a practical level, but I shall try to indicate some of the lines of criticism which could be advanced.

4.5   LIBERTY AND POWERS

First of all I shall take the issue of liberty, partly because this has historically been important in the attempt to provide a moral foundation for the welfare state, partly because a good deal of recent thinking on the left has taken up the matter again, and partly because the neo-liberals' argument about liberty reveals something both important and controversial about their characterisation of the market and the possibility of providing a moral critique of the market.

As we saw earlier, there are several strands to the critique. Primarily the argument turns on a very vigorous defence of negative liberty as the absence of intentional coercion which, when combined with the argument that the outcomes of markets are unintended, entails that market outcomes cannot restrict freedom.

It might be accepted that overall market outcomes are not intended, but they are clearly foreseeable. Indeed, if this were not so the neo-liberals would be at a very considerable disadvantage. Their own arguments in favour of extending markets depend for their plausibility on the claim that market outcomes are in fact foreseeable, at least in some macro sense. So, for example, when the neo-liberals argue in favour of extending the market in rented accommodation as a solution to the housing shortage, this assumes that we can make very good guesses about the outcomes which would arise from such a change, namely that the supply of accommodation would in fact be increased. Market outcomes are foreseeable therefore, but does this make any difference to the question of whether they can restrict the liberty of the worst-off if such outcomes are not intended? In micro situations involving personal morality we can be held morally responsible for the foreseeable, although unintended, consequences of our actions. This provides for instance the conceptual basis for a crime such as manslaughter. I can be held to restrict your freedom if I undertake an action which could reasonably be foreseen to restrict your ability to do something which you would otherwise do, even if such a restriction was not part of my intention in acting. However, can this tell us anything about the moral status of foreseeable market outcomes? The neo-liberal will argue that the issue at the level of personal morality cannot throw any moral light on the macro issue. The crucial difference is that at the micro level the outcome of the action can be reasonably foreseen in relation to individuals, but this does not hold at the macro level. It may well be that we can foresee that if we were to extend the role of markets against the background of existing inequalities, then those who enter the market with least are likely to leave it with least. Obviously, this cannot be foreseen at the individual level and therefore the analogy does not hold.

Nevertheless, if it is possible to make probabilistic judgements of this sort for a large number of the worst-off members of society, namely that some will bear greater costs in the extension of markets than others, then there is a case for arguing that, if there is a collective commitment to extend markets, we bear some responsibility for the poverty which some groups will experience as the result of this policy, given that it is undertaken against a background of initial inequality. The reason for stressing this is that, while the market is in some respects like an impersonal force, it is nevertheless unlike impersonal forces in the sense that there are in fact alternatives, and the impact of markets on groups can be changed by mechanisms such as welfare states.[11]

However, this argument still assumes something which the neo-liberal will wish to deny, namely that freedom has something to do with ability and the resources which the exercise of those abilities requires. As we saw earlier, this is a central argument. The neo-liberal case is that being free to do X is quite different from being able to do X, and therefore that the lack of resources is not a restriction on freedom.

However, it is doubtful that this case can be maintained. First of all it can be argued that we cannot understand the worth of negative liberty without linking it to an idea of ability and agency. If we ask the negative libertarian why liberty is valuable, then the obvious reply is that if we are free from the intentional coercion of others then we shall have space in which we can live a life shaped by our own projects and plans. However, if it is this which makes liberty valuable to us, and worth struggling for, can freedom be seen as logically distinct from ability to act on our purposes and our projects? Can an understanding of the meaning of liberty be detached from an account of what makes liberty valuable? This could be avoided only if one argued that liberty is an intrinsic good that is not valuable for any other purpose. However, this is an unappealing move since, if one does not share this intuition about the nature of liberty, then there is no possibility of further argument about the role of liberty in human life. If what makes freedom valuable is in fact connected with enabling us to pursue our own projects, then a free society cannot be indifferent to the question of whether people actually possess the material goods which are necessary conditions of action.

At this point the neo-liberal will usually deploy two arguments. The first is that negative liberty can be detached from the idea of the worth of liberty, those features of human life which make liberty worthwhile and the resources necessary to attain these. Secondly, in a morally pluralistic society we have no way of coming to an agreement on what are the necessary conditions of action, or what needs have to be fulfilled for someone to be able to act as an agent. However, I believe that there are plausible responses to each of these arguments. In the first case I would argue that we cannot detach an understanding of negative liberty from a conception of the good or of human flourishing. There are three reasons for this. The first is that, if we could, then the distribution of liberty would indeed depend entirely on identifying all those examples of intentional coercion. However, this would have a very paradoxical outcome, namely that a society such as Albania, to take Charles Taylor's example,[12] may have very few regulations governing movement such as traffic regulations and traffic lights. But if the existence of negative liberty is established by identifying the number of coercive acts, rather than by looking at the range of things and the quality of things which we are free to do, then it might be difficult to argue that Albania is less free than the UK or the USA. Liberty has to be connected with a notion of the value of liberty, with the type of actions which we are free to perform and the role they play in human flourishing, and not just with the incidence of coercion.

The second argument against the negative liberty view is that, except on the most restrictive account of coercion, it cannot work without invoking human powers and capacities which bear on human flourishing. If we regard threats as coercive then they can only be coercive in relation to a view about what people value. If I am threatened with the loss of something valuable unless I do what someone else wants, then, if this is coercive, it is so only because I value one thing more than another in my life. However, this links freedom, coercion and desire in a way that the negative libertarian regards as objectionable when discussing positive liberty.

Finally, it is also arguable that liberty is predicated on powers and abilities and that we cannot just say that freedom is one thing and power or ability another. For example, the question of liberty does not arise when someone is quite unable to do something. The paralysed man is neither free nor unfree to walk. The issue of whether one is free to walk depends upon being able to walk and then whether one is prevented from doing so by another person. If this is so then far from freedom and ability being separate things, freedom is actually predicated of capacities. If freedom is predicated of powers then the question of the distribution of powers and associated resources is an essential aspect of freedom.

4.6 PLURALISM AND HUMAN NEEDS

All these arguments imply the view that we cannot produce an account of freedom without some reference to both human flourishing and basic human interests, powers and capacities in a way that the proponent of negative freedom denies. The negative libertarian will argue that in a pluralistic society no conception of human flourishing is sufficiently widely shared for us to be able to link an account of freedom to it, or that we do not have a sufficiently consensual account of the needs which would have to be satisfied in order for an agent to be able to act. I want to leave on one side the first form of this argument because it is not directly relevant to thinking about the role of the welfare state. The second version of the argument is much more central however. The defender of the welfare state will argue against the neo-liberal that freedom is linked not just with our ability to fulfil particular desires, for, if it were, then the neo-liberal would be right in thinking that freedom would become wholly subjective, depending as it would upon the particular desires that we have. Rather, liberty should be connected to the possession of those goods which are necessary conditions of action at all, not therefore to particular desires but to the needs which would have to be satisfied in order for us to act so as to satisfy our desires at all. These would be the basic goods of welfare.

Neo-liberals argue that in a pluralistic society we do not have sufficient agreement on what these necessary conditions of action or basic needs would be as a basis for the welfare state. This is certainly the view which John Gray takes for example in his essay in *Dilemmas of Liberal Democracies*.[13] There are however two responses to this. First of all it is not clear that there is any empirical evidence to suggest that it is true, and certainly none is advanced by thinkers such as Gray and Hayek. Is it really the case in the UK that there is no agreement that income, health, nourishment and housing are not part of basic needs, or the generic conditions of action? If this is claimed it would be interesting to see the empirical evidence on which such a claim is based.

It could be argued against this, that we disagree not about basic needs, but about how collective means should be able to meet them. However, this argument fits badly with the neo-liberal account of poverty I described earlier. The neo-liberal rejects a relative view of poverty in favour of an account of poverty based upon an idea of need rather than on the degree of inequality or relative deprivation.[14] However, if this is so, then their position is paradoxical. How are we to arrive at a characterisation of poverty as the basis for a depoliticised, absolute account, if we do not share a conception of basic needs, which is what, as the criticism in the previous paragraph assumes, we do not have agreement about? Secondly, on their own understanding of political dynamics, to say that the state should meet basic needs however defined, is likely to mean that such needs will be bid up by interest groups and pressure groups within the political process. Even assuming that there was a distinction to be drawn between basic and other sorts of needs, the boundary between the two will be broken down by political pressures.

4.7 THE CASE FOR SOCIAL JUSTICE

The basis for trying to answer the neo-liberal critique is implicit in what has already been argued. There are two aspects of the claim. The first, as we saw, is that injustice can only be caused by intentional action, and the outcomes of markets are unintended. The second is that social justice cannot be a guide to public policy because there are no consensual norms of social justice in a modern complex society.

The answer to the first claim depends, as we saw in the case of the neo-liberal account of freedom and markets, upon the claim that we can bear moral responsibility for the foreseeable consequences of actions in relation to groups when such actions could have been different and are alterable. If this point is accepted in relation to freedom, then it also goes through in relation to social justice. However, there is another way of making the point. On the neo-liberal view, the question of injustice depends crucially upon the nature of the process which led to the alleged injustice. The action of the weather in destroying crops or of the genetic lottery in causing spina bifida is not an injustice because it is the result of an impersonal force. Similarly the action of the market in perhaps lowering the standard of living of some groups is also not an injustice for the same reason. Leave aside for the moment the points already made about the foreseeability and the alterability of market outcomes, it is still worth asking whether this is in fact all that there is to identifying injustice. Does not injustice depend also on our response to a situation which is alterable and not just on whether that situation was brought about by an impersonal force? Take again a micro example. Imagine that we have discovered a cure for a genetically transmitted disease. There is no doubt that the disease is transmitted through the impersonal genetic lottery. However, assume that we prefer not to market the product which would alter the quality of life of these people. Is the question of justice really to be settled by arguing that, since the problem was caused by an impersonal force, the issue of justice cannot arise? Does not injustice also arise in our response to the problem and not just in how it was caused? So again at the macro level, if some people are made worse off by our actions and we fail to compensate them – even if their being made worse off was not part of our intention – then we could argue that an injustice has occurred. Hence, my claim is that criteria relating to social justice are a salient basis for criticising market outcomes and these cannot be dismissed as irrelevant to the welfare state, as the neo-liberal claims.

Of course, we have to meet the second criticism of social justice deployed by the neo-liberal, namely that there is no point in invoking the principle as a guide to public policy if we cannot formulate criteria of social justice. However, I have already argued in the case of need, which is the dimension of social justice of concern to the welfare state, that the neo-liberal has no consistent line here. Need is invoked as a basis for the claim about the absoluteness of poverty on the one hand and yet needs are regarded as open-ended on the other. If needs are indeterminate and open- ended, then they cannot be used as the neo-liberal wishes to use them to produce a depoliticised, absolute conception of poverty. Needs are always going to be a matter of political negotiation and bargaining and this is going to be true whether the role of government in welfare is to use the claims of need as an instrument of social justice, or whether it is to see welfare as a residual category. If neo- liberals were consistent in their strictures on needs then they would take Nozick's path and reject the idea of the welfare state altogether.

4.8   WELFARE RIGHTS AND SCARCITY

The neo-liberal rejects the idea of welfare rights and argues that they are fundamentally different from civil and political rights, which can be defined in procedural terms which do not imply the commitment of resources. Again, I think, for the neo-liberal, but again not for a consistent libertarian such as Nozick, this is a very shaky argument. The discussion here is capable of endless ramification and I shall concentrate on just one point. The neo-liberal concentrates upon the problem of scarcity. There cannot be rights to welfare because of scarcity. However, the problem of scarcity is much more pervasive than the critic will allow. Negative rights, like positive rights, require resources, once it is allowed that there is a right to the safeguarding or the enforcing of negative rights. If I have a right to have my negative rights protected, then clearly this requires the state as the guarantor of rights to commit resources to their enforcement. These resources will include the police, courts, legislation, prisons and so on. This is because in the real world there is a scarcity not just in terms of material resources, but also in motivation relating to forbearance in respecting negative rights. Take two examples of paradigmatic negative rights such as the right to privacy and the right to security. The fact is that people do not forbear. They do infringe such rights and to prevent such infringements there is a need for such safeguards as street lighting, or security checks at airports, which go as far as possible to protect such rights. But these are rights to scarce resources and the demands embodied in such rights come up against this constraint. Debates about the appropriate level of resources to be committed to securing such rights become highly politicised – see for example the debate about the number of inspectors needed under the new Airport Security Bill. Recall the argument that the duties relating to such negative rights are supposed to be clear and categorical. Obviously this claim does not hold in the sense that securing the implementation of such rights is going to involve highly political disputes. We cannot therefore hold, as some neo-liberals do, that civil and political rights are depoliticised and not subject to political bargaining as welfare rights are. Bargaining about how to secure rights is a central feature of all these cases and we cannot therefore draw a hard-and-fast distinction between the two sorts of rights on this basis.

Several conclusions follow from this. The first is that the argument that positive rights involve open-ended commitments in the way that the securing of negative rights do not, is fatally flawed. For example, in the medical case it is argued that there can be no right to medical care because of the open-ended nature of medical needs, which grow with technological change. But the same is true of the right to privacy and security. There was no need for the Data Protection Act before the computer; there was no need for elaborate security at airports before the invention of plastic explosive. The enforceability of such rights is therefore always changing and open-ended, subject to technological change in exactly the same way as welfare rights. However, this is not seen as an insuperable objection to continuing to claim such rights. We are assured for example that there is no such thing as absolute security, but it is still thought worthwhile for the state to do what it can to ensure that travel can occur as safely as possible. Why cannot the same be true for social and economic rights? Clearly there cannot be thought to be a right to some kind of absolute level of medical provision. But why is this thought to be a fatal argument against the idea that there can be a right to health care and not the right to security?

The obvious point to make is that we can, through the normal processes of political bargaining, arrive at some kind of consensus about what at a particular time is an adequate level of public provision to protect rights such as privacy and security. If we can do this with those rights why cannot we do the same for rights such as health care and education?

However, there is still an important issue to be faced in thinking about rights in the context of the welfare state. It is argued correctly that such rights are not individually enforceable. There cannot be individual rights to scarce resources: they must be distributed in a discretionary way by service providers rather than according to a rule of law defining individual entitlements.

The claim that negative rights should be enforced encounters the same difficulty. As an individual I do not have a right to the services of a policeman or a security official at an airport. If we argue that welfare rights are not individually enforceable we cannot treat that as being fatal to the claim that there are welfare rights unless we also say the same about the enforceability of negative rights. I believe that there is a way forward here in trying over time to link rights to performance indicators and for exit from locally provided services or compensation if the educational system or the health service fails to meet performance targets. One other benefit of the approach would be that individually enforceable rights in welfare would also meet one of the other objections of the neo-liberals to the welfare state, namely – drawing upon the Public Choice School – their strictures on the power of producer interest groups within welfare bureaucracies. In their view this power will be constrained if more of welfare is made over to the market. The idea of individually enforceable rights would be one way in which there could be a non-market alternative solution to what I believe is a genuine issue. If there can be such rights then their enforceability would in fact constrain the behaviour of professionals within the welfare state and put much more power into the hands of the consumers of the services.

4.9   CITIZENSHIP, OBLIGATION AND DEPENDENCY

The argument about dependency is that the able-bodied poor have become locked into a culture of dependency and this can only be changed by either trying to link them into something like the disciplines of work through schemes like workfare, or by linking benefits to a more stringent interpretation of being available for work or being prepared to take a place in a training scheme. This approach is already in place, although it is not called workfare, for the 16–18 year old group. The other more stringent approach would be to argue that benefits should actually be reduced in order to create a more effective incentive to take a job, however low paid, as a way of getting onto the employment ladder. I believe that these ideas about remoralising the poor may well loom larger in future debates about the welfare state, largely because of the influence of American welfare theorists such as Charles Murray, who favours cutting back on benefits, or Larry Mead, who is a strong advocate of workfare as part of the obligation of citizenship, that the receipt of a benefit as a right should be conditional on discharging a concomitant obligation. The Mead approach raises some deep issues about the nature of citizenship, which again, I think, turn upon the idea that there is a categorical difference between civil and political rights on the one hand and social and economic rights on the other. We do not regard civil and political rights as conditional on discharging particular obligations or having a particular kind of moral character, and it is unclear why we should regard welfare benefits in the same way, unless we assume that the rights in question are fundamentally different. Public opinion might favour conditional rights in the welfare field but it is unclear whether there is a difference of principle here.

Indeed, the argument about dependency could be turned on its head. In the case of Charles Murray, who advocates reducing benefits, it could be argued that given that the intended effect of this is to throw the individual onto networks other than the state – relatives, friends, neighbourhoods, voluntary charities etc. – such an approach only redistributes dependency away from the state and on to private charity and families. It does not eliminate dependency, but only redistributes it.

In the case of the Mead/Novak proposals about workfare/learnfare, the same argument holds. If state benefits have to be linked to work or training, then against a background of unemployment the state will have to become the employer or the trainer of last resort. It would be quite unjust to link benefits to discharging such obligations if these obligations were not available to be discharged. However, in some ways this could be regarded as redistributing dependency from the Department of Social Security to the Department of Employment, which presumably would have the duty to be the employer or trainer of last resort. The public expenditure implications of such a programme could be horrendous. This could be coupled with a further point about workfare/learnfare in these circumstances, namely that the assumption behind the argument is that a job confers a sense of dignity and self-reliance, but assuming that this is true it is surely only true in those circumstances in which one has got a job for oneself. It is not at all clear that this would be so if the job was provided by the state and the individual was dependent on such state provision.

The second point to be made is that the argument for the remoralisation of the poor fits very badly with some other aspects of the neo-liberal case about the lack of moral consensus in society. However, when it comes to claiming that the poor need to be remoralised, this alleged lack appears to be overlooked. This links up with two aspects of the neo-liberal view of the role of the state. First of all it is argued that because of moral diversity it is necessary for the state to be neutral between different conceptions of the good, a claim which cannot be sustained if part of the job of the state is to remoralise the poor. Secondly it is argued that the state has a very limited capacity. Collective action always gives rise to unintended consequences and it is better for the state to stay its hand when tempted to intervene in the lives of citizens. However, this argument seems not to apply when it comes to claims about using workfare or changing the incentives of the social security system to remoralise the poor. We know very little about individual motivation, and for the state to try to inculcate a particular set of attitudes towards the economy and individual motivation within it is fraught with difficulties, difficulties which in other contexts neo-liberals are only too keen to recognise.

The remoralisation argument brings us round full circle. I have been concerned with the moral critique of the welfare state deployed by the New Right critics, and in my view it is to be found wanting.

NOTES

1. I have in mind thinkers such as Hayek (1960, 1976); Seldon (1990).
   For a summary see Green (1987).
2. For details see Vincent and Plant (1984).
3. See Joseph and Sumption (1978).
4. See the discussion in Hayek (1960).
5. See Gray (1988).
6. This is the argument in Hayek (1976) p 2.
7. See Gray (1984).
8. Murray (1984).
9. Mead (1986).
10. Novak (1987).
11. For further analysis of the debate between myself and the neo-liberals see Barry (1990).
12. Taylor (1987) p 211ff.
13. See Gray (1983). Here he argued that the 'objectivity of basic needs, is equally delusive' p 182.
14. Plant (1990).

REFERENCES

Barry N (1990) *Welfare*, Open University Press, Milton Keynes.

Gray J (1983) Classical Liberalism, Positional Goods, and Politicisation of Poverty, in Ellis A and Kumar K (eds) *Dilemmas of Liberal Democracies: Studies in Fred Hirsch's Social Limits to Growth*, Tavistock, London.

Gray J (1984) *Hayek on Liberty*, Blackwell, Oxford.

Gray J (1988) *Liberalism*, The Open University Press, Milton Keynes.

Green D (1987) *The New Right*, Wheatsheaf, Brighton.

Hayek F (1960) *The Constitution of Liberty*, Routledge, London.

Hayek F (1976) *Law, Legislation and Liberty*, vol 2, *The Mirage of Social Justice*, Routledge, London.

Joseph K (undated) *Stranded on the Middle Ground*, Centre for Policy Studies, London.

Joseph K and Sumption J (1978) *Equality*, J Murray, London.

Mead L (1986) *Beyond Entitlement: The Social Obligations of Citizenship*, Macmillan, New York, USA.

Murray C (1984) *Losing Ground, American Social Policy 1950–1980*, Simon Schuster, New York, USA.

Novak M (1987) *The New Consensus on Family and Welfare*, American Enterprise Institute, published by Marquette University, Wisconsin, USA.

Plant R (with Barry N) (1990) *Rights in Thatcher's Britain*, Institute of Economic Affairs, London.

Seldon A (1990) *Capitalism*, Blackwell, Oxford.

Taylor C (1987) What's Wrong with Negative Liberty, in *Philosophical Papers*, vol 2, Cambridge University Press, Cambridge.

Vincent A and Plant R (1984) *Philosophy, Politics and Citizenship*, Blackwell, Oxford.

5 Merit Goods and Benefits in Kind: Paternalism and Liberalism in Action
Alan Ryan

5.1 INTRODUCTORY: THE LAYOUT OF THE CHAPTER

This chapter is concerned with the question whether, and when, a welfare state ought to deliver benefits in kind rather than in cash. I begin with two other issues that bear on it. The first is the argument between Amartya Sen and Peter Townsend concerning the 'relativity' or 'absoluteness' of the concept of need – and thus of related concepts such as that of welfare or the standard of living.[1] The moral of the argument is that we must discriminate between the *causal* and the *symbolic* impact of goods and services. It is not the bare fact of being 'worse off' than others that counts, nor what the prevailing conception of the good life happens to be, but the impact of those things upon the welfare of the individual.

What matters is the way in which resources are resources for those who employ them (or choose not to employ them). This brings benefits in kind above the horizon in virtue of the thought that the welfare state's task is to *enable* its beneficiaries to play the social game rather than to ensure any particular outcome in welfare or utility terms. This in turn demands attention to the physical and psychological effects of what is provided by the welfare state on its recipients' capacity to act as they themselves choose. This 'enabling state' understanding of the 'welfare state' has only recently appeared, but it is a notion which it is now hard to do without.[2] Its detailed connection with arguments over cash versus kind is explored at the end of the chapter.

In the second part of this chapter, a list of sweeping moral justifications for the welfare state is canvassed. This is not in order to say anything novel about them, but to show the role of 'enablement' among possible justifications of the welfare state. This in turn ties in to the question of merit goods and their role in justifying government action.[3] Lastly, I turn to the question whether an emphasis on enablement supports a régime generally built upon cash benefits or whether it rather demands the provision of benefits in kind. I proceed tentatively. The approach is to show what sorts of considerations press one towards deciding for cash or benefits in kind, and only in the very last paragraphs do I tie together a conception of merit goods as enabling goods with the thought that different aspects of a concern for individual liberty may drive us either towards cash or benefits in kind.[4]

5.2 RELATIVISM AND ABSOLUTISM IN STANDARDS OF LIVING

One reason why people weary of arguments about the welfare state may be that they become sceptical about the whole notion of 'welfare', perhaps because they are taken in by the merits of a relativist dismantling of the idea that there is a determinate condition to be described as someone's welfare. Arguments to this effect come in many shapes and at many levels of sophistication. A plausible starting place is the eighteenth-century observation that what it takes to enjoy a reasonable 'standard of living' differs dramatically from one place and time to another. Achilles possessed slaves, weapons and fame, but didn't have a clean set of underclothes to his back. Only the very poorest inhabitant of eighteenth-century Glasgow would have been short of those. Are we therefore to conclude that Achilles enjoyed a 'low standard of living'? It seems obvious that we should not.[5]

The same conclusion is readily reached by many routes. What is often rather swiftly inferred is that the divergence between resources and welfare shows that welfare is 'relative'. But this thought is ambiguous between the harmless claim that *what* makes for well-being depends a good deal on the environment in which it is enjoyed or employed – a fur coat being more use in a Canadian winter than a Nigerian summer – and the less harmless claim that well-being is itself a matter of one's own well-being *relative to that of others*. The difference between these two propositions is what has been at stake between Professors Sen and Townsend.[6]

Noticing the difference does not supply all the answers because the way *beliefs* and *values* enter into our own well-being reintroduces a form of relativism even within an absolutist conception of welfare. This terse statement needs expansion. The simple relativist position holds that well-being is a question of one's relationship to the general level of well-being. Some or perhaps all statements about how well we are doing contain an implicit reference to how well other people are doing. To have 'enough' is to have 'such and such a proportion of the average or mean'; to be adequately housed is to be housed adequately by the local standards. As Marx long ago observed, it is when someone builds a palace next door that the peasant's humble but adequate cottage becomes a hovel instead.[7]

The counter to this claim is in its way decisive. The concept of well-being is not relative, but absolute. Suppose we grant that one component of what clothing does for us is to produce self-respect; Achilles had it without clean underwear, we cannot have it without clean underwear. None the less, what we are after is not some *proportion* of the local average of self-respect; we are after self-respect *simpliciter.*[8] Similarly, once it is impossible to obtain employment without being literate, it becomes essential to self-respect to be literate, but not because self-respect operates on the same sliding scale as degrees of literacy. Rather, once we have become literate enough to secure stable employment, and can keep our self-respect, we have achieved one of the components of well-being, regardless of where we feature on any scale.

This counter-claim is in essentials Sen's response to Townsend's espousal of a relativist conception of welfare. Still, one may think that the matter cannot be decided quite so swiftly; Townsend has returned to the charge, and one may agree that if the direct argument for relativism is inconclusive, there is something left to be dug out. The first thing is straightforward and not contested. The impact of different goods upon our welfare varies with the conditions of consumption because the way everyone else behaves makes a difference to the good our consumption does. The most obvious examples are such old favourites as the need of the poorest portions of society for what were once luxuries – such as telephones and television. These have now become necessities of consumption. The reason lies in the effects of other people's possession of these things on the environment of the non-possessor. If *almost everyone* has a telephone, anyone seeking employment has to leave a telephone number where he or she can be reached by employers. Those not on the telephone are to all intents and purposes out of the labour force.[9] What it is about the telephone that makes it essential is non-relativistically connected to the good it does. That is, the underlying proposition runs: 'Employment is essential to self-respect; communication with employers is a *sine qua non* of being employed; a telephone is the only means of effecting such communication.' A television set might similarly be defended as essential; where *almost* everyone possesses one, entertainment, information and social participation are channelled through it.

If 'sufficient social interaction' is an absolute rather than a relative concept, the defence of an absolutist approach to welfare is made out. Within these limits it is impossible to resist the argument that self-respect and well-being are intrinsically absolute rather than relative. Yet, we cannot bypass the question of how whoever it may be whose well-being and self-respect are in question relates to those around him or her. To put it simply, it is not obvious that the absolute conception of welfare *interestingly* survives the observation that he or she has standards, values, beliefs and aspirations which would be senseless in the absence of comparison with others of his or her own kind.[10] We can acknowledge that what a person enjoys is an adequate level of welfare or an adequate level of self-respect – absolutely – but still find everything interesting lurking in the question of how that standard gets set.

Now we can go further. When we dig into the ways in which well-being, self-respect and agency are related to the doings of others than the agent, we encounter the considerations that sometimes make us think the welfare state should operate only as a system of cash support, and sometimes make us think it ought mostly to provide non-tradeable goods and services to its clients. The starting point is what we have just left behind us, the observation that the utility of a good cannot be determined by barely inspecting it, and that we need to be sensitive to the effects of others' consumption or use of it. The example of the telephone is a paradigm case.

Other goods fall into a similar category both for the same and also for rather different reasons. Take literacy. The trickiness of the argument about relative and absolute values can be seen here. On one view, literacy is like access to a telephone; if everyone is illiterate, employment is readily available to the illiterate, and nobody suffers. Literacy is a luxury, and no individual's human rights are violated if he or she is left illiterate. Once enough people are literate, it is rational to organise economic life around written instructions which only readers can follow. Once most people can read and write, the illiterate is at a disadvantage which has nothing to do with the intrinsic pleasures of literacy or with the social esteem in which literacy is held.[11]

In a competitive economy, however, what is needed is likely to be not so much literacy as *as great a degree of literacy as one's competitors possess*. Here there is a genuinely comparative element, but again that is not because of the esteem in which literacy is held; rather, against the background of a genuine competition for employment, merely being qualified to be employed at all is not enough. One must compete on equal terms. Our first thoughts assumed that any literate person can get employment; now we have dropped that assumption. The change makes all the difference.

Arguments about 'relative' versus 'absolute' aspects of welfare raise the issue of how goods and services affect well-being *as a causal* rather than as a *symbolic* matter. To separate causality and symbolism as well as to understand their interaction is sometimes a formidable task. Estimating just what they imply for any given person or group of people is appallingly complex. I would turn this point around. The welfare state is well suited to increasing the welfare of individuals in non-complex cases. The complexity of estimating well-being in complicated cases, on the other hand, provides pragmatic support for the idea that the welfare state's task lies not in *securing* the welfare of members of society but rather in *enabling* members of society to secure it for themselves.[12]

We should focus, that is, not on the utility of what someone gets but on the question of what it enables them to do. It is, we might say, the job of the welfare state to deliver the resources to enable people to attain a degree of self-respecting well-being that nobody ought to fall below, but it is neither possible, nor is it in the end the state's job, to see that people actually attain that level. As will appear below, it is not part of my case that we should avoid paternalism at all costs. Compared with Wiseman, for instance, I am tolerably happy to allow the better-informed to second guess the less-informed. None the less, if we wish to avoid both inefficiency and claustrophobic intervention, a state that conceives itself as operating at arm's length to provide enablements is an attractive proposition.

Thus, when we ensure that the bus actually stops outside the old people's home, that the walkways to the bus stop are well lighted and smoothly paved, and that the bus itself has wheelchair access for the disabled but active elderly, we have delivered an enablement. If someone persists in visiting relatives whom she can't stand, or goes to films she dislikes, or in other ways uses the facilities so provided in a way that gives her no pleasure, it is not a defect in the welfare state. The fundamental thought is that against a background of ordinary competence, we incline for libertarian and practical reasons only to enable people to look after their own well-being, not to take over that task for them.

'Enablement' may push us in two very different directions. The first is that of simply making cash transfers, on the grounds that that enables individuals to do whatever they wish with the money they have been given and maximises their freedom of action. The other is that of providing aid in the form of benefits in kind on the grounds that it is the causal properties of the goods or services in question that enable the recipient to do what the recipient has a mind to do. It is to this second argument that the final section is devoted, using the obvious example of the National Health Service. Before turning to it, I should like to interpose a few thoughts on the place of enabling goods in arguments for the welfare state – indeed in arguments for the public provision of goods and benefits more generally.

5.3 GROUNDS FOR WELFARE STATE PROVISION: UTILITARIAN AND OTHER

Not all intervention is 'welfare state' intervention, but there is so little point in discussing what is and what is not a task of the *welfare* state rather than the state *simpliciter* that we may risk lumping together things that many people would consider to be in different categories. To think of the welfare state in terms of enablement is not always to think in terms that *compete* with other conceptions of the welfare state. To suppose that the welfare state exists to allow people to escape the nagging fear of hunger, bad housing, ill health and the like is not to choose between enablement and a utilitarian or rights-based view. The utilitarian certainly has one gloss on the purpose of policies designed to avert these evils; but an enablement theorist may well think that the *point* of the capacities he hopes to secure to people is to allow them to lead a life freed of the evils the utilitarian identifies as his target.

There are two things that are distinctive about arguing from enablement. The first is that it offers a way of fending off critics of the welfare state who concentrate their fire on the limitations said to be imposed by the welfare state on individual freedom of choice.[13] If anyone can be rendered freer by being equipped to make a wider range of effective choices it must be admitted that the state can increase freedom by intervention in various ways. The discussion of the fair value of liberty in John Rawls's *A Theory of Justice* is, in these terms, a discussion of enablements.[14]

The second distinctive feature of talk about enablement has emerged once already, and will emerge again later. This is the way it allows us to deal with welfare itself at arm's length. To see the welfare state as concerned with the provision of enabling goods both allows us to draw back from too minute an inquiry into the actual use people make of the resources they have, and allows us to concentrate on improving people's broad-gauge potential for activity as well as on defeating manifest evils of one or another kind. Whether this makes much difference doubtless depends upon context, and upon our imagination. Still, in the context of arguments about cash and kind it is a point to be borne in mind, because the advantage of cash is its translatability into an indefinitely wide range of goods and services; a concern for broad-gauge enablement would choose benefits in kind which secure a wider rather than a narrower scope for action.

Of all defences of the welfare state the simplest is utilitarian, for the utilitarian view of the welfare state is the utilitarian view of the state, period. This is consistent with the historical fact that many utilitarians were for a variety of reasons opposed to most forms of public provision. The state exists to do whatever good it can, so all states are welfare states. Mill and Bentham were straightforward defenders of just this view, different though they were in their ultimate judgements about what the state might achieve and how it might achieve it.[15] 'Welfare state' is a pleonasm; any rationally organised state is a welfare state, since there is no other goal or purpose to the state beyond its people's welfare. All the interesting arguments turn on delicate sociological questions about the means inevitably employed by the state and about the nature of the goals they are supposed to serve. In essence, however, the question boils down to one that animates Mill's *On Liberty*, the works of de Tocqueville, and those of many other anxious liberals.[16]

Suppose one considers the provision of education a task of the welfare state. Perhaps the inculcation of certain sorts of moral and intellectual character can only be assisted by arm's-length state assistance – bureaucratically administered heroism and moral independence are hard to imagine, and one respect in which British public education has been superior to American public education has until lately been the absence of political control over the syllabus. Such considerations, however, are internal to a utilitarian approach to the question of public provision. The claim is that whatever the state *can* usefully do, it should.

Utilitarian considerations are not the only ones we may invoke and lately have not been the most popular. Welfare state provision is also a matter of justice between those in need and those not. One appropriate conception of justice invokes the notion of compensation. Take unemployment benefit, which many writers treat, as I do below, as a matter of insurance. This is by no means the only possibility. We might, as Richard Titmuss did, think of unemployment benefit not in terms of cashing in a policy for which one might not in fact have paid the premiums, but as exercising a right against the employed, a right founded on the fact that the unemployed person had played his or her part for society in bearing the risks of the market-place, and was entitled to a reward for having done his or her bit for the market economy.[17] This conception is both engaging and idiosyncratic, but its merits are not at issue; more to the point is the limited range of the benefits it seems to cover – unemployment benefit and little else.

More obviously appealing are arguments from egalitarian justice. Both cash transfers and benefits in kind can be defended in terms of their redistributive impact, as doing something to make the distribution of goods and services less unequal. Even so, it is equally important to see how narrow is the egalitarian impact of welfare state thinking. The welfare state does not alter whatever inequality stems from different employments. On the contrary it reflects its existence in any system of earnings-related benefits.

Egalitarian *justice* is not to be confused with the egalitarianism implicit in traditional utilitarianism. The utilitarian case is that if people had identical tastes and received identically patterned diminishing marginal utility from their consumption, an equal distribution of goods would be required to maximise utility. The argument from justice is different. It is that some, or many, or for the really strenuous egalitarian *all*, of the various factors that create different degrees of well-being between one person and another do so arbitrarily. There may be countervailing reasons for leaving many of these arbitrary unfairnesses untouched, but where there are not, they should be remedied. The inequalities stemming from unpredictable ill health or unemployment, and from all too predictable old age and incapacity, can be remedied without damage to the productive efficiency of society, and should be.

The most eloquent and most widely read defence of the liberal welfare state since the war must be John Rawls's *A Theory of Justice*. Because Rawls's account of 'maximin justice' comes embedded in an elaborate theory of political institutions, it is an ill-advised move simply to lift the principle of 'make the worst-off as well-off as possible' out of context. Still, we may remark four features of Rawls's account which tie it in to the concerns of this section. First, it shares with what we have just described as egalitarian justice the thought that where differences result from arbitrary considerations, the disadvantaged have a right to have their disadvantages made up. To the question who has the duty to make up these disadvantages, the only rational answer is that the rest of us collectively have such a duty, and each of us distributively has the duty to stand ready to contribute our fair share to a workable scheme for meeting that duty. Second it shares with an 'enablement' theory a concern with *resources* rather than outcomes. Its account of the primary goods which are at stake in questions of distributive justice is linked to 'wealth and power' by Rawls himself, but in theory to any resources needed for self-respect, whatever they are. Thirdly, it is quite clear that the property institutions of a society take second place to these considerations, and are meant to be shaped by them; they do not, as in libertarian, anti-welfare-state theories place a constraint on them. Finally, it resembles, but is not identical with, a 'baseline' conception of social justice which holds that there is some absolute level of well-being which everyone is entitled to enjoy as of right. It is more ambitious than 'baseline' theories. It asks that the worst-off should be as well off as possible; baseline theories ask only that they should attain some respectable level.[18]

Another form of justification more characteristic of Titmuss even than the compensation theory, is communitarianism. Almost all the benefits of the welfare state – the health service, unemployment payments, old age pensions at any rate – can be seen as the expressions of a common intention to pay for the minimum requirements of our common humanity. This is a distinctively communitarian defence and elucidation of welfare state provision, captured by the thought that at some level we are all in the same boat and all ought to have some minimum defence against the ills to which we are commonly and inescapably prey. It tells us nothing, of course, about how much provision, nor about how it is to be provided, nor in what shape it is to come. The one thing that is clear is the moral model behind it. A community is to be understood as a group whose *raison d'être* is its ability to defend each of its members against common hazards in a way each of us could not do individually.[19]

This may be understood negatively as a matter of fending off the worst that may happen to us. Still, even this negative task gives rise to all sorts of positive moral virtues such as solidarity and mutual concern, which are themselves valuable and to be cherished as such. Indeed, some defenders of the welfare state seem inclined almost to subordinate the primary tasks of the welfare state to the achievement of these secondary solidaristic goods. Public provision is to be valued, not so much for its efficiency, or even its egalitarianism in a welfare-based sense, as for its collective character.[20] It may be thought that a concern for enablement is foreign to such a perspective. Certain forms of individualist liberalism surely must be. None the less, a view of individual liberty that was sensitive to the facts of socialisation would not be uncommunitarian, and a concern for enablement would be in like case.[21]

Institutionally, the welfare state has been commonly and rather satisfactorily conceived of as a system of compulsory insurance; in this vein, we may elucidate its role by considering the benefits that we should (if we were well informed) buy in the insurance market if we could. Health care and unemployment benefit fall into this category easily enough. The provision of pensions, though it may be channelled through insurance companies in the private sector, and is often coupled with life insurance, involves compulsory saving for a known event, rather than insurance against an event whose likelihood is unknown. Providing pensions for dependants, on the other hand, is a matter of meeting obligations which we would wish to see to ourselves, but fear that accident may prevent us doing, and really is a matter of insurance.

The state's role in this may be market-improving or market-supplanting, and is probably best thought of as a combination of both. It is market-improving if it is a question of giving people insurance benefits of a sort they would purchase in an ideal market, and charging them prices they would be willing to pay in such a market. It is market-supplanting when it extends insurance to people who would quite rationally choose not to spend their income on insurance, or who are too intermittently employed or too frequently ill to build up the resources with which to purchase insurance. One thing that is worth noticing in this connection is how uncontroversial most of these activities (as distinct from their financing) are, and how large a proportion of the welfare state's budget they occupy. Countries vary a good deal, of course, but in the USA the provision of old age pensions and health care to the old and the indigent takes up almost all the social budget.[22] In Britain, too, income maintenance in the face of misfortune, illness and old age takes up the largest share of strictly welfare activities.

From these sweeping moral justifications for a welfare state, we must home in on one less sweeping thought. This is the role of the state in the provision of merit goods. Merit goods are goods whose value is estimated differently by governments and individuals, so that individuals would, left to themselves, consume less of the merit good than governments think they ought (and, in the case of a demerit good, more). The view that the state should provide such merit goods, or should push up their consumption by subsidising them, is easily defended in a utilitarian framework, though not in a utilitarian framework which follows Bentham in thinking the individual the best judge of his or her own interests. Mill, once more acting as Bentham's fiercest critic, was emphatic that 'the uncultivated cannot judge of cultivation', and employed the principle to some effect in defending state support for – though not state provision of – education at all levels.[23]

By the same token, if one thinks that some portion of the population is more likely than the rest to undervalue merit goods, there are redistributive arguments for their provision. Education might operate in either framework; we might think that *everyone* would get more from being educated than they suppose, and that total utility will be increased by free or heavily subsidised compulsory education, or we might think that the illiterate and ignorant poor were peculiarly likely to underestimate the good it would do them, and so target it at them. For our purpose here, the link between merit goods and the issue of benefits in kind is simply that one 'merit' a merit good may have is that it enables the possessor or enjoyer of it to fend for himself or herself in a larger, more interesting and less dependent fashion, the topic to which we now finally turn.

5.4   MERIT GOODS, BENEFITS IN KIND AND ANTI-PATERNALISM

The elementary arguments about benefits in kind versus cash transfers are not difficult to spell out. The empirical issues surrounding the argument are of a degree of complexity which might daunt anyone. What follows is simply an arrangement for explaining some of these complications. The case for cash transfers is straightforward. On utilitarian grounds, where there is a presumption in favour of the consumers' own preferences, it is better to give consumers resources they can employ in whatever way they choose. They are the best authority on what will yield them maximum utility. The basic thought is very simple. For any good, there may be another available for the same cash outlay which the consumer prefers; if consumers are given non-tradeable goods they are denied access to the other good; if they are given cash they have access to it and any other good at the same price. To these arguments from the standpoint of general utility and individual freedom of choice, we may add another one of some force. It is simpler and cheaper for governments to transfer cash to recipients than to hand over physical goods or services. Moreover, it takes less information to be sure of handing over enough money than it does to be sure of handing over the optimal bundle of gifts in kind.

Arguments of a utilitarian or libertarian kind for cash transfers must avoid falling foul of the obvious fear that the goods and services needed may not be available, or may be of poor quality. So a third argument in favour of cash is simply the belief in consumer sovereignty. The consumer or consumers collectively will secure the best provision of goods and services by demanding what they want and rejecting what they do not. This is the argument in favour of a system of private health care. That is, since it is the patient who decides whom to consult, and what treatment to accept, doctors and providers of other medical services have to be attentive to their patients' demands.

The difference between types of health care provision would still remain striking were the United States to extend Medicare Insurance for the elderly to members of population below the age of sixty-five. For patients would behave like all other privately insured patients do; it would remain up to them to shop for the specialists, consultants and hospitals they needed. Whether the actual condition of American health care is a conclusive empirical refutation of the trust placed in consumer sovereignty is another matter. What seems rather dispiritingly to be true is that where the privately insured are tolerably well educated, live in areas where there are plenty of specialists to consult, and in communities which sustain good hospitals, consumer sovereignty is a reality. And it is for such people that consumer sovereignty tends to be a reality under the British National Health Service, without their paying to achieve it.

Counter-arguments to the case for cash rather than provision in kind fall into a similar pattern. We may think consumer sovereignty is a dubious notion in the contexts in which the welfare state operates. Health care is again an obvious instance. Though some systems allow the patient a freer hand in choosing his or her own physician or surgeon, no system can do much to alter the fact that as patients we are at the mercy of the expertise of our healers. In an age of CT scans, Magnetic Resonance Imaging, and the rest, the patient has little scope for informed choice, and little room to shop around for treatment. Consumer sovereignty is almost wholly limited to giving one a sporting chance of finding physicians, surgeons and the rest with whom one feels comfortable – and the individual choices that get made along these lines have little effect on the quality of treatment.

Besides health, many other areas show the same features. Consider the problem of housing the elderly. The chances of a somewhat defenceless elderly person getting a bad deal on the open market are uncomfortably high. Nor is this because landlords are out for what they can get. The elderly can make difficult tenants; they may become feeble and fail to look after the property, or cantankerous and a nuisance to the neighbours, or fall ill and need a lot of help. Adding in one thing with another, we may doubt whether the ordinary operations of the market-place will produce adequate accommodation for the elderly at a reasonable price. We may wonder how far the category of sovereign consumer overlaps with the natural beneficiaries of the welfare state.

A government which confined itself to putting cheques in the post might operate more cheaply and more controllably than a government which went in for the direct provision of benefits in kind. Still, the contrast between them may not be so sharp. A welfare state which provides benefits in kind may operate in almost any manner from merely purchasing goods and services which the beneficiaries then receive free or cheaply to operating public facilities through its own employees. More than likely it will adopt one method with certain goods, and another with other goods. In many national health systems the providers of services are self-employed but paid directly by government; in others, they are paid by their clients, who recover the money from the state. Both systems deliver what is in one sense a benefit in kind, since nobody can sell on their entitlement to the services they get, and the state will not provide income *instead* of medical treatment. Again public housing may be what that term usually connotes, or may be housing rented by some public authority from private landlords and allocated on a subsidised basis to appropriate tenants; either way, it would be the supply of benefits in kind.

The point which a very long line of writers has made is that we must beware of starting from assumptions only satisfied in the ideal world of economic theory. The world may be the best world we have got, but it is not one that satisfies simple economic models. Once those models are complicated for the vicissitudes of the real world, we cannot assume that doing something much like we should have done in the first best situation will achieve a second best. We may need to start again and think up a different strategy.

The case for benefits in kind emerges from these considerations. Wherever there is what we may non-pejoratively label consumer incompetence – that is, the failure of the conditions required for consumer sovereignty – cash is no more attractive than benefits in kind. The one additional argument for benefits in kind – or non-tradeable goods and services – which we ought to note is the argument from the existence of merit goods. We should divide merit goods into two classes. First is the kind of merit good associated with all the existing literature. Here, we have a case where we know that the consumer will turn cash into goods which the government rates less highly than the consumer does. There are only two alternatives. Either we adopt a system of cash transfers and subsidise the merit good to the point where the consumer will consume as much of it as we think he or she ought to – for example by handing over income supplements *and* subsidising food rich in vitamins which we know would be consumed in too small quantities otherwise – or we act directly by handing out the appropriate food for free and forbidding its resale. The only objection to such a policy, whichever way we frame it, must be the kind of principled antipathy to paternalism explained by Wiseman in Chapter 3. The paternalist has at least two replies. In the first place, people often are just inept about matters of diet. In the second place, the argument from fair shares suggests that anyone who proposes to benefit from free health services can hardly complain if he or she is prevented from becoming a needless burden on the system out of ineptitude in their dietary choices. This is not a directly paternalist argument, though paternalism lurks in the background if we are not willing to let people choose to neglect their health and opt out of the medical care system.

The more interesting case is the second case. This is where the merit good is what I call an enabling good, where it is instrumental to some future capacity which we desire the recipient to have. Education is an example. Free compulsory education *can* be defended as a pure merit good, but is better defended as an instrumental good of the sort I have in mind, and delivered as particular services. This, if it is paternalism, is a novel version of Rousseau's intention to force people to be free – and a great deal less alarming. If we are entering a period in which job opportunities for the illiterate and innumerate are diminishing while opportunities for the reasonably numerate and literate are expanding, it is only the right sort of education that will get people back into the workforce. Other enabling goods may not fit into the 'merit' goods category in so simple a way.

To those of us who have long looked to J.S. Mill for guidance, both positive and negative, there is one fact about Mill himself that might give us pause. The welfare state both as constituted in practice, and as it could be imagined in any of the societies to which it is appropriate, would have been anathema to Mill.[24] It would have been anathema for two sorts of reason, one usually to be found in the mouths of conservatives, the other in the mouths of radicals of the left. The first objection to the welfare state is that it makes its clients dependent on itself; it substitutes its judgement for theirs; it breaks the linkage between rational self-control and its consequences which Mill wanted to preserve, to encourage the provident and fore-sighted and to discourage the feckless and the weak. Mill certainly allowed for acts of public charity which were the forerunners of the welfare state we know today, but his whole moral outlook was at odds with anything like a principled defence of the welfare state.

This was not because he wished to see the reign of *laissez-faire* and the triumph of an unfettered capitalist economy. Mill wanted to do away with those and institute a system of market socialism in which the main economic institutions would be producer cooperatives together with whatever political and public management they required. This change would simply render the welfare state obsolete. So, it is with a strong sense of writing against the *letter* of Mill's prescriptions that I observe that we need to ask ourselves what sort of implementation of Mill's *goals* one might aim at in a welfare state context. Granted that we sin against the letter of his doctrine, can we act in its spirit?

The answer is rather brief. There are two aspects of liberty involved. The simpler boils down to the negative libertarian assertion that we must minimise interferences with people's actual choices. All who do not suffer some clearly specified disability which renders them unable to choose for themselves should be left to choose for themselves. They will make errors, sometimes grave errors. But *Liberty*, if it is anything, is a stern injunction not to be so distressed by the immediate accidents and mischances that befall free choosers that we succumb to the temptation to put them on leading strings. In the light of this picture of liberty, we are asked to err on the side of taking risks with the welfare of the dependent for the sake of making them less dependent in their dealings with the welfare state itself.

Mill's aspiration was to go to great lengths in equalising property, abolishing the distinction between owners and managers on the one hand and their employees on the other, but otherwise to avoid redistributive tinkering. He was opposed as a matter of principle to progressive taxation, and spoke in the harshest terms of attempts to tailor taxation to 'ability to pay'. By extra-polation, the welfare state should provide some financial support, and offer such advice as is useful. After that, it should cease to interfere.

One may doubt all Mill's assumptions. The elderly and the confused are not only numerous but increasingly numerous in our own day: in their case the line between incapacity and shortage of information may not always be easy to draw, especially when some of the people they have to deal with have a vested interest in making information harder to come by and less accurate into the bargain. In the light of such thoughts, the desire to do all one can by cash transfers plus information looks factually ill-founded and morally narrow, even if it exhibits one sort of liberal or libertarian impulse.

But there is another way of looking at it. This is not to reject or despise the impulse that leads to this view, but to extend the notion of liberty involved to embrace the general, all-in capacity to 'play the social game'. This might sometimes lead in just the same direction; if people can fend for themselves, but lack only the cash to make their wishes effective, then cash support is all we need or ought to think about. Take housing as a concrete illustration. It is an open question whether housing assistance for any but the elderly ought to proceed in any other way than by cash assistance, perhaps backed up by legal assistance for tenants's cooperatives. Elsewhere, there are other arguments to bear in mind. An alternative to 'workfare' thinking about unemployment benefit would be 'edufare'; we should spend our un-employment money on compulsory education for the unemployed. Work-fare is one way of satisfying the moral demand that the unemployed show themselves willing to work; but edufare satisfies the expanded liberal goal of giving assistance in such a way that it maximises the capacity of the pre-viously dependent to be subsequently independent.

Other than educational services it is not easy to think of ways of giving assistance via benefits in kind that have quite this character. The merits of this approach cannot in any case be argued briefly. If it carries some degree of *prima facie* plausibility, it cannot carry more than that until one sees how it fares in detail. To do that, a wholly different sort of paper from this is required, one that goes into the detail of welfare state provision and assesses the plausibility of this kind of moral stance towards it carefully and flexibly in the light of its detailed applicability. The best this chapter can do is provide some reason to embark on that task.

NOTES

1. Townsend (1985); Sen (1985).
2. Gilbert and Gilbert (1988).
3. Ryan (1989).
4. This eclecticism is well developed in Goodin (1988); see, too, Moon (1988).

5. Smith (1976).
6. See Note 1 and Sen *et al* (1987).
7. Marx (1962).
8. Sen (1985).
9. Jencks (1976).
10. Readers of Veblen (1969) will find it hard to swallow any form of absolutism, of course.
11. Again, a distinction Veblen (1969) would mock.
12. Goodin (1988).
13. Nozick (1974).
14. Rawls (1971).
15. Mill (1965).
16. Mill (1974).
17. Harris (1987).
18. Rawls (1971).
19. Harris (1987).
20. Taylor (1990).
21. Taylor (1989).
22. Their untouchability was amply displayed in the Budget negotiations of the autumn of 1990.
23. Mill (1965).
24. Mill (1974).

REFERENCES

Gilbert N and Gilbert B (1988) *The Enabling State*, Oxford University Press, Oxford and New York, USA.

Goodin R (1988a) *Reasons for Welfare*, Princeton University Press, Princeton, USA.

Goodin R (1988b) Reasons for Welfare, in Moon D (ed) *Rights, Welfare and Responsibilities*, Westview Press, Denver, USA.

Griffin F (1987) *Well-Being*, Clarendon Press, Oxford.

Harris D (1987) *Justifying State Welfare: The New Right and The Old Left*, Blackwell, Oxford.

Jencks C (1976) *Equality*, Basic Books, New York, USA.

Marx Karl (1962) *The German Ideology*, Foreign Language Publishing House, Moscow, USSR.

Mill J S (1965) *Principles of Political Economy*, University of Toronto Press, Toronto, Canada.

Mill J S (1974) *On Liberty*, Penguin Books, Harmondsworth.

Moon J D (1988) Moral Justifications of the Welfare State, in Gutman A (ed) *Democracy and the Welfare State*, Princeton University Press, Princeton, USA.

Nozick R (1974) *Anarchy, State and Utopia*, Basic Books, New York, USA.

Rawls J (1971) *A Theory of Justice*, Harvard University Press, Cambridge, Mass., USA.

Ryan A (1989) Value Judgements and Welfare, in Helm D (ed) *The Economic Borders of the State*, Oxford University Press, Oxford.

Sen A (1985) A Reply to Peter Townsend, *Oxford Economic Papers* **37**, Oxford.

Sen A *et al* (1987) *The Standard of Living*, Cambridge University Press, Cambridge.

Smith A (1976) *An Enquiry into the Nature and Causes of the Wealth of Nations*, Clarendon Press, Oxford.

Taylor C (1989) *Sources of the Self*, Harvard University Press, Cambridge, Mass., USA.

Taylor C (1990) Cross-Purposes, in Rosenblum N (ed) *Liberalism and the Moral Life*, Harvard University Press, Cambridge, Mass., USA.

Townsend P (1985) A Sociological Approach to the Measurement of Poverty: A Rejoinder to Professor Amartya Sen, *Oxford Economic Papers* **37**, Oxford.

Veblen T (1969) *The Theory of the Leisure Class*, Penguin Books edn, Harmondsworth.

Part Three

Questions of Practice

6   Constraints
Charles Carter

All activities of government in a democracy must in a general way be expected to add to the welfare of citizens – that is, to be conducive to good fortune, happiness or well-being – since it would be perverse to elect to the service of government those who would reduce the welfare of electors. There are obvious exceptions to the generalisation: electors may be mistaken about the likely results of the policies they are offered, and be unable to correct the mistake until there is another election; governments may be mistaken in their assessment of external forces and events; particular measures may advance the welfare of some citizens but subtract from that of others; the losers may be a majority, if for some reason the gainers have political clout. But such exceptions do not affect the conclusion that there is no need to hijack the word 'welfare' to apply only to what is described in Chapter 1 as the conventional core of 'the welfare state'. That core consists of social security payments, health, education and housing, but there is no firmly drawn boundary line even in conventional usage. These activities compete for attention with others which claim to add to the general welfare of citizens. Choices have to be made.

What can be done for the welfare of citizens depends on the size of the national product. If we bring into the balance the welfare of future generations as well as of this one, the pursuit of short-term gains in the national product may be wrong. Such gains may, for instance, be achieved only at the cost of lasting environmental damage or the exhaustion of irreplaceable natural resources. We need to cultivate the economic garden so that its fertility remains unimpaired in future years. But such an aim is quite consistent with an improvement in our present gardening efficiency which would yield an increase in welfare. Thus, though in past years the Eastern European states made large claims about their concern for the welfare of their citizens, many people felt that they frustrated their own good intentions by the inefficiency with which they managed their economies. Japan leaves substantial areas of welfare to the private sector: but, guided by intelligent government policy, its economy grows so fast that there is room for large gains in welfare.

We need, therefore, to consider whether public expenditure, on the services mentioned above, impairs national efficiency and therefore limits the scope for a real increase in general welfare. We shall need also to ask whether 'excessive' government expenditure of any kind harms the national product. That belief was strongly held by government in the 1980s; it implies that 'welfare state' expenditure must face enhanced competition for its share of a limited amount of state finance.

A large part of these welfare activities take the form of transfers of money: they join with progressive income taxation in altering the distribution of income so that it is seen to be more just. Transfer payments financed from taxation or contributions apparently constitute no extra call on the national product, since they simply remove purchasing power from A to give it to B. They will tend, however, to alter the balance between spending and saving, and that may affect economic growth directly, or indirectly through the reaction of government to an enhanced danger of inflation. They may also reduce the incentive to work, and thus harm the national product – though the evidence on this is confused. But, if we take a wider definition, we bring in welfare activities such as the National Health Service, which make a large real call on the national product, and in doing so are in competition not only with other kinds of government expenditure but with all the other ways in which people would like to spend their money.

6.1   GOVERNMENT EXPENDITURE CHOICES

Let us look first at the choices which have to be made within the total of government expenditure. For 1989, taking central and local government together, total expenditure (before taking account of privatisation sales of nationalised industries) divided as shown in Table 6.1.

Table 6.1 Government expenditure 1988/9

Defence, public order and safety	16%
Economic services (e.g. roads, agricultural and industrial subsidies)	8%
Social security and personal social services	29%
Education, health and housing	27%
Community amenities, recreational and cultural affairs	4%
General public services (e.g. finance, executive and legislative organs, external affairs)	5%
Other expenditure (mostly debt interest)	11%

Source: United Kingdom National Accounts, 1989 edn, HMSO, Table 9.4

Table 6.1 makes it clear that the main competition for the taxpayer's money is between social security and other welfare state services. Debt interest has to be paid; recently the national debt has been reduced, so it is reasonable to hope that the average level of this item will fall. The 'general public services' do not make a large claim on expenditure, so – even if one believes that they could be run more efficiently – the share of expenditure released would not be very significant. In principle, the economic services should be capable of justification as increasing the national product, and therefore the fund from which welfare can be provided. In practice, they are heavily burdened with aid to lame ducks and to favoured sectors such as farming, but they do also include spending vital to national efficiency, for example on the roads. If savings can be made in the economic services, there would be a strong case for using the share of expenditure released to develop additional ways of stimulating the national product, for instance by more support for industrial research.

The competition for resources with defence, public order and safety is of a rather different kind. It is not easy to judge whether larger defence forces improve the likelihood of international peace; they may simply produce a balancing increase in the forces of other powers. It is not even easy to prove that spending more on the police, or sending more people to jail, improve public order. But the important factor is that public opinion generally favours an 'adequate' defence, and strongly favours more spending on law and order and on safety. Some, probably modest, reduction in defence expenditure did indeed seem possible with the ending of the cold war; but the savings were likely to be no greater than the cost of the environmental protection measures which the public increasingly demands. Subsequent events in the Middle East illustrated the precariousness of forecasts about savings in defence expenditure. The prospect of a sizeable movement of resources from defence, public order and safety in favour of other forms of welfare does not therefore seem likely.

In the competition between social security and the other welfare services, the advocates of more expenditure on social security can use the strong argument that transfer payments are economically less significant than calls on real resources. But those who wish to spend more on education, health and housing can all argue that they are dealing with fundamental social evils which contribute to the poverty which social security relieves merely as a palliative. A better system of education and training would reduce the numbers of those who, even in good times, find it impossible to obtain satisfactory employment, and therefore call on unemployment benefit or income support. The National Health Service admittedly has some difficulty in *proving* that, apart from a select list of diseases such as tuberculosis, it actually improves the nation's health very much: but that improvement is its aim, and, if it is achieved, the calls on sickness and disability benefits will be less (though the same process would increase the call on retirement pensions and on services to care for the very elderly). Various social evils which give rise to demands for cash relief, notably those related to the break-up of families, are linked to unsatisfactory housing conditions, among other things; if we can find ways of building houses which show a proper regard for the physical and psychological needs of families, these social evils might be reduced.

These arguments in favour of the welfare services which use real resources are in line with gut reactions of the public. Spending which improves health services is very popular; parents readily support extra public spending on education and there begins to be a sense of public shame about homelessness and inadequate housing. In contrast, attitudes to social security spending are equivocal. There is an undercurrent of gossip which suggests that some of the unemployed do not seriously look for work, that there is widespread cheating about benefits (a view made plausible by the large number of applicants who withdraw when special investigations are mounted), that single parents should have taken more care with their marital affairs, and so on. The public image of social security is perhaps not far from that presented by the television series *Bread*. Much of the gossip is cruel and unjustified, but the fact remains that in the 1990s there would be few votes in the further expansion of the social security system – except perhaps for an increase in the real value of retirement pensions, a measure which would be a very inefficient way of deploying funds for the relief of poverty. These are matters further examined below.

Thus far, then, it appears that there is a serious constraint on all kinds of welfare state spending if these are seen as competitors for a share of a fixed total of government spending. But why should the total be fixed? It can surely go up as national product increases, and why should it not go up faster? In December 1945 Colin Clark published a paper in the *Economic Journal* whose argument he later summarised as follows:

> There is good economic evidence to show that the figure for the safe upper limit of taxation is 25 per cent of national production. This figure of 25 per cent is based on the experience of a number of countries. It is found that, when taxation exceeds this proportion of the national income for more than two or three years, a devaluation of the currency and a rise in prices will ensue.[1]

In order to get taxation within his limits, Clark proposed to 'privatise' a large part of the welfare state, including in his proposals compulsory insurance with private organisations to cover needs in old age, sickness or unemployment. For many years all this was regarded as self-evident nonsense. In 1954 Clark claimed that taxation as a proportion of national income was over 40 per cent (though it is not quite clear which figure he used); in 1988 taxation, including social security contributions, was 43.1 per cent of gross national product at factor cost. Surely any figure like 25 per cent could only be valid in relation to the social attitudes of a particular time; perhaps at another time the economy would work perfectly well with 40 per cent or even 50 per cent taxation.

But the supposed nonsense concealed a real point. Taxation by governments is an interference with the ability of individuals (and companies) to spend income as they wish. That interference is tolerated if the public goods so obtained are seen as having an importance which compares well with the private goods given up. But if the point of tolerance is passed, the taxpayer can act in various ways to frustrate the intentions of government: for instance, by working less because marginal income does not seem worth having; or by diverting effort to tax avoidance, which may distort or weaken the economy; or by demanding large pay increases, to restore personal purchasing power – even though that intention is likely to be frustrated when everyone does the same, and there is a general inflation of prices. It is no answer to claim that taxation must be broadly acceptable, since it is determined by the representatives of the people: for those representatives, once elected, will often see an advantage in the enlargement of the role of government and the provision of bounteous favours for the electorate. Ministers in charge of spending departments do not usually argue that they should have less money.

In the mid 1970s, governments in many countries became aware that the upward trend of state spending had passed the point of tolerance. Since 1979 the British government has held that lower taxation would improve the productivity of the economy and lessen the pressures of inflation – though in fact the efforts to reduce the overall tax burden have been singularly unsuccessful. But it is important not to see this policy, with its associated annual efforts to restrict government expenditure, as particularly 'Thatcherite'. It is in fact the conventional wisdom of most of the developed world, reinforced by the admonitions of international bodies such as OECD. In every democracy, opposition parties of course rail against the meanness of government spending, and make large promises about the extra spending which they would authorise on coming to power; but these are not promises which, in the present climate of opinion, they could successfully carry through.

Now it is conceivable that in the 1990s the point of tolerance may shift again, and public activity financed from taxation will be seen to be an honourable, efficient and proper way of tackling new problems. There is already evidence that some electors say they would be prepared to pay more taxes in exchange for better services; though they are not perhaps as numerous as those who favour someone else paying more taxes. On the other hand, there is widespread cynicism about the efficiency of public bodies and about the willingness of public sector unions to allow change. My guess is that the timescale over which large changes take place in the conventional wisdom is a long one, and that, at least until the end of the century, governments of whatever party will be trying to keep the lid on public expenditure and to hold, or if possible to reduce, the ratio of taxation to the national product.

Even so, it remains possible that the growth of the national product will provide some leeway for extra expenditure on welfare services – in addition, of course, to the improvements which the 'real-product' services can achieve by advances in their own efficiency, and which the cash benefit services can achieve by better targeting. But the sharpness of competition for public funds which rise by 2 or 3 per cent per year (in real terms) will be almost as great as for funds which are constant; the National Health Service alone will have a 'shopping list' capable of absorbing several years' increase in the finances available, and there would be a large potential demand for extra monies if cash benefits were to be restored to their earlier proportions of the average wage, after many years of being indexed for prices alone. If the 1990s prove to be a period of considerable prosperity, it may become more difficult to persuade people that social security has a proper function beyond acting as a safety net which keeps people from an absolute level of poverty. For instance, it may be asked why it is the duty of the state to provide an indexed pension at the present level for those who have already made adequate private provision. The question of whether the welfare state should 'wither away' with rising prosperity may again become a real one, affecting cash benefits before it touches the real-resource services.

6.2 CHOICES FOR THE USE OF THE NATIONAL PRODUCT

The limit to social tolerance of taxation, which constrains each item of government expenditure, can be looked at another way. The nation can spend on its current and capital needs the value of its product, together with what it can earn or borrow from abroad. Thus, in 1989 the UK had a gross national product of £440 billion, but domestic expenditure, supported by an excess of imports over exports, was about £459 billion. The 'real' expenditure on the welfare services – that is, paying wages and salaries, buying materials, building and repairing hospitals and so on – is a claim on the total of feasible expenditure, and that expenditure cannot depart far, or for long, from the national product; and that in turn, if we take out the effect of price rises, can be expected to rise only slowly, perhaps by 2 per cent a year, as a result of rising productivity. The choices about the use to which the total of feasible expenditure will be put are predominantly made in the market system, and derive from the actions of individual consumers: thus, in 1989, consumers spent £255 billion (excluding indirect taxes), plus another £56 billion in indirect taxes. To make continued and growing production possible, businesses and individuals spent £86 billion on capital investment and replacement, while central and local government spent another £14 billion.

Now it can be argued that people will generally be most satisfied if they are able to make their own free and personal decisions about what goods and services they obtain, having regard to each person's income and to the prices with which they are faced. But some goods and services have to be taken outside the market system and supplied communally. The cost of defence is an example – we could not have people buying their own bit of the army. In the area of the welfare services, however, the case is not so clear-cut. Health services could be bought in the market, with insurance against the cost of major disasters, and a redistribution of income through the tax and benefit system to ensure that the poor could still meet essential health needs. Indeed, apart from the fringe of private medicine, general areas such as dentistry and optical care are increasingly charged out to the consumer. Education could be bought in the market, given a redistribution of income through a system of education vouchers; indeed, with some schools opting out of local education authority control, with new self-standing institutions such as City Technology Colleges, and with increasing numbers of individual schools controlling their own budgets, the further step to a market system would be a short one. With the transfer of polytechnics, and higher education and teacher training colleges, to an independent status, and the proposed increases in finance through fees, a market system for higher education is already half-way here.

Over three-fifths of housing has been purchased in the open market, and a tenth is leased at market rents from private landlords. The size of the residue of 'social housing' needed from housing associations and local authorities depends on a choice between providing housing 'in kind', that is to say at a subsidised cost, or helping families with money so that they can pay market rents. The personal social services obviously meet some special needs unlikely to be tackled by the market, but even there a major activity, residential homes for the elderly, is paralleled by a large private market provision, made possible by the special arrangements for income support.

The 'transfer payments' for social security are not a direct call on the national product, but they also give rise to choices between public and private provision. Private pension and annuity payments to households are now a very considerable part of total pension provision. The increase has been fostered by tax exemptions, and it results in a much more adequate pension for people in the middle and upper range of incomes (though the benefit is slowly being felt lower down the income range). It would be conceivable for the state to dispose of its liability to finance pensions for those also in private schemes, by making a transfer to the private sector. It would even be conceivable (and has indeed been suggested) that unemployment and sickness benefits could be derived from private industry-based insurance.

These examples are given, not to express any political view on the desirability of moving things into the private sector, but to illustrate an essential feature of the welfare state activities. The word *state* indicates that we are talking about communal services, to be taken outside the market system and financed from taxation. But in most cases that involves a choice, and in consequence a constraint which depends on the strength of the argument for doing things communally rather than in the private sector. What is the nature of this argument?

We can largely discount the assertion that private sector services are inferior because they involve the payment of profits to private investors. Most services require some capital: public services commonly obtain this by borrowing money at fixed interest. This is not necessarily cheaper than paying dividends to ordinary shareholders – indeed at times it can be much more expensive; and, whereas the ordinary shareholder takes the risk of having no dividend in bad times, the public service has no such way of passing on risk – it must pay the interest bills in good times and bad. Of course, if a public service is handed over to a private unregulated monopoly, there is a risk that users of the service will be exploited; but such a possibility can be foreseen and prevented.

It is often claimed that there is an essential and important difference in attitudes. A public service will be staffed by people having a concern to do the very best for the users, whereas a private one will give its main attention to profit, and will tend to cut costs and lower the standard of service. But there are two things wrong with this argument. A public service does not have access to a blank cheque; it has to do the best it can with limited resources, and that involves choices which are essentially the same as those made by a private owner. Furthermore, concealed in the argument is a paternalist assumption that someone other than the consumer knows best what standard to provide; so that, even if consumers have fully adequate resources, their choice in the market place will not be 'really' what they ought to have. That is occasionally true; but in many cases the public service operates under the disadvantage that it does not receive signals about what the user wants. The link between the payer and the producer has become a roundabout one through the tax system; and the signals provided by democratic control in central or local government are confused by the static of political controversy.

There may be cases in which it is possible to claim that a public service is more efficient, for instance by reason of its size or its integration with other parts of government. Equally, there may be cases in which the opposite claim can be made: that the public service is too large and unwieldy to be managed properly, and that it is too liable to inefficiencies arising from the domination of public sector trade unions. Such matters have to be assessed on a case-by-case basis, and there is no ground for a general conclusion favouring one view or the other.

But there is a much more important argument which is common to most of the welfare services. The intention is to provide for a particular 'need', for all who suffer that need. That implies, either that the provision should be free or subsidised if the person in need is poor, or that there should be a money transfer which enables that person to provide for his or her need in the market. Nowadays we do not generally provide welfare food or welfare clothing in kind; we give assistance in cash so that people can choose for themselves what food and clothing to buy. They may still feel poor, but the chances of increasing their satisfaction are seen to be best if they are left to make their own choices. But we do provide welfare housing (subsidising its cost to produce what are called 'affordable rents'); we provide free schooling (available even to the rich) in preference to topping up family incomes so that full school fees could be paid; we provide a free health service (again, also available to the rich) in preference to giving people incomes from which they could insure against health risks. On the other hand, we do top up incomes of the elderly to a point at which they can (or could until recently) afford to live in private sector residential homes.

These differences of treatment appear to relate to the degree of difficulty in providing for need by giving help in cash (and thereby opening the door to the use of private sector services) as against provision in kind. Full insurance against health needs would be difficult to provide, and probably very expensive: cash help to meet the premiums would very probably be spent on other things, so that there would still be a residue of people experiencing serious illness and having no insurance cover (and perhaps injuring others by spreading disease). The assurance of universal help is also a considerable psychological advantage. The majority of people therefore support the idea of a health service which (with some exceptions, such as prescription charges for drugs) is free to all; it is less hassle than trying to run a market system in health with financial support for the health expenses of the needy, as in the United States. (However, since a free service generates excess demand, it suffers continuously from the quarrels and poor morale produced by working within cash limits which are always seen to be too low.) The case for free education is less clear; it would not be very difficult to give standard cash help to families with children, though the help might have to be earmarked in some way (e.g. by the use of education vouchers) to make sure that it was in fact spent on school fees. The housing case is also unclear; but a system of cash help for housing, right up to true market rents, is liable to encourage exploitation by local monopolists and the wasteful use of housing space. And, although it would be theoretically possible to provide for certain social security needs by genuine insurance, few would regard the trouble and the administrative cost as worthwhile.

The preceding paragraphs trespass on arguments more fully examined in other chapters. From the point of view of this chapter, the point is that the case for welfare *state* provision of services, as against providing for welfare needs as we provide for food needs, is of varying strength; and therefore the size of the welfare state is constrained, like the area controlled by a beleaguered garrison, by attacks at the margin. One may conjecture that, with increasing prosperity, these attacks will become more numerous and effective, because alternative private sector provision will grow in importance.

6.3   THE EFFECTS OF REDISTRIBUTION

Some parts of the welfare state (for example free secondary education) are more heavily used by the middle classes than by the poor; but in general the tendency of the services-in-kind, and the purpose of the cash benefit services, is either to transfer resources to those who are poor, or (as in the case of retirement pensions) to give benefits to all classes on uniform principles. The redistribution so achieved has to be considered as part of a wider transfer of resources: by income tax, which takes more from the rich and less or nothing from the poor; by taxes on commodities, which sometimes bear more on the rich and sometimes more on the poor; by the community charge for local authority services, which (being in any area at the same rate per adult) takes a smaller proportion of the incomes of the rich; and so on. It is important to look at the picture of redistribution as a whole, because it is not technically possible for an ideal philosophy of redistribution to be applied to every separate part – for instance by selling beer cheaper to the poor than to the rich.

This implies that one cannot say whether the redistribution through the welfare services is too little or too much; that would be to look at only one piece of the jigsaw. It might appear, therefore, that one could ignore the economic consequences of the redistribution, since they could always be offset by balancing action in some other area of government policy. But this is not quite true. It is characteristic of the welfare services that they are long-term commitments, and the size of the redistribution may alter considerably in response to underlying demographic or other factors which the government cannot change. Thus, there is a greatly increasing commitment to the support and nursing of the frail elderly; lower birth rates reduce the numbers of children to be educated; high divorce rates inevitably lead to a large bill for the support of single parent families. It is conceivable that balancing action in other areas of policy may be difficult to achieve, and that in consequence some area of the welfare services may be constrained.

However, examples of this would be hard to identify, except perhaps for the action taken in Britain to limit future commitments to State earnings related pensions, which had promised to become unduly expensive. And even if there was an increase in redistribution through the welfare state, what of it? The economic consequences of Robin Hood (taking from the rich and giving to the poor) are a fall in savings and a rise in consumption, and this is reasonable, since the purpose of the exercise is to enable the poor to consume or to be provided with more. Such a shift is potentially harmful if the economy is overstretched, and the government is battling to contain inflation, but potentially beneficial if the economy is underemployed, and needs the stimulus of a bigger demand for consumer goods. In the former case it may harm economic growth, by adding to the requirement on the government to (for instance) keep interest rates high, or run a big budget surplus. In the latter case it may help to stimulate growth.

But these are very theoretical points. In the real world the redistribution through the welfare services only varies slowly (different services moving in contrary directions), and its significance tends to be eroded by increases in general prosperity. Thus, social security payments as a proportion of household disposable income were 15.0 per cent in 1978 and 14.8 per cent in 1988 – a fall produced by the policy of uprating benefits by reference to prices rather than average earnings. Health services provided from taxation can be regarded as providing a free addition to the consumption of individuals; and they amounted to 7.8 per cent of consumers' expenditure in 1978, and 7.8 per cent in 1988. The stability of the welfare state redistribution implies that there has been plenty of time for an adjustment in other parts of redistribution policy, if the balance were held to be wrong.

6.4 DIRECT EFFECTS ON EFFORT AND SAVING

However, it is sometimes argued that welfare policies should be constrained because they reduce the effort which people expend in helping themselves. The familiar examples relate to people with low earning capacity who are better off on social security than if they tried to support themselves, the so-called 'unemployment trap'. A related issue is the 'poverty trap', that is to say a range of income in which, as people earn more, they lose as much or more in social security benefits as they gain in earnings; so they have no incentive to try to earn more. Now plainly one should not design a social security system with needless disincentives of this kind; but equally one should not suppose that all such disincentives can be removed. Under any system, the unskilled labourer with twelve children is rather likely to be better off if he relies on state assistance than if he works. Some of our problems in this area are due to uprating benefits until the gap between benefits and low wages almost disappears. The policy response of uprating benefits for inflation only while wages increase at a greater rate (with rising prosperity) may lessen the disincentives. But perhaps not enough thought has been given to the right ways of helping those whose *capacity* for work is very limited. A minimum wage law, applied to those people whose value to the employer is less than the minimum, will simply force them into unemployment. But the supplementation of low wages, systematised by the Berkshire Justices at their meeting at the Pelican Inn at Speenhamland in 1795, and more recently attempted in our social security system through the means-tested family credits paid to low-wage working families, has always proved difficult to work with justice and uniformity, and avoidance of temptation to employers to exploit the low-paid.

For present purposes, let us accept that it may be difficult or impossible to devise a welfare system which is free of all disincentives to effort. But this matters only if the numbers affected are significant, and if those affected understand the situation and react by actually reducing their effort. Despite stories in the tabloid press about 'shirkers', and a considerable fuss about the poverty trap, there is very little evidence that these conditions are fulfilled. The numbers potentially involved are not very large – many of them would certainly not understand the choice before them, and, even if they could be richer by not working, it is clear that many prefer to get a job if it comes up. That is reasonable: work offers social and psychological benefits, in addition to the wage – notably the sense that someone wants you – and those who get a foothold in the labour market, however poorly paid, increase their chances of doing better tomorrow. There may still be some effects on effort – for instance, it is thought that the availability of benefit causes people who fall into unemployment to 'shop around' longer before getting a new job – but there is no good evidence at all that the British economy is being rotted by an idleness produced by the welfare state.

But that does not quite dispose of the issue. In considering constraints on the size and development of welfare services, what matters is (as suggested earlier) not the objective facts so much as the gut feelings of ordinary electors. There is little problem about the services which are available to all and used by the great majority. Thus, although the development of the health service or of school education may be constrained by budgetary or resource difficulties, they are not held back by lack of public support. No government will lose popularity if it spends more on health. Nor is there much of a problem about special services for people whose hardship is due to natural causes beyond their control – for instance, the blind. But it is much more difficult to sustain public support for the general relief of poverty, especially in a country which is evidently becoming much richer – consumers' expenditure in Britain in 1989 was more than 70 per cent higher, in real terms, than twenty years earlier. The majority of families support themselves, by their own efforts or foresight, well above the poverty line. They find it easy to believe that those dependent on welfare relief are so either because they do not try hard enough, or because they have acted with foolishness and improvidence. They notice, though often without great sympathy, outward evidence of poverty, such as those who sleep rough in the London streets; but they notice much more easily the family which can manage to run a car or to have holidays in Spain, while apparently dependent on social security. Such attitudes are a serious constraint on the upgrading of services for the relief of poverty, and indeed provide considerable pressure for their reduction or stricter supervision. 'I manage very well – why can't you?' is a more common attitude than 'There but for the grace of God go I.'

This uncharitable approach is not readily altered by an appeal to the facts – not even to the statistics so deftly presented by the poverty lobby. It is not easy for people to be clear about what the facts are. It has always been true that there are 'undeserving poor'; a century and a half ago, the Benthamite principle of 'less eligibility' was invented to deal with them. It has always been true that *merely* to hand out more money may make the underlying problems worse rather than better; that is why the great social reformers have tended to look for the underlying causes of poverty rather than for schemes for its relief. And no mere academic argument will make much headway against the feeling that, if the country becomes 70 per cent richer in twenty years' time, there ought to be less poverty to be relieved.

An interesting test of public attitudes may perhaps be provided, in coming years, by attitudes to the basic retirement pension. This is a benefit available to rich as well as poor, structured in a manner which makes it appear (falsely) that the pensioner has paid for his pension by his contributions. It is suggested above that it might therefore be popular to increase it. But a different view may perhaps emerge. Large numbers of people now supplement the retirement pension by an occupational pension or other private pension. That is indeed what Beveridge intended, as the means by which the elderly would share in rising prosperity – a basic subsistence level only was to be provided by the state pension. On a strict economic calculation, the state pension ought to be seen as better value to the recipient than any private provision. But with a growth in the numbers of those with occupational pensions, the state pension will possibly acquire the image of a hand-out mainly intended for those who, through a supposed lack of providence, have not made provision for themselves; in which case there may be a lack of sympathy for increasing it. It is the pattern of life of the relatively affluent majority which will determine the attitude that will emerge.

Much of welfare provision cannot avoid rewarding the improvident and passing by the provident. There would be a great row if income support was provided for a man known to have £100,000 in the bank. Such support, and access to a variety of welfare services, depends on being able to show that your capital resources are small or zero. This implies, for instance, that saving for old age can be foolish, unless you are going to be able to save quite a lot; modest savings may leave you worse off than none at all. This conflicts with a strong public feeling that saving is virtuous – that it is an expression of a willingness to help yourself and to avoid being a burden on others. Despite occasional credit-based booms, net personal saving – gross savings less new personal borrowing – has recently been rather low. But over the longer period, the net wealth of the personal sector has increased. Thus it rose by more than 70 per cent in real terms over the ten years from 1977 to 1987, helped on, not only by house-buying, but by large investments in building societies, in ordinary shares, and in pension schemes. There is thus little doubt that saving and accumulating are very popular; and the continuance of this trend will tend to sharpen the division between those who have capital behind them (whose interest in the welfare benefits will mostly relate to the universal services) and those who have none. Twenty years ago the latter would have been a majority, but they are so no longer, and this again is a change unfavourable to the expansion of the poverty-relieving services.

Nothing in the preceding paragraphs is intended to imply that people are right to take such uncharitable and unsympathetic attitudes to parts of the welfare state, and, of course, there will be many who do not. But political facts have to be faced. At one time the majority of the electorate lived close to the poverty line and owned practically nothing. That is so no longer. The change is bound to have profound consequences for the political acceptability of some parts of public welfare provision.

NOTE

1.   C Clark (1954) *Welfare and Taxation*, Catholic Social Guild, Oxford, pp 4–5.

7 A National Minimum? A History of Ambiguity in the Determination of Benefit Scales in Britain
A.B. Atkinson

7.1 INTRODUCTION

The objective of securing a national minimum is a major consideration in the determination of benefit scales. In a social security system dominated by flat-rate benefits, as in Britain, this relation is particularly close. From the choices made about the level of benefits, it may be possible to make deductions about the objectives which lay behind them – a revealed preference argument – and it may be possible to learn from the expressed intentions of governments. The first half of this chapter provides a review of the considerations which appear to have influenced the determination of benefit scales at a national level in Britain. It covers pensions and National Insurance benefits since 1908 and the scales applied in a succession of national means-tested schemes dating from the Unemployment Assistance Board established in 1934.

From this review of the historical record, it is evident that the determination of benefit scales has been characterised more by ambiguity than by clarity. Empson (1953) distinguished *Seven Types of Ambiguity*; in the treatment here in the second half of the chapter I limit myself to three types. First, the decisions made by governments may reflect not just a concern to establish a national minimum but also a balancing of this objective against others, including the reduction of the cost of social security programmes and the avoidance of disincentives. There may be a compromise between different objectives. This compromise is often left implicit rather than made explicit, governments hoping that a blurring of the goal (a national minimum) with the instrument (a level of benefit) would leave the impression that the objective had in fact been fully achieved, without any need to compromise with other policy concerns. The first type of ambiguity therefore concerns the relation between the target and the constraints.

The second type of ambiguity concerns the degree of responsibility accepted by the government for the achievement of the goal of a national minimum. Are benefits to be a *contribution* to securing such a minimum, with the recipient dependent on self-help or support from relatives to make up the balance? Where state benefits are seen as the principal source of income, is the provision of a minimum *conditional* on the other resources of the claimant by means of a means-test, so that state help is the last resort? Or is there an *entitlement* to benefit irrespective of means, as under an analogy with private insurance? At any one time there has been a variety of conceptions, giving rise to ambiguity in the way in which benefits have been viewed, particularly the extent to which *insurance* benefits should provide an acceptable minimum without recourse to means-tested *assistance*, and the degree to which individuals in a family are liable to support one another.

Thirdly, there is ambiguity about the justification given for the provision of a national minimum. Much of the early discussion focuses on *well-being*, with the objective being to ensure that no one falls below some specified standard of living. Benefits have been related explicitly to studies of 'subsistence needs', such as those of Seebohm Rowntree and Sir Arthur Bowley. More recently, there has been reference to notions concerned with minimum *rights*, or the capacity of people to participate effectively in society. The abolition of poverty is a precondition of securing positive freedom. By revealed preference, and from their expressed intentions, governments appear to have had in mind elements of both well-being and rights when making decisions about benefit levels.

The significance of these ambiguities becomes particularly clear when we consider the uprating of benefits over time, and this is taken as a case study to illustrate the earlier analysis. Uprating poses questions of major long-term significance for the welfare state, but ones which are often lost from sight in discussion of more short-term policy. At this point, I refer not just to historical evidence from this century but also to the policy issues that are likely to arise over the first part of the twenty-first century.

Clarification of the ambiguities surrounding the achievement of a national minimum is a key contribution of social policy analysis, but it must be recognised that such ambiguities have a role to play in political discourse. This is the subject of the concluding section.

7.2   A NATIONAL MINIMUM? BENEFITS IN BRITAIN SINCE 1908

The aim of this section is not to provide an exhaustive review of the history of social security in Britain over the twentieth century but to highlight some of the key episodes when the form and level of benefits have been determined. I concentrate on *national* benefit scales, starting in 1908 when state old age pensions were introduced by the Asquith government. It should also be noted that I do not consider housing benefits and the related question of the treatment of housing costs under social assistance.

OLD AGE PENSIONS 1908
The first state old age pension was paid at the rate of 5 shillings (5s)[1] per

person per week. The pension was non-contributory and available to all aged seventy or over, subject to an income test which reduced the amount payable to those with incomes between 8s and 12s a week.[2] No pension was paid when income exceeded 12s. For a couple, the pension was double, as were the parameters of the income test (applied to their joint income). Whereas the government had originally proposed that a couple should receive only 1.5 times the single pension, this was defeated by back-bench opposition.[3] The payment of the old age pension had moralistic overtones, in that a claimant had to satisfy the authorities that he was not guilty of failing 'to work according to his ability, opportunity, and need, for the maintenance of himself and those legally dependent on him',[4] but the income test was applied quite separately from the Poor Law (pension officers were in the service of Customs and Excise) and, unlike the Poor Law, there was no obligation on relatives to contribute.

The introduction of state old age pensions had been the subject of debate for several decades. In this debate, one of the principal concerns had been the possible cost of the new pensions. The pensions proved in fact to be very popular, and by 1909 half a million old persons were in receipt. The resulting rise in public expenditure was one of the factors which led to the 1908 'People's Budget', which Lloyd George described as:

a War Budget. It is for raising money to wage implacable warfare against poverty and squalidness. I cannot help hoping and believing that before this generation has passed away we shall have advanced a step towards that good time when poverty and wretchedness . . . will be as remote to the people of this country as the wolves which once infested its forests.[5]

There can be little doubt that the cost was a crucial factor in determining the level of the pension. As a result, it fell short of being adequate on its own to guarantee a national minimum. Of the rate of 5s per person, Booth had earlier written:

It does not pretend to be 'an adequate provision' but is the contribution of the State towards it, being about the sum (and less rather than more) which the bare maintenance of a destitute person actually costs.[6]

That this was less rather than more is borne out by the estimates of Rowntree (1901) in his study of poverty in York of the minimum expenditure for the 'bare necessaries', which came to 7s per person (including an allowance for rent). It does not appear that the architects of the scheme saw it as providing more than a contribution to a minimum level of income. Lloyd George, for example, 'claimed that the pension was not intended to give full subsistence, merely an addition'.[7] According to Clarke,

Pensions, at 5s a week, were meant to be supplementary to the resources of the righteous man. They were to be the reward of virtuous living rather than any token of communal responsibility for the well-being of the enfeebled citizens.[8]

The figure of 5s per week may also be compared with the average earnings of manual workers in the 1906 earnings inquiry, which for adult males ranged from 26s 4d to 34s 4d.[9] On this basis, the single pension was around one-sixth of average earnings of adult male manual workers.

This first major departure from the Poor Law was followed in 1911 by the introduction of contributory National Insurance. Part I of the Act provided sick pay for insured workers, at a rate of 10s a week for male workers and 7s 6d for female workers, together with medical benefits; Part II provided for unemployment benefit in selected industries at a rate of 7s per week. Relative to the average earnings figures just quoted, the sickness benefit was around one-third, and the unemployment benefit was around one-quarter. It may be noted that these rates of benefit are different from that paid to pensioners, and that (for sickness) the rates are different for men and women. Both of these points are taken up below.

UP-RATING OF BENEFITS AFTER THE FIRST WORLD WAR

After the First World War, the level of state benefits was discussed against a background of a price level which had approximately doubled and of expectations that, as a result of the war, living standards would have to be reduced. The Secretary to the Treasury, Sir John Bradbury, described the position in 1919 with regard to the level of old age pensions as follows:

I doubt whether the active working classes short of a social revolution will be content with a lower standard of comfort. You must therefore make economy elsewhere, and I want to make the economy principally at the expense of the wealthier classes. I want to prevent people riding in motor cars; I want to prevent people wearing expensive furs; I want to prevent people buying unnecessary clothing, and very soon the Income Tax will have that effect. [But] I think it quite impossible to restore people like Old Age Pensioners who are not part of the industrial machine to as favourable a position as they occupied before the war.[10]

This is taken from a statement to the Adkins Committee, which also heard evidence about the living standards of pensioners. As a result of its recommendations, the state pension was set at 10s a week in December 1919. The purchasing power of the pension increased in subsequent years as prices fell, but nonetheless the subsistence calculations by Bowley and Hogg (1925) suggested that a rate of 10s allowed very little margin to cover housing costs once allowance had been made for food, clothing and fuel. The level of the pension was again lower than the unemployment benefit set in 1920, which was 15s a week for men and 12s a week for women.

UNEMPLOYMENT ASSISTANCE BOARD 1934

The provision of income support for the unemployed was one of the major political and economic problems of the inter-war years. In 1934 the Government carried out a large-scale reconstruction of unemployment insurance and unemployment assistance. In the latter case, the newly created Unemployment Assistance Board (UAB) took over the functions of Public Assistance, which had itself replaced the Poor Law in 1929. For the first time in Britain there was, for one category of claimants, a national system of means-tested relief operated on a uniform basis. This immediately raised the acute problem of setting the national scale, in view of the previous variation across local Public Assistance Committees in the amounts of benefit which they paid.

As Veit-Wilson has argued, one of 'the principal considerations in the minds of members and officials' of the UAB when determining the new scale was:

> to implement the traditional Poor Law principle of 'less eligibility', that is, to pay benefits below the level of wages which the manual workers would in general earn if they were in full time work.[11]

Similarly, Lynes concluded that:

> It will be apparent from this account of the Board's deliberations that throughout the period from July to October 1934 the relationship between the scale rates and the wages of unskilled workers was a dominant consideration.[12]

The rates originally set for single persons were 15s for men and 14s for women (raised to 15s in 1936). Compared with average earnings of 69s for adult male manual workers in October 1938,[13] from which we have to deduct 1s 10d contributions to old age pensions, health and unemployment insurance,[14] the benefit of 15s represented some 22 per cent of net earnings. For a couple, the rate was 24s a week, and there were additions for children, ranging from 3s to 6s depending on their age.

Lynes goes on to say that calculations of subsistence needs played a relatively minor role in the determination of the benefit scales:

> From the start, the Board tended to be sceptical of the scientific approach to the problem of establishing a minimum income scale for the unemployed and their families.[15]

The relationship between the benefit scales and subsistence calculations may be illustrated by reference to Rowntree's *The Human Needs of Labour*, published in 1937. For a family consisting of a couple plus three children (of average age), with rent of 9s 6d he estimated the minimum needed to be 53s a week (or 49s 11d if travel-to-work expenses and other costs of working were deducted). The UAB scale would have given this family 37s 6d a week if the children were aged 11 to 13. The benefit level was significantly below the level which Rowntree described as that 'below which no section of the community should be compelled to live'.[16] Later he contrasted the human needs scale with his earlier 'primary poverty line', this being 'a standard of bare *subsistence* rather than *living*'.[17] This would have been 38s 6d, so that the benefit scale was nearer to this primary poverty line.

The impact of the UAB scales was also affected by the rigorous way in which the Board attempted to enforce the household means test, taking account of all income coming into the household and in effect transferring responsibility for support of a claimant to parents, children and other relatives. This is discussed further below.

BEVERIDGE REPORT 1942

The work of Rowntree, Bowley and others received greater prominence in the Beveridge Report, and both served on the Sub-Committee which advised on benefit rates. The Report stated in an apparently uncompromising fashion that 'social insurance should aim at guaranteeing the minimum income needed for subsistence'.[18] It went on at once to recognise that 'what is required for reasonable human subsistence is to some extent a matter of judgement', and it is in the translation of the concept into actual levels of benefit that the objective ceased to be unambiguous. Beveridge himself, in a memorandum for the Committee, drew attention to the difference between Rowntree's human needs scale and his lower primary poverty scale.

The motives underlying the choice of benefit scales in the Beveridge Report are the subject of controversy. Beveridge's biographer has argued that he came down on the side of the more generous Rowntree human needs scale, quoting from the Memorandum a statement by Beveridge that the more stringent scale would 'be rejected decisively by public opinion today'.[19] Some grounds for believing that this was the case is provided by the fact that the recommended scale for a couple with three children including rent is identical to Rowntree's 53s. Veit-Wilson (1989b) on the other hand has drawn attention to the much larger proportion of this amount which is assumed to be allocated to food (Beveridge adopted the higher League of Nations dietary) and the lower amounts for other items. As a result the scales for other family types differ quite significantly. In broad terms, Beveridge allocated less to single adults and couples without children and more to families with more than three children. Veit-Wilson argues that, as a result of minimising the amount allocated to 'social expenditures', Beveridge was returning to the bare subsistence notion, rather than allowing for the costs of social participation.

Certainly there is evidence that concerns other than that of securing a national minimum played an important role in the determination of the scales recommended by Beveridge. A memorandum by the Committee's Secretary (D.N. Chester) discussed the relation between the benefit standard and the level of wages:

> If this standard is attacked for being too low, it would raise the much wider question of minimum wages and the raising of the standard of living of the working classes.[20]

Consideration of the cost of benefit provision was indicated in Beveridge's use of evidence from the 1930s poverty surveys. He noted that the total surplus income of working-class families above the poverty line was eight times as great as the total deficit of those below, concluding that poverty could be abolished 'by a re-distribution of income within the working classes'.[21]

NATIONAL INSURANCE AND NATIONAL ASSISTANCE 1946 AND 1948

The legislation of 1946 established the present system of flat-rate National Insurance benefits covering major contingencies and retirement, and that of 1948 set up National Assistance as a unified means-tested safety net. As has been described by Thane:

> The Labour legislation together with the wartime introduction of family allowances came closer to the introduction of a national minimum than any previous government action.[22]

There were however several reasons why this celebrated legislation fell short of providing an unambiguous national minimum.

The first shortcoming lay in the departure from the key Beveridge principle that the national minimum should be guaranteed by social insurance, with social assistance playing a residual and diminishing role. As was explained by Ernest Bevin (then Foreign Secretary), the government

> rejected Sir William Beveridge's argument that benefit rates under the insurance scheme should be related to the cost of maintenance . . . applicants who proved need would be entitled to obtain higher rates of assistance from the Assistance Board.[23]

The National Assistance scale for a single person was set at 24s a week, in addition to which housing costs were met, whereas the National Insurance retirement pension was 26s a week. This meant that a single person with housing costs of more than 2s would have been below the National Assistance level if he or she had no other income. The minimum was a conditional one.

The second controversial issue is the extent to which the benefit levels matched those proposed by Beveridge when allowance was made for the inflation that had taken place during the war. In the case of the National Assistance scale, the official description of its determination indicates that it was considered to be more generous:

> they constructed a new dietary, the cost of which was much higher than that used by Beveridge (some staple items in pre-war diets were then rationed or unobtainable), and allowed a bigger margin for non-essential expenditure.[24]

On the other hand, Veit-Wilson (1989a) has argued that the unpublished memoranda of the Board in 1948 reveal it to be concerned about the inadequacy of the provision and that it 'presupposed only short-term dependence on assistance'.[25] Outside Whitehall, there was contemporary concern about the level of benefits:

> The rates of that benefit payable under the National Insurance Act are not alone sufficient to maintain a family above the poverty line even if other welfare measures are taken into account.[26]

As far as the comparison with Beveridge is concerned, the official Cost of Living Index shows the rise in prices for all items between 1938 and 1948 (linking with the Interim Index) to be 44 per cent. According to this, the National Insurance pension of 26s for a single person introduced in 1948 corresponded more or less in real terms to Beveridge's recommendation of 17s 6d in 1938 prices. However, the London and Cambridge Economic Service estimates[27] show the increase in prices as 75 per cent. This is clearly a major difference, and would mean that the National Insurance scale was some 15 per cent lower in purchasing power.

There is of course a difference between *prices* and *earnings* as a basis for comparison. In the latter case, allowance has to be made for the increased burden of contributions and income tax. In terms of the net earnings of an adult male worker at the average, the Beveridge recommendation for the single pension had amounted to 26 per cent in 1938; the actual benefit level of 26s in 1948 was 23 per cent of the April 1948 figure.[28] This suggests that in terms of net earnings the scale was more comparable to the pre-war proportion.

Finally we should note that the unification of National Insurance involved not only a unified administration but also the payment of benefits which were largely uniform in amount. The earlier separate systems had paid a level of benefit to pensioners which was typically lower than that paid to those below pension age. This could have been rationalised in terms of the lower food and other requirements of the elderly, as assessed in the studies of Rowntree (1941) and others. There are also issues concerned with the length of time for which a person is dependent on benefit. A government spokesman explained in 1948 that

> The existing differences in the scales for unemployment and the aged are considered to be no longer justified in conditions of full employment, when the great majority of persons who may be expected to require assistance will be either right outside the employment field or . . . only on the fringe of it, and will be likely . . . to need it for a long period.[29]

It should be noted that this argument is inconsistent with the presupposition, referred to earlier, that people would only be dependent on assistance for a short period. It reveals ambiguity as to whether the scales are intended to cover short-run or long-run needs.

THE UPRATING OF INSURANCE AND ASSISTANCE BENEFITS

In the uprating of benefit levels over the post-war period, there was a distinct shift of emphasis at the end of the 1950s, as was indicated in the announcement in the White Paper *Improvements in National Assistance* that the government had been:

> considering the position of those on National Assistance and have reached the conclusion that the time has come when it is right to move to a higher standard, so giving them a share in increasing national prosperity.[30]

Whereas the earlier upratings had been broadly in line with price changes, this introduced a commitment to raise benefits in line with rising standards in the community as a whole. As an objective, it lacked precision, as was later noted by an Opposition spokesman (D. Houghton):

> There is no index for a share in increasing national prosperity. It could be a full share or a proportionate share. It could be something less.[31]

What was agreed was that it represented a real improvement in the scales, a change of policy which has been interpreted as signifying a shift in the way that the role of benefits has been viewed:

> While the conventional idiom was that of the pseudo-absolute poverty line,

and class cultural stratification was taken for granted . . . from the 1950s one detects a decline in the use of this language. Citizenship rather than class increasingly seemed to become the status criterion of adequacy.[32]

Or, to quote a contemporary account:

While the Webbs were concerned to use social security to make the working classes less poor by singling them out for State grants, now it is planned to treat the working classes like the middle classes treat themselves.[33]

In considering the uprating of benefits in more recent years, account has to be taken of the distinction introduced in 1973 between 'long-term' and 'short-term' benefits. The ambiguity concerning the function of the benefits has been noted earlier, but it was not resolved by this distinction, since the unemployed were classified as 'short-term' recipients irrespective of the duration of their unemployment. The basis for the distinction appeared to lie in the principles thought appropriate for uprating over time. The long-term benefits between 1975 and 1980 enjoyed statutory indexation to whichever was the faster rising of earnings and prices, and since 1980 have been guaranteed indexation to prices. In practice, the same principle has often been applied to the two types of benefit; none the less a gap has opened up between the Retirement Pension and short-term benefits such as that for unemployment. Whereas these benefits were aligned in 1948, an unemployed person now receives only 80 per cent of the National Insurance rate for a single pensioner. Differentiation in the treatment of pensioners relative to that of those of working age has been reintroduced – in the reverse direction from that which existed before the Second World War.

The principles to govern benefit uprating were discussed in an unusually explicit manner in the 1978 *Annual Report* of the Supplementary Benefits Commission:

It is right that society should determine through Parliament and the elected Government what level of support should be afforded to pensioners, the unemployed, the sick, and others. That level should be decided by sensitive use of the subjective test that beneficiaries must have an income which enables them to participate in the life of the community. *That means a standard which rises in line with any rise in the general standard of life in the community.* We do not believe it is sufficient to increase benefits in line with the movement of prices.[34]

This principle was endorsed by the incoming Conservative government,[35] but in recent years the policy has been different. The policy has been that of indexation of benefits to prices. For example, in his statement about the

1990 uprating, the Secretary of State made mention of the increase in retail prices,[36] but there was no reference to shares in rising national prosperity.

Examination of the actual movements in benefit levels relative to earnings over the past two decades shows that for long-term benefits there was a discrete upward shift in 1975.[37] This was maintained for the best part of ten years, but since 1985 the pension has fallen relatively as net earnings have increased in real terms while benefits have been indexed to prices. For short-term benefits, upratings in the 1970s broadly maintained their relation with net earnings, but they too have fallen since the mid-1980s.

7.3 AMBIGUITIES IN THE DETERMINATION OF BENEFIT SCALES

What can be learned from government decisions on benefit levels about the motives which lie behind social policy? In effect, this represents a 'revealed preference' approach to government objectives, seeking to draw conclusions about the nature of social objectives from the policy choices made. The main point which I wish to stress here is the need to come to terms with the ambiguities which characterise government policy in this area.

AMBIGUITY I: THE SCALES AS A COMPROMISE BETWEEN DIFFERENT OBJECTIVES?

The first source of ambiguity concerns the extent to which the policies chosen reflect a compromise between different objectives. The Government, however well intentioned, pursues the objective of a national minimum *subject to constraints*. The resultant benefit policy may be attributable as much to constraints as to goals and there may be ambiguity as to which is the determining factor.

On this view, it would be quite consistent for the government to have as a target a national minimum level of income, Y^*, but to face a trade-off between the level of benefit B, and the contribution rate required to finance the transfer scheme. Increases in the contribution rate reduce the net income of those in work, as indicated by the downward-sloping line in Figure 7.1 (for a person with average earnings). Suppose that the government has a view of the maximum acceptable contribution, as in Figure 7.1. This determines the maximum level of benefit, B^*. If, as shown in the diagram, this is less than the target Y^*, then there is indeed a compromise. The government is in effect setting the level of benefit with an eye to the resources available – which is one interpretation of how the old age pension was determined in 1908. A variation on this is illustrated by the belief of Sir John Bradbury that in 1919 net earnings could not be reduced, so that any increase in the pension would have to be financed by other sources of revenue, effectively limiting the extent to which the value of the pension could be restored after the war.

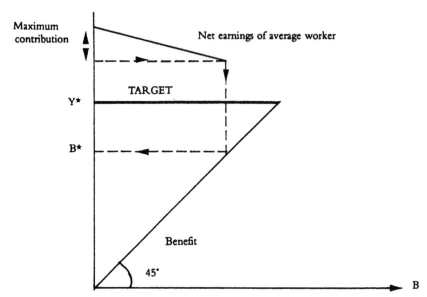

Figure 7.1: Choice of benefit constrained by the maximum acceptable contribution rate

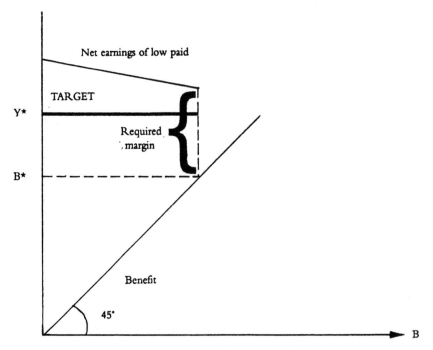

Figure 7.2: Choice of benefit constrained by the less eligibility criterion (required margin between benefit and income in work)

The constraint in Figure 7.1 arises from the total burden of financing. A second important constraint is that arising from considerations of less eligibility. Here the comparison is made not with average earnings but with the position of the low paid. As shown in Figure 7.2, there is a required margin between benefit levels and the take-home pay of the low paid, and this may introduce a second upper bound on the permissible benefit level. We have seen the role played by such factors in the determination of the 1934 UAB scales.

How can we interpret the observed policy choices? In some cases it is assumed that the benefit level in fact corresponds to the target national minimum, neither the less eligibility nor the financing constraints being binding. This appears to be the interpretation where the benefit level is used as a poverty line, as in studies of low incomes based on the supplementary benefit level. (The fact that some people fall below is an indication that the benefit system is not being fully effective.) It appears to be the case where benefit scales are justified by reference to estimates of subsistence needs, as with Beveridge's use of the work of Rowntree, Bowley and others. On this interpretation, the Beveridge Report is seen as arguing that the attainment of a national minimum was 'affordable'; the benefit level $Y^\star$ could feasibly be financed (as in Beveridge's discussion of the surplus of working–class incomes relative to the poverty deficit quoted earlier).

However, in general, the level of benefit chosen is the smaller of $Y^\star$ and $B^\star$, and we are not able to deduce simply from the observed policy which is the determining variable. The maximum acceptable contribution may cause B to be set below $Y^\star$, as shown in Figure 7.1. Considerations of less eligibility may be a binding constraint, as in Figure 7.2. Both of these have been referred to in a recent official statement:

> Even if it were possible to arrive at some general consensus on a minimum acceptable income, this would not necessarily provide a determination of the level of benefits to be paid . . . rates are not set in isolation: the Government gives due regard to the relationship between benefit levels and the rewards available to those in work, and to the total resources available for public spending.[38]

In such a situation, to use the benefit scale as a poverty line would be quite misleading. A new government, say, which took the view that the acceptable level of contribution was higher than in the past would allow the benefit scale to rise relative to earnings. This would tend to reduce the number with incomes below the desired national minimum, but measured taking the benefit scale as a poverty line, poverty might increase – a fact that successive governments have emphasised.

AMBIGUITY II: WHAT DEGREE OF RESPONSIBILITY?

Recognition that the level of benefits falls short of an adequate minimum is implied where the government describes the role of state support as only a 'contribution' to securing that minimum. The old age pensions of 1908 were seen in that light by the government of the day. The benefit level was governed by the cost of the scheme and calculations of subsistence needs did not enter the picture.

The move to the idea of benefits providing a subsistence minimum represented a major shift in responsibility, but the state has always appeared ambivalent as to the degree to which this minimum has been accepted. Two aspects in particular stand out. The first is the extent to which others have a prior responsibility for the support of individual claimants. There is a marked contrast between social insurance, providing a benefit which is conditional on the efforts of the individual (for example to find work) but which does not demand any contribution from other family members, and the successive versions of means-tested assistance. Under the Poor Law, there had since 1601 been a liability to contribute to support poor relatives unable to work (not the able-bodied unemployed) imposed on parents, grandparents and children. This was taken over by Public Assistance in 1930 and then by Unemployment Assistance. The household means test was one of the most unpopular features of social security in the 1930s, and its scope was considerably narrowed in the 1941 Determination of Needs Act. There remains however the liability to support within the inner family of husband, wife and dependent children.

The lack of certainty with regard to support from relatives arises on account of the fact that this support may not in reality be provided. The situation in the 1930s was described by Bowley as follows:

> The process of comparing the aggregate of incomes of members of the family with the family needs assumes that the whole income is pooled if necessary. Where family ties are strong, or where additional earnings come from the wife or young workers, the assumption is justified; but when the income is that of elder brothers or sisters, they may not be willing to hand over all surplus above their special needs to the support of an employed parent or other children.[39]

In more recent times, it has come to be questioned how far incomes are shared between husbands and wives. Pahl (1983) reports that a sizeable proportion of women who have left their husbands report being 'better off' living alone on benefit than living with their husbands, the figures ranging from 18 per cent to one-third. This has to be interpreted with caution, not least because the personal circumstances may colour recollection, but there is clearly no guarantee that obligations of support are met. We have a situation where the state is appearing to offer a safety-net level of income but is leaving the claimant exposed to the risk that others will not contribute their share. There is of course a great deal of difference between a social security system where the state assumes that others contribute, deducting the assumed contribution or denying eligibility, and one where the benefit is paid in full and the state seeks reimbursement from those deemed liable.

The degree of responsibility is also relevant to the time period for which benefit is paid, and this is the second aspect considered here. If the responsibility of the state is to tide people over short periods of low income, then the levels of benefit can be set such that claimants draw down their reserves. These reserves may be monetary assets, and because most means tests reduce benefit by an amount which exceeds the interest on savings, capital must be used up. (The means test applied to the 1908 old age pension took 10 per cent of capital above a certain level, when interest rates were about 2.5 per cent.) Or the reserves may be stocks of goods, whether stores of food or clothing being worn out and not replaced. Or the reserves may be less tangible, as with postponing social obligations (such as presents), or presuming on the help of neighbours/relatives. There is ambiguity as to whether the state is accepting responsibility for long-term support or whether the safety net is meant as a stop-gap measure. This ambiguity is to be observed in the discussion of the adequacy of benefit levels, as we have seen, and in the changing policy with regard to one-off provisions to allow the replacement of durables.

AMBIGUITY III: STANDARD OF LIVING OR MINIMUM RIGHTS?

The third ambiguity concerns the justification for a national minimum. Much of the early discussion was in terms of a subsistence minimum, or the standard of living. More recently, there has been the shift to a vocabulary of 'citizenship' or 'participation', where considerations of minimum rights enter the picture.

This may appear a rather theoretical distinction, but it has important implications for the benefit scales and their structure. Take for example the benefits for men and women. A minimum rights approach would suggest that they should be identical for men and women, as a matter of principle, and that a couple should receive the same as two individuals. This was indeed the case with the old age pension of 1908, which was paid at the same rate to both men and women, and a couple received twice the amount for a single person. Notions of a subsistence minimum, on the other hand, pointed to lower benefits for women than for men and to a couple receiving less than twice the scale for a single person. Rowntree's scale of 1936 for pensioners allowed 15s 3d to a single man but only 12s 6d for a woman. For a couple, the Rowntree scale was 22s 4d. Differential treatment of men and women may also be justified on the grounds of the difference in pay rates, whether on account of the earnings-replacement motive or because of less eligibility constraints. The 'low paid' line in Figure 7.2 may be lower for a woman than for a man. The rates of unemployment insurance benefit were indeed different up to 1948; and Beveridge, far from starting from any presumption that the rates of men and women should be the same, only came down against making a distinction on the grounds that the calculated subsistence amounts were relatively close.[40] Beveridge set the rate for a couple two-thirds higher than that for a single person, a relativity which has remained very little changed since that time.

The difference between a standard of living approach and one based on minimum rights also becomes evident when we consider the uprating of benefits.

7.4   A CASE STUDY: THE ADJUSTMENT OF BENEFIT SCALES OVER TIME

The systematic comparison of benefit scales at different dates requires more space than I have here, but from Section 7.2 it appears that there has been a tendency over the century for benefits to rise at least as fast as average net earnings. Those on benefits have shared in rising national prosperity. In the case of the unemployed, National Insurance benefit has declined relative to net average earnings since the mid-1980s, but it is still the case that in April 1989 it represented 22 per cent of net earnings for a person at the average for *manual workers* (not *all* workers), or virtually the same as in 1948 – and also in 1911 when unemployment insurance was introduced. In the case of the retirement pension, there has been a distinct improvement over the century. Since the basic pension before the First World War was below the benefits paid for sickness or unemployment, and is now above, it is apparent that it has risen more than proportionately. The single pension began at around one-sixth of average net earnings for male manual workers and is now about one-quarter. However, present policy is to link benefits to prices and this is likely to mean that people entirely dependent on state benefit will find their incomes falling progressively further and further behind those of the working population. If real net earnings rise at the rate of 2 per cent per annum but pensions remain unchanged in real terms, then the retirement pension will be back to one-sixth in the second decade of the next century.

How can these different policies with regard to the uprating of benefits be related to the earlier analysis? Suppose first that the actual level of benefits represents a compromise between the desired national minimum and the constraints of either financing or less eligibility. It then seems quite possible that these constraints are eased as incomes rise, allowing benefits to rise. If for example the benefit is limited to some percentage of the take-home pay of the low paid, then a rise in pay would allow the benefit to rise proportionately. Or, if National Insurance contribution revenue rises on account of rising total incomes, then the pensions can be raised proportionately. (In the case of the 1980s, the revenue from National Insurance contributions has indeed risen in real terms, but it has not in general been used to pay higher basic pensions. The increased revenue has in large part been used to reduce the Treasury Supplement and hence to finance tax cuts elsewhere.)

The dynamics of this process may be such that, as the economy becomes richer, the constraints cease to bite, and the target level of benefits becomes attainable. On this optimistic view, we may indeed reach a situation where the poor become as rare as Lloyd George's wolves. This means that the principles governing benefit uprating may change. During the constrained period, benefits rise in line with the easing of the constraints, but then are governed by the target national minimum. If the latter is taken to be a fixed standard of living, we may then see earnings indexation during the constrained phase followed by price indexation once the target is attained.

Can this provide a justification for the observed change in policy in Britain with regard to uprating? This is not at all evident. To begin with, the relation between the desired national minimum and rising incomes depends on whether one adopts a standard of living approach or one based on minimum rights. If benefits are justified on a minimum rights basis, then this may lead to the prescription that benefits increase with rising incomes. In the United States, for example, Fuchs (1965) proposed that the poverty line should be set at half the family median income. The Supplementary Benefits Commission in 1979 argued that the standard should rise *in line* with the general level of incomes; this would be Mr. Houghton's 'proportionate share' in rising national prosperity referred to earlier.

It may be that current policy represents a return to a standard of living approach. However, it is not evident that this implies that the target level of income should be fixed in real terms, taking a fixed bundle of goods adjusted only for the change in prices of these goods. First of all, in applying the standard of living approach there is the question of the *availability* of these goods. Reference was made earlier to rationing after the war and the fact that certain goods could not be purchased. In the longer term, goods which were once widely available may cease to be so as new goods are introduced. The range of goods may depend on the general level of incomes. As the community becomes better off, the cheaper goods may be taken off the market; the poor may not be able to buy cheap cuts of meat or to buy small quantities of perishable goods. Rowntree noted in 1937 that

> Unfortunately, fresh skimmed milk, which was largely consumed by the lower paid workers in 1918, cannot easily be bought today.[41]

The interdependence between the living standards of different income groups becomes even more important when we consider what consumption involves and the implications of recent theories of household production.

We have been talking in terms of 'goods', whereas the literature on house-hold production has rightly pointed to the need to see goods as inputs into household activities, with the level of such activities being our concern, not the purchase of goods as such. On this basis, the objective has to be rewritten as a target level of *activities*, for which the required goods inputs may vary over time. The significance of this approach is that even when we take a fixed set of activities, the required goods may be changing because of changes in the input matrix, and this in turn may be influenced by the general standards of living. This point has been expressed by Sen as follows:

> in West Europe or North America a child might not be able to follow his school programme unless the child happens to have access to a television. If this is in fact the case, then the child without a television in Britain or Ireland would be clearly worse off – have a lower standard of living – in this respect than a child, say, in Tanzania without a television. It is not so much that the British or the Irish child has a brand new need, but that to meet the same need as the Tanzanian child – the need to be educated – the British or the Irish child must have more commodities.[42]

Applied to changes in benefit scales over time, the same argument means that – even on a standard of living basis – there may be a case for a rising real standard. In 1970 it would not have been a handicap to a child that his or her family could not afford a home computer; in 1990 the child will find it more difficult to follow lessons than his or her classmates with their computers.

To sum up, the current policy of price indexation of benefits may be seen as a return to a standard of living basis for the national minimum, rather than some notion of minimum rights, but even in these terms it is not evident that increases in the real value of benefits are ruled out. To take account of the changing range of goods available, and of the changing re-quirements of household activities, a rise in the real value of benefits may be justified. And to the extent that present benefits represent a compromise between the target national minimum and economic constraints, increased real earnings may be expected to ease these constraints and to permit those on benefit to share in rising national prosperity.

7.5 CONCLUDING COMMENTS: THE PLACE OF AMBIGUITY

The central theme of this paper has been the ambiguity surrounding the determination of benefit scales in twentieth century Britain and their rela-tion to the notion of a national minimum. It might be thought that this ambiguity could readily be dispelled. However, we have to recognise that *within* individuals there is often ambivalence about the objectives to be pursued and that *between* individuals there are considerable disagreements about the ends and means of policy. There is both plurality and diversity of individual judgements. In this situation, it is scarcely surprising that ambiguity is characteristic of political discourse.

The plurality of objectives which any one individual would like to see pursued is not typically taken into account in welfare economics, but it seems very much present in reality. People feel that the state should take responsibility for securing a national minimum and at the same time see how considerations of self-help point to the state only making a contribution. Their conception of the national minimum is based on elements both of well-being and of rights. There may be conflicts between the elimination of poverty and the reduction of inequality; and the relation between these two objectives is far from transparent.[43] The objectives of an individual may not be reducible to a simple welfare function; nor is there necessarily an internal 'umpire', as supposed by John Stuart Mill (1843), adjudicating between conflicting concerns, such as justice and freedom.

The differences between people are evident. There are those who reject any concern with poverty – either because they feel that any state intervention is unjustified or because they feel that it distracts attention from more fundamental distributional goals. But even among those who are concerned about poverty, there may be disagreement about the weight to be placed on poverty as against inequality. There may for example be different views about the desirability of an anti-poverty programme if the cost falls on those with incomes above the line but below the average, thus accentuating the gap between this group and the wealthy. This is likely to be an issue if there is a 'redistribution of income within the working classes', as referred to by Beveridge.

Those making a case for social policies to secure a national minimum have naturally sought to appeal to the widest possible audience and to give each person the widest possible range of reasons to support their proposals. It is scarcely surprising therefore that this appeal contains elements of ambiguity. The definition of the minimum income has had to be made with an eye to its acceptability as much as to its statistical foundations. To talk, as the Macmillan government did, of giving those on National Assistance a share in rising national prosperity conveys a general intent, while leaving open the precise extent to which there would be real increase in benefits. That the Beveridge plan was based on firm numbers did not mean that it was not capable of different interpretations. Beveridge was writing for a variety of audiences (not least within Whitehall itself) and to meet a variety of concerns. The art lay in the way in which they were interwoven. As Empson has argued, 'if an ambiguity is to be unitary there must be "forces" holding its elements together'.[44] As far as British social policy over the course of this century is concerned, this has been achieved with varying degrees of success.

In identifying ambiguity in attitude towards benefits in Britain, I am not therefore seeking to be critical. There is a key role for ambiguity in the presentation of political argument. But, equally, such ambiguity has no place in the scientific analysis of social policy, and one aim of this chapter has been to indicate the dimensions along which clarification is necessary.

NOTES

This paper is based on research which forms part of the Welfare State Programme at the LSE supported by the ESRC (Programme Grant reference X206 32 2001). The author would like to acknowledge the stimulus which he has received from reading the recent papers (1989a, 1989b and 1989c) of John Veit-Wilson, and has drawn heavily on his work. He is grateful to Dorothy and Tom Wilson, and other contributors, for their comments on the first version of this chapter.

1. There were twenty shillings (s) in a pre-decimal pound and twelve pennies (d) in a shilling.
2. J J Clarke (1939) p 630.
3. Fraser (1984) p 153.
4. J S Clarke (1948) p 167.
5. H C Debates (1909), 29 April.
6. Booth (1892) p 236.
7. Thane (1982) p 83.
8. J S Clarke (1948) pp 167-8.
9. HMSO (1971) Table 37.
10. Thane (1982) p 336.
11. Veit-Wilson (1989a) p 27.
12. Lynes (1977) p 42.
13. HMSO (1971) Table 40.
14. HMSO (1942) p 217.
15. Lynes (1977) p 43.
16. Rowntree (1937) p 159.
17. Rowntree (1941) p 102, author's italics.
18. HMSO (1942) p 14.
19. Harris (1977) p 394.
20. Quoted by Veit-Wilson (1989b) p 14.
21. Harris (1977) p 393.
22. Thane (1982) p 254.
23. Quoted in Fraser (1984) p 231.
24. HMSO (1977) p 8.
25. Veit-Wilson (1989a) p 32.
26. Rowntree and Lavers (1951) p 45.
27. Feinstein (1976) Table 65.
28. HMSO (1971) Table 40, with a deduction of 4s 11d for NIC and 16s 7d income tax.
29. H C Debates (1948) 16 June, col 559.
30. HMSO (1959) p 3.
31. H C Debates (1962) 14 November, col 18.

32. Veit-Wilson (1989a) p 34.
33. Abel-Smith (1959) p 363.
34. HMSO (1979) p 20, their italics.
35. H C Debates (1979) 6 November, cols 167-8.
36. H C Debates (1989) 25 October.
37. HMSO (1988) Table 46.15.
38. HMSO (1989) p 5.
39. Bowley (1937) p 63.
40. HMSO (1942) p 89.
41. Rowntree (1937) p 85.
42. Sen (1984) pp 336-7.
43. Atkinson (1989) Chapter 2.
44. Empson (1953) p 234.

REFERENCES

Abel-Smith B (1959) Social Security, in Ginsberg M (ed) *Law and Opinion in England*, Stevens, London.

Atkinson A B (1989) *Poverty and Social Security*, Harvester Wheatsheaf, Hemel Hempstead.

Booth C (1892) *Pauperism and the Endowment of Old Age*, Macmillan, London.

Bowley A L (1937) Wages and Income Since 1860, Cambridge University Press, Cambridge.

Bowley A L and Hogg M H (1925) *Has Poverty Diminished?*, P S King, London.

Clarke J J (1939) *Social Administration*, 3rd edn, Pitman, London.

Clarke J S (1948) The Assistance Board, in Robson W A (ed) *Social Security*, 3rd edn, Allen and Unwin, London.

Empson W (1953) *Seven Types of Ambiguity*, 3rd edn, Chatto and Windus, London.

Feinstein C H (1976) *Statistical Tables of National Income, Expenditure and Output of the UK 1855–1965*, Cambridge University Press, Cambridge.

Fraser D (1984) *The Evolution of the British Welfare State*, 2nd edn, Macmillan, London.

Fuchs V (1965) Toward a Theory of Poverty, in *Task Force on Economic Growth and Opportunity, the Concept of Poverty*, Chamber of Commerce of the United States, Washington DC, USA.

Harris J (1977) *William Beveridge*, Clarendon Press, Oxford.

HMSO (1942) *Social Insurance and Allied Services*, Cmnd 6404 (Beveridge Report), London.

HMSO (1959) *Improvements in National Assistance*, Ministry of Pensions and National Insurance, Cmnd 782, London.

HMSO (1971) *British Labour Statistics*, Department of Employment, London.

HMSO (1977) *Low Incomes*, Department of Social Security, Supplementary Benefits Administration Papers 6, London.

HMSO (1979) *Annual Report (1978)*, Supplementary Benefits Commission, Cmnd 7725, London.

HMSO (1988) *Social Security Statistics*, Department of Social Security, London.

HMSO (1989) Benefit Levels and a Minimum Income, in House of Commons Social Services Committee Minimum Income, House of Commons Paper 579, HMSO, London.

Lynes T (1977) The Making of the Unemployment Assistance Scale, Appendix 1 in Department of Health and Social Security, *Low Incomes*.

Mill J S (1843) *A System of Logic*, J W Parker, London.

Pahl J (1983) The Allocation of Money and the Structuring of Inequality within Marriage, *Sociological Review* **31**: 237–62.

Rowntree B S (1901) *Poverty*, Longman, London.

Rowntree B S (1937) *The Human Needs of Labour*, Longman, London.

Rowntree B S (1941) *Poverty and Progress*, Longman, London.

Rowntree B S and Lavers G R (1951) *Poverty and the Welfare State*, Longman, London.

Sen A K (1984) Poor, Relatively Speaking, in *Resources, Values and Development*, Harvard University Press, Cambridge, Mass., USA.

Thane P (1982) *The Foundations of the Welfare State*, Longman, London.

Veit-Wilson J (1989a) The Concept of Minimum Income and the Basis of Social Security Scales, seminar paper.

Veit-Wilson J (1989b) Memorandum, in House of Commons Social Services Committee *Minimum Income*, House of Commons Paper 579, HMSO, London.

Veit-Wilson J (1989c) Genesis of Confusion: The Beveridge Committee's Poverty Line for Social Security, seminar paper.

8 The Objectives and Attainments of Pension Schemes

Nicholas Barr

What are the objectives of old age pensions, and to what extent have pensions in the UK since the war met them? The starting point (Section 8.1) is to list possible aims (by no means all of them compatible). Section 8.2 discusses some major issues of principle: the case for and against compulsion; arguments about the relative desirability of funded and pay-as-you-go (PAYG) schemes;[1] and the place, if any, of actuarial principles. Section 8.3 looks at various reforms, implemented or proposed, since 1948 and shows how they relate to the objectives in Section 8.1. The bulk of the discussion concerns the National Insurance system and its relation with the private sector. For reasons of space two major areas receive little attention: there is no detailed discussion of the vast numbers of occupational and private pension schemes; nor is there any analysis of the position of widows.

INSTITUTIONAL BACKGROUND

In brief, individuals with an appropriate National Insurance contributions record are entitled to a pension if (a) they become permanently disabled, or (b) they reach retirement age. As a good approximation, such a pension is an entitlement awarded without means test. Under the National Insurance Act 1946 individuals made flat-rate contributions, which entitled them to a flat-rate pension. In the early 1960s a small additional graduated pension was grafted on to those arrangements, and the long-term disability pension was introduced as a National Insurance benefit in 1971.

After various reform proposals by different governments the 1973 Social Security Act and the 1975 Social Security Pensions Act overhauled both contributions and pensions. Contributions became fully earnings-related. The basic, flat-rate pension was retained, but superimposed upon it was the State Earnings Related Pension Scheme (SERPS) to be phased in by 1997, with further changes to take place round the turn of the century.[2]

8.1 THE OBJECTIVES OF OLD AGE PENSIONS

8.1.1 AT THE LEVEL OF THE INDIVIDUAL/FAMILY

The objectives of retirement and disability pensions, as in any other area of

economic policy, are efficiency, equity and administrative feasibility. However, it is useful to adopt a more detailed categorisation which at times may
cut across the efficiency/equity divide. At an individual level pensions have
three strategic purposes: income maintenance, including poverty relief; the
reduction of inequality; and social integration. As discussed later, these aims
can be in conflict and some writers deny that one or more is an appropriate
objective.

The first strategic goal is income maintenance, which has at least three
aspects.

(i) **Poverty relief:**
   *No elderly or disabled individual/household should fall below some minimum
   standard of living.* The basic National Insurance pension has this objective. The poverty line for the relevant groups can be defined in
   terms of subsistence; alternatively, it can be defined relative to average living standards, for example a participation definition of poverty.
   Once the poverty line has been decided, the effectiveness of the basic
   pension in relieving poverty is measured by statistics relating to *how
   many* pensioners are in poverty (so-called 'headcount' measures) or to
   how much they fall below the poverty line (so-called 'poverty gap'
   measures).

(ii) **Protecting accustomed living standards:**
   *No one should face an unexpected and unacceptably large drop in their
   living standards.* Since retirement is not unexpected, this objective
   is not immediately relevant to old age pensions, but is acutely
   relevant to disability pensions. This aspect is measured by the replacement rate, which shows a person's income when receiving
   pension in comparison with previous income (net of taxes and
   benefits) when working.

(iii) **Income smoothing:**
   *Pension schemes should make it possible for individuals to reallocate consump-
   tion over their lifetime.* Schemes with this objective can take the form,
   at least notionally, of individuals redistributing income from themselves at one stage in the life cycle to themselves at another, an objective which lies at the heart of the proposals in the 1942 Beveridge
   Report:

   > Management of one's income is an essential element of a citizen's
   > freedom. Payment of a substantial part of the cost of benefit as a
   > contribution irrespective of the means of the contributor is the
   > firm basis of a claim to benefit irrespective of means (para. 21)

A genuinely actuarial pension scheme[3] fulfils just such a function.
Alternatively, there can be provision out of general taxation (that is,
with no pretence of individual contributions) to groups whose stage
in the life cycle suggests that they are likely to be financially con-

strained. An example is a pension scheme run on pay-as-you-go (PAYG) lines, in which benefits bear no actuarial relation to an individual's past contributions. The success of pensions in smoothing out income has to be measured by comparing the incomes of elderly people with their incomes at other stages of the life cycle.

The smoothing objective has a major efficiency role, in that pensions are a mechanism to enable individuals to make choices about the time path of consumption over their life cycle. In principle, individuals are able to do this through private institutions such as savings and insurance; but there is an efficiency role for state intervention in the case of risks against which the private market cannot, for technical reasons, supply insurance.[4] Additionally, the state may have a distributional role, in that income smoothing might be impracticable for lower-paid people, whose savings during working life would be insufficient to raise their retirement income above the poverty line. Note that objectives (ii) and (iii) are different. Objective (ii) seeks to protect individuals against an unexpected reduction in living standards (that is, it is mainly an insurance objective); objective (iii) concerns the protection afforded individuals in the face of a predictable fall in their income (that is, it is more of a savings objective).

The second strategic goal is the reduction of inequality, both as between otherwise equal households with different incomes (vertical equity) and as between households at a given income but differing in some other respect (horizontal equity).

(iv) **Vertical equity:**
Pensions should redistribute towards individuals/ families with lower incomes. This is a highly contentious goal. Redistribution can arise in at least three ways. All means-tested benefits contribute to a greater or lesser extent to the vertical equity aim (e.g. poor pensioners in Britain are eligible for Income Support).[5] So, too, do non-means-tested benefits whose recipients have lower incomes (the basic National Insurance pension being a case in point). A third form of redistribution towards lower incomes arises where the benefit formula pays more benefit per pound of contributions at lower incomes. This can occur in a number of ways: any flat-rate benefit financed by a contribution proportional to earnings will redistribute progressively, for example the British basic, flat-rate pension; another example is the redistributive formula built into the combination of the basic and earnings-related state pensions in Britain;[6] and another is the redistribution built into the US Social Security retirement pension.

The success or otherwise of pensions in reducing inequality in incomes can be judged by the inspection over time of aggregate inequality measures such as the Gini coefficient or Atkinson measure,[7] though it should be remembered that the distributional impact of the cash benefit system is complex, and summary statistics should be treated with caution.

(v)   **Horizontal equity:**
Groups should be treated equally, irrespective of factors which are regarded as irrelevant, such as race and gender. In the case of pensions, a particular problem arises in defining what is meant by equality between men and women, given women's greater average life expectancy, a topic discussed shortly.

A third strategic goal is social integration, which has two aspects.

(vi) **Dignity:**
Benefits should be given so as to preserve individual dignity and without unnecessary stigma. Beveridge emphasised the importance of contributions in this context: it was not only less means-testing which fostered dignity, but also the making of contributions. Benefits which were given, not earned, implied some loss of dignity. The basic pension and SERPs, being based on a contributions record and paid without means test, both contribute to this aim.

(vii) **Social solidarity:**
Benefits should foster social solidarity. The aim has two aspects. First, to the extent possible, benefits should depend on criteria such as age which are unrelated to social status (in contrast with means-tested benefits). The basic pension is a case in point. Second, and separately, benefits should be paid at a level which allows pensioners to participate fully in the life of the society in which they live. This aspect completes the circle by bringing us back to objective (i), one aspect of which is the payment of pensions sufficiently high to allow pensioners full participation.

8.1.2   AGGREGATE OBJECTIVES

In any discussion of cash benefits, a major strategic objective is efficiency.

(viii) **Efficiency:**
'The design of benefits, and of the taxes necessary to finance them, should be such as to minimise any adverse effects on the incentive to work and save' (Meade).[8] Pensions at an aggregate level are a mechanism for dividing national output between workers and pensioners in such a way as to minimise efficiency losses. As discussed in Section 8.3, the future reduction in SERPS (HMSO, 1985b) was motivated by worries that an excessive pensions burden would adversely affect labour supply and output growth after the turn of the century, when the proportion of elderly people is set to rise sharply.

A final strategic objective, administrative feasibility, has two aspects, as explained by Meade.

(ix) **Intelligibility:**
'The whole system should be as simple, as easy to understand and as cheap

to administer as possible.' Examples are the computerisation of contributions records and the attempts which have been made from time
to time to pay pensions directly into the bank accounts of individual
pensioners.

(x) **Absence of abuse:**
'The benefits from the system should be as little open to abuse as possible.'
The objectives of efficiency, intelligibility and absence of abuse can
be thought of either as goals in their own right, or as constraints on
the state's ability to pursue the earlier objectives. To some extent the
weight they are given is ideological: Labour governments have
tended to emphasise income maintenance, inequality reduction and
social integration; since 1979 Conservative governments have laid
more emphasis on efficiency aspects.

8.1.3 *DEFINITIONAL PROBLEMS AND INCONSISTENT OBJECTIVES*

Problems of definition and measurement
Defining the various objectives and measuring their achievement raise major
problems. This section does no more than sketch out the most serious ones.
Defining and measuring poverty ((i) above) raises the problems discussed in
Chapter 7. (Atkinson): in particular, how does one define the poverty line,
and how do we measure how many individuals/families fall below it, and
by how much? Protecting living standards raises the question of how large a
drop in income is 'unacceptable'. The appropriate extent of vertical redistribution and of 'equal treatment of equals' has occupied economists, philosophers and political theorists for centuries, and has plagued policy makers at
least since the Poor Law Act of 1601. Even the term 'equality' is difficult to
define unambiguously.[9]

A particularly difficult area in the case of pensions is the meaning of
equality as between men and women. An ambiguity arises because women
tend to live longer than men. Consider a man and a woman with identical
earnings profiles, who both retire at 65 and both live exactly their life expectancy. Since the woman lives longer, she collects her pension for longer;
and if she pays the same contributions and receives the same weekly pension
as the man, she collects more pension in total over her retirement. Thus
equality defined in terms of the *weekly pension* implies that women receive
more pension per pound of contribution than men. Alternatively, if each has
the same earnings profile, the man and the woman each has an identical
lump sum on retirement: if this were used to buy an actuarial annuity, the
woman would receive a lower weekly pension than the man over more
weeks, such that the present value of her pension stream was the same as
that of the man's. Thus equality defined in terms of the *present value of the
pension stream* implies that the woman receives a lower weekly pension. The

ambiguity is genuine. Fortunately, it can be resolved for policy purposes because there is a consensus that horizontal equity requires the equal-weekly-pension definition.

Concepts such as 'dignity', 'stigma' and 'social solidarity' (objectives (vi) and (vii)) are also far from easy to define and in addition defy measurement. Individualist writers such as Hayek argue that the term 'social solidarity' is wholly devoid of meaning, and that its pursuit is therefore pointless, and also dangerous (Hayek 1976). Efficiency (objective (viii)) has a precise analytical definition in economic theory, but measurement problems such as the incidence of taxes and benefits make policy applications very difficult.

Conflicting objectives

Even if these difficulties were somehow resolved, major problems remain in that some objectives are inherently in conflict, and others may be. In the latter category, efficiency may be enhanced by competitive wage differentials and low taxes, both of which can conflict with distributional goals. The pursuit of equity, if it complicates the system, could conflict with administrative simplicity; for instance, attempts to tailor means-tested benefits very precisely to family circumstances usually have serious administrative implications.

Some objectives are in conflict almost by definition. The smoothing of lifetime income implies that an individual with higher earnings should have a higher pension, an objective which does not sit easily with the requirement that pensions should redistribute towards those with lower incomes, nor with the objective that pensions should contribute to social solidarity. On one interpretation of horizontal equity, everyone should receive a pension proportional to past contributions; according to this view, it is inequitable if some people receive more pension per pound of contribution than others. But that rules out redistribution towards lower incomes, and so conflicts with vertical equity, and possibly also with social solidarity objectives. It is because some objectives conflict that hard decisions have to be made. A key choice is whether pensions should have a larger redistributive role; many of the debates about pensions since 1948 have, directly or indirectly, been rooted in that question.

8.2 ISSUES OF PRINCIPLE

As a background to the evaluation of the various UK pension régimes since the war this section discusses a number of issues of fundamental principle. The theoretical arguments for and against compulsory membership of National Insurance are set out in Section 8.2.1. Section 8.2.2 considers whether the state, as well as making pensions compulsory, should also provide the pension itself. Section 8.2.3 discusses the desirability or otherwise of the actuarial principle, whereby the pension of a representative individual is strictly proportional to past contributions.[10]

8.2.1 VOLUNTARISM VERSUS COMPULSION

An individual who makes inadequate pension provision will be poor in old age. This situation imposes costs on others; the cost of non-contributory support for poor pensioners falls upon the taxpayer; alternatively, if elderly people who made inadequate pension provision for themselves were simply allowed to starve, the costs would fall on society as a whole (hazards to public health, and so on). More generally in dealing with externalities, a possible theoretical solution is an appropriate tax or subsidy; for example, paying a subsidy (or charging less tax) on lead-free petrol encourages drivers to use cleaner fuel.[11] But the objective here is not marginally to influence pension provision but, more simply, to ensure that everyone makes provision at least at some minimum level. Thus a more effective solution is to make membership of a pension scheme compulsory for all individuals, at least up to some minimum level.

Compulsion can therefore be defended in *efficiency* terms. There is little disagreement with the argument as it applies to pensions at a subsistence level, that is in pursuit of poverty relief. Nor is there serious disagreement with its application to the basic, flat-rate pension, even though this is above bare subsistence, to protect accustomed living standards and to enhance income smoothing and social solidarity. However, the applicability of compulsion to ensure pensions related to the recipient's previous income is much less clear. A possible justification is that individuals, including the non-poor, are systematically myopic, and should therefore be required to smooth their lifetime income.

But there are objections. First, earnings-related schemes preserve in old age some of the inequalities of working life. This has three results: it conflicts with social solidarity; the redistributive formula may be regressive, as in SERPS, which conflicts with vertical equity and social integration; and compulsion is inappropriate if one denies that the pursuit of redistribution or social solidarity are appropriate objectives for pensions. The second and third arguments do not apply to occupational pensions.

A second problem is who determines the level of compulsory earnings-related provision. Perhaps people should be allowed to spend more when they are younger, either because they might enjoy it more (*si la jeunesse savait, si la vieillesse pouvait*), or because they need it more (for example families with young children). It is sometimes suggested in other countries (Sweden is a case in point – Chapter 11) that retired people are *too well* provided for compared with working families with children. Third, even if policy makers achieve the right answer on average, there will be a variance about that average since individual tastes differ. Individuals who would prefer more consumption now and a lower pension later will not be allowed to make that choice; individuals who would prefer more future consumption can make additional voluntary provision, though not necessarily with the advantages (tax and otherwise) accruing to compulsory schemes.

What case for compulsion then remains? One argument is that, because of myopia, compulsion is necessary to ensure that people make what they will later, in old age, regard as sufficient provision. An entirely separate argument is that in the face of uninsurable uncertainty (for example, over future rates of inflation) people should be compelled to belong to a scheme which gives them a reasonable guarantee of future benefit levels.

Where either argument applies, there is a case for compulsion so as to maintain accustomed living standards and to avoid large falls in income on retirement. In the case of SERPS, additionally, compulsory membership makes it easier to reduce inequality of pensions between men and women, and may help to preserve the dignity of individual pensioners, in that membership of the scheme is not the sole preserve of the poor.

8.2.2   THE CASE FOR PUBLIC PRODUCTION: FUNDING VERSUS PAY-AS-YOU-GO

The fact that the state makes something compulsory does not mean that the activity must be publicly organised. The externality argument in the previous section applies to automobile insurance (where, quite correctly on efficiency grounds, compulsion is restricted to damage to third parties). But having made it compulsory for drivers to insure, the state does not then feel it necessary to organise a National Car Insurance system. There are four sets of reasons why government might provide pensions itself, as opposed simply to regulating the conduct of pension provision in the private sector: if indexation is not possible in the private sector; if the state can cope more efficiently with demographic change; if redistribution is a major objective; and if state pensions can be administered more cheaply than private pensions (which British experience suggests is the case).

(i)   Indexation

Individuals can make efficient inter-temporal choices only where they can act with certainty or where any uncertainty is insurable. Not least for efficiency reasons, therefore, pensions should be tied to an appropriate index (leaving to one side for the moment whether that index should be changes in prices or in earnings). PAYG pensions are financed out of the contributions of the current workforce; and since wage rises generally outstrip inflation, pensions rest on a buoyant tax base. Under PAYG it is therefore generally easy to index pensions at least to the rate of inflation. With funded schemes, pensions are financed out of the previous contributions of current pensioners. Pensions can be indexed only if the assets on which they are based *always* pay a rate of return at or above the rate of inflation. The only such asset guaranteed is indexed government bonds. In such cases, the pension can be private and funded, but the indexation component is public and financed by current levies on the tax-paying population. Income smoothing, it can be argued, is enhanced by public provision of the whole pension or by state provision of indexed assets for the use of the private pensions industry.

(ii) Pensions and demographic change

The impact of demographic factors on pension finance is well known, but sufficiently important to merit a sketch of the main arguments (Aaron 1982; Barr 1979, 1987; Falkingham 1989). There was a large 'bulge' in the birth rate in the late 1940s and another in the early 1960s. Thereafter birth rates fell sharply. A similar pattern occurred in most other advanced industrialised economies. Currently, therefore, the UK has plenty of workers (the 1940s cohort being in their early 40s and the 1960s cohort in their mid 20s); and since birth rates were fairly low in the 1920s and 1930s, there is not an excessive number of pensioners. But increasingly after 2008 the 1940s cohort will start to retire, a process which will be exacerbated in the years after 2025 when the 1960s cohort retires. Since birth rates after the late 1960s have been low, there will be few workers and a large number of pensioners. In the late 1980s there were 3.4 people of working age for every person over pension age; by 2025 this is projected to fall to 2.6. With PAYG finance, other things being equal, an increase in the ratio of pensioners to workers (the so-called dependency ratio) requires a larger tax on each worker to finance a given real pension. Funded schemes, according to some commentators, avoid this problem (Feldstein 1974); other writers argue that the problem is largely the same however pensions are organised.

To start with what is non-controversial, there are three (and only three) possible outcomes to a decline in the relative number of workers: (a) pensions must fall if the contribution rate stays constant (that is, the purchasing power of pensioners is reduced); or (b) contributions must rise if the real pension is maintained (that is, the purchasing power of the working population is reduced); or (c) output rises sufficiently to increase the tax base, so that a constant rate of taxation can finance an unchanged real pension. The desirable solution, rather obviously, is to increase output. That can be done in only two generic ways: by increasing the output produced by each worker; and/or by increasing the number of workers. To increase output per worker, relevant policies are increased investment, increased expenditure on research and development[12] and better education and training for the workforce. Measures to increase the number of workers include reducing the rate of unemployment, encouraging married women to rejoin the labour force (for example by providing more child care facilities),[13] raising the retirement age and importing labour. An obvious solution under this last head in the case of the UK would be generosity in awarding passports to the Hong Kong population; similarly, western Germany can absorb workers from the (younger) eastern German population.

The argument in the previous two paragraphs is not controversial. What *is* controversial is whether funding does or does not lead to higher output growth than PAYG. Funding has no bearing on policies to increase the number of workers. It is true that pension provision affects labour supply; but to the extent that that is relevant to married women's labour-force participation, what matters is the *level* of the pension not whether it is paid from a fund or out of current revenues. If funding has any impact on output it must be through increased investment and more expenditure on research and development. This entails three causal links: (a) aggregate savings will increase; (b) the increase in saving will lead to an increase in investment; (c) the increased investment will lead to an increase in output.

The empirical evidence on the first link is, to say the least, far from definitive. The key question is whether increased pension savings do or do not cause an offsetting reduction in other savings. Aaron surveys the evidence for the USA and suggests that conclusive empirical evidence is unlikely, mainly because actual behaviour depends crucially on how expectations are formed – something which cannot be measured. He concludes

> that a person determined to find a respected theoretic argument to support a preconception will find one, and that a person without preconception will find a bewildering diversity of answers in economic theory about whether social security (i.e. pensions) is more likely to raise or to lower consumption or labour supply.
> To get by this theoretical impasse, one turns with hope to the empirical research . . . As will become clear, most of these hopes remain unfulfilled. (1982: 28)

Nor does it necessarily follow that increased savings lead to more investment – the second link; pension funds could instead be used to buy old masters. So far as the third link is concerned, the object of the exercise is to channel resources into their most productive investment use. But it cannot just be *assumed* that pension managers make more efficient choices than other agents. Nor do state-funded schemes necessarily fare better. Based on the evidence from Sweden and Japan, the only two industrialised countries with publicly organised funded pensions, Rosa concludes that such schemes

> offer powerful evidence that this option may only invite squandering capital funds in wasteful, low-yield investments [which] should give pause to anyone proposing similar accumulations elsewhere. (1982: 212)

Where does this leave us? The need to increase output is not in dispute. But the contribution of funding is controversial; so is the choice of appropriate policies. The answer depends in part on the weight given to different objectives. If the efficiency objective is given heavy weight, and redistribution much less, one might argue in favour of funding on the grounds that no one has argued that funding *reduces* economic growth.[14] Alternatively, if redistribution is thought important, one can agree with Aaron's conclusion that there is no evidence that funding makes any major efficiency contribution, whereas PAYG makes it possible to redistribute towards the pensioner generation. He therefore argues that PAYG has no (or little) efficiency cost and major equity gains. That gives a case for state PAYG schemes, albeit a controversial one.

(iii) Redistributive aspects of public provision

If everyone were well informed and rational, and provided suitable indexed assets were available, the protection of accustomed living standards and income smoothing could be achieved by voluntary, private schemes. Vertical equity objectives require compulsion to prevent high earners from opting out. To achieve equity between men and women, similarly, requires compulsion to prevent 'men only' pension schemes, with higher pensions for a given contribution because men on average have a shorter life expectancy than women. Dignity and, especially, social solidarity objectives require both compulsion and a state scheme.

A different aspect of redistribution concerns the relative treatment of older and younger people. PAYG brings out the intergenerational conflict explicitly: horizontal equity relates not only to equity as between different pensioner groups but also to that between pensioners and workers. Public provision of pensions makes it easier for the state to tip the balance between the different groups in pursuit of horizontal as well as vertical equity objectives, an example being the reduction in the generosity of SERPS in the years after 2000.[15]

It is in this context, as well as in connection with inter-temporal efficiency, that it is necessary to ask whether pensions (or at least the flat-rate pension) should be indexed to prices or to earnings. The answer depends largely on the weight accorded the social solidarity objective: the more important is that aim, the greater the tendency to adopt a poverty line defined in terms of a participation standard, and the stronger the argument for indexing to earnings rather than prices.[16] Under an individualistic view, *per contra*, social solidarity is unimportant, suggesting a subsistence (or thereabouts) poverty standard.

The choice between (a) PAYG state pensions, and (b) compulsory membership of private schemes backed by indexed government bonds therefore depends on the answers to two sets of questions. First, there is a technical efficiency issue of whether funding does or does not contribute to economic growth. Second, there is the ideological question of the weight attached to redistributive and social solidarity objectives.[17]

8.2.3   THE ACTUARIAL PRINCIPLE

The usefulness of the actuarial principle is best discussed in terms of three views of the world.

View 1: a private, funded, actuarial world: the major objectives are poverty relief, protection of accustomed living standards and income smoothing; redistributive goals are strictly off the agenda. There remains a case for compulsion at least up to a subsistence level; and there is a role for the state in helping the private sector to offer protection against inflation through the issue of indexed gilts.

In such a world, pensions would be private and funded, and benefits would bear a fairly strict relation to contributions. In a *strictly* funded world, pensions would be 'money-purchase', as opposed to being related to 'final salary'.[18] According to this view, there is no case for a scheme which is either (a) publicly organised; (b) PAYG (except, possibly, for the indexation component of private pensions); or (c) redistributive from rich to poor within a given generation. The actuarial principle is alive and well and living in the private sector. This first view is adopted by those who argue that funding contributes to economic growth (a technical issue), and who are of an individualistic persuasion (an ideological matter).

View 2: a public-sector, PAYG actuarial world: the objectives and ideology here are identical to those underlying View 1. The difference is purely technical. If inflation is regarded as a major problem and the private sector is unable to offer adequately indexed pensions, it is possible in principle to have a state-organised PAYG scheme in which benefits are strictly related to individual contributions. In such a scheme individual A, who earns twice as much as otherwise identical individual B, would pay twice as much in contributions and receive twice as large a pension.[19] From the viewpoint of the individual, the situation would be identical to that in an occupational scheme, save that indexation would be complete. Again, the actuarial principle remains intact.

View 3: a non-actuarial world: major objectives now include vertical and horizontal equity, and possibly also dignity and social solidarity. Could these objectives be achieved through compulsory membership of heavily regulated private schemes? The argument is best spelled out in steps.

If people are free to join their chosen scheme, there will be schemes restricted to lawyers and accountants, and no professional would join the shopworkers' pension scheme. As a result, there would be little redistribution beyond that between more and less rich lawyers and accountants, and more and less rich shopworkers.

To make redistribution possible it is therefore necessary to make it more or less compulsory for everyone to belong to the same scheme. A single, monopolistic, notionally private-sector scheme would have to be so heavily regulated that it would, in effect, be acting as an agent of the state.

Since membership is compulsory, better-off people cannot opt out, and it becomes possible, without *major* inefficiency, to break the link between contributions and benefits. Once that link is broken, pensions (including SERPS) have become *de facto* a tax-transfer scheme.

In short, to the extent that redistribution is one of the objectives of pensions, the logic leads inexorably to compulsory membership of a state or quasi-state scheme in which pensions bear no actuarial relation to contributions. There does not have to be the same answer for all pension schemes; it would be possible to have a redistributive basic pension and an actuarial earnings-related scheme. But systematic redistribution and actuarial principles are fundamentally incompatible. Thus View 3 determines the appropriate institutions where funding is not thought to contribute to economic growth, and/or where redistribution is a major objective.

8.3 HISTORICAL REVIEW

In the light of previous discussion it is possible to shed some light on why pensions policy in the post-war years took the shape it did.

The original Beveridge scheme was in many ways actuarial. Individuals paid a flat-rate contribution and received flat-rate benefits. The premium did not reflect differences in individual risk; but since membership was compulsory it did reflect the *average* risk. In contrast with later arrangements, the weekly stamp can be regarded not as a lump sum (and hence regressive) tax, but as a compulsory insurance premium. The one major non-actuarial element was the inclusion alongside the pension of unemployment compensation, even though unemployment is an uninsurable risk. This is anomalous if one adheres to strictly actuarial View 1, but natural if one adopts View 3, which includes both redistribution and social solidarity as goals. Since Beveridge wished to minimise distortions to actuarial principles, redistribution was not a *major* objective (though there was some redistribution, in that the scheme was partly financed by progressive tax revenues); but much of the purpose of his proposed arrangements was to foster dignity and social solidarity. It was adherence to these aims in the aftermath of the collapse of unemployment compensation in the 1930s which explains the inclusion of support for the unemployed in the 1946 National Insurance Act, and also the fact that the new arrangements were compulsory and universal.

The introduction of graduated pensions: the flat-rate contribution in the 1946 Act bore more heavily on individuals with lower incomes, leading to pressures to keep it small. In consequence, benefits, too, were low, a source of increasing dissatisfaction over the 1950s. As a result, from 1961 a compulsory additional earnings-related contribution was levied above a certain level of earnings, giving entitlement to a graduated (that is, earnings-related) pension on top of the flat-rate pension. The additional pension bore a strict actuarial relation to the additional contribution. Each £7.50 of graduated contribution entitled a man to an extra 2.5 pence of weekly pension; for women the extra 2.5 pence per week cost an additional £9 of contributions because of their greater average longevity.

Clearly the major aim was income smoothing. A subsidiary objective was horizontal equity: there had always been state assistance for earnings-related pensions through tax expenditures (tax allowances) for occupational pensions; but these went mainly to salary earners. One view of graduated pensions (and *a fortiori* of SERPS) is that they reduced inequality between salary earners and wage earners. Graduated pensions, in other words, improve horizontal and vertical equity by correcting (or at least reducing) a lack of symmetry in graduated provision.

The Joseph plan: a 1971 White Paper, published under the auspices of Sir Keith Joseph, provoked considerable discussion and formed part of the basis of the 1975 Social Security Pensions Act. The full Joseph proposals, however, were never implemented. The White Paper proposed a state flat-rate pension supplemented by a (mostly private) earnings-related pension. The flat-rate benefit was to be paid out of an earnings-related contribution, as for instance in the Netherlands – an explicit overthrow of even the pretence of actuarial principles.

The basic pension was thus motivated by the first objective – the relief of poverty – in that the pension, in conjunction with means-tested assistance with housing costs, was just above the poverty line defined in terms of Supplementary Benefit.[20] It also had a vertical equity aim, since a flat-rate benefit paid out of an earnings-related contribution is highly redistributive from rich to poor. In addition, social solidarity might have been a motive, since the pension was to remain a non-means-tested entitlement for individuals with the necessary contributions record. In contrast, the earnings-related pension was to be organised in the private sector (apart from a residual state scheme) on a funded and broadly actuarial basis. The underlying aim in this part of the package was income smoothing, but emphatically not vertical redistribution.

The 1974 Labour government, as soon as it gained office, pursued poverty-relief and social-solidarity objectives by increasing the basic pension in fulfilment of an election pledge. Later that year, it published a White Paper (Cmnd 5713) which kept the Joseph flat-rate arrangements, on which it superimposed SERPS. The explicit aims of the White Paper were: to avoid means-testing (in pursuit of dignity and social solidarity); to pay indexed benefits (income smoothing); to pay earnings-related benefits (income smoothing and the protection of accustomed living standards); to redistribute towards the less well-off (vertical equity); and to offer equality for women (horizontal equity).

Since most of these objectives are hard to achieve in a private scheme, it was almost inevitable that the Labour White Paper should advocate the (more or less compulsory) state earnings-related scheme implemented in the 1975 Social Security Pensions Act. The Joseph plan was motivated mainly by actuarial principles, which were abandoned in the 1975 legislation.

As discussed already, the increase in the basic pension in 1974 reflected greater stress on poverty relief; on the face of it, so too did the emphasis on indexation, which ensures that the poverty line is not eroded by inflation. In many ways, however, the change was more one of form than substance. The 1946 National Insurance Act made no mention of uprating benefits in line with inflation, and benefits in the early years were uprated only infrequently.[21] Under the 1975 Social Security Act and Social Security Pensions Act, the level of SERPS and various other benefits was to be reviewed annually and uprated in line with prices or, in the case of the basic pension, with earnings or prices, whichever was the larger.[22] The requirement to review benefits annually, it can be argued, made little difference. Benefits between 1948 and 1975 had in practice remained a constant fraction of average pre-tax earnings so exactly that it is clear that successive governments had an unwritten behavioural rule to maintain the relativity.[23]

The Fowler review: in 1985 the results of 'the most fundamental examination of our social security system since the Second World War' were published as a Green Paper (Cmnd 9517) and in a White Paper (Cmnd 9578) later in the same year, under the auspices of the then Secretary of State for Health and Social Security, Norman Fowler. Notwithstanding the claim that it was a fundamental review, the bulk of the proposed changes – apart from substantial changes in SERPS – was little more than housekeeping improvements (for example measures to reduce the likelihood of poor families losing more in benefit than they gained in extra earnings). *Parturiunt montes, nascitur ridiculus mus.*

Nevertheless, the Green and White Papers gave a valuable insight into the government's objectives: '[T]he social security system must be capable of meeting genuine need' (that is, the objective of poverty relief); '[T]he social security system must be consistent with the Government's overall objectives for the economy' (the efficiency objective); '[T]he social security system must be simple to understand and easy to administer' (Cmnd 9517, para. 1.12).

These objectives are consistent with private, non-redistributive, actuarial provision of the earnings-related pension (View 1, above). It is therefore not surprising that the Green Paper (Cmnd 9517) proposed the abolition of SERPS and its replacement, for the most part, by occupational pensions. The proposal was hotly opposed, not least by the pensions industry, worried that it might be expected to offer pensions not only to salaried professionals in stable jobs but also to the less well-off. A subsequent White Paper (Cmnd 9518) was more circumspect, retaining SERPS but reducing benefits in later years (see Note 6).

Alongside the Fowler reforms, further incentives were given to individuals to contract out of SERPS in order to join occupational schemes; and other legislative changes allowed individuals, subject to certain regulations, to opt out of both SERPS and occupational provision and make their own pension arrangements either through an insurance company or, even more individually, by building up a portfolio of assets with some freedom of choice. These changes, especially the latter, extended the actuarial element in earnings-related pensions.

So far as pensions are concerned, the Green Paper proposal to abolish SERPS was an attempt to shift earnings-related pensions from the non-actuarial stance of the 1975 legislation (View 3, above) back to the actuarial principles which underpinned the Joseph proposals. Because of widespread concern at the proposed abolition of SERPS the White Paper represented a much smaller move in an actuarial direction. The changes after 2000[24] reduce the weight put on equity objectives. For instance, the calculation of benefits over a whole working life rather than over the best twenty years works to the disadvantage of individuals with fluctuating incomes, particularly those individuals (mainly women) who have spells in and out of the labour force.

However, though the redistributive element in the state scheme was reduced, the move towards actuarial principles was only very partial. Whether such a move is good or bad depends on the answers to two questions: first, and ideological, is whether one believes that pensions should be redistributive; second, and largely technical, is whether or not a move towards funding is an effective response to demographic prospects. On the latter point, earlier discussion focused on two issues: whether or not the demographic problem is serious; and what policies might improve matters. The Green Paper's response was largely to duck the problem by advocating that earnings-related provision should be mainly a private-sector activity; the White Paper, as we have seen, retained SERPS but reduced benefits in later years.

It can be argued that this was the right policy. Either the SERPS promise of 1975, with hindsight, was too generous or it was not. If output were to grow sufficiently to allow the original SERPS promise to be kept, pensions could be raised in future years (with PAYG it is easy to increase pensions, but politically difficult to lower them). If, on the other hand, the original promise was indeed too generous, then the strategy of making the promise less generous has much to commend it in comparison with the Green Paper alternative of replacing SERPS by private, funded schemes. The 1975 Social Security Pensions Act was based on nearly two decades of debate, with considerable all-party support for the final outcome. Little has changed since 1975, save that the scheme has (perhaps) turned out to be unrealistically generous, given likely demographic trends and their effect on output. The proposed changes should reduce the most acute cost (i.e. demand-side pressures), particularly if buttressed by the supply-side policies discussed earlier (p 151). In the USA similar changes, in the form of future increases in contribution rates and in the retirement age, have already been announced.

Changing the age of retirement: finally, some dogs that did not bark. The UK, unusual amongst industrialised countries, has a retirement age for women (60) which is lower than that for men (65). The differential was introduced in 1940 when the retirement age for women was reduced to 60, partly because of a campaign by women's organisations.[25] In today's terms, the differential violates horizontal equity. First, a woman who retires at 65 receives a higher pension than a 65-year-old man with an identical earnings record, because she has worked beyond her normal retirement age.[26] Second, there is the discrimination against women who would prefer to work longer than 60; this is both inequitable and inefficient. Various lawsuits, particularly at a European level, are putting the differential under increasing pressure; and the demographic outlook implies that a common retirement age of 65 (or higher) is likely. To date, however, notwithstanding pressures to the contrary, the differential retirement age remains.

The power of the state over pensions: in 1920, public spending on the welfare state (all cash benefits plus benefits in kind) was around 6 per cent of GNP; in 1948 the figure was 10 per cent; by 1989/90 it had risen to 23 per cent. Pensions in 1989/90 comprised more then one-fifth of all social spending, and some 5 per cent of GNP. The power of the state over pensions has clearly become very great.

Is such a development good or bad? In terms of *realpolitik* there was, for most of the period since 1948, little worry about the state's power over benefits for two reasons: the post-war system was so much better than the system it replaced; and the demographics until recently were very favourable, so that generous pensions could be paid without a substantial impost on the working generation.

As an analytical matter the answer depends on whether one gives greater weight to actuarial principles or to redistributive objectives. According to actuarial View 1, described earlier, pensions should be funded and non-redistributive, with the state's role limited to the provision of indexed assets for the use of private schemes. This approach is taken by those who believe that funding contributes to economic growth, and who place little weight on redistribution. To such individuals the growing power of the state is a matter for regret. According to View 3, however, pensions should be PAYG and redistributive; this is the approach when funding is believed to contribute little to economic growth, and where redistributive goals are both legitimate and important. From this perspective the increased role of the state is benign.

NOTES

I am grateful to Sir Alec Atkinson, Jane Falkingham and the editors for helpful comments on an earlier version and to Fiona Coulter for her part in joint work on which Section 8.1 draws heavily. Remaining errors are my responsibility.

1. Funded pensions are paid from a fund built up over a period of years out of

the contributions of its members. Pay-As-You-Go (PAYG) pensions, in contrast, are paid by the state out of current revenues, rather than from an accumulated fund.

2. For further institutional description see Barr (1987) ch 9, and for compendious detail Tolley (1989).

3. In an actuarial scheme the present value of the real-benefit stream for a representative individual equals the lump sum accumulated over working life.

4. Depending on the type of risk involved, the state scheme might embrace actuarial principles, or might simply consist of transfer payments. For more detailed discussion, see Barr (1987) chs 5, 8 and 12.

5. The 1948 National Assistance Act introduced *National Assistance*, a means-tested benefit of last resort for those whose income from all other sources left them below some benchmark level. The benefit was reformed and renamed *Supplementary Benefit* in 1966. Under the 1988 reforms, Supplementary Benefit was replaced by *Income Support*. For further institutional detail see Tolley (1989).

6. Current British arrangements are summarised in Barr (1987) pp 205–8. The State Earnings Related Pension Scheme (SERPS) pays a pension of one-quarter of the excess of an individual's average earnings over the lower earnings limit. Thus an individual with twice the earnings (and hence twice the contributions) will receive less than twice the total pension (basic pension plus SERPS). The present arrangements will be changed in three major ways, starting in 2000. From 2010 the pension will be one-fifth rather than one-quarter of the relevant amount, the reduction having been phased in over the previous ten years. Second, average earnings will be measured not over an individual's best twenty years, but over full working life. Third, the surviving spouse will inherit up to half, rather than all, of the spouse's earnings-related pension. These changes increase the importance of the basic, flat-rate pension, and hence increase the redistributive tilt in the state pension scheme.

7. The Gini coefficient is a measure of overall inequality in income, which varies from zero (implying complete equality) to one (implying complete inequality). The Atkinson measure is another such statistic. For further discussion, see Atkinson (1983) ch 3, or Barr (1987) ch 6.

8. See, for instance, Meade (1978) p 269.

9. Le Grand (1982) pp 14–15.

10. Fuller discussion of the economics of pensions can be found in Aaron (1982) and Barr (1987) ch 9.

11. In the presence of an external benefit, an unrestricted private market will supply an inefficiently small quantity. One way of restoring supply to its efficient level is to pay a subsidy. Similarly, an appropriate tax discourages excessive supply in the presence of an external cost.

12. Robots are an example of more and better capital equipment; they enable a smaller labour force to produce more output. They have the added advantage that they do not require a pension when they retire!

13. Though this would increase output, it would also reduce the pool of informal carers; in this case there is a tension between income maintenance (the pension) and care for the elderly.

14. An advantage of funding is that it disciplines pension promises, since pensions promised for the future require the imposition of additional contributions in the present. On the other hand, complete funding of the state pension is not prac-

ticable, given the size of the fund which would be necessary, and the fact that the cost of funding would have to be added to the cost of financing PAYG pensions already in payment.

15. See Note 6.

16. Under current British arrangements, the basic pension is indexed to changes in prices; SERPS entitlement during contributors' earning years build up in line with earnings, but SERPS *in payment* is indexed to changes in retail prices.

17. It is interesting (and perhaps depressing) how often those whose ideology places little weight on social solidarity can find support for the efficiency gains from funding, and *vice versa*.

18. Under a money-purchase scheme, the present value of the expected stream of pension payments depends on the size of the individual's accumulated lump sum upon retirement *and on nothing else*. Most occupational schemes, however, pay pensions related to the number of years of contribution and to the individual's salary in the last few years of employment. The latter involves a PAYG element if, when under pressure, the pension fund is 'topped up' out of current revenues.

19. In principle, such a scheme could be organised in the following way: individuals would pay contributions proportional to their earnings; on retirement they would be awarded a pension of £X, where £X is what they would have received from a private funded scheme for the same contribution; pensions in payment would be uprated each year out of current tax revenues in line with changes in the appropriate price index.

20. See Note 5.

21. The retirement pension, for instance, was £1.30 per week for a single person in 1948; over the next fifteen years it was uprated five times, reaching £2.875 in April 1961.

22. The result of the indexation formula for the basic pension was to create a 'ratchet' whereby the effect if price inflation exceeded the rate of earnings increase in any one year was to give an unintended increase to the real pension. The operation of the ratchet is best shown by example. Suppose that pensions are £100 in period 0; that in period 1 earnings rise by 100 per cent, with no increase in prices; and that in period 2 prices rise by 100 per cent with no increase in earnings. Over the whole period real earnings remain unchanged, but pensions have been increased to £200 in period 1, and to £400 in period 2. The real pension, unintentionally, has doubled whilst real earnings remained constant. The effect operated on a number of occasions in the later 1970s.

23. Benefits were not necessarily uprated each year; nor was each uprating necessarily exactly in line with earnings increases. Benefits were raised more rapidly than earnings just before some elections (for example 1959 – 'You've never had it so good') or, as in 1974, just after an election in fulfilment of a manifesto pledge. But the effect in the long run was to maintain the relativity of benefits to pre-tax average earnings almost exactly. See Barr (1981).

24. See Note 6.

25. The Old Age Pensions Act 1908 established a common retirement age of 70. It was reduced to 65 under the Old Age and Widows and Orphans Contributory Pension Act 1925. For details of the events leading to the change in 1940, see Thane (1982) p 245.

26. The real pension is increased by 7.5 per cent for each year of work beyond

normal retiring age; thus a woman retiring at 65 receives a pension 37.5 per cent higher than that of an identical 65-year-old man.

REFERENCES

Aaron H J (1982) *Economic Effects of Social Security*, The Brookings Institution, Washington DC, USA.

Atkinson A B (1983) *The Economics of Inequality*, 2nd edn, Oxford University Press, Oxford.

Barr N A (1979) Myths my Grandpa Taught Me, *Three Banks' Review* no 124, December, pp 27-55.

Barr N A (1981) Empirical Definitions of the Poverty Line, *Policy and Politics* **9**(1) January.

Barr N A (1987) *The Economics of the Welfare State*, Weidenfeld and Nicolson, London.

Barr N A (1988) *The Mirage of Private Unemployment Insurance*, London School of Economics, Welfare State Programme, Discussion Paper WSP/34.

Barr N A and Coulter F (1990) Social Security: Solution or Problem? in Hills J (ed) *The State of Welfare*, Oxford University Press, Oxford.

Falkingham J (1989) Dependency and Ageing in Britain: A Re-examination of the Evidence, *Journal of Social Policy* **18**(2): 211–33.

Feldstein M S (1974) Social Security, Induced Retirement and Capital Accumulation, *Journal of Political Economy* **82**: 905–26.

Hayek F A (1976) *Law, Legislation and Liberty*, vol 2, *The Mirage of Social Justice*, Routledge and Kegan Paul, London.

HMSO (1942) *Social Insurance and Allied Services*, Cmd 6404 (Beveridge Report), London.

HMSO (1971) *Strategy for Pensions: The Future Development of State and Occupational Provision*, Cmnd 4755, London.

HMSO (1974) *Better Pensions: Fully Protected Against Inflation*, Cmnd 5713, London.

HMSO (1985a) *Reform of Social Security*, Cmnd 9517, London.

HMSO (1985b) *Reform of Social Security: Programme for Change*, Cmnd 9518, London.

Le Grand J (1982) *The Strategy of Equality*, Allen and Unwin, London.

Meade J E (1978) *The Structure and Reform of Direct Taxation*, Allen and Unwin, for the Institute for Fiscal Studies, London.

Rosa J-J (ed) (1982) *The World Crisis in Social Security*, Fondation Nationale d'Economie Politique, Paris, France, and Institute for Contemporary Studies, San Francisco, USA.

Thane P (1982) *The Foundations of the Welfare State*, Longman, London.

Tolley (1989) *Social Security and State Benefits, 1989*, Tolley Publishing Company, Croydon, Surrey.

Part Four

Some Issues of Policy in Europe

9 Political Change and the Objectives of the Continental Welfare State
S.P. Mangen

9.1 INTRODUCTION

The question of whether new goals have displaced long-held welfare objectives in France, the Federal Republic of Germany and Spain forms the basis of this chapter. These countries were selected because, institutionally, they conform to the 'continental' welfare model; also important, the elections of new governments in the early 1980s were accompanied by promises of fundamental change in social policy. Moreover, the longevity of these governments has provided a sufficiently long period for at least the major social goals to be implemented, since government leaders elected at the beginning of the decade were still in office in 1990, although in France, President Mitterand in the mid 1980s had to 'cohabit' with the conservative Prime Minister Chirac.

Each government head had promised a change of direction: in West Germany the Christian Democrat (CDU) Chancellor Kohl in 1982 promised a 'Wendepolitik' – rolling back the limits of the state after what he argued had been the excesses of government dominated by the Social Democrats (SPD). His rhetoric, although more cautious, was evocative of the Thatcherite style. On the other hand, both Mitterand in 1981 and Gonzalez in 1982 were elected on socialist manifestos raising popular expectations of 'progressive' social change.

This chapter briefly outlines the principal features and objectives of these three welfare systems and examines political responses to the broad issues in health and social security that arose in the 1980s. The conclusion is that, in the event, policy innovation at the institutional level has been limited. Furthermore, simplistic left–right party political differences are not substantially supported by the evidence, at least for this limited sample of 'most similar' countries in terms of welfare systems, for these policy sectors and for the limited review period. What will emerge is that, despite their distinct vocabularies of justification, cost containment has been a shared and enduring preoccupation of these political leaders, a concern that can be traced back to the oil crises of the mid 1970s. On the other hand, although a broadly similar package of retrenchment measures has been employed in all three countries, there have not been significant indications of a closer convergence of institutional arrangements. What is apparent is that the high-profile, vote-catching promises of the early 1980s were short-lived and have been progressively displaced in social policy debate by the promotion of a 'technically oriented' strategy.

9.2   CONTINENTAL WELFARE SYSTEMS: PRINCIPAL FEATURES AND OBJECTIVES

Social protection arrangements in the three countries maintain the traditional distinction between: (1) contributory insurance which determines entitlements for the majority of the population; (2) non-contributory benefits enjoyed by civil servants; (3) means-tested social assistance awarded on proof of need; and (4) certain universal benefits such as child allowances. Although the 'continental' model of the welfare state is broadly shared – and, in the case of Spain, was consolidated during the transition to democratic government – there are significant differences in the degree of central government control, the reliance on corporatist policy-making processes and the extent of pluralist arrangements for the supply of welfare. In terms of broad objectives, Esping-Anderson (1990) has classified Germany and France as conservative and strongly corporatist welfare states. Redistributive effects are comparatively weak in the face of the strong adherence to what is termed the equivalence principle (see below), and, equally, social security policy allocates a major role to the social partners. The principles of solidarity, equivalence, devolution of responsibilities and self-administration are the fundamental objectives of these welfare states and are discussed more fully below.

Social catholicism has been an important historical determinant of welfare arrangements. The instrumental papal encyclicals *Rerum Novarum* and *Quadragesimo Anno* identified the appropriate responsibilities of the state, the family and the individual in providing welfare and in regulating relationships between capital and labour. In essence, the state was to play a subsidiary role and preference was to be given to lower-tier authorities, to a plurality of citizen initiatives and to social insurance and other welfare arrangements negotiated between employer and worker. This influence is perhaps most clearly manifest in the German social market economy. Here the operation of the free market is subject to important checks, such as rights to worker participation, and the social partners play an important consultative role in social and labour market policy-making and are also responsible for the administration of the social insurance scheme.

An attempt to demonstrate the resultant complexity of these welfare systems is provided by Table 9.1, which reproduces the EC categorisation of social security arrangements. But even this limited classification conceals the full complexity of the system. Generally, most social risks are indemnified by

Table 9.1 Welfare pluralism – the organisation of social insurance

	FR Germany	France	Spain
Sickness & maternity	Local funds or company schemes or occupational schemes or mutualities	General scheme Occupational schemes Employers' schemes Mutualities	
Sickness			INSALUD (national health agency) or occupational and company schemes
Invalidity & old age	Federal white-collar scheme Local state blue-collar schemes	General scheme Occupational schemes Complementary schemes Employers' schemes	INSS (national social security agency)
Industrial accident & occupational diseases	Trade co-op. Federations or federal, state or local schemes depending on employment sector	General scheme or occupational schemes or employers' schemes	INSS or employers' mutualities
Unemployment & family benefits	Federal Labour Office State Labour Offices Local agencies		
Unemployment		Occupational schemes Complementary schemes	INEM (national agency)
Family benefits Maternity benefit Child benefit	See above	National fund Farmers' scheme	INSS or employers' schemes

(*Sources*: Comparative Tables of the Social Security Schemes in the Member States of the European Communities, Brussels, Commission of the European Communities (undated); Murard N (1989) *La Protection Sociale*, Editions la Découverte, Paris, France)

separate insurance funds which, in the case of France and Germany, are varyingly organised at local, regional and national level. However, insurance schemes are not organised solely by geographical areas. In each country there are also separate schemes for certain occupations such as rail workers, miners, merchant sailors and, in the case of Spain, bullfighters! In Germany it is also possible to contract out of statutory health insurance by contributing to so-called 'replacement funds' (*Ersatzkassen*) and in France there is widespread voluntary insurance to offset the patient's treatment charges. The full extent of this plural provision may be judged by the fact that in the German health system there are over one thousand sickness funds, and French social security incorporates about five hundred schemes. Before 1978 Spain, too, relied on a more plural organisation, and the national social security system still retains important pre-existing arrangements, notably separate employer schemes in certain occupational sectors. Elsewhere in the welfare system a variety of health and social services are supplied by municipalities and a large number of voluntary agencies.

9.2.1 THE EQUIVALENCE PRINCIPLE

As has been demonstrated, the structure of continental welfare systems preserves social differentiation. Equally important in preserving status differences has been the strong adherence to the 'equivalence principle' in social insurance. This means the offering of earnings-related entitlements at a level intended to guarantee a more or less equivalent standard of living in or out of work. Inevitably this principle, jealously guarded by the trade unions, means that the inequalities of the labour market are faithfully reproduced in the welfare system, to the obvious disadvantage of low-paid workers and, therefore, of the majority of women. Yet poverty and inequality as serious political issues have emerged only comparatively recently in the form of a debate about the 'new poverty' afflicting groups in society that welfare states do not – or no longer – serve well.

9.2.2 SOLIDARITY

Social insurance is predicated on the solidarity principle by which individual risks are pooled. As an objective this principle was subject to certain modifications during the 1980s. In France, for example, the term solidarity was also applied to *ad hoc* general taxation measures adopted to clear social insurance budgetary deficits. The generational and gender contracts implied by solidarity were sorely tested in the 1980s and are still burning political issues. Low birth rates in most EC countries – Germany and Italy now have the lowest in the world – and the growth of the elderly cohort, which will accelerate into the first couple of decades of the next century, have endangered the post-war generational contract which is the cornerstone of statutory pay-as-you-go pension schemes. That is to say the currently employed working generation has its contributions to social insurance passed on to the currently retired instead of being accumulated for its own later benefit in a fund. The implicit assumption is that the next generation would do as much for them when their time came – an assumption rather than a contract, and one that is now viewed with some reserve. The gender contract is endangered by the increase in female labour market participation and by the relatively poor economic rewards afforded to women through family policies. Growing differentiation of the welfare system, including increased use of private for-profit services, together with the growing dependence by a minority of the population on means-tested non-contributory benefits, have raised questions about the lack of transparency in the system and the appropriateness of collective 'solidarity' provisions as the basis for future development.

The solidarity principle has also been challenged because of the prominence of differential contribution–benefit ratios within the same insurance risk, which results in unequal treatment for similar individuals. This inequality is further exacerbated by the regressive effect of income ceilings in assessing the insurance contribution rate. Differential treatment has been a predominant feature of the French system and has given rise to a privileged group of *cadres*. Furthermore, both contributors to funds linked with ailing industries and the self-employed are subsidised by the other funds and frequently receive preferential treatment. In Germany white-collar workers contributing to 'replacement' sickness funds are in a favourable position with regard to contribution levies when compared with contributors to the statutory sickness schemes that legally must accept any applicant for membership and must consequently have a heavier risk profile.

9.2.3 REDISTRIBUTION

The element of vertical redistribution in continental social security is limited, though there is an obvious horizontal redistribution in sickness insurance from the contributing well to the recipient ill. In fact, right-wing sources, such as the German Kronsberger group of economists, reject a strong redistributive role for social insurance and argue that, where such an objective is indicated, it is more appropriately pursued through fiscal policy.

During the 1980s the issue of redistribution as an objective has emerged politically in relation to the question of 'new poverty', which has been most clearly highlighted by the fate of the long-term unemployed whose insurance entitlements have expired, or the young unemployed who have never worked to qualify for benefits. Yet new poverty extends to other groups and has strong spatial and gender dimensions in that inhabitants of inner cities and certain regions, together with women (and particularly single mothers and the elderly), are most affected. Although some governments attempted to play down the issue, it is clear that the First Poverty Programme of the EC gave impetus for research into a problem that in several member states was badly neglected. The criterion used was half the average per capita disposable income for a single-person household with a 70 per cent addition for every additional member. By this measure the EC study indicated that one in seven French households were living 'in poverty' in the mid 1970s, compared to over one in twenty in both Germany and the UK (CEC 1981). The EC measure is essentially an index of income inequality rather than a subsistence minimum, which is why certain governments reacted unfavourably to the findings (Brown 1986). In this regard it is important to note that income inequalities in France (and Italy) in this period were the largest of OECD European countries. As a then non-member Spain did not participate in the first programme, but a review of national surveys in the 1980s indicates between 14 and 20 per cent living at or below the EC level (Munoz de Bustillo 1990).

Perhaps it is the regional aspect of inequality that has the greatest political consequences. In *France*, the formerly prosperous North and Lorraine, where heavy industry is concentrated, have been particularly hit since the recession of the 1970s; in *Germany*, the Hansa towns and the Ruhr. This is reflected in the spatial distribution of social assistance expenditure, and, in France, of the recently introduced national income benefit (RMI) (*Données Sociales* 1990). A similar situation pertains in the Basque Territories and Catalonia, but in *Spain* it is the South that has been most adversely affected by the legacy of profound underdevelopment, in part due to the failure to implement land reform and, thus, eradicate *latifundismo*. Carabantes (1984) for example reports that in 1984, 80 per cent of Andalusian peasants were hirelings and that half of all irrigable land was owned by only 2 per cent of landlords. In this region over 46 per cent of households were poor in 1984 according to the EC criterion (Munoz de Bustillo 1990).

9.2.4   EFFICIENCY AND COST-CONTAINMENT

An overarching objective of social policies formulated in the 1980s was the search for greater efficiency in the use of welfare resources. This was progressively incorporated into the wider goal of restraining the growth of social expenditure, most typically by limiting increases in expenditure to the annual growth rate in GDP. In France and Germany social protection now accounts for over one quarter of total GDP. In Spain it still consumes less than one-fifth. Table 9.2 contains details, and there is further discussion of financing later in the chapter. The problem of cost-containment after previous heavy expansion is the best-documented international aspect of the welfare state 'crisis'. A common strategy has been an increasing reliance on state subsidies (note that Table 9.2 lists data from the EC for the whole of *social protection activity* and not specifically for *social insurance*). The creeping fiscalisation of the system has now become a permanent feature, the objective, in part, being to stabilise funding and to reduce employer contributions, which some have argued will be a serious curb on international competitiveness in the wake of the Single Market.

Table 9.2 Continental welfare states in the eighties: a comparative audit

		BRD	F	E	UK
A:	Per capita GDP US $ 1987 purchasing power parities	13323	12803	8681	12340
B:	GDP average annual volume growth, 1982-7 (%)	2.1	1.6	2.9	3.2
C:	Total social protection expenditure, 1988 % GDP *	28.1	28.3	17.7	23.6
D:	Total health expenditure % GDP, 1986	8.1	8.5	6.0	6.1
E:	Social protection funding, 1987				
	% employer	41.1	52.2	52.2	27.9
	% employee	30.4	27.0	19.4	17.0
	% public funds	25.2	18.2	26.0	43.4
	% other[†]	3.2	2.6	2.4	11.8
F:	Social protection benefits per inhabitant in terms of purchasing power parities, 1987 ECU	4603	4279	1906	3452
G:	Unemployment rate 1988 %[‡]	6.2	10.3	20.1	8.3
H:	Female unemployment rate 1987 (%)	31.9	45.5	61.9	42.6
J:	Male youth unemployment rate 1987 %	31.9	45.5	61.9	42.6
J:	Male youth unemployment rate 1987 %	7.0	17.6	31.3	13.5

(*Sources*: C, E, F: *Rapid Reports: Population and Social Conditions*, no 3, Eurostat, Commission of the European Communities, 1990. A, B, D, G, H, J: OECD in figures, supplement to *OECD Observer*, no 158, Paris, OECD, 1989)
*UK and Spanish statistics are for 1987
[†]This category comprises receipts from interest on capital, which in the case of the UK is derived from occupational pension funds
[‡]OECD Standardised Unemployment Rates except for Spain, where national definition applies
For information on terminology see Note 2 on p 189.

Successive governments in *France* have adopted a cocktail of familiar retrenchment measures in welfare policy. Chapellière (1989) notes that between 1976 and 1989 there were five restrictions imposed on social security entitlements and ten increases in the contribution rate. Except for large families, most sections of the population have been affected in one way or another by expenditure curbs. Although French GDP growth rates in the 1980s have been below the OECD average, total public social expenditure in 1987 amounted to nearly 30 per cent of GDP, a figure slightly inferior to that for 1985, but still higher than that for 1981 (OECD, 1989a). Moreover, insurance funds were again in serious deficit in 1988, and a special tax levy together with increases in pension premiums were among the short-term measures adopted, pending the recommendations of a commission of enquiry which was to propose comprehensive social security reform.

In *Spain*, public expenditure has increased rapidly since 1975 as a consequence of efforts to construct a post-Franco democracy. The Spanish economy, a high-flier before the oil crisis, was especially adversely affected in the late 1970s, which was precisely the period when democratic arrangements were being institutionalised. However, entry into the Community stimulated economic growth and in the late 1980s it averaged over 4 per cent per annum, the highest recorded by any OECD state. Yet Gonzalez's prime objective has been to avoid a speedy expansion of the welfare state in the interests of consolidating these economic gains. Thus, Spanish social expenditure remained well below the OECD European mean, consuming in 1986 only 20.4 per cent of GDP (OECD 1989b). This modest welfare effort in the face of relatively healthy economic performance prompted the OECD to exhort the Spanish government to increase social expenditure as part of a wider national infrastructural investment.

By the early 1980s public social expenditure in *Germany* (see Note 2) reached 25 per cent of GDP. But the goal of budgetary retrenchment consistently pursued by Chancellor Kohl is reflected in subsequent trends and by 1986 OECD data indicate that total public social expenditure was 1.4 percentage points less than in 1980, pensions and education having taken the brunt of the cuts (OECD 1990). In the late 1980s budgetary pressures were relieved somewhat by improved economic performance, although OECD projections, made, significantly, before unification, indicated slower growth in the 1990s.

9.2.5 THE ADMINISTRATIVE EFFICIENCY OF THE WELFARE STATE

During the 1980s there was popular disenchantment with the alienating effects of large-scale bureaucratic welfare states. In the countries reviewed here, as in others, there has been growing concern about quality, flexibility and the choice offered by welfare services. Extensions of coverage all too often led in some countries to a 'massification' of service delivery, particularly in health and education. Consequently, there has been increasing resort to the private sector and a deepening institutionalisation of dual welfare systems in which the public sector may ultimately become the sole preserve of those who lack the ability to buy their way out. Disillusionment has been compounded in southern Europe by the popular scepticism about state and local authorities and their ability to intervene fairly and effectively. Politicians and public bureaucracies have generally been held in poor regard. The importance of political 'families' and the prime concern to safeguard the interests of 'lo nuestro' extends to the nomination of officials according to local party strength and permeates discretionary judgements about welfare entitlements, particularly as regards pensions and the distribution of regional aid.

In the light of these negative attitudes the objective of improving the administrative capacity of welfare systems has been pursued through a variety of policies which have different emphases and meanings as one moves through the political spectrum. Among these strategies are the promotion of self-help and mutual-help, the improvement of public participation in social planning, decentralisation of policy-making responsibilities, greater contracting-out to the private and voluntary sectors, and moves to establish a more locally based delivery of health and social services in part relying on community care.

Regional decentralisation, for example, became an important issue in many countries in the late 1960s. In *France*, an extensive debate launched since the 'events' of 1968 about *autogestion* eventually led in 1982 to the national implementation of devolution. Decentralisation to the regions (autonomous communities) was guaranteed in *Spain* under the 1978 constitution in an attempt to reconcile political and cultural competition between the centre and certain regions where a strong separate national identity persists. *West Germany*, since its inception, was a federal republic. Prime responsibility for policy making in health care, education and the personal social services lay with the federal states, the Länder, although the federal government employed a variety of devices to promote harmonisation of service provision.

There have been misgivings about the ultimate intentions of governments in espousing these new policies. Self-help and community care, for example – particular favourites of Chancellor Kohl – are suspected of being cost-cutting exercises, the latter to the detriment of women, who provide most of the caring. Similarly, selective privatisation is viewed as a means by which the state can surrender responsibilities. Furthermore, decentralisation policies may have exacerbated the task of effective planning by significantly expanding the range and tiers of agencies that need to be incorporated into the process.

9.3   SOCIAL SECURITY: A SELECTIVE COMPARISON

Cross-national comparisons of social expenditure are fraught with problems of reliability and should be very broadly interpreted, since there is a lack of functional equivalence in definitions both among national data sources and between major international organisations such as the OECD and EC (see Note 2). Table 9.2 provides a broad comparative welfare audit of the three countries and also includes data for the UK.

It is apparent that, according to EC definitions, social protection benefits per inhabitant in 1987 were highest in Germany (4603 ECU) and France (4279 ECU), both being substantially above the Community average. The corresponding figure for Spain is one of the lowest in the EC. Total social protection expenditure as a percentage of GDP in 1988 in both Germany and France (at 28 per cent) was significantly above that of the UK and well in excess of that of Spain, one of the welfare laggards among the Twelve. Total volume of expenditure is determined by four factors, each of varying significance in this sample of countries: demographic trends, maturation of social insurance schemes, extension of coverage and the quality of entitlements. In assessing the adequacy of benefit provisions, of course, account also needs to be taken of the availability of allied services in kind.

A particular feature of continental insurance systems is the heavy reliance on employer contributions' which, by international standards, are exceptionally high in France and Spain (and, incidentally, Italy). In *France* these contributions in 1987 represented almost 21 per cent of GDP, which was higher than in any other EC state. As stated earlier, since the mid 1980s French governments have instigated a policy of reducing the employer insurance burden. For example, the unemployment scheme which is employer-funded receives a 45 per cent state subsidy (Murard 1989). Other action taken in the 1980s included the removal of income ceilings, criticised for their regressiveness, in the calculation of contributions (except for pensions).

Social security contributions in *Spain* amounted to 13 per cent of GDP in 1987, having risen sharply since the 1970s. Improvements in the quality of benefit and extension of entitlements have resulted in mounting social security deficits, which have had to be made good by government subsidies. Government contributions to the insurance system increased by over 100 per cent between 1983 and 1987 to peak in 1986 at almost one-quarter of total expenditure. Cost-containment measures, implemented most notably in health and pension reforms, reduced the rate to about 20 per cent. However, total outlays on pensions and health care are likely to increase more than GDP, given their modest baseline at the time of Franco's death and the subsequent political pressures to extend coverage and improve standards. In fact, health expenditure already doubled between 1975 and 1990, albeit from a low base in international terms. In the 1990s, the government's medium-term plan is progressively to fund health care, social assistance and personal social services largely from general taxation.

German social insurance contributions accounted for over 17 per cent of GDP in 1987 and, although being contained in the 1990s, are, like the French, among the highest of the OECD countries. Unlike in France and Spain, social security budgets in West Germany were in surplus in the late 1980s, although the balance was subsequently reduced by half owing to improvements in benefit levels and increases in the number of pensioners. Deficits in the unemployment funds have arisen, partly as a consequence of the assumption by the Länder of responsibility for employment training programmes, previously financed by the federal government. Federal subsidies of social insurance in recent years have averaged about 12 per cent of their expenditure, but this is set to rise with major reforms in health provision and in pensions which were introduced in the late 1980s (see below).

9.3.1 PENSIONS SYSTEMS

France has a complex pensions system. Although most of the insured are members of the statutory general funds (régime général), complementary pensions play an important role. These schemes, jointly administered by the social partners on a pay-as-you-go basis, have been obligatory since 1972 for members of the general fund (Lynes 1985). Many of the larger companies offer generous complementary schemes and some also offer *ex gratia* benefits which, combined with the statutory and complementary pensions, can amount to up to 80 per cent of final salary. The administrative complexity of the system is illustrated by the fact that many pensioners receive several separate entitlements. In 1983, for example, 40 per cent of pensioners received almost two-thirds of the total number of pensions disbursed (IRES 1984).

French pensions are among the most generous of the OECD countries. During the 1980s the difference between contributory and non-contributory benefits declined sharply, as the result of the Socialists' attempt to honour their commitment substantially to improve the means-tested minimum pension paid to those without or with only partial entitlements under social insurance. In their first two years in office the level of this benefit rose by 50 per cent and the majority of other pensioners have seen their entitlements increase more than average wages. As well as reducing the pension age, the Socialists initially also encouraged early retirement. Thus expenditure on these schemes was among the highest in the EC in the mid 1980s (Kessler and Masson 1985).

The maturation of pensions has become increasingly important in France. Pension expenditure is projected to double in the period 1990 to 2030, the maturation effect being the prime determinant until 2005, with the demographic factor being more significant thereafter. OECD projections estimate that pensions as a proportion of GDP will rise from 12 per cent in the early 1990s to 17 per cent in 2010 and 27 per cent in 2040 (OECD 1989a).

Despite the change of policy in favour of cost-containment, French governments have been unable to control pensions expenditure. Stricter indexation criteria and contribution increases have both been rapidly absorbed. In the Tenth Plan (1989-92) the implications of increasing the pension age were considered, but at the time of writing no ultimate decision on this sensitive political issue has been forthcoming.

Since the Transition, electoral pressures in *Spain* to improve the value of pensions have resulted in a substantial increase in expenditure although, by international standards, expenditure ratios remain low. Projections in the mid 1980s suggested that expenditure on the state schemes would reach 11 per cent of GDP by 1993, when persons of pensionable age would comprise about 15 per cent of the population. The consequences of current demographic trends are only now beginning to be fully appreciated. Until the 1980s, the percentage of pensioners in the population was comparatively low, but subsequently it has been increasing at an annual rate of about 5 per cent (McVicar 1985).

The problems of financing pensions have become increasingly difficult politically. In the early 1980s benefits and eligibility rules were relatively generous, allowing recipients, for example, to choose their best income years in calculating entitlements. Under the 1984 Social and Economic Accord (AES) between the government and the social partners, a tripartite system was envisaged which in the long run would comprise the state scheme, a complementary occupational scheme and voluntary private pensions. In the event a contentious reform was implemented in 1985 which reduced state benefits by about 10 per cent. The qualifying period for a full pension was increased to (a still generous) 15 years and the number of 'best years' taken into consideration was also increased. Indexation was based on official inflation targets rather than actual rates. In advance of the achievement of the Single Market the government has also legislated for private pension plans and, for the first time, companies that wish to introduce such a scheme will have to offer coverage to all their staff and not, as has largely been the practice, only to white-collar workers.

The lack of equity remains a persistent feature of Spanish pensions. A survey in Barcelona revealed that the position of elderly women was particularly precarious: 28 per cent of women in the sample of over-65-year-olds did not receive a social security pension, compared with only 4 per cent of men, and many were in some form of residential care only because they lacked the means to lead an independent life (Barcelona 1985). Nationally, government statistics indicated that in 1988 there were 400,000 old people who did not receive any form of public pension. In 1989 the government announced its intention of extending the minimum pension to them.

German pension entitlements can reach 80 per cent of previous average income after a minimum of 25 years of contributions, or 5 years for women. Although pension schemes were in deficit in the late 1970s and again in 1982 and 1983, these problems have been less acute than those in the health sector. None the less, it is estimated that by 2030 there will be 117 pensioners for every 100 workers, a situation that, under existing arrangements, would impose such a penalising contribution rate as to raise serious questions about the equity and sustainability of the intergenerational contract. Consideration was given throughout the 1980s to a variety of solutions to stabilise the system. The reform eventually announced in 1989 will progressively increase the retirement age to 65 for both men and women by 2012 (2006 for men). Henceforth, indexation will be based on net wage levels and although early retirement will still be possible, it will be made less attractive. Moreover, there will be incentives for people of pensionable age to continue working. The new pensions formula reduces the projected increases in contribution rates; however, they are still set to rise from 18 to 21 per cent of the total wage bill. The federal subsidy will amount to almost 20 per cent of pensions expenditure, compared with 14.5 per cent subsidy under the old system. Other elements of the reform include the upgrading of low pensions, the phasing in of a second and third 'baby year' for mothers, and pension credits for carers of the elderly and disabled in the community. On the other hand, students are to lose their rights to pension credits.

There has been a large measure of collusion among the major parties to portray pension problems as essentially 'technical' rather than 'political'. Even so, critics – and they include some within the progressive 'social' wing of the Christian Democratic Union – fear that the reforms implemented will prove to be no more than a short-term palliative since they have failed to confront fully the fundamental issue of intergenerational equity.

9.3.2 UNEMPLOYMENT PROTECTION

Table 9.2 provides an indication of the dimensions of the intransigent problem of long-term unemployment, the common lot of the three countries reviewed here. Some governments have sought to make the problem look less serious by stressing the importance of the 'submerged economy', claiming that official statistics greatly underestimate true economic activity rates. This sector of the economy in southern Europe incorporates a large part of the traditional *doppio lavoro* and represents a serious leak of fiscal resources. For example, the submerged economy is estimated by the OECD to account for 20 per cent of Spanish GDP (OECD, 1989b).

Despite electoral promises of job creation, the number of unemployed in *France* increased by over half a million during the first four years of the Socialist government, to reach almost two and a half million in 1986. The official rate peaked in 1987 at 10.7 per cent, though by April 1990 it was down to 9.1 per cent. The high rate of youth unemployment, particularly among females, has also declined, with the OECD reporting a figure of 18 per cent. However, long-term unemployment has continued to rise, with the consequence that coverage provided by unemployment insurance declined substantially in the early 1980s. The research institute IRES (1984) calculated that in 1984, 46 per cent of women and 49 per cent of men were not indemnified by unemployment insurance, although the subsequent introduction of the national minimum benefit (RMI) has improved their lot.

In real terms, French unemployment compensation is below the EC average. In 1984, in the face of pressure from the employers' federation, the government divided the benefits system so that insurance funds provided allowances for those whose eligibility has not expired and a less generous scheme funded by the state from general revenue provides for others, the majority being the young unemployed whose entitlement to benefits is linked to job training schemes, or the long-term unemployed. In 1988, over one and three-quarter million people participated in public labour market schemes and the expenditure allocated, though now declining, remains one of the largest in GDP terms among OECD nations. The government has acted to make the employment of older workers more attractive by assuming responsibility for the payment of the employer social security contributions for new hirings of workers over 50. The increase in the number of unemployed in this age group has largely been due to the relaxation of redundancy rules in 1986 (OECD, 1989a).

For much of the 1980s the unemployment rate in *Spain* remained above 20 per cent and was one of the chief indictments of the Socialist government, despite its activity in substantially extending the public training schemes. It has been estimated that over half of all new employment opportunities in 1988 were provided by job creation schemes (OECD 1989b). The official unemployment rate for the first quarter of 1990 declined to just over 16 per cent, although much of this was due to a sharp increase in part-time and temporary work and to the allocation of the young unemployed to training programmes. In 1990 about one-quarter of all wage earners held temporary contracts, which was almost double the EC average. The government can, however, claim some success in reducing the rate of long-term unemployment. In 1987, over 60 per cent of claimants had been registered for more than one year, whilst in 1990 the rate was about 35 per cent. Again, gender, age and regional factors are significant: in 1990, for example, one third of the Andalusian economically active population was registered unemployed.

The unemployment benefit system was reformed and extended in 1984, with an apparent government commitment to increase eligibility for unemployment benefits to 48 per cent of the unemployed. However, five years later only about one-third of the unemployed were entitled to benefit. The issue of unemployment has maintained a higher political profile than in northern countries, contributing significantly to the disillusionment with the achievements of the post-Franco state. The unions claimed that the Socialists had reneged on their promises of 1984, but the government responded that their agreement had referred to an absolute figure and not to a percentage. In 1984 this figure had corresponded to a 48 per cent level, but this percentage had been overtaken by subsequent expansion in the labour market. The resentment rumbled on until the 1988 general strike, when, as stated earlier, the eligibility issue was a central factor. The government has consistently refused to give in to the demand but, more recently, has attempted reconciliation with the unions by policies designed to increase the number of temporary contracts being transformed into permanent jobs, and by subsidising to the tune of 50 per cent the employer's social insurance contributions.

Perhaps the persistence of long-term unemployment in *Germany* demonstrates most forcibly the intransigence of the problem. Even though GDP growth in 1988 was the highest achieved for a decade, unemployment declined only slowly. In the first quarter of 1990 it stood at just over 6 per cent. Critically, the proportion of the long-term unemployed rose slightly to comprise about 35 per cent of the total. German unemployment trends share with other countries a strong regional dimension: the 1988 rate was only 5 per cent in Baden-Württemberg, a third of that recorded in Bremen. The problem of expiry of entitlement reached serious proportions in the 1980s. In 1985, for example, only about one-third of the unemployed received the full unemployment benefit, 28 per cent received the unemployment assistance which follows on when rights to full benefit have expired, and is paid at lower rates. No less than 38 per cent were dependent on local means-tested social assistance, women being over-represented in this latter category. The government limited the earnings-related component of unemployment benefit in the mid 1980s and, generally, real increases in benefits and social assistance during the decade compare unfavourably with those in pensions (Alber 1986).

More positively, a partial retirement scheme, replacing the previous early retirement policy, was introduced and there has been at least a doubling of the unemployment benefit eligibility period of entitlement to two and a half years for the older worker. There has also been a reduction in contribution period, and a range of job creation and training schemes has been introduced by federal and local authorities. The amount spent on these schemes increased by three-quarters between 1985 and 1988 and in GDP terms is well above the OECD average (OECD 1990). Finally, the government announced new subsidies to employers for the hiring of the long-term unemployed.

9.3.3   FROM SOCIAL 'ASSISTANCE' TO SOCIAL 'REINSERTION'

German social assistance has continued to be a 'passive' benefit funded by Länder and local authorities, although since the late 1980s substantial federal subsidies have been forthcoming for Länder hard-hit by heavy calls on their resources, largely as a result of claims by the long-term unemployed. There have been innovations in social assistance through the introduction of a second generation of discretionary benefits which diverge from the traditional 'passive' notion of assistance by incorporating the principle of social 'reinsertion', a broad concept that extends beyond mere occupational rehabilitation measures.

In *France* the most significant development has been the introduction of the *revenu minimum garanti d'insertion* (RMI) in 1988. Prior to its enactment, France lacked a national generalised social assistance scheme and provided only local *aide sociale* to limited categories of the poor. The promise to create the RMI was one of the major social policy proposals of the 1988 presidential campaign and was intended to exemplify Mitterand's commitment during his second septennate to concrete action designed to promote new ideas of citizenship that would address the growing problem of social exclusion. Legislation followed soon after, although there had been concern during parliamentary debates about the vague notion of 'insertion' and some feared that, in operation, the benefit would have more to do with social control than with social compensation. There was also concern that the introduction of the RMI could run the risk of institutionalising social marginalisation by creating a permanent underclass of dependent recipients. In the event, the measure was unanimously adopted by the National Assembly.

The RMI is based on the premise that marginalisation is more a function of the deficiencies of social policies than of moral shortcomings on the part of the individual. Conceptually, it occupies the middle ground between welfare assistance and active labour market policy. The RMI derives its logic from three distinct welfare principles: the citizen's right to work; entitlement to benefit through citizenship; and – as it is financed by a wealth tax – the principle of social solidarity. The benefit is available to all French people over the age of twenty-five and to those under that age who have responsibilities for children. The younger age groups were excluded because they had preferential entitlement to employment training programmes. The scheme, to be evaluated after three years, is administered by the *départements*. Local committees formulate a practical 'contract of reinsertion' appropriate to the individual applicant, on the basis of which the benefit, set at 80 per cent of the SMIC national minimum wage, is awarded. However, the use of the word 'contract' has been criticised, since in the case of the RMI the agreements are not legally binding. In the first year of operation there were almost half a million beneficiaries, 80 per cent of whom were the long-term unemployed (Milano 1989).

In *Spain* the creation of the French RMI attracted considerable interest with pressure on the government to adopt a similar measure. This has been resisted on the ground that the benefit entails the serious danger of actually according official recognition to marginalisation. Nevertheless, some autonomous communities (regions), utilising their constitutional powers, have adopted the policy. The Basque Territories and Cantabria have already implemented their own versions of the RMI. Similar plans in several other regions are at an advanced stage.

9.3.4   HEALTH

France and West Germany have been relatively generous spenders on health care when compared with other EC states, and Spain has been below average. Table 9.2 provides further details. During the 1980s pressure on health budgets came from both demand and supply factors. The increasing number of the elderly, for example, has had serious implications for the provision of long-term facilities, and, critically, their distribution between the sectors of medical 'treatment' and of social service 'care', with the corresponding issue of the appropriate division of financial liability between social insurance, on the one hand, and social assistance on the other (see, for example, Mangen

1985). Inflationary factors in health service supply have in part derived from the 'hospital-centred' health systems which have restricted the development of cheaper preventive and primary care alternatives. But equally indicted were the methods employed to finance treatment. The fee for each 'item-of-service' payable to doctors, particularly in the private sector, together with the payment to hospitals of a daily fee for each occupied bed, provided an obvious stimulus to over-supply. From the mid 1970s, governments acted to reduce these perverse supply incentives: France and Germany introduced annual global budgets, initially for the public hospital sector; and Spain is in the process of transferring health costs to general tax revenues. All have taken measures to contain annual increases in out-patient fees and to scrutinise the fee schedule more carefully. A further stimulus to supply has been the rapid growth of the private sectors, in part due to the perceived low quality of public services, but also in part to the serious over-supply of new doctors whom the statutory sector cannot absorb. The combined effect of these factors was evident in the continual rise in health expenditures over the 1970s and 1980s at a rate considerably in excess of GDP growth. Critically, most countries can report only modest or short-term success in containing these trends.

In *France* health expenditure in the 1980s, already among the highest in GDP terms, increased more rapidly than the EC average. Despite below-average economic growth rates of less than 2 per cent between 1982 and 1987, annual health expenditure increased by over 7 per cent and, in some years, by as much as 10 per cent. After an expansionary phase, cost-containment has been a prime consideration since 1983. For example, there have been 'exceptional' tax levies in certain years to compensate for budgetary deficits. There have also been increases in patient contributions to treatment costs and hospital 'hotel' costs, restriction of reimbursable medical and pharmaceutical treatment and the adoption of global budgeting in the in-patient sector. Yet, in combination these measures have had only temporary effect. One reason is that, because the French now have to pay a substantial proportion of their treatment fees, almost three-quarters take out mutuality insurance which covers these costs, thus weakening what is supposed to be a demand-limiting reimbursement system. Despite the wide-reaching rationalisation plan enacted by the Chirac government, which included the controversial policy of limiting full reimbursement for that distinctively French category of 'long and costly' illnesses, expenditure has once again been increasing. Nor – an important point – have pharmaceutical disbursements shown any long-term signs of abating.

In *Spain*, the health system retains features of the Franco era. One of the most significant developments since the Transition has been the decentralisation of policy making. Unlike in France, expenditure was more stable in the 1980s than in the 1970s. By 1989 three-quarters of expenditure was derived from the state budget, with only a quarter coming from social security contributions. The medium-term objective is to reduce the insurance element to about 15 per cent of total expenditure (de Miguel *et al* 1989). Treatment is free in facilities affiliated to the social security régime. However, many of the larger companies run private insurance schemes that employ their own doctors. The private sector as a whole has grown in the 1980s, despite the government's aim of stemming the tide of two-tier medicine by moving towards a universal socialised system and establishing more public services to reduce the need to contract out to the private sector. However, the 1986 reforms, which were primarily designed to control expenditure, failed to honour a commitment to achieve universal coverage and this objective was pushed further into the future, to be phased in gradually. A new emphasis in policy was the contracting-out of public sector responsibilities to the private health and care sector. Previous reservations about promoting these facilities now appear to have been overcome and subsidies have been allocated to private services, principally for the long-term care of the elderly.

In *Germany* annual increases in health expenditure in the 1980s on occasions reached 8 per cent, which, as data in Table 9.2 indicate, was several times greater than annual GDP growth. Apart from constraints imposed by the financing system, powerful health supply lobbies among medical practitioners, drug companies, health facilities and the insurance funds have reduced political opportunities to implement comprehensive reform. Pharmaceutical products account for a significant proportion of German health expenditure; prescription costs are the highest of any EC country, and in percentage terms are twice those of France, the second highest spender.

In 1985 an annual budget for hospitals was established and the sickness funds are no longer required to make good any excessive in-patient expenditures. In the 1980s demand for private treatment grew and there was also increased reliance on private facilities for long-term care, especially for the elderly (Brauns and Kramer 1989).

The most important reforms of the health system were implemented in 1989. Thenceforth, increases in the insurance premium were to be held strictly in line with average salary rises. Restrictions in respect of certain reimbursable treatments were also introduced and an 'approved' medication list was established. Moreover, a temporary 20 per cent prescription charge was levied. The government's objective was to achieve savings of up to 14 billion DM, half of which was reserved for a 1 per cent reduction in insurance premiums, whilst the remainder was allocated to improve facilities for preventive health and to a new scheme for long-term community care for the elderly and severely handicapped. Informal carers were offered tax incentives and an attendance allowance. Up to twenty-five hours a month of professional care was guaranteed, supplemented by four weeks' annual holiday relief. The package, which was clearly aimed at serving a variety of objectives in health and welfare policy, was criticised by the Social Democrats and the Greens for what they viewed as the shirking of essential structural reforms and for being a meretricious attempt to transfer the burden of chronic care to the family. Concern was also expressed that savings would not accrue in anything but the short run, and once the package was in operation, the government would be unable to resist demands to subsidise the community care programme from general taxation.

9.4 POLITICAL CHANGE AND WELFARE OBJECTIVES: THE 1980S AND BEYOND

9.4.1 MITTERAND'S FRANCE
In comparison with Germany the process of social policy making tends to be more adversarial in France and also appears more loosely coordinated. In fact, Heidenheimer and his colleagues (1990) argue that the French central government has acquired a 'thoroughly ambivalent status as regards welfare policy making'.

When they assumed office in 1981 the Socialists were confronted with the effects of austerity measures implemented by the outgoing Prime Minister, Barre. Mitterand's electoral programme – the 110 Propositions – had heralded a 'new citizenship' which would radicalise the nature of French social policy and create a 'France of the People'. Swiftly dispensing with Barre's National Plan, the new government embarked on a short-term flirtation with an increasingly unfashionable Keynesian economic strategy. The first year of the septennate was to be the main period during which electoral promises were fulfilled; policy thereafter progressively deviated from the election propositions. Substantial increases in family allowances, disability benefits, the minimum pension and housing allowances were announced. The retirement age was reduced to sixty. A policy of decentralisation, long discussed, was finally implemented in 1982 and was to prove the 'grand affair' of the first septennate. Under the new arrangements most of the responsibilities of the government-appointed prefect were transferred to the elected councils of the départements, with a planning function being undertaken by regional authorities.

Economic realities were soon to catch up with the government. Official growth projections, on which social expenditure plans had been based, proved over-optimistic. In the face of a growing budgetary deficit, cost-containment displaced welfare expansion as the highest priority. In 1983 Beregovoy, a fiscal conservative, replaced Questiaux as head of a newly formed superministry combining health and social security. His austerity measures contributed to the growing dissension within the Cabinet which, with Mauroy's replacement as Prime Minister by Fabius in 1984, signalled the end of communist participation in government. Critics argued that socialist principles were being sacrificed and that, in essence, the Socialists were implementing Barrist neo-liberal policies. None the less, even in this period, there were welfare gains. Thus, a new child benefit was introduced, and a special education allowance for parents with three or more children.

There is a general consensus that the achievements of the Socialists up to the 1986 parliamentary election defeat were only modest when compared with what had been promised. Kessler and Masson (1985) identify a positive redistributive effect of policies in the initial years in favour of low income groups and large, though not necessarily poor, families. However, during this period real disposable incomes declined for the first time since the Second World War (Cerny and Schain 1985) and austerity policies produced a decline of 1 per cent in social expenditure in both 1985 and 1986 when compared with 1984. It must be conceded that the early and mid 1980s were scarcely a propitious time to implement radical and expensive social programmes and both Collins (1987) and Freeman (1990) concur that the Socialists' views on welfare were more appropriate to the economic climate of the late 1960s. Crucially, they had failed to get to grips with the complexities of the social security system and its structural deficiencies which rendered budgetary deficits a chronic rather than a short-term problem.

The Socialists had hit their own constituency hardest, since they had encouraged wage restraint in return for promises of improvements in the social wage that, to a large extent, did not materialise. They were rewarded with the loss of the parliamentary elections in 1985 in which the conservative RPR-UDF was returned to government. Under Chirac the policies of 'modernisation' and 'consolidation' enacted by the previous government were continued. Certain symbolic gestures were legislated for: private pay beds were restored in publicly funded hospitals, and Chirac, in what were often crudely pro-natalist exhortations, invested in family policy with, for example, the introduction of allowances for child-minders. As regards social security policy, the conservative government was not very productive. The recommendations of an advisory committee and an inquiry were largely ignored, in the wake of the presidential campaign. These recommendations were for an increasing privatisation of the system, but Social Minister Seguin favoured a more cautious consensual approach to reform. These contentious problems and the likelihood that unpopular long-term decisions would have to be made with a presidential election imminent persuaded Chirac to hive off the issue by appointing an expert advisory committee and calling an 'estates general' of social security. In the event, a range of contribution increases and special tax levies were announced but neither of the two bodies had any significant impact, since Chirac's attention was diverted to the presidential campaign.

Mitterand's second presidential success and the return of a Socialist government in 1988, albeit without an absolute majority, saw the social democratic 'Rocardian' wing of the party consolidate its position. Social security issues featured prominently in the election, with a promise to introduce the national minimum benefit (RMI) described above. On the other hand, the Tenth Plan (1989–92) contains only modest aims for improving the quality of services within existing institutional arrangements.

9.4.2 SPAIN: 'EL GIRO SOCIAL'

Following the Caudillo's death in 1975, Spain experienced a rapid social transformation that, by necessity, included dismantling Franco's corporatist welfare system. The principal aims of this process were to achieve administrative unification of the complex organisation of welfare, to depoliticise its administration, decentralise policy making, and to increase public sector responsibilities (Casado 1987). Existing government ministries were reorganised and a new social ministry was set up to supervise the control of the social security system by the social partners.

Mounting economic problems – originating within the last governments of the old régime, but played down politically – gained pace during the period of the Transition. In an attempt to sustain a broad consensual political approach the centrist government continued to minimise the urgency of the situation and between 1977 and 1982 social expenditure increased from 12 to 17 per cent, the extra monies being obtained by running a large public deficit.

With an electoral campaign promoting their image as the party of social change and a promise to create 800,000 jobs, the Socialists (PSOE) were elected with an absolute majority in 1982, an event which many feel represented the final legitimisation of the new Spanish democracy. Once in office and faced with the straitened circumstances of a country that was already one of the poorest in Western Europe, Gonzalez adopted a cautious policy. From the beginning he was to be no Mitterand, and in the course of the decade he progressively embraced an unambiguous neo-liberalism. Rather than committing himself to substantial increases in social expenditure, Gonzalez opted for selective targets, the prime consideration being to reduce mounting public deficits. Welfare reforms, when they came, were scarcely radical and the manner in which they were introduced upset the socialist trade union, the UGT. For example, union leaders protested that the 1985 pensions reform had been introduced without the consultation with the social partners that was required under the agreement of 1984. Both this reform and new health policies announced a year later were dismissed by the unions as cost-control measures designed to encourage private provision by making the statutory services less attractive.

Despite their increasingly unpopular measures, the Socialists secured a second absolute majority in 1986, in part due to the disarray of the centre-right. Gonzalez continued to pursue policies that many thought indistinguishable from those of the centrist UCD government in the late 1970s. Trade union compliance in moderating wage claims led to widening income inequalities and, consequently, to a deepening rift within the government.

Apart from general disenchantment with the growing disparity between wages and profits, the unions were aggrieved by proposals for what they regarded as an exploitative youth employment scheme. There were also complaints about increases in taxation and other levies in return for what were regarded as poor-quality public services. Among union demands were improvements in the minimum wage and the extension of eligibility for unemployment benefit discussed earlier. Popular discontent culminated in the one-day general strike late in 1988, which received almost total support from the working population but, in the event, did not force any significant change of position on the part of government. However, after his third election victory in 1989, albeit without an absolute majority, Gonzalez became more conciliatory. Social expenditure increased, largely due to the increased public financing of health care and the growing number of pensioners. Pension and minimum wage increases were also announced, but the government resisted demands for the creation of a national minimum benefit, which, as discussed earlier, has been implemented at the regional level by several of the autonomous communities.

9.4.3 KOHL'S 'WENDEPOLITIK'

In West Germany, which provides the epitome of 'middle way' consensus politics, social policy-making over much of the past forty years has been typically characterised by an administrative rather than adversarial approach. This consensus tradition is common to both broadly based major parties, and is also reflected in relations between the social partners (Bulmer 1989).

Some cracks in this placid cross-party consensus on welfare issues began to appear in the late 1970s. First, there was the increasingly vocal disenchantment of the junior coalition partner – the liberal party (FDP), whose neo-liberal wing was in the ascendancy – with Schmidt's economic and social policies. Later, a fledgling political force, the Greens, was to present a challenge from the left. Late in 1982 the FDP deserted its alliance with the Social Democrats and, again as junior partners, formed a government under the conservative (CDU) Kohl. Kohl promised the politics of change (*Wendepolitik*): the rigidities of an over-regulated market were to be swept away and the social excesses of the '*Vaterstaat*' were to be eradicated by a renewed emphasis on self-help. However, despite his pronouncements, it soon became apparent that Kohl would not institute radical welfare reform, but limit himself to extending the retrenchment measures imposed by his predecessor. There were cuts in the federal budget allocated to labour market and unemployment measures. Subsidies to pension funds were reduced and stricter entitlement criteria were announced. Pensioners became liable to pay sickness insurance contributions. There were also cuts in health service entitlements.

After his initial two years in office the Chancellor refrained from further substantial cuts. His room for manoeuvre in a plural welfare system that allocates such a strong role to the Länder was in any case limited. Thus, Alber (1986) assesses that by the mid 1980s Kohl had implemented only half of the public expenditure curbs he had originally been seeking. Indeed, as a result of embarrassing political defeats in Länder elections, he conceded some welfare advances. Thus, an early retirement scheme was announced and older claimants' unemployment entitlements were extended. Family policy also moved into the centre ground of welfare priorities; growing concern with demographic problems encouraged the government in 1986 to introduce a special child-rearing allowance, in addition to the existing child benefit, which was intended to benefit parents in employment. Significantly, to alleviate the poor pensions profile of women, another 'baby year' credit was added in calculating pension entitlements of mothers (Mangen 1989).

Following the federal election success of 1987, the conservative government's activity centred on reforms of pensions, health care and personal tax. The overall objective was to reduce public expenditure to under 40 per cent of GDP, the level pertaining in the late 1960s. Overall, social expenditure under Kohl more closely followed GDP growth than was the case during Social Democratic governments and especially those of Brandt. But what is most striking is the high level of cross-party consensus that has been maintained – or, at least, regained – the only remaining major parliamentary dissent coming from the Greens. This has been particularly true since the mid 1980s, after the worst years of retrenchment were past. Once again, German parties adopted a technical approach in resolving welfare issues, especially as regards health and pensions. In anything but the short run, it was inevitable that Kohl's *Wendepolitik* would be long on rhetoric and short on reality. Given the status of the CDU as a *Volkspartei* and the pluralism of the German political system, which generates many points at which interest groups can make an impact on policy formulation, it would have been foolhardy for 'a government dominated by a catch-all party . . . [to] run the risk of dismantling the [welfare system] for the political risks . . . seem too high' (Schmidt 1985).

9.5   THE WELFARE STATE: A LEGITIMACY NOT LOST, BUT WEAKENED

Within the 'continental' model, at least as represented by the three countries reviewed here, there have been few critical differences in the performance of governments, whether of left or right. That is not to deny that there have been politically distinctive policies which often assumed real as well as symbolic importance: the reintroduction of pay beds by Chirac and Mitterand's commitment to the national minimum benefit are examples and, to some degree, education and family policy would be others. But, in each of these plural welfare systems, political leaders have faced specific economic and social constraints that ultimately dictated that their approach to reform would be within existing institutional arrangements.

Neither a radical dismantling nor a substantial expansion occurred and it had become a truism to say that the welfare state in the 1980s was not 'in crisis' but 'in process of change'. There was some reordering of welfare objectives, most notably related to the promotion of greater efficiency in the use of resources and in cost-containment. And there was a certain reappraisal of individual goals, the reconsideration of the 'intergenerational contract' being a case in point. But the essential features of the welfare state in France, Spain and Germany have remained intact. Electorates have learned that welfare expenditure could not continue the exponential growth of the early 1970s and have accepted limited retreats on certain fronts. Significantly, they have re-elected Kohl, Mitterand and Gonzalez on several occasions, albeit if not so enthusiastically as in the past.

Periods of recession are not opportune moments to enact major change for, in the face of economic uncertainty, there are political pressures to defend as much of the status quo as is feasible. Demographic, maturation and cyclical factors, combined with the effects of decentralisation policies, have ensured that social expenditure has largely kept pace with GDP growth. As for the real value of welfare benefits, the situation is more complex. There have been winners and losers, the latter particularly among the unemployed.

Social security policy in the 1980s has been shaped by the overriding consideration of cost-containment, initiated through a by now familiar repertoire of measures. Chronic structural problems of the social insurance funds have meant that state support has become a permanent feature. Disaffection with the quality of public services has stimulated a further expansion of the welfare mix and elements on the left seem to be reconciled to the permanent existence and expansion of the private sector. Private welfare provision, often through voluntary insurance, will accelerate what has been a growing disparity between the majority of individuals who have access to benefits by way of insurance and an increasing minority of marginalised individuals, long dependent on social assistance. Popular preference for the private sector and certain misgivings about social solidarity as the basis of collective provisions have represented an assault on intellectual traditions but, equally, this assault should not be overstated. For, after all, the welfare state's 'legitimacy is not lost, but weakened' (Ringen 1987, p 68).

NOTES

1. EC calculations of the number of households in poverty employed the following criteria:
    (i) The weighted average net income per adult equivalent unit was calcu-

lated using a weight of 1.0 for household heads and 0.7 for additional members.

(ii) The poverty line for a single-person household was set at 50 per cent of net income per adult equivalent unit.

(iii) The poverty line for households consisting of more than one person was calculated by adding 70 per cent of the poverty line income of the head of household for each additional member.

For further details see CEC (1981) p 91.

2. Social expenditure is normally understood as including all forms of public financing of health, housing, education and personal social services, as well as social insurance, social assistance and tax concessions. Social protection data normally refer to expenditure on statutory social insurance, social assistance, employment promotion measures and housing benefits.

Apart from different national accounting traditions in the production of welfare data, there are important disparities in the denotation of social expenditure employed by the EC and OECD. EC data include the costs of administration of social security whilst OECD data do not. Furthermore, the OECD incorporates only statutory insurance expenditure, thereby excluding certain important occupational and voluntary provisions. Categorisation according to insurance risk is also different. Other important distinctions relate to divergent treatment of such expenditure as housing allowance in defining global family benefit funding. These differences produce important disparities in the published statistics: for example, between EC and OECD data sets for 1981 there is a difference of five percentage points for Belgium, four for the UK and two for France. (For further details see *La Protection Sociale*, Cahiers Français, no 222, 1985).

REFERENCES

Alber J (1986) Germany, in Flora P (ed) *Growth to Limits: The Western European Welfare States Since World War II*, De Gruyter, Berlin, Germany.

Barcelona, City of (1985) *Els Anciens de les Residencies Municipals*, Social Services Department, Barcelona, Spain.

Brauns H-J and Kramer D (1989) West Germany – the Break-up of Consensus and the Demographic Threat, in Munday B (ed) *The Crisis in Welfare: An International Perspective on Social Services and Social Work*, Harvester Press, Hemel Hempstead.

Brown J (1986) Cross-National and Inter-Country Research into Poverty: the Case of the First European Poverty Programme, in Mangen S and Hantrais L (eds) *Doing Cross-National Research* vol 2: *Research Methods and Problems of Comparative Public Policy*, Aston Cross-National Research Papers, Birmingham.

Bulmer S (1989) *The Changing Agenda of West German Public Policy*, Dartmouth Press, Aldershot.

Carabantes A (1984) *Balance y Futuro del Socialismo*, Ed Planeta, Madrid, Spain.

Casado D (1987) *Introduccion a los Servicios Sociales*, Acerbo, Madrid, Spain.

CEC (1981) *Final Report from the Commission to the Council on the First Programme of Pilot Schemes and Studies to Combat Poverty*, Commission of the European Community, COM (81) 769, Brussels, Belgium.

Cerny P and Schain M (1985) *Socialism, the State and Public Policy in France*, Pinter, London.

Chapellière I (1989) *Où Va la Protection Sociale?*, Editions la Découverte, Paris, France.

Collins D (1987) A More Equal Society: Social Policy under the Socialists, in Mazey S and Newman M (eds) *Mitterand's France*, Croom Helm, London.

Données Sociales (1990), INSEE, Paris, France.

Esping-Anderson G (1990) *The Three Worlds of Welfare Capitalism*, Polity Press, Cambridge.

Freeman G (1990) Financial Crisis and Policy Continuity in the Welfare State, in Hall P, Hayward J and Machin H (eds) *Developments in French Politics*, Macmillan, Basingstoke.

Heidenheimer A J, Heclo H and Teich-Adams C (1990) *Comparative Public Policy: The Politics of Social Choice in America, Europe and Japan*, 3rd edition, St Martins Press, New York, USA.

IRES (1984) *La Protection Sociale*, Cahiers Français, no 215.

IRES (1985) *La Protection Sociale*, Cahiers Français, no 220.

Kessler D and Masson A (1985) What are the Distributional Consequences of the Socialist Government in France? *Journal of Social Policy* **14**: 403–418.

Lynes T (1985) *Paying for Pensions: The French Experience*, London School of Economics, Suntory-Toyota International Centre for Economics and Related Disciplines, London.

McVicar N (1985) Social Security in Spain, *Social Security Journal*, Canberra, Australia, pp 57–64.

Mangen S (1985) Germany: The Psychiatric Enquête and its Aftermath, in Mangen S (ed) *Mental Health Care in the European Community*, Croom Helm, London.

Mangen S (1989) The Politics of Welfare, in Smith G, Paterson W and Merkl P (eds) *Developments in West German Politics*, Macmillan, Basingstoke.

de Miguel J, Porta M and Rodriguez J (1989) Socialist Health Policies and Politics in Spain, in Albrecht G (ed) *Advances in Medical Sociology*, JAI Press, Greenwich, USA.

Milano S (1989) *Le Revenu Minimum Garanti dans la CEE*, Editions PUE, Paris, France.

Munoz de Bustillo R (1990) Distribucion de la Renta, in Instituto Sindical de Estudios (ed) *Reflexiones sobre Politica Economica*, Ed Popular, Madrid, Spain.

Murard N (1989) *La Protection Sociale*, Editions la Découverte, Paris, France.

OECD (1989a) *Economic Survey: France*, OECD, Paris, France.

OECD (1989b) *Economic Survey: Spain*, OECD, Paris, France.

OECD (1990) *Economic Survey: Germany*, OECD, Paris, France.

Ringen S (1987) *The Politics of Possibility: A Study in the Politics of the Welfare State*, Clarendon Press, Oxford.

Schmidt M (1985) Budgetary Policy: A Comparative Perspective on Policy Outputs and Outcomes, in von Beyme K and Schmidt M (eds) *Policy and Politics in the Federal Republic of Germany*, Gower, Aldershot.

10 The Welfare State in the USSR
Alastair McAuley

10.1 INTRODUCTION

There are three ways in which the Soviet conception of social policy and
the welfare state differs from that in Western Europe. (These differences also
apply to conceptions of welfare in post-war Eastern Europe.) First, Soviet-
style socialism has meant that the state is the main if not the only employer.
The state sets wage rates and salary scales; its decisions exercise a major
influence on the so-called primary distribution of income. Earnings differentials are a reflection of the state's preferences. In a sense, therefore, the
authorities can be assumed to have chosen the degree of inequality that
results. This affects the scope for income redistribution.

It also affects the intellectual justifications that can be advanced for state
intervention. There is no reason to introduce a progressive tax system.[1] The
perceived roles of the social security and social insurance systems are different as well. They are not seen as the means whereby the authorities correct
injustices, reduce inequality or alleviate poverty; rather, they serve as a complement to the wage and salary system. Finally, when all institutions that
produce goods and services are state-owned (and the state can set the prices
that it wishes), the arguments that can be advanced in favour of the provision of particular services free of charge or at subsidised prices take on a
different character.

The second reason why the Soviet conception of social policy differs
from that to be found in Western Europe is that Soviet ideas about the
welfare state have developed largely in isolation from the trends in social
thought that have shaped institutions and policies in a country such as Britain. Soviet theories of social policy can be traced back to Lenin and Marx.
They thus originate in the same nineteenth-century European socialist tradition that lies behind much of British or Scandinavian social policy. But the
suppression of social science under Stalin meant an end to the coherent
analysis of social problems, to constructive proposals for their solution.
When economics and sociology were reborn in the 1950s, continued political isolation meant that the academic community was largely ignorant of the
intellectual debates found in Western journals. Even today, restrictions on

travel and the legacy of ideological censorship serve to cut off Soviet policy makers and their academic advisers from the ideas that prompt change in other industrial societies.

Third, it must be remembered that in 1917 Russia was a poor agrarian society; in many respects this was still true of the USSR in the 1950s. Economic conditions were very different from those in Britain – and from those that socialist theorists had assumed would prevail after the revolution. The resources available for social policy were limited; these limits were accentuated by the Soviet preoccupation with defence. As a result, socialist commitments in the field of social policy were not honoured; or they were modified and distorted.

On the other hand, since 1930, the Soviet Union has experienced an industrial revolution. This has led to changes in demographic and social structure similar to those experienced in other industrial economies. These changes have resulted in similar social problems. In certain ways, Soviet institutional responses have paralleled those of other advanced societies. Also, failures in the delivery of social policies in the 1970s have resulted in widespread popular scepticism about the advantages of socialism. As in Britain after 1979, there is a preparedness to question the assumptions upon which social consensus has been erected. There is a new willingness to propose radical alternatives. Perhaps, then, the Soviet experience of the welfare state can provide an instructive contrast to that of mixed economies such as Britain. This chapter has been written in the belief that this is so.

The rest of the chapter is organised as follows: Section 10.2 deals with the objectives of Soviet welfare policy and the way that these have evolved. Sections 10.3 and 10.4 deal with the achievements of that policy, looking first at the formal structure of programmes and then at evidence of performance.[2] The final section considers prospects for future change in the context of *perestroika*.

10.2 OBJECTIVES OF WELFARE POLICY

In the USSR the population obtains a variety of services such as education free of charge; others are available at subsidised prices. The social security and social insurance systems provide a range of transfer payments to particular groups. Soviet economists and statisticians refer to resources committed to these uses collectively as expenditures from social consumption funds (hereafter SCF). The term SCF was introduced into Soviet academic discourse (and economic statistics) in the 1950s; before the Second World War, economists had talked about the social wage or socio-cultural funds.[3] This concept forms the basis of discussion for the rest of the chapter.

The editors of this volume (Ch. 1) have suggested that the objectives of the welfare state include protection against poverty, reduction of inequality and the attainment of higher standards of consumption in certain areas. These three propositions form a convenient framework around which to organise a discussion of the objectives of Soviet social policy, although one should bear in mind what was said above about inequality. It is also difficult to distinguish between the reduction of inequality and the relief of poverty.

The *Critique of the Gotha Programme* forms the starting point for all Soviet discussions of inequality and social policy. In this pamphlet, Marx drew a distinction between two phases of post-revolutionary society that is fundamental to the understanding of subsequent Soviet discussion. In the second (or higher) phase, there is material abundance; distribution will be characterised by: from each according to his ability, to each according to need. This is what Soviet economists call communism. In the first phase, however, goods will still be scarce and people will not yet want to work simply for works sake. Distribution is characterised by: from each according to his ability, to each according to his labour (although this phrase does not itself occur in the *Critique*). This is what is meant by socialism.[4] This distinction between communism and socialism will recur again and again in the debates that I describe below.

10.2.1   THE SATISFACTION OF MERIT WANTS

Marx also suggested that a future socialist society would set up a centrally administered fund to support those unable to work and another to finance communal satisfaction of needs such as schooling, health care and so on.[5] This is the basis for the SCF given in Soviet statistics.

In the 1950s, it was frequently asserted that the distribution of goods and services included in this centrally administered fund was 'according to need'. It was thus in accordance with communist principles and more progressive than that of other goods (access to which depended on ability to pay). It was suggested that as society gradually approached the phase of full communism through continued economic development, the share of such goods and services in total consumption would grow. This perception is embodied in the 1961 Party Programme, which claimed that in the following years such things as bread, housing, urban transport and meals in factory canteens would be included in SCF – and thus be made available free of charge.[6]

These arguments were criticised in the 1960s. Their most articulate opponent was Boris Rakitskii. He pointed out that in the USSR (and in any *socialist* society) resources were scarce; it was not possible to distribute goods 'according to need'. Marx had suggested that, as a general rule in a socialist society, ability to pay would determine access to goods and services; it was, therefore, necessary to ask why he had singled out a particular group of goods and services for special treatment – and base policies on this analysis.[7]

Rakitskii argues that socialist governments are committed to the most rapid possible rate of economic development; this will ensure the earliest possible attainment of communism. Economic development depends upon investment in human as well as fixed capital. This will involve expenditure on education, on health care, on rational and progressive lifestyles. Because tastes are determined by experience, there is no reason to assume that individuals, if free to spend their incomes in the market, will choose to invest optimally in human capital. Rather, we may assume that families will reveal a myopic taste for current consumption. In such circumstances, the state is justified in overriding individual preferences and imposing an alternative pattern of consumption upon its citizens.[8]

These ideas of Rakitskii's are similar to Musgrave's concept of merit wants and the government's obligation to supply merit goods (Musgrave 1959). In some respects they are superior. Rakitskii is more explicit in his ascription of priority to the preferences of the state. He is more convincing in his explanation of why individual tastes might be found wanting. Finally, it should be noted that Rakitskii is aware of some of the social and political implications of his theory.[9]

Since the late 1970s, Rakitskii's thesis that the state was entitled to override individual preferences and that the satisfaction of these so-called merit wants determined the scale and structure of expenditure on welfare services has itself been criticised. The assumption that the state's preferences are superior to those of individuals has been questioned. It has been argued that state provision of education, medical care and housing involve non-price rationing. This imposes unwarranted restrictions on individual choice; it results in social injustice. It is suggested that state provision of such services should be confined to that minimum required for individuals to participate in a society's life; quantities in excess of this social minimum should be sold on an expanded market for consumers' goods. Such a policy would be more efficient as well as more equitable.[10]

This Soviet thesis about the provision of a socially guaranteed minimum of certain goods and services is similar in many respects to the French proposals for *sécurité sociale à deux vitesses*, according to which the same minimum protection would be guaranteed for all, but individuals would be encouraged to top up the benefits to which they were entitled through participation in contributory schemes. Those who advocate the *sotsialno garantirovannyi minimum* in the USSR do so for two reasons: they have despaired of the possibility of creating efficient non-price delivery systems; they also believe that social justice requires greater differentiation of rewards. They are thus no longer committed to the egalitarianism of the European socialist tradition.[11]

From a Western perspective, the analysis of the scope of welfare services offered by both the Rakitskii and Zaslavskaia schools is incomplete. Soviet discussion of the principle of ability to pay assumes that goods will be distributed through markets; but Soviet analysis shows no awareness of the possibility of market failure. There is no discussion of the problems caused by externalities, by asymmetric information, by uncertainty and the possibility of imperfect capital markets. Soviet economists thus demonstrate their ignorance of much of the Western technical literature on markets that has played an important role in debates about the appropriate limits of the welfare state.[12]

10.2.2 THE REDUCTION OF INEQUALITY

In a socialist society, it is not possible to separate policies for the reduction of inequality incorporated in the welfare state from the more general question of the desirable distribution of income.

There is a long-standing tradition among Soviet leaders (and their economic advisers) of emphasising the need for inequality as long as socialism lasts. Lenin stressed the link between inequality and labour force participation. He wrote in the margin of his own copy of Marx's *Critique* the biblical judgement, 'he who does not work, neither shall he eat'. Stalin, too, criticised the egalitarianism of pre-revolutionary trade unionists – who were still in control of the movement in the early 1930s. He called such attitudes petty-bourgeois. At the time, he emphasised the importance of wage differentials in providing an incentive to acquire desirable industrial skills. In the 1960s and 1970s, academic economists were still warning against attempts to reduce earnings differentials prematurely. Excessive equality was said to threaten the main objective of socialist society – the building of communism.[13] The threat of excessive equality continued to be a favourite theme for labour economists and those who supported *perestroika* in the 1980s.[14]

The desirability of maintaining appropriate incentives to participate in the labour force and to acquire industrial skills constrains the socialist state in its choice of social security and social insurance systems. It might be thought that in circumstances where available resources are limited, as they have been over much of the Soviet period, the fairest social security system to adopt would be one in which all receive the same pension or benefit. But such was not the Soviet view.

Opposition to uniform pensions and other benefits is based on two grounds. First, it is argued that such schemes must inevitably result in low levels of support since it is generally accepted that the pension or benefit a person receives cannot exceed earnings while in employment without undermining labour incentives and reducing participation rates.[15] Second, the differentiation of benefits provides a desirable reinforcement of the so-called socialist distribution principle; workers are encouraged to acquire the skills needed to obtain both higher earnings and increased benefits. To this purely instrumental justification of differentials some would add an equity argument: it is only fair that those who have worked harder, whose contribution to society and social production has been more valuable while able-bodied, should receive a larger share of social output when incapacitated or retired. 'The state's evaluation of the past activity of those no longer capable of work is shown in [their] pensions'.[16]

A desire to promote equality – or at least to reduce social differentiation – has also been cited as a reason for the state's provision of free education or health care. (This argument is in addition to the satisfaction of merit wants discussed in Section 10.2.1 above.) Rakitskii and others have suggested that the free provision of education ensures that 'all individuals enjoy a real possibility of acquiring the highest qualifications and, as a result, can conceivably occupy any position in production or society'.[17] The provision of opportunities for free education will lead to the reduction of earnings inequality in the long run. More important perhaps, it counters tendencies towards elitism and social exclusivity that can still be found in socialist society.[18]

10.2.3   PROTECTION AGAINST POVERTY

Until the 1950s, protection against poverty was reduced to this: compensation for loss of earnings for those who had suffered a temporary or permanent loss of working capacity. In the last thirty years, however, it has come to be recognised that the causes of poverty are more complex. Consequently, the state has adopted a more nuanced set of anti-poverty measures.

In the 1930s, under the influence of Stalin, the state's responsibility to protect its citizens against poverty was subordinated to the need to ensure high levels of labour force participation. Stalin's ideas about social policy were accompanied by anti-peasant prejudice and by severe limits on available resources. As a result, the social insurance and social security systems were restricted to state employees; the peasantry (and, perhaps surprisingly to those unfamiliar with Soviet history, members of collective farms) were expected to rely upon their own resources – or those of the extended family. Even among state employees, social insurance was effectively reduced to the provision of disability pensions for the victims of industrial accidents (and wartime injuries after 1941). This restriction of the role for measures designed to alleviate poverty was also the result of a belief that, in conditions of full employment, poverty was voluntary. It was the result of idleness, of a wilful refusal to work.[19]

This view of poverty and its causes was challenged after the Second World War. Attempts were made to define a poverty line, to determine how many families lived in poverty and to find out why families were poor. The results of these studies made uncomfortable reading for policy makers in Moscow. But they did result in changes to the Soviet welfare state. The first attempts to measure poverty in the post-war period were made in the 1950s, but we know virtually nothing about either the methodology or the results of this exercise. Presumably it was thought to be unsatisfactory since the exercise was repeated in 1963-7. The results of this second study were published.[20]

In the 1960s, Soviet researchers and policy makers did not talk about poverty; that was a condition to be found only in capitalist societies. Rather, their work was directed towards establishing a minimum material standard

(MMS) budget. The Soviet approach to this involved experts in the specification of the quantities of goods and services needed by an unskilled labourer and his family if he was to be able to keep healthy and do his job properly. These were then priced and the necessary income calculated. The estimates were based on a notional family of four living in the central industrial region of the country. This exercise was repeated in the middle 1980s, using more or less the same methodology and a new MMS budget was published. Experts' views on what an unskilled labourer needs increase as output, productivity and average earnings rise; the Soviet conception of poverty is thus relative.

In 1965, researchers at the Research Institute for Labour suggested an MMS budget of 50 roubles a month per capita. At that date, average earnings in the state sector were 96 roubles a month. Hence an average worker could barely support one dependant – and most members of unskilled worker-families lived in poverty. In fact, calculations suggested that some 47–53 million state employees and their dependants were living below the poverty level (as were 30 million *kolkhozniki*).[21] This was out of a total population of 230 million. I believe that this study embodied an excessively liberal definition of the MMS budget. The 1986 study proposed that the MMS budget should be raised to 60 roubles a month per capita.[22] Rimashevskaia has proposed a poverty level of 75 roubles a month and a public opinion poll seems to favour something even higher.[23] In June 1989, the Prime Minister, Nikolai Ryzhkov, reported to the Soviet parliament that there were almost 40 million persons living below the poverty line – but it is not clear which poverty line he used.[24]

This work on the poverty level was accompanied by attempts to identify the causes of poverty. Social studies suggested that there was a high incidence of poverty among families with children; family breakdown almost invariably led to poverty.[25] The need to support elderly relatives was also associated with material deprivation.

These results led to calls for a more differentiated approach to social security and an extension in the level of support for the family.[26] Initially, these were rejected; the authorities, worried about the impact of extensive child allowances upon labour force participation, preferred to increase the minimum wage.[27] But poverty was the result of limited labour force attachment as much as low wages *per se*; social studies continued to reveal a high incidence of poverty among families with children. In 1974, the government conceded and introduced a special allowance payable to those families with children under the age of eight whose per capita income was below the MMS level. It was suggested that free school meals would alleviate the position of those above eight years of age!

Increases in disability pensions and changes in the regulations governing entitlement to maternity pay and other allowances, which occurred at more or less the same time, are evidence that the authorities attached greater priority to protection against poverty after the early 1970s.[28] At the official level this concern persists; at the first session of the newly elected Congress of Peoples' Deputies, the Prime Minister said:

> Speaking of social policy, I think that it is essential to stress . . . the issue of the state's and society's responsibility for the material welfare of the least socially protected groups of the population like pensioners, the disabled, young families and those with many children.[29]

Among academics, however, particularly those associated with the new preoccupation with social justice, this focus upon the poor has been questioned. For example, Natalia Rimashevskaia, an economist who has specialised in the study of inequality and living standards, has recently written:

> The supposed existence of an independent problem of low-paid workers and impoverished families requiring purposeful measures for its solution . . . proved to be unfounded.[30]

She suggests that the programmes of the 1970s have failed to reduce the incidence of poverty; and hence, by implication, must have been based on an inadequate theory of income determination. But she also argues that this should not be cause for too much concern: there will always be relatively low-paid workers and relatively impoverished families. Social policy should focus upon other objectives. In particular, more attention should be paid to ensuring an appropriate structure of wage and salary differentials. It is not clear how widely held are views like those of Rimashevskaia. But it is certainly conceivable that they will exert a significant influence on the direction of official policy in the next five years or so.

The Soviet welfare state has evolved as a result of interaction between ideological preconceptions and the revived study of Soviet society and its problems. This has affected the way in which objectives were conceived and the way in which priorities were established. Policies have also been constrained by the scarcity of resources. These issues are explored further in the next two sections.

10.3   THE STRUCTURE OF SOCIAL CONSUMPTION

Soviet expenditures from social consumption funds reveal the dual structure suggested by Marx. First, they cover the cost of providing certain goods and services either free of charge or at subsidised prices. Second, they include cash transfers. In this section, I describe the major components of each of these categories.

10.3.1 WELFARE SERVICES

Published statistics refer to three areas of activity: education, medical care and housing. The nature of the services provided under each of these headings is described briefly in (i-iii) below. After that, I report a Soviet debate about the desirability of including food subsidies in social consumption expenditure.

(i) Education:

At the present time, education is provided free of charge for all children from 7 to 17 or 18 years of age. Children who complete ten or eleven classes are said to have a complete secondary education; those who leave at 15 (or who repeat one or more years and fail to graduate from tenth grade) are said to have an incomplete secondary education. All children follow the same curriculum, but there are special schools for the academically gifted. There are also schools where some of the instruction is provided in a foreign language; these are sought after by the intelligentsia. Finally, there are vocational schools where the emphasis is placed on the acquisition of industrial skills. Increasingly, these PTUs, as they are called, also provide their students with a complete secondary education.

A complete secondary education is necessary for admission to further and higher educational establishments. Tuition at these institutions is also free and the state provides student stipends. Eligibility for financial assistance depends upon course of study and parental income; but the terms are relatively generous and a majority of students receives support. The amount received varies with academic performance: those attaining first-class grades receive higher grants; those who fail courses may forfeit financial support.

Educational expenditures also cover part of the cost of pre-school child care.[31] Most urban children attend kindergartens or day nurseries. Many rural children do so as well; but in the countryside, such facilities are more likely to operate for only part of the year. The fees for kindergartens and day nurseries also depend upon parental income but it is claimed that most families pay at the top rate.

(ii) Health care:

Primary health care delivery is organised through polyclinics. Attendance at these is free; for those referred to hospital, medical consultation is free as well. But out-patients may be required to contribute to the costs of any drugs prescribed for them. There are special restricted-access polyclinics and hospitals for members of the élite and certain other groups. It is claimed that the quality of equipment and service in these establishments is far better than in the general service.

(iii) Housing:

There are three forms of tenure in the Soviet Union. Some families own their own homes, others belong to housing cooperatives and a third group live in state-owned accommodation. In 1987 (the latest year for which detailed estimates are available) about two-thirds of the stock of housing in rural areas and two-ninths of that in towns was privately owned. Published statistics do not distinguish between cooperative and state-owned apartments.

Soviet accounting conventions make it difficult to work out the cost of housing – and who bears it. It appears that no charge is made for land. The state provides non-repayable grants to cover the costs of construction and of state housing; it also lends money to cooperatives. The rents paid by tenants only cover part of the costs of the upkeep of the housing stock; the balance is covered by a subvention from the state budget. It is this that appears as 'housing subsidies' in SCF. If this analysis is correct, the economic cost of Soviet housing support is much greater than the published figure.[32]

Food subsidies:
It has been claimed that the decision to maintain low and constant prices on certain items of consumers' expenditure, notably meat and dairy products (which applied for the period 1962–89 and to some extent still operates) constituted an addition to the real incomes of the Soviet population; expenditure on the subsidies involved should therefore be included as part of SCF.[33] This suggestion has also been challenged; Rakitskii and Shokhin argue that it confuses the problem of measuring real income accurately with that of identifying elements of the Soviet welfare state. They argue that price subsidies are a consequence of the failure of policies designed to improve efficiency in agriculture; they bear no relation to the satisfaction of merit wants (Rakitskii's criterion for the inclusion of expenditure programmes in SCF). The two authors also propose that housing subsidies should be excluded from SCF on the same grounds.[34]

10.3.2 CASH TRANSFERS
Published statistics of the cash transfers provided by the Soviet state suggest that these serve two purposes: income maintenance and child support. The elements that make up these two categories are described in more detail in (i) and (ii) below. I also comment on the insignificance of public assistance.

(i) Income maintenance transfers:
Pensions are paid to those Soviet citizens who suffer permanent loss of capacity to work. More precisely, the Soviet social insurance system provides for the payment of old age and disability pensions and also support for those families who have lost a breadwinner. Such pensions are non-contributory, being financed by a payroll tax and out of general budget revenues. Benefits depend upon employment record; they also relate to terminal earnings.[35]

Sickness benefit is paid to those who suffer a temporary loss of working capacity. It is paid on the attestation of a physician. Benefit levels depend upon employment record and union membership. Sickness benefit may also be paid to those who take time off work to care for sick relatives.[36] *Unemployment benefit* has not been available in the USSR since the early 1930s. It is argued that such transfers are unnecessary since full employment is guaranteed. This is not strictly true, but in the last twenty or thirty years, unemployment has been primarily frictional and of short duration. Only in Central Asia and one or two other regions have there been substantial pockets of structural unemployment. As part of *perestroika*, however, the authorities want to encourage more rapid structural change; this is expected to result in the shake-out of significant numbers of workers. In 1988, the government took the first tentative steps towards providing a system of support for those declared redundant. They will normally be entitled to one month's wages as redundancy pay; in certain circumstances, workers receive payments equal to their previous wages for a period of three months after being declared redundant. After that, nothing![37] Expenditure on this benefit does not yet figure in the statistics, although there is some evidence to suggest that the level of unemployment has begun to creep up.[38]

(ii) Child support payments:
Three categories of expenditure are grouped under this heading: maternity grants and allowances, conventional child allowances and payments in respect of children living in low-income households.

Maternity benefits are paid to employed women while they are on maternity leave. In the 1955 law, the level of benefit was linked to union membership and employment record. In 1973, entitlement conditions were relaxed: now all women receive their full pay while on leave. In 1981-3, employed women who chose to remain at home until the baby's first birthday became entitled to a flat-rate benefit.[39] Employed women are also entitled to a maternity grant – of 50 roubles for the first child and 100 roubles for each subsequent one. The husbands of non-employed women receive a grant of 30 roubles on the birth of the first three children.[40]

Child allowances are paid to women with four or more children. The amounts paid increase as the number of children in the family goes up – until the tenth child. Allowances are payable from the child's first until its fifth birthday. Mothers also receive a lump sum payment on the birth of the third and subsequent children; this too increases with birth order. Single mothers are entitled to an additional allowance in respect of all children; this is paid until the child's sixteenth birthday (or eighteenth for those in full-time education). The system of child allowances was first introduced in the mid 1930s – as compensation for the decision to make abortion illegal. The present framework of payments and entitlements was decided upon in 1947, although it has been modified since then. But benefit levels have changed remarkably little![41]

Income supplements have been payable since 1974 to families with children under the age of eight whose per capita income is less than 50 roubles a month.[42] The rate of benefit is 12 roubles a month. There is no evidence about rates of take-up on this or other benefits. But, since the procedures for establishing entitlement seem to me to be fairly bureaucratic, I would be surprised if all those who qualify for a particular allowance in fact receive it.

(iii) Other benefits:
The Soviet social security system contains provision for other forms of assistance as well as those mentioned above. These include such payments as burial grants and assistance to those in need. These latter are the equivalent of public assistance and make up the ultimate safety net provided by the Soviet welfare state. Statistics show that expenditure on these programmes is relatively small.[43] This may come as something of a surprise to those familiar with the British system. This difference reflects the fact that the Soviet system offers much less scope for discretion than does the British.

There are three reasons for this. The central authorities are suspicious of the motives that would govern the decisions of local officials; there is a feeling that they would be too willing to provide assistance and thus undermine the incentive to participate in the labour force. As a result, there is a preference for explicit rules and clear categories of entitlement. Second, the Soviet administrative structure does not contain a large body of officials capable of exercising discretion; this is a consequence of the Soviet failure to develop personal social services. Most social security programmes are administered by the trade unions or by the salaries and wages departments of state enterprises. Finally, until the 1950s or perhaps later, the USSR remained an agrarian society; in such circumstances, it was assumed that the extended family would take responsibility for its members. Such an assumption was embodied in Soviet family law. It continues to influence the development of the welfare state.

10.4   THE SOVIET WELFARE STATE: PERFORMANCE

In this section, I examine the way in which the various components of the Soviet welfare state have evolved since 1940. This is intended to illustrate the way in which priorities have changed. I also attempt to assess the effectiveness of the various programmes that these expenditures support.

10.4.1   THE GROWTH OF EXPENDITURE
Table 10.1 provides estimates of aggregate expenditure on SCF both in current roubles and as a proportion of net material product (NMP). The table also contains information on the way in which components of SCF have changed through the years.

The figures in the table relate to Soviet statistical concepts. No attempt has been made to make them comparable with Western analogues; this should be borne in mind when casual comparisons are made with figures for other countries. Second, the entries in the first row of the table are in current prices and those in the rest of the table make no allowance for changes in relative prices. Thus, no allowance has been made for inflation. One reason for this is that the academic study of inflation in the USSR is in disarray. Soviet government statisticians continue to claim that it has been almost non–existent since the mid 1950s; academic economists suggest that there has been a significant increase in the price level since 1960 or 1965, but there is no appropriate deflator available.

The following observations may help in the interpretation of the entries in Table 10.1. The official retail price index in 1960 was 40 per cent above its 1940 level; in 1950 it had been 80 per cent higher. These figures are thought to be reasonably accurate, although they make insufficient allowance for the widespread shortages of individual goods that persisted throughout the 1950s. For the more recent past, a senior Soviet economist, Bogomolov, asserted that the price level has more than doubled since the end of the 1950s.[44] Again, this makes no allowance for repressed inflation.

The figures in Table 10.1 show that expenditures out of SCF have increased rapidly in the past forty or fifty years. Even allowing for inflation, expenditures doubled between 1940 and 1950. They doubled again in the next decade as elements of Khrushchev's welfare state were put into place. In 1965, expenditure out of SCF amounted to 42 billion roubles in 1965

Table 10.1 Composition of social consumption expenditure, 1940–89

	1940	1950	1960	1970	1980	1989
Social Consumption Funds (bn roubles)	4.6	13.0	27.3	63.9	117.0	187.0
SCF as percentage of Net Material Product	–	18	19	22	26	29
Welfare services (as percentage of SCF)	65	54	50	49	47	45
education	39	34	27	27	25	24
health care	22	17	18	16	15	15
housing subsidies etc.	4	4	6	6	7	6
Cash transfers (as percentage of SCF)	35	4	49	51	54	55
holiday pay and stipends	17	18	14	16	16	13
income maintenance	6	18	31	32	34	36
child support ⎫	11*	9*	4	2	3	5
other ⎭			0.4	1	1	1

Sources: NK SSSR (1989) pp 15, 82, 615; NK SSSR (1980) pp 523, 525; NK SSSR (1970) pp 535, 537; Iu V Peshekhonov, Nekotorye problemy formirovania i ispolzovania obshchestvennykh fondov potreblenia, Izvestia Akademii Nauk: seria ekonomicheskaia no 5 (1976) pp 80, 88; Vestnik statistiki (1987) no 1, p 79
* Includes sickness benefits

prices; allowing for inflation at the rate suggested by Bogomolov, real expenditure out of SCF has doubled again in the past quarter of a century.

The growing importance of the Soviet welfare state is reflected in the figures in the second row of the table. These show SCF as a percentage of NMP. NMP is the conventional Soviet Marxist concept of aggregate output. Because it excludes value added in the services sector (and because of the way it accounts for capital consumption) it tends to be less than GNP. The figures in the table may therefore give the unwary reader an exaggerated impression of the relative importance of the Soviet welfare state.

I have been unable to locate an estimate of NMP in current prices for 1940, but it is unlikely that the share of SCF fell between 1940 and 1950. Hence, at the end of the 1930s, the Soviet welfare state probably accounted for about one-sixth of NMP. The share had risen by 1950 because the authorities were obliged to provide pensions for the very large numbers of war-disabled. In 1960, SCF accounted for almost one-fifth of NMP; in the last thirty years, its share has risen to more than one-quarter.

Figures on the composition of SCF show that in 1940, welfare services accounted for two thirds of the total.[45] This was in line with prevailing views about the desirability of communal satisfaction of particular needs. Since 1940, the share of these services in the total has declined continuously – as attitudes to income maintenance and the relief of poverty have changed. The decline has also been brought about by demographic and social change. Now, welfare services account for little more than two-fifths of the total. This trend reveals the failure of Khrushchev's vision of a welfare state as set out in the 1961 Party Programme.

10.4.2   EXPENDITURE ON WELFARE SERVICES

Changes in the relative importance of expenditure on health, education and housing reflect changing official priorities and the demographic and social evolution that has occurred in the last half century.

Continuing decline in the birth rate – and hence in the share of school-age children in the population – has led to a fall in the relative importance of expenditure on education despite a growth in educational standards. In 1940, only 11 men in a thousand had higher education and a further 116 had complete or incomplete secondary education; in 1987, the figures were 94 and 647 respectively. Over the same period, the USSR succeeded in closing the educational gap between the sexes: in 1987, of the employed population, 890 men per thousand had an incomplete secondary education or better; for women, the figure was 888. (In fact, sex equality in secondary education was achieved as early as 1959; equality in higher education came by 1979.[46])

The ageing of the population has led to an increase in the demand for medical services over and above that which has resulted from the progress of medical knowledge. There is a widespread feeling in the USSR, however, that state medicine has failed to respond adequately to the demands that society puts upon it. Despite the availability of resources (the number of physicians has risen from 1.5 per thousand population in 1950 to 4.3 per thousand in 1987), mortality and morbidity remain high.[47] The 1960s and 1970s witnessed a reduction in life expectancy; this was particularly marked for men. There was also the scandal of the increase in infant mortality.[48]

As real earnings have risen, so has demand for housing; the state's response has resulted in an increase in the relative importance of housing subsidies. The urban housing stock has trebled since 1960; the rural stock has doubled. Despite this impressive growth, there is still considerable overcrowding in the USSR. In 1980, Soviet citizens had an average of 13 to 14 square metres of usable space per capita. Assuming that living space, *zhilaia ploshchad*, accounts for 70 per cent of usable space, the Soviet population in that year attained the sanitary norm set by the government in 1926! There are, of course, significant variations about this average – with workers and those who live in large cities tending to receive less space. Also, statistics on space say nothing about the availability or otherwise of amenities such as running water or mains drainage.[49] There is, consequently, widespread dissatisfaction with the performance of socialist housing policy.

10.4.3   EXPENDITURE ON CASH TRANSFERS
The figures on cash transfers, given in Table 10.1, are dominated by the inexorable growth in expenditure on income maintenance. This has risen from 6 per cent of SCF in 1940 (or 11 per cent if one assumes that sickness benefit accounts for half of recorded expenditure on child support etc. – which was true in 1960) to 36 per cent in 1989. This increase is a reflection of changing attitudes towards the obligations of the state to provide support for the disabled and the elderly as well as changes in the structure of the Soviet population.

In 1912, Lenin and the Bolsheviks advocated the introduction of an all-risks, no-fault, non-contributory state insurance scheme covering all employees and providing benefits at a level equal to lost earnings. Although a pension law was one of the first pieces of legislation to be adopted after the October revolution, it did not implement this programme. The Soviet system still does not approach it.

Soviet pension schemes have been restricted in various ways: until 1966, pensions and social security were available only to state employees; collective farmers and their dependants received no state protection. Even after 1966, the rates of benefit paid to *kolkhozniki* were lower and conditions of entitlement were stricter than for state employees. Among state employees, pensions were largely confined to those who had suffered industrial accidents (or had been injured in the second world war). As a result, in 1960 only a quarter of persons of pensionable age received old age pensions. It was not until the late 1970s that the bulk of the elderly were covered.

Table 10.2 Inequality of earnings and income, 1956–85

	1956	1965	1970	1980	1985
Minimum wage (roubles)	27–35	40–45	60	70	70–80
Average earnings	72('55)	96	122	169	190
K (earnings)*	4.4	3.7	3.1	3.0	3.3–3.4
K (per capita income)†	3.6('58)	3.3('67)	3.7('72)	3.1('82)	

Sources: Janet Chapman Income Distribution and Social Justice in the Soviet Union, *Comparative Economic Studies*, **31** 1 (spring 1989), pp 16, 19; *NK SSSR 1987*, p 390; *NK SSSR 1968*, p 555; McAuley (1979) p 248

*K is the ratio of the ninth and first deciles; it is the inequality coefficient most commonly quoted by Soviet labour economists
†K (per capita income) relates to the distribution of Soviet wage-earner and salaried employee families by per capita money income

Table 10.3: Inequality of pension incomes, 1987

	Roubles per month	As a percentage of average earnings in the state sector
All pensions	78	38
Old age – state	92	45
– kolkhoz	47	23
Other	55	27

Source: NK SSSR 1987, p 399

The rates at which pensions were paid, moreover, were low. In 1940, the average pension amounted to one-fifth of average earnings; in 1950, the position was worse. The situation improved with the introduction of the new pension law in 1956 – but collective farmers continued to suffer. Even in 1987, rates of support were modest, as Table 10.3 shows.

Not surprisingly, there is a high incidence of poverty among pensioner households; and the presence of elderly relatives increases the probability that families will fall below the MMS standard.

10.4.4 WELFARE AND INEQUALITY

The tone of the last few paragraphs may have been excessively negative. The USSR has built up a system of services and benefits that is similar in many ways to those found in Western Europe. Despite its shortcomings, the Soviet welfare state can claim substantial achievements in the alleviation of poverty and the reduction of inequality. This is brought out by the figures in Table 10.2 – although from a methodological point of view these perfor- mance indicators are less than ideal.

In 1965, the minimum wage was less than the state's MMS budget; substantial numbers of workers must have been condemned to poverty through low pay. Given what is known about changes in the price level in 1955–65, the same must have been true in the 1950s. Since 1968, however, the minimum wage has been kept above the MMS budget. This has surely reduced the number of employed workers in poverty.

Figures in table 10.2 also show that there was a significant decrease in earnings inequality between 1956 and 1980.[50] This had been translated into a more equal distribution of family income in the 1980s. What is not clear, however, and what available statistics cannot show, is how far this greater equality had been achieved by the Soviet welfare state and how far it was a consequence of Soviet wage determination procedures.

10.5   PROSPECTS FOR THE FUTURE

In the late 1970s, the Soviet economy experienced the beginnings of an economic crisis that threatened the Party's ability to attain its policy objectives. When Mikhail Gorbachev took over as leader, the government embarked on a radical reform programme which has accentuated the economic crisis – at least in the short run. The changes in the economy and society that reform will bring about will create new problems for the Soviet welfare state. The new thinking that underlies the reform programme (and which can be traced back to the academic literature of the 1970s) calls into question some of the assumptions underlying Soviet social policy and sets new objectives. These topics are discussed briefly in this concluding section.

10.5.1   GLASNOST AND PERESTROIKA
There is a new frankness about the public debate of social problems. There is also much greater diversity in the views expressed. Real debates are taking place on the small screen and in the columns of newspapers. One can begin to identify alternative programmes. Alternative political groupings and even parties are beginning to emerge. This may lead to substantial changes in the Soviet welfare state.[51]

Perestroika involves the introduction of markets – and, indeed, elements of the mixed economy – in the place of central planning. This means that households will face a more uncertain environment. As pointed out above, unemployment has already begun to increase. It is to be expected that income inequalities will increase also as the enterprising (or the lucky) take advantage of new oportunities. Change in economic structure will define a new role for the state: rather than determining the distribution of income through its control of wage rates, it will have to influence outcomes through instruments of redistribution, direct taxes and transfers. Further, if the government and planners abdicate responsibility for deciding the level and structure of output as a whole, the authorities will have to fix the level of 'public sector' activity – and obtain the resources to finance the necessary programmes. In these respects too, the Soviet welfare state can expect to acquire new responsibilities.

10.5.2 NEW THINKING

Changes in institutions have been preceded by the development of new views about the appropriate role for the state and the objectives of social policy. Elements of this new thinking can be found in the academic literature of the 1970s; it is much more obvious in political discussions since 1985. In what follows, a distinction is made between problems created by the transition to a market economy and the arrangements that would be appropriate once a market economy has been introduced.

The main strands of this new thinking have already been described. I have already referred to the argument that the distribution of income has become too equal and that this undermines the effectiveness of the labour market. These views surfaced among economists in the late 1960s. Proponents have become much more insistent on the need for a radical increase in differentials in recent years. It is claimed that the state's failure to raise the salaries of engineers and middle managers has resulted in increasing numbers of qualified individuals choosing not to practise their professions. This is inefficient; it is also claimed to be unjust – since those who do work as managers do not receive rewards that correspond to the quantity and quality of the labour they supply. Soviet economists complain about the inconsistency of Soviet public opinion; privilege (and hence differentiation) has existed for a long time in the USSR and is regarded by many as acceptable. But earnings differentials are held to be 'anti-socialist'. As one observer remarked, 'so far experience shows that we are more ready to accept black market incomes than tax deductible incomes'.[52]

As I have pointed out elsewhere, there has been a shift in Soviet conceptions of equality. There is less emphasis on equality in the *ex post* distribution of income and more on equality of opportunity.[53] This view is particularly common among economists who support *perestroika*. For example, Tatiana Koriagina (of the Gosplan Economic Research Institute) was reported as arguing that 'the main thing . . . is to provide people with the opportunity to earn properly and to buy goods with the money that they have earned. People would then be able to solve many of their own problems and won't need some social programmes'.[54] She is particularly opposed to present Soviet policies governing the distribution of housing. This advocacy of the need for greater inequality of incomes has provoked a response; some sociologists now argue for the adoption of radically egalitarian policies.[55]

The willingness to countenance greater inequality is associated with a greater toleration of poverty. This is brought out clearly in Rimashevskaia's recent work. It is also apparent in the Koriagina interview referred to above.

She suggests that a Scandinavian-style welfare state is only possible when labour productivity has reached Scandinavian levels. At the present time, Soviet goals should be more modest: the focus should be on the provision of minimum consumption for the poorest of the poor. These, she claims, are single pensioners – especially those who live in the cities.

Finally, economists have questioned the desirability of state allocation of such goods and services as health and housing. Non-price rationing is inefficient; it is also inequitable. Reformers seem to favour the provision of a socially guaranteed minimum, either free of charge or at heavily subsidised prices, and the introduction of a market on which individuals could purchase additional quantities – provided their incomes were sufficient. In this proposal, one detects a certain convergence of views between Soviet reformers and the British radical right. For example, the Institute of Economic Affairs would surely approve of the following comments: 'Only with a normal market economy shall we be able to solve social problems too'. And again, 'Free housing should become the exception, not the rule'.[56] From different starting points, both appear to have come to the conclusion that the social consequences of market failure are not as bad as those of the failure in state provision mechanisms.

If this view prevails, we may expect considerable change in the scope of the Soviet welfare state in the next five or ten years, including the introduction or extension of means tests and a wave of privatisation *à la russe*!

NOTES

1. Such a system would be necessary only if the authorities were unable to calculate the effects of different wage rates upon the distribution of family income. To admit this, however, undermines the Communist Party's claim that economic processes are planned.
2. I have dealt with the issues discussed in Sections 10.2–10.4 in greater detail elsewhere. See McAuley (1979) chs 4 and 11; McAuley (1980); McAuley (1981) ch 9; McAuley (1982).
3. Rakitskii and Shokhin (1987) p 126. This Soviet concept corresponds roughly to the definition suggested in Chapter 1: the provision, usually to identifiable persons, of benefits in cash or kind as a contribution to meeting their 'needs' and not as a payment for any current productive effort.
4. See Marx (1970) p 10.
5. *Ibid.* p 7.
6. Rakitskii and Shokhin (1987) p 129.
7. Rakitskii (1966) pp 17–19.
8. Rakitskii (1966) pp 119–121; Rakitskii and Shokhin (1987) p 130.
9. McAuley (1980) pp 246–7.
10. Zaslavskaia (1986) pp 69ff; Rakitskii and Shokhin (1987) p 130.
11. Crosnier (1986) p 64.
12. These are summarised in Barr (1987) for example, especially chs 4–5 and 12–14.

13. Kulikov (1972) pp 58–9; Rabkina and Rimashevskaia (1972) pp 13–19.
14. Rimashevskaia (1988) pp 37, 48; Shatalin (1986) p 60.
15. Lantsev (1976) p 100.
16. Acharkan (1967) p 58.
17. Maier and Rakitskii (1976) p 192.
18. *Ibid.* p 192; Mamontova (1975) p 217.
19. It was recognised, however, that large numbers of children might impose a strain on the family budget. Cash benefits for the fourth and subsequent children were introduced in 1936, when abortion was made illegal.
20. See *Potrebnosti* (1967).
21. McAuley (1979) ch 4.
22. Kriazhev (1986) p 2.
23. Rimashevskaia (1988) p 46; Millar and Clayton (1986) p 11.
24. T Koriagina, of the Gosplan Economic Research Institute, suggests that the figure of 40 million relates to the 75 rouble poverty line; she also claims that, due to inflation, the equivalent figure might now (1989) be nearer to 80 roubles. But the official adoption of such a figure would reduce the amount of assistance that the state could give to the poorest members of Soviet society (*Moscow News*, no 32, 1989).
25. This suggests that Soviet arrangements for the payment of alimony do not work well. The legal system and its influence on financial arrangements between individuals is normally excluded from the definition of the welfare state; I ignore it here as well. But it can have a significant impact upon the incidence of poverty.
26. Lantsev (1974) p 129.
27. See McAuley (1979) ch 4.
28. See McAuley (1979) ch 11; McAuley (1981) pp 173ff.
29. *Izvestia* 8 June 1989, p 2.
30. Rimashevskaia (1988) p 46.
31. Part of the cost of day nurseries (for the under-threes) comes from the medical care budget. Parents pay fees for both day nurseries and kindergartens. For more detail, see McAuley (1981) pp 178–82.
32. Those living in privately owned accommodation are responsible for the full costs of maintenance; members of cooperatives must also repay loans from the state. There are two reasons why Soviet households join cooperatives: the quality of construction is higher and space allowances are greater. Such property can also be passed on to heirs or sold (subject to the approval of other members of the co operative).
33. Peshekhonov (1976) p 80.
34. Rakitskii and Shokhin (1987) p 128.
35. McAuley (1979) pp 269–76; *Sotsialnoe* (1986) ch 4.
36. McAuley (1979) p 276; *Sotsialnoe* (1986) pp 111, 161.
37. *Izvestia* 20 January 1988.
38. Soviet Economic Performance (1989) p 5.
39. In fact, this is paid at two rates: 50 roubles per month in the North and East where the cost of living (and wage rates) are higher; 35 roubles a month elsewhere (Sotsialnoe, 1986, p 98).
40. McAuley (1981) p 175; *Sotsialnoe* (1986) p 98.
41. McAuley (1979) p 281; *Sotsialnoe* (1986) pp 453–62.

42. Since 1984, a higher cut-off income of 75 roubles a month has applied to families living in the North and East of the country. (*Sotsialnoe*, 1986, p 428).
43. Madison (1968) pp 206–8; George and Manning (1980) p 54.
44. See Bogomolov (1987) p 12.
45. The structure of expenditure is affected by the Soviet convention of including holiday pay in SCF. The formal justification for this is that holiday pay is not a reward for current productive effort and so is logically equivalent to sick pay or maternity benefit. But suspicion exists that it was originally included to inflate the size of SCF (since it is also included in the statistics of average earnings). Conservatism at the Central Statistical Administration has led to its retention despite frequent criticisms from academic economists. If it is excluded, the share of welfare services in SCF has evolved as follows:

	1940	1950	1960	1970	1980	1989
Welfare services/(SCF - HP)(%)	75	63	57	57	54	51

The starting level at the end of the 1930s was higher; the decline in the post-war period has been sharper too.
46. McAuley (1981) ch 8.
47. See Feshbach (1982).
48. See Davis and Feshbach (1980).
49. Matthews (1979), pp 105–18.
50. More detailed statistics show that minimum earnings inequality according to K (earnings) was attained in 1968. Since then, differentiation has increased (Chapman 1989, p 19).
51. Analysis of the first Congress of Peoples' Deputies identifies four tendencies: reformers, conservatives, radicals and populists. The reformers, who predominate among the central leadership, are committed to the introduction of a market. They (and the radicals) would like to see a substantial reorganisation of the welfare state whereby benefit levels were restricted and access limited. Conservatives, who predominate in the middle levels of the administration, would like to see much of the present system preserved; so would the populists. But the latter are also in favour of an attack on élite privilege. For more detail see Kliamkin (1989) p 12; Ie Iasin (1989) p 4.
52. This contradiction between existing policies and the requirements of social justice was a common theme of articles on wages policy in the 1980s; all advocated an increase in differentials. See Koriagina (1989) p10; Matthews (1978).
53. McAuley (1979) pp 310–17; McAuley (1980) p 254.
54. Koriagina (1989) p 10.
55. See, for example, Rogovin (1985).
56. Koriagina (1989) p 101.

REFERENCES

Acharkan V A (1967) *Gosudarstvennye pensii*, Iuridicheskaia literatura, Moscow, USSR.

Barr N (1987) *The Economics of the Welfare State*, Weidenfeld and Nicolson, London.

Bogomolov O T (1987) Skolko stoiat dengi, *Literaturnaia gazeta*, no 38, 16 September, Moscow, USSR.

Chapman J (1989) Income Distribution and Social Justice in the Soviet Union, *Comparative Economic Studies* **31** (1), pp14–45, London.

Crosnier M A (1986) Les Transfers Sociaux en Economie Socialiste: Le Modèle Sovietique, in Duchène G *Les Transfers Sociaux en Europe de l'Est* mimeo, pp 17–70, Centre d'Economie Internationale des Pays Socialistes, Université de Paris I, France.

Davis C and Feshbach M (1980) *Rising Infant Mortality in the USSR in the 1970s* series P–25, no 74, US Bureau of the Census, Washington DC, USA.

Feshbach M (1982) Issues in Soviet Health Problems, in *Soviet Economy in the 1980s: Problems and Prospects* **2**, pp 203–27, Joint Economic Committee, USGPO, Washington DC, USA.

George V and Manning N (1980) *Socialism, Social Welfare and the Soviet Union*, Routledge and Kegan Paul, London.

Iasin Ie (1989) Populists: A Neglected Force, *Moscow News*, no 32, 6 August, Moscow, USSR.

Kliamkin I (1989) What Lies Ahead, *Moscow News*, no 27, 2 July, Moscow, USSR.

Koriagina T (1989) Free Benefit is Utopian since the Treasury Cannot Solve all Social Problems, *Moscow News*, no 27, 2 July, Moscow, USSR.

Kriazhev V (1986) Obshchestvennye fondy potreblenia i sotsialnaia spravedlivost *Ekonomicheskaia gazelà* no 52, December, Moscow, USSR.

Kulikov V S (1972) *Rol finansov v povyshenii blagosostoiannia sovetskogo naroda*, Finansy, Moscow, USSR.

Lantsev M S (1974) Sovershenstvovanie sistemy sotsialnogo obespechenia v usloviakh razvitogo sotsialisma, *Sotsialisticheskii trud*, no 9, pp 129–37, Moscow, USSR.

Lantsev M S (1976) *Sotsialnoe obespechenie v SSSR: ekonomicheskii aspekt*, Ekonomika, Moscow, USSR.

Lapidus G and Swanson G (1988) *State and Welfare USA/USSR* Research Series no 71, Institute of International Studies, University of California, Berkeley, USA.

Madison B (1968) *Social Welfare in the Soviet Union*, Stanford University Press, Stanford, California, USA.

Maier V F and Rakitskii B V (1976) Obshchestvennye fondy potreblenia i rost blagosostoiania naroda, in *Oplata truda pri sotsializme: voprosy teorii i praktiki*, Ekonomika, pp 190–206, Moscow, USSR.

Mamontova T I (1973) Povyshenie roli obshchestvennykh fondov potreblenia v reshenii sotsialnykh problem, in Sarkisian G S *Dokhody trudiashchikhsia i sotsialnye problemy urovnia zhizni naselenia SSSR*, Nauka, Moscow, USSR.

Mamontova T I (1975) Vlianie obshchestvennykh fondov potreblenia na differentsiatsiu v urovne zhizni rabochikh i sluzhashchikh, in Shevtsov A *Sotsialisticheskii obraz zhizni i narodnoe blagosostoianie*, pp 294–302, Izdatelstvo Saratovskogo Universiteta, Saratov, USSR.

Marx Karl (1970) *Critique of the Gotha Programme*, International Publishers, New York, USA.

Matthews M (1978) *Privilege in the Soviet Union: A Study of Elite Lifestyles under Communism*, Allen and Unwin, London.

Matthews M (1979) Social Dimensions in Soviet Urban Housing, in French R A and Hamilton F E *The Socialist City*, pp 105–18, John Wiley, Chichester.

McAuley A (1979) *Economic Welfare in the Soviet Union*, Allen and Unwin, London.

McAuley A (1980) Social Welfare under Socialism: A Study of Soviet Attitudes to Redistribution, in Collard D *et al, Income Distribution: The Limits to Redistribution*, Colston Papers no 31, pp 238–58, Scientechnica, Bristol.

McAuley A (1981) *Women's Work and Wages in the Soviet Union*, Allen and Unwin, London.

McAuley A (1982) Social Policy, in Brown A and Kaser M *Soviet Policy for the 1980s*, pp 146–69, Macmillan, London.

Mikulskii K I, Rogovin V Z and Shatalin S S (1987) *Sotsialnaia politika KPSS*, Izdatelstvo Politicheskoi Literatury, Moscow, USSR.

Millar J and Clayton E (1986) *Quality of Life: Subjective Measures of Relative Satisfaction* mimeo SIP Working Paper no 9, University of Illinois, Champain-Urbana, USA.

Musgrave R (1959) *The Theory of Public Finance*, McGraw Hill, New York, USA.

Peshekhonov I V (1976) Nekotorye problemy formirovania i ispolzovania ob-shchestvennykh fondov potreblenia, *Izvestia Akademii Nauk: seria ekonomicheskaia* no 5, pp 75–89.

Potrebnosti i dokhod semi, Ekonomika (1967) Moscow, USSR.

Rabkina N E and Rimashevskaia N M (1972) *Osnovy diferensiatsii zarabotnoi platy i dokhodov naselenia*, Nauka, Moscow, USSR.

Rakitskii B V (1966) *Obshchestvennye fondy potreblenia kak ekonomicheskaia kategoria*, Mysl, Moscow, USSR.

Rakitskii B V and Shokhin A N (1987) *Zakonomernosti formirovania i realizatsii tru-dovykh dokhodov pri sotsializme*, Nauka, Moscow, USSR.

Rimashevskaia N M (1988) Public Well-Being: Myth and Reality *Problems of Economics*, **31**(12), pp 34–50. (This is a translation of Naroadnoe blagosostoianie: Mify i Realnost, *EKO* no 7, pp 3–19.)

Rogovin V Z (1985) *Lichnaia sobstvennost*, Komsomolskaia Pravda, 12 November.

Shatalin S (1986) Sotsialnoe razvitie i ekonomicheskii rost, *Kommunist*, no 14, pp 59–70.

Sotsialnoe obespechenie v SSSR: sbornik normativnykh akotov (1986) Iuridicheskaia Lit-eratura (1986), Moscow, USSR.

Soviet Economic Performance during the First Quarter of 1989, *PlanEcon Report*, vol 5, no 17.

Zaslavskaia T (1986) Chelovecheskii faktor razvitia ekonomiki i sotsialnaia spravedli-vost, *Kommunist* no 13, pp 61–73.

11 Lessons from the Swedish Pension System
Ann-Charlotte Ståhlberg

11.1 INTRODUCTION

At an early stage of its development, the Swedish labour movement rejected the idea of a detailed and frequently personally offensive testing of individual means, to which applicants for poor law relief, the only source of assistance for the needy, had to submit. Instead the Social Democratic Party emphasised the need to establish a system of social security that guaranteed each individual a basic minimum income. The elderly were the first to benefit when old age pensions were introduced in 1913 as a right of citizenship. These pensions, however, were very meagre and had to be extensively supplemented on a means-tested basis out of national and local relief funds. For the next half-century pensions policy was largely concerned with improving the basic pension to provide an adequate income for the elderly without recourse to poor relief. Eventually in 1960 the introduction of the national supplementary pension (ATP) initiated a new phase in the development of the Swedish welfare state. As a result of this reform, pension rights above the basic pension became income-related. This shift towards providing compensation for a reduction in income rather than merely guaranteeing a basic minimum level of provision meant that the public social security system became of increasing importance to the growing numbers of highly paid employees. Benefits related to middle-class income levels are one of the factors underlying the explosive growth of social expenditure and taxation from the 1960s onwards.

On the basis of an international comparison, the Swedish system of social insurance provides a generous level of benefits. This might be partially explained in terms of the need to win support for the public social insurance system from the white-collar groups who had already negotiated advantageous insurance benefits under the terms of collective agreements. It was the considered opinion of Social Democrats that if this proved to be successful, the welfare state would be in a better position to count on the loyalty of middle-class taxpayers.

This represents something of a dilemma for the Social Democratic government in the 1990s. On the one hand, the realities of the economic climate exert pressure on the government to reduce expenditure. At the same time, the government hopes to retain the support of the middle class for the welfare state, a support that the Social Democratic Party believes has been largely bolstered by the idea of compensation in the event of loss of income.

However, even if the government maintains a passive role, the principle of income compensation will be eroded. Benefit levels in the Swedish pension system are subject to a pensionable earnings ceiling, linked to the consumer price index. When this limit was first established, only a limited number of individuals reached this ceiling. Consequently the principle of income compensation was able to operate without restriction. However, the growth of real wages has raised the incomes of an increasing number of individuals, including manual workers, up to the ceiling. This process will tend to accelerate as real wages continue to rise. The strict application of a principle of income compensation without a ceiling would give rise to a substantial increase in expenditure over and above that required by automatic price adjustments. In other words, the situation is unstable.

11.2   THE NATIONAL SUPPLEMENTARY PENSION SCHEME (ATP)

This new scheme was preceded by an intense debate in the 1950s, which not only led to a referendum but also to a government crisis and new elections. The referendum was based on three different alternatives: (1) a statutory occupational pension constructed as a pay-as-you-go system, (2) raising the level of the existing basic old age pension, and (3) measures to encourage the growth of negotiated and private funded pensions. Finally, alternative 1 – the policy favoured by the Social Democrats and the Trade Union Confederation (LO) – narrowly won the day in the Riksdag after new elections had been held and a member of the Liberal Party had abstained from voting on the question.

The ATP scheme has been modified in several ways since its introduction in the early 1960s. The basic flat-rate pension has been raised; there is a new special pension supplement available to persons with no or only a low ATP pension, and there is also an income-tested housing subsidy. It has become easier to receive early retirement pensions, and part-time pensions have been introduced. Further, recent decades have seen the introduction of negotiated occupational pensions in addition to the two national pensions in areas of employment where such benefits did not previously exist. The entire labour market is thus covered in practice by negotiated pensions, which in the private sector are not financed on a pay-as-you-go basis but as funded systems or a combination of both. Hence the present pensions system consists of three parts: the flat-rate pension, the ATP earnings-related pension and private occupational pensions.

Table 11.1: Expenditure on social welfare 1987

Object of expenditure	Share of social expenditure (%)	Share of expenditure (%) covered by contributions from:				
		The State	Local authorities	Employers	Insured persons	Funds
Sickness and occupational injury	37.3	10.5	60.1	26.8	0	2.6
Sickness insurance	11.8	14.5	0	77.1	0	8.3
Public health, hospitals etc.	21.1	8.5	91.5	0	0	0
Care of mentally retarded	2.1	8.8	91.2	0	0	0
National dental service	0.7	0	100.0	0	0	0
Dental care insurance	0.8	15.0	85.0	0	0	0
Occupational injury insurance and industrial safety	0.8	4.0	0	87.9	3.8	4.3
Unemployment	5.7	52.0	1.6	43.3	3.1	0
Unemployment insurance and benefits	2.3	32.3	0	60.0	7.7	0
Employment exchanges, vocational guidance	0.1	100.0	0	0	0	0
Retraining of unemp- loyed persons etc.	1.9	38.5	4.7	56.7	0	0
Public works	1.4	100.0	0	0	0	0
Old age, disability etc	36.8	12.4	12.1	65.8	5.2	4.5
National basic pension	15.6	15.5	7.3	74.3	2.9	0
National supplementary pension (ATP)	15.6	0	0	80.1	9.4	10.5
Partial pensions	0.2	100.0	0	0	0	0
Care of disabled	1.4	88.0	0	12.0	0	0
Assistance for aged and disabled	4.1	17.9	82.1	0	0	0
Families and children	16.1	50.0	36.5	13.4	0	0
Parent cash benefit	2.4	15.0	0	85.0	0	0
General child allowance	2.9	100.0	0	0	0	0
Advances of maintenance allowances	0.5	100.0	0	0	0	0
School meals	0.8	0	100.0	0	0	0
Child care	5.6	47.4	52.6	0	0	0
Other assistance	3.9					
Other	4.1					
Total	100.0	21.9	33.3	40.1	2.1	2.6

(*Source*: Swedish Statistical Yearbook 1989)

The public budget for all expenditure on social welfare corresponded to 34 per cent of GNP in 1987. Cash transfers from social insurance (including sickness and unemployment benefits) amounted to 17 per cent of GNP. National pensions alone stood for 11 per cent of GNP. In terms of social benefits in kind, health care expenditure accounted for 8 per cent of GNP.

Table 11.1 shows the distribution of social expenditure in 1987, one-third of which was cash transfers to pensioners.

As much as 40 per cent of social expenditure is financed by proportional payroll taxes on employers. In total, payroll taxes amount to 37.47 per cent of the payroll, of which 20.45 per cent goes to pensions and 10.1 per cent to sickness cash benefit insurance. Negotiated non-statutory benefits are financed in a similar manner. For private sector salaried employees these contributions amount to close on 9 per cent of the payroll, while the corresponding amount for private sector blue-collar workers is 6 per cent. Negotiated benefits are narrower in scope than statutory ones, partly because negotiated benefits are mainly a complement to the statutory ones, partly because statutory benefits are aimed at a much wider group of beneficiaries. Even people who have never worked are entitled to national insurance benefits.

The basic pension is a fixed amount, the same for everyone irrespective of previous earnings, which is pegged to the consumer price index. It is financed on a pay-as-you-go basis and payroll taxes (9.45 per cent in 1989) account for 80 per cent of expenditure, while the remainder is covered out of general tax revenues. The basic pension, including the special pension supplement, is roughly 30 per cent of the average income for full-time male employees. The second-tier ATP is income-related and is in principle financed by payroll taxes. Together with the basic pension, ATP replaces 60-65 per cent of a person's previous income in real terms, while pensions provided by employers replace a further 10 per cent, so that ATP clearly comprises the largest part.

The problems associated with ATP are many. One of these concerns the demographic changes that have resulted in a reduced number of economically active persons supporting a growing number of pensioners. Another and more important problem is the way in which the pensions scheme was constructed. It is now possible, after thirty years, to evaluate the economic and redistributional consequences of the various characteristics of the ATP scheme. This chapter, therefore, is intended to describe the Swedish national supplementary pension scheme and its shortcomings.

11.3   THE STRUCTURE OF THE PENSION SCHEME

The public transfer payment system is constructed on the basis of two main principles: the idea of basic social security and the idea of restitution in the event of loss of income. The idea of basic security guarantees pensioners a given standard. The basic pension is an expression of this principle. The idea of compensation for loss of income guarantees a person his or her previous standard of living, the amount of compensation being dependent on previous earnings. ATP is based on this latter principle. However, only incomes from employment up to a stipulated level (indexed only for price rises) are counted as pensionable, i.e. giving credits for ATP. (In 1989 14 per cent of men and 2 per cent of women had incomes over the ATP ceiling.) Employees are also covered by the negotiated pensions schemes, which complement the basic pension and ATP, partly by raising the level of compensation within the income range covered by the public pension scheme, and partly by giving pension rights to incomes earned above the ATP ceiling. Negotiated pensions are also based on the income compensation principle.

An ATP pension is the equivalent of 60 per cent of pensionable income at constant prices during the 15 best-paid years of earnings. Pensionable income is income from employment within the range of 1 to 7.5 so-called base amounts (one base amount in 1989 being equivalent to roughly 20 per cent of an average industrial worker's wage). The base amount is an interesting statistical device introduced in 1957 to provide a common base for the calculation of the two national pensions and, being constantly readjusted in accordance with changes to the consumer price index, keeps pensions inflation-proof. Normally, 30 years of earnings are necessary in order to gain full ATP and the size of the ATP pension is reduced by $\frac{1}{30}$ for each year below 30 at the time of retirement. The rules were more generous during a transitional period for those who were already quite old when the ATP scheme was introduced in 1960. ATP credits can be earned from the age of 16.

The ATP is a pay-as-you-go system financed by payroll taxes, at a rate of 11 per cent in 1989. In a pay-as-you-go system, pensions are financed out of the incomes of the presently employed generation. A build-up of funds as in an actuarially fair (funded) system is therefore unnecessary. Up to the end of 1981, pensions and contributions were based on the same body of income. Since then, however, contributions have been levied on total incomes while there are stipulated limits on incomes which count for pensions.

The basic pension, which like ATP is automatically adjusted for inflation, is 96 per cent of one base amount for single pensioners and 78.5 per cent of one base amount each for married pensioners where both spouses are pensioned. For persons not eligible for ATP or with a very low ATP, there is a special pension supplement. This was introduced in 1969 and has successively been increased to a level that is now at its maximum of 54 per cent of one base amount.

ITP, the negotiated supplementary pension scheme covering privately employed white-collar workers, is devised as an actuarially fair funded system. Premiums paid by employers amount on average to 8 per cent of the payroll.[1] An ITP pension consists of two parts: 10 per cent of final salary up to the ATP ceiling and 65 per cent of earnings up to a very much higher ceiling than the ATP. The right to a partial ITP pension can be earned by persons who have worked for as little as 40 per cent of full time from the age of 28. Thirty years of earning are required in order to gain a full pension.

STP, the corresponding scheme for privately employed blue-collar workers, is organised as a compromise between the funded and the pay-as-you-go systems. Each year the employer pays a premium equal to the amount needed to provide lifelong pensions for those workers being pensioned that year. The rate of premium, which is the same for all employers, amounted to about 3 per cent of payroll in 1989. A pension from STP is 10 per cent of average income during the 3 best-paid years of employment between the ages of 55 and 59. At the end of the 1960s, maximum blue-collar wage levels were achieved between the ages of 55 and 59. The rules for STP, introduced in 1973, were drawn up accordingly. Incomes over the ATP ceiling are not counted as eligible for STP, 30 years of earnings are normally necessary in order to gain a full pension, and pension rights can be earned from the age of 28. Only 10 per cent of full-time employment is required to qualify for inclusion in this scheme, and to earn a partial pension.

Occupational supplementary pensions for state and municipal workers are structured on the pay-as-you-go principle and financed by ordinary taxation out of the state and municipal budgets. They are coordinated with the national pension scheme in order to guarantee a pension of 65 per cent of final salary up to a very much higher ceiling than the ATP. As in the case of the ITP scheme, 40 per cent of full-time employment is required to be eligible. In the municipal schemes, credits are earned from the age of 28, but in the state schemes from the age of 20. In both cases, 30 years of earnings are required to gain full pension rights.

11.4   ATP AFTER THIRTY YEARS

In 1960, ATP contributions were 1.9 per cent of the payroll. These have risen to 11 per cent in 1989. Given the present definition of the rules, ATP contributions will have to be raised substantially in the future in order to meet pension payment demands. According to computations by the National Social Insurance Board in 1987, an annual real income growth rate of over 2 per cent must be achieved if a dramatic rise in contributions is to be avoided. This is shown in Table 11.2. Zero growth means that contributions in the year 2025 must be close to 40 per cent of the payroll in order to finance pensions, while a 2 per cent annual growth rate will keep the contribution rate at just over 20 per cent. The structure of the ATP scheme, with consumer price indexation and earnings-related pensions, makes it extremely sensitive to real wage fluctuations. However, as more and more people become eligible for ATP benefits and at higher rates, the need for the special pension supplement will gradually disappear along with the related contributions. This can be seen in Table 11.3, which shows total national pension contributions as a percentage of the payroll.

The payroll upon which ATP contributions are calculated depends partly

Table 11.2: ATP contributions as a percentage of the payroll

Year	Real wage growth			
	0 %	1 %	2 %	3 %
1990	14.6	13.8	13.7	13.6
1995	17.4	15.7	14.9	13.7
2005	24.0	19.6	17.1	14.2
2015	33.8	26.5	21.0	15.9
2025	38.2	29.1	20.8	14.2
2035	39.5	30.0	18.8	11.4

(*Source*: National Social Insurance Board 1987)

Table 11.3: The national pension schemes (basic pension, special pension supplement, and ATP) contributions as a percentage of the payroll

Year	Real wage growth			
	0 %	1 %	2 %	3 %
1990	24.0	22.8	22.5	21.7
1995	27.5	23.9	22.8	20.2
2005	35.0	27.2	23.7	17.9
2015	44.1	32.0	24.0	16.5
2025	52.4	36.3	22.8	14.6
2035	52.5	37.9	21.8	12.5

(*Source*: National Social Insurance Board 1987)

on how many employees receive incomes chargeable for contributions at any one time, and partly on how large these incomes are, which is in turn dependent on the numbers of hours worked and wages per unit of time. The number of pensioners has increased substantially since the 1960s. This is partly a result of the maturation of the scheme and partly of the fact that the number of elderly persons has increased. We live much longer now than we did 30 years ago; the normal retirement age has been lowered from 67 to 65, and the rules for early retirement pensions have become more lenient – early retirement pensions can in 1989 be taken at the age of 60 in the event of an individual being unable to find employment. The average retirement age is thus in practice 62.

According to the forecast of the National Social Insurance Board in 1987, the number of persons in the age groups 20-64 will increase until shortly after the turn of the century, to fall again up to the end of the forecast period in 2035. The number of persons of 65 and over is expected to rise until 1990, to fall somewhat towards the year 2010, but to rise again sharply to 2035. Given the assumptions on which the forecast is based – a histori-cally low fertility rate, a small immigration surplus and low mortality risk – the ratio between the number of persons aged 20-64 and the number of persons of 65 and over will shrink from 3.3 in 1985 to 2.5 in 2035. If early retirement or disability pensions drawn between the ages 20 and 64 are also taken into account, the ratio will be further reduced from 2.5 in 1985 to 1.9 in 2035. This means that from about the year 2010, a reduced number of economically active persons will have to support a growing number of economically non-active persons. In its 1989 population forecast, Statistics Sweden foresees a higher fertility rate and greater immigrant surplus than in the prognosis above. However, this is of marginal importance in relation to the systemic problems of the ATP system being discussed here. An increased dependency ratio will of course place a great strain on the pension scheme. It is, however, the structure of the scheme itself which is its own worst enemy. The method of inflation protection, the rules for earning ATP, the scheme's conception as a pay-as-you-go system etc. are all characteristics which were hotly debated before the 1960 Bill. The results are now, thirty years later, evident to see.

11.5 THE STANDARD OF LIVING GUARANTEE

A full pension from ATP is 60 per cent of pensionable income during the fifteen best-paid years of earnings in real terms. Inflation protection means that the pensioner is guaranteed an income related to his or her previous standard of living. The income compensation principle, however, has become a bit chipped around the edges through the imposition of the ATP ceiling, since only incomes up to a certain level may be counted as eligible for pension.

The rules guarantee that the pensioner is compensated for price increases but not for general improvements in living standards in the society as a whole, as in the event of an increase in real wages. On the other hand, their already achieved standards would not be affected by any fall in the real wages of the economically active section of the population. Thus, if real wages fall, the pensioners' standard of living improves compared with that of the working population, while in periods of rising real wages, there is a relative deterioration in the standard of living of pensioners. The present definition of the rules causes the income distribution between the working population and pensioners to be very sensitive to changes in the growth rate of wages. This is illustrated in Table 11.4, which presents calculations of the average gross and net pension in relation to the average gross and net wages of the working population on the basis of different real wage growth assumptions. In these calculations, the average tax on earnings is assumed to be 50 per cent and on ATP income to be 40 per cent.

Without growth in the economy, the average pension would in 35 years' time be 99 per cent of the average gross wages of the working population, as against at present barely 60 per cent. The net pension would on average

Table 11.4: Average basic pension plus ATP as a percentage of the average wage for the working population aged 20–64

Year	Pension and wages *before* tax Real wage growth		Pension and wages *after* tax Real wage growth	
	0 %	2 %	0 %	2 %
1990	58	55	70	66
1995	65	51	77	61
2005	98	56	118	67
2015	92	56	111	68
2025	99	51	119	61
2035	96	43	116	51

(*Source*: National Social Insurance Board 1987, own calculations)

be all of 119 per cent of the net mean wage after tax. If real wages were to rise by 2 per cent per annum, in 35 years the average gross pension would be 51 per cent of the average gross wage and the average net pension would be 61 per cent of the average net wage. Above all, it is the method of adjusting pension levels by the consumer price index together with the 15-year rule which cause the wide variations in income distribution between pensioners and the working population.

Too wide a gap between pensions and wages would lead to tension between the two groups. If this gap is felt to be unfair, demands will be made either for compensation or for a change in the rules. In periods of positive growth, it is easy to raise pensions. But if growth falls, the pensioners' share of the pie increases, and at the same time it becomes more difficult, politically, to reduce benefits already in payment.

If pensions were indexed to real wages instead of to prices, more flexibility could be achieved in adapting the pension scheme to economic growth. In periods of falling real wages, for example, a rapid accommodation of costs to the new economic situation could easily be arrived at. When the pensions level is a fixed share of the wages of the working population, the amount of contributions exacted will only be affected by changes in the dependency ratio. When a pension, as is presently the case, is a fixed share of pensioners' previous earnings in real terms, contributions are affected both by changes in the dependency ratio and by changes in the real wages of the working population. Contribution increases on account of changes in the dependency ratio would then be dampened by real wage increases but further increased by real wage decreases.

The question of whether pensions ought to follow changes in prices or changes in wages has been discussed by various commissions of inquiry both before and after the adoption of the ATP reform. At the time that the decision to introduce ATP was adopted, optimism was great about the future. It was thought that a reform which tied pension rights to previous earnings (in real terms) and pensions in payment to the consumer price index would be cheaper in the long run than linking both to a wage index.

Today, however, this linkage of pensions in payment to the consumer price index has come under fire and demands are being made for a change-over to some form of wage indexation. Let us therefore take a closer look at what this could mean. To begin with, let us suppose that age distribution, that is to say the ratio between the number of pensioners and the number of economically active persons, remains constant. If pensions were then to follow changes in real wages, the mean pension would always be a fixed share of the mean wage of the working population. If, for example, the rules are such that the mean pension is to be 60 per cent of the mean wage and real wages increase by 2 per cent, then pensions would also rise by 2 per cent. Correspondingly, pensions would fall if real wages were to fall. Let us say that there were three economically active persons to each pensioner, the payroll tax would then be 20 per cent per year.

Normally, however, the ratio between pensioners and the working population is not constant over time. When changes in the ratio occur, on account of demographic changes, changes in the retirement age, in the labour supply etc., the balance is disturbed. Let us now suppose that there are two economically active persons to each pensioner. If pensioners are to retain their share at 60 per cent, payroll taxes must be increased to 30 per cent. If, instead, taxes are kept unchanged at 20 per cent, pension benefits must correspondingly be reduced to 40 per cent of the average wage.

Even if pensions were to follow changes in the working population's wages, a continuous adjustment would still be necessary, either of the contributions or of the pension level or of both, since the relationship between the number of pensioners and the number of the gainfully employed is constantly changing. Just where the adjustment is to be made, however, whether in the contributions, in the pension level, or in both, is not self-evident.

Let us imagine that the ratio between the number of pensioners and the number of persons in the working population is reduced on account of *changes in the birth rate*, so that for a few years many more children are born than in the preceding and the following years (cf. the large cohorts of the 1940s in Sweden). When these cohorts enter the labour market, the addition to the labour force will be unusually large. A not unreasonable consequence of this would be a relative shortage of capital, which will tend to reduce labour productivity and depress wage levels (see Auerbach *et al*, 1988). It would then seem reasonable to allow the reduction in the dependency ratio to have its effect in a reduction in contributions, in order to improve the situation of the working generation *vis-à-vis* the pensioned generation. For the same reason, adjustment could also take place by way of contributions (an increase) when these large cohorts are pensioned and the ratio between the number of pensioners and the number of working persons rises.

Let us now imagine that the ratio between the number of pensioners and the number of the working population rises because *the retirement age has been lowered*. We would here have to differentiate between the elderly, the middle-aged, and the young. Young persons would have to pay more in contributions because they will be supported for more years as pensioners. Those who are already pensioners should not have to pay by reduced pensions for benefits that they will never enjoy. But the middle-aged will not have adequate time in which to pay for their pensions, even if contributions are raised. For the latter, a combination of raised contributions and reduced pension benefits may be a possible solution.

As a third example, let us choose *fewer working hours*. In this case, adjustment could also be made by means of increased contributions. The pensioned generation can of course not share in this benefit, while the working generation ought to pay for this extension of their free time.

What these examples show is that *wage indexing like price indexation cannot be expected to be totally free of objections*. Neither the rate of contribution nor the pension level can be considered as given once and for all. Sources of friction will therefore still exist between the working and the pensioned generations.

11.6   OVERCOMPENSATION

The introduction of a pay-as-you-go system such as the ATP scheme overcompensates the older generation in the sense that this generation is expected to receive more in benefits than it has contributed to the system. The generation becoming pensioned in the period of transition have only had time to contribute for a few years, at the same time as the pension rules governing their retirement become more generous so that they nevertheless have the chance of getting a reasonable pension. The size of the fund and the related amount of overcompensation was an important question in the 1950s pensions debate. The unfairness of too large a degree of compensation was pointed out. Initially a higher contribution was charged than was strictly necessary in a pure pay-as-you-go system, and in this manner the National Pension Insurance (AP) Fund was built up.

Today we know the outcome of this in terms of overcompensation. In Ståhlberg (1990a, 1990b), I have calculated for a random sample of 6000 persons what each person could be expected to receive as pension during his or her lifetime and how much each person could be expected to contribute (by the incidence of payroll taxes) to the ATP Scheme during his or her working life. Data on each individual's factual pensionable and chargeable incomes have been taken from longitudinal registers, where annual data for each person are available for a consecutive period of about twenty-five years. Future incomes have had to be estimated. On the basis of this combi-

Table 11.5: The benefit/contribution ratio and net transfers as a proportion of life-cycle incomes in ATP

Cohort born in	Benefit/contribution ratio	Net transfers as a proportion of life-cycle income
1905-14	5.9	0.02
1915-23	3.7	0.04
1924-33	2.0	0.04
1934-43	1.2	0.01
1944-50	0.8	−0.02
1964-70	0.8	−0.02

(*Source:* Ståhlberg 1990a)

nation of factual and estimated incomes I have then computed each individual's expected life-cycle benefits and ATP contributions.

In Table 11.5, computations are presented of what different generations contribute to the ATP scheme and what they receive from it. The results are shown in the form of benefit/contribution ratios and as the net transfers' share of life-cycle incomes. The net transfer means the difference between the present value of what a generation expects to gain from the scheme and the present value of what they expect to contribute. It has been presumed that wage earners will in the long run bear the burden of ATP contributions. The real rate of discount is assumed to be 2 per cent, a reasonable assumption in view of the fact that average growth in the past one hundred years has remained constant at about that level. Sensitivity analyses using other rates of interest show that the order of precedence between the cohorts is not changed, only the absolute amounts.

For those who were middle-aged or elderly when the ATP scheme was introduced, the effect on life-cycle incomes is, as expected, positive. The ratios between benefits and contributions are greatest for the very oldest cohorts. Benefits are nearly six times as much as contributions. ATP has thus increased individual life-cycle incomes by on average 2 per cent. For a person who has been employed for forty-five years, this corresponds to one year's average income. Up until the 1933 cohort, benefits are at least twice as much as contributions, which means that ATP has increased life-cycle incomes by on average 4 per cent − an increase of about two years' average incomes.

Those who were young at the time that the scheme was introduced, and successive generations, on the other hand, are forced to contribute much more than they can expect to get back in the form of benefits. The 1944 cohort is the first one not favoured by the transition period, since they may have to pay during their whole life cycle. ATP reduces life-cycle incomes by on average 2 per cent for today's 40-45 year olds, as it did for the generation born 20 years after. We can make the assumption that these transfer subsidies are instead placed in an actuarially fair scheme with an average real rate of interest of 2 per cent. Life-cycle incomes would then, on average, have been one year's income higher. That the benefit/contribution ratio turns out to be less than 1 for these generations is partly a result of an unfavourable population and real wage growth, and partly due to the higher contributions paid during the first twenty-year period (in order to build up the National Pensions Fund) than would normally have been the case in a pure pay-as-you-go system.

In order for a pension scheme to function in the long run, it ought to be constructed in such a manner that it can be accepted by the average citizen for many generations to come. If everyone in a generation stands to gain by the scheme in the sense that they can count on getting out more than they put in during their working lives, one would expect that almost everyone in that generation would support the scheme. If, however, it is obvious for a generation that they will never get back as much as they contribute, *it is doubtful whether the majority of that generation will feel inclined to support the scheme*, especially in a situation where contributions are rising.

11.7   THE 15- AND 30-YEAR RULES

The rules of ATP are such that pension size is determined by incomes earned during the 15 best-paid years of working life at constant prices (the 15-year rule) while 30 years of earnings are enough to give entitlement to full pension (the 30-year rule). (During the period of transition, after ATP pensions were first introduced, 20 years' contributions were considered enough.) These are rules 'inherited' by the ATP scheme from earlier occupational pensions schemes. The idea was that even women who remained at home with small children, or university graduates with many years of studies, would have time to accumulate 30 years of working life. But since blue-collar workers normally did not reach their highest earnings just before retirement, like most white-collar workers, it was decided that the ATP scheme would be assessed on the basis of the 15 best years of earnings rather than the final years as in the occupational pensions schemes.

Thus, a working life of more than 30 years does not in itself add to the size of one's pension. Furthermore, it makes no difference at what stage in working life the best 15 years have occurred, nor how small an income may have been earned in the remaining years. A person who has worked full-time all his or her life may still have a lower ATP than a person who has only worked full-time for 15 years, and part-time for a further 15 years. Yet ATP contributions are levied on income for all the years of working life, and the full-time worker may therefore have contributed far more to the scheme during his greater number of working years.

In 1969, the special pension supplement was introduced to complement the basic pension for those with a very low or no ATP. Since 1982, the upper and lower income limits for contributions have been removed so that these are now paid on total income.

The 15- and 30-year rules are advantageous for persons who have an uneven distribution of lifetime income and fewer years of earning, so that the tendency is to favour women and high-income earners. The ATP ceiling on pensionable earnings, on the other hand, is favourable to low-income earners, and the special pension supplement is advantageous to those who have low or no ATP. The situation is such that the rules can work in a contradictory fashion from the point of view of redistribution policy. Consequently, only empirical study can reveal the true patterns of redistribution.

Social insurance always contains some element of risk sharing. The impossibility of knowing how long each person will live means that both payments to and withdrawals from the pension scheme are subject to a degree of uncertainty. One person in the workforce may die before reaching retirement age and may therefore have made substantial contributions, while another person may live for many years as a retiree and therefore receive a very high 'dividend' on payments made, as some income redistribution in every insurance system always occurs *ex post facto*. Such transfers are random, however, and from the point of view of redistribution policy less interesting. What is interesting from this viewpoint are the *systematic* transfers brought about by the working of the rules. Is it the case that everyone contributes as much or do some categories pay more than others for an expected pension benefit of the same size?

In Ståhlberg (1990a, 1990b) I have computed for each person in the study his or her expected benefits from and contribution to the ATP scheme (see also p 224). The analysis shows that for the currently economically active generation, the regressive tendencies inherent in the 15- and 30-year rules (the rules are disadvantageous to those who work for a greater number of years and have an even distribution of lifetime income – frequently low income earners) are stronger than the progressive influence of the ATP ceiling. (So far, relatively few persons have incomes above the ATP ceiling.) The opposite is true for most of the younger generation (see Tables 11.6 and 11.7).

In Table 11.6 the transfers are illustrated, as in Table 11.5, partly through the benefit/contribution ratio and net transfers as a proportion of life-cycle income, and partly through the non-redistributive pension contributions. The first measure is based on the assumption that the tax is proportional to the wage. In the case of the second measure, this assumption is not necessary. This measure indicates the annual percentage tax on wages that the individual would have to pay to ATP, that is to present-day pensioners, if no income redistribution was allowed.

It is clear that ATP redistributes incomes between the social classes and that this redistribution is regressive. Incomes are transferred from the lower

Table 11.6: The benefit/contribution ratio, net transfers as a proportion of life-cycle income and the non-redistributive, neutral pension contribution to ATP for the cohort born in 1944–50

Sex and social class		Benefit/contribution ratio	Net transfers as a proportion of life-cycle income	The non-redistributive (neutral) pension contributions (%)
Men	I	0.88	−0.01	8.0
	II	0.80	−0.02	7.0
	III	0.78	−0.02	6.6
	I+II+III	0.80	−0.02	7.0
Women	I	0.94	−0.01	8.5
	II	0.82	−0.02	7.3
	III	0.65	−0.03	5.9
	I+II+III	0.77	−0.02	6.9
Men + women		0.79	−0.02	7.0

(*Source*: Ståhlberg 1990a)

Note: Social class I is here defined as higher-grade salaried employees and large-scale businessmen. Social class II consists of lower-grade salaried employees and smaller-scale businessmen. Social class III is made up of workers (Erikson and Åberg 1987). Income earners in social class I have on average the highest life-cycle incomes, while earners in social class III have the lowest.

to the upper classes, the benefit/contribution ratio being higher in social class I than in social class II and greater in social class II than in social class III, and this is true of both men and women. If the ATP scheme had been neutral from a redistribution viewpoint and had consequently not given rise to any income transfers, the pension contribution/burden of payroll tax would have been greater for social class I than for II and III, and the working class would have paid the lowest contribution. How large the difference would have been is illustrated by the non-redistributional contribution column in the table. In reality, however, the contribution percentage is equal for all.

Table 11.7 makes clear that transfers are no longer regressive for those who today are in their twenties. The rate of progression is even stronger than depicted, as the way in which life-cycle incomes are computed tends to under-estimate this trend. As we can see, the benefit/contribution ratio is greater in the lower social classes than in the upper. (The exception is working-class women, whose ratio is the same as men's in the same class, but less than the women of both other classes. The reason for this is that women have not come up to the ATP ceiling on pensionable earnings to the same degree as men.) It follows that in a non- redistributive system, the working class would pay a larger proportion of their incomes than would the other classes. Since this is not the case, for that generation the direction of transfer is from the upper to the lower class.

Table 11.7: The benefit/contribution ratio, the net transfers as a proportion of life-cycle income and the non-redistributive, neutral pension contribution to ATP for the cohort born in 1964-1970

Sex and social class		Benefit/contribution ratio	Net transfers as a proportion of life-cycle income	The non-redistributive (neutral) pension contributions (%)
Men	I	0.71	−0.03	6.4
	II	0.74	−0.02	6.5
	III	0.77	−0.02	6.6
	I+II+III	0.75	−0.02	6.6
Women	I	0.83	−0.02	7.5
	II	0.91	−0.01	8.1
	III	0.77	−0.02	7.0
	I+II+III	0.85	−0.01	7.6
Men + women		0.79	−0.02	6.9

(Source: Ståhlberg 1990a)

Although ATP is regressive today it cannot be assumed that this will remain unchanged on a longer perspective. This is because pensionable earnings, but not contributions, are limited to a ceiling.

11.8   THE CEILING IN THE ATP SCHEME

If real wages increase, an increasing number of persons will come to have incomes above the stipulated ceiling of ATP pensionable earnings, which will soon reduce ATP to no more than a basic pension for employees, albeit at a higher level than the present one. Today, about 14 per cent of men and 2 per cent of women have incomes above this ceiling. According to the National Social Insurance Board's calculations, 74 per cent of men and 50 per cent of women will have incomes above this ceiling by the year 2025, given an annual real wage growth rate of on average 2 per cent. If growth is less – say 1 per cent – the figures will be 40 per cent of men and 11 per cent of women (see Table 11.8). This will be to the disadvantage of blue-collar workers employed in the private sector (belonging to the STP scheme) who unlike other groups do not have negotiated pensions that compensate for loss of income above the ceiling. If nothing is done, the situation will revert to one resembling the period before the arrival of ATP.

The fact that the income compensation principle is rapidly being under-mined and that ATP is gradually reverting to becoming a basic pension for employees at a higher level than the present, is contrary to original inten-tions. *However, any raising of the ceiling, as we have seen, would be entirely at the expense of low-income earners as income transfers will then work to the advantage of high-income earners.*

Table 11.8: The percentage of the working population with incomes above the ATP ceiling on different assumptions as to rates of growth in earnings

	Real annual growth in earnings (%)	1985	1995	2005	2015	2025	2035
Men	0	9.2	9.0	7.5	6.9	6.8	8.0
	1	9.2	17.2	23.0	29.5	39.5	50.4
	2	9.2	21.3	41.5	60.6	74.2	80.6
	3	9.2	30.1	62.3	77.6	83.8	87.0
Women	0	0.7	0.6	0.5	0.4	0.5	0.6
	1	0.7	2.0	3.4	6.1	11.2	19.4
	2	0.7	2.9	10.9	29.8	50.2	66.3
	3	0.7	6.2	31.1	58.7	74.7	81.7
Men + women	0	5.0	4.9	4.1	3.7	3.7	4.4
	1	5.0	9.7	13.3	17.9	25.5	35.1
	2	5.0	12.2	25.4	45.4	62.3	73.6
	3	5.0	18.4	46.9	68.2	79.3	84.4

(*Source*: National Social Insurance Board 1987)

Raising the ATP ceiling would mean a corresponding increase in ATP contributions. Table 11.9 shows the payroll taxes required when the ATP ceiling is raised in step with the real rate of growth. Compared to present rules (see Table 11.2), the differences in the contribution rates in the event of growth above 1 per cent will be most evident.

11.9   ATP AND SAVING

The effect of ATP on saving in the economy is as acute a question in the 1990s as it was in the 1950s. Now, as then, the view is that Sweden needs to save more. The ATP scheme's overcompensation of both the elderly and middle-aged, in the form of increased life-cycle incomes, created increased consumption at the expense of saving. Private saving fell dramatically during the 1960s. On the other hand, a high level of savings was maintained in the public sector throughout the 1960s and early 1970s. This largely coincided with the build-up of the National Pension Insurance Fund. Since then, however, public saving has been negative and private household saving has fallen even further and is at its lowest level during the entire post-war period.

We have seen that when real wages rise, ATP gradually evolves into a new basic pension for employees. If ATP pensions are to be income-related even in the future, an upward adjustment of the ceiling is necessary. Another possibility is to allow the ceiling to remain at the same real level as

Table 11.9: ATP contributions as a percentage of the payroll when the ATP ceiling is raised in step with real GNP

| Year | Rate of annual growth in GNP in real terms | | | |
	0 %	1 %	2 %	3 %
1990	14.6	13.8	13.7	13.6
1995	17.4	15.7	15.0	13.9
2005	24.0	19.7	17.2	14.6
2015	33.8	27.5	22.4	18.4
2025	38.2	31.1	24.5	19.8
2035	39.5	33.6	25.8	21.3

(*Source*: National Social Insurance Board 1987)

today but instead to let negotiated pensions meet compensation above that level. This is already the case for salaried workers in industry through the ITP scheme and for state and local government employees. It should also be possible to upgrade the STP scheme for blue-collar workers in industry to fit this model.

There are advantages to giving negotiated pensions a more important role instead of raising the ATP ceiling. One vital characteristic of any pension scheme is the manner in which it influences capital supply and thereby economic growth. *An increase in capital supply in order to meet future pension demands is facilitated by a system constructed on the basis of funding.* Both of the private sector's negotiated pension schemes, ITP and STP, are funded schemes.

11.10   INSURANCE VERSUS TAXATION

On its introduction in 1960, the ATP scheme was more of an insurance and less of a tax-transfer system than it has become today. In other words, there was a closer correlation between benefits and contributions. It was also easier than today to see the ATP contribution as a deferred fringe benefit. The gradual extension of the system to its present fully functioning stage together with changes in the rules have also brought with them a shift in emphasis, whereby the taxation policy aspects of the ATP contributions have received greater prominence.

Only incomes between stipulated levels are pensionable. The ATP contribution, however, is levied on total income. This means that ATP contributions levied on those portions of income above and below this range are pure taxation. This tax came into force in 1982. Previously, pensionable income and income chargeable for contributions were one and the same amount. The ceiling construction, in combination with real wage growth, has tended to raise the incomes of an increasing number of persons above the ceiling. *Consequently, there is constant growth in that part of the ATP contribution which is pure taxation.*

ATP contributions on individual incomes beyond 30 years and in principle also beyond the 15 best years of earning are also pure taxation, since 30 years are sufficient for full pension rights and these are only computed on the basis of the best 15 years. A reduction in working hours during other years is of no importance for the person's ATP. Those who retired in 1974 – those born in 1908 or later – are the first individuals who can have had incomes eligible for ATP for more than 15 years. Persons born after 1924 are the first who can have satisfied the 30-year rule for a full pension. Thus the taxation share of ATP contributions increases as the ATP scheme approaches its fully functioning stage. Individuals will then have had at least a theoretical possibility of having qualified for ATP benefits during the maximum number of years. The taxation element will then have achieved full force.

Since pensions and ATP contributions are not computed on the same income, reduced working hours need not mean a reduced pension. Those who choose a greater amount of free time are favoured by the system.[2] Reduced working hours lower the taxable payroll and cause an increase in the rates of ATP contributions. For this reason, therefore, shorter working hours, longer vacations, or a lower retirement age impose a great burden on the pensions system.

As a result of the 15-year and the 30-year rules and the ATP ceiling, a distinction has been drawn between *pensionable* and *chargeable* income. From either the standpoint of efficiency or of redistribution, this is undesirable. *A stronger correlation between benefits and contributions is a precondition for the achievement of a stable system.* Each year of contributions would then add to each future pension an expected increase proportional to the contribution. Those who choose more free time could not then be subsidised by the system. It is true that income transfers from high- to low-income earners would then not take place. However, by the same token, there would not be any income transfers, as at present, from low- to high-income earners. Part-time employees and those who have not worked for very many years, however, would lose by such a change in the 15- and 30-year rules. In practice this would strike hardest against women in the workforce, as the present ATP rules are generous towards part-time employees, who are mainly women.

11.11   THE PROBLEMS OF ATP AND SUGGESTIONS TOWARDS A SOLUTION

Let us recapitulate the problems and see what solutions appear logical in our context.

(i)   The protection of pensions against inflation by means of the consumer price index is under question. Should some form of wage index be chosen instead? It has, however, been made clear that the use of a wage index is also not without its problems and that a change-over to such an index might well result in an equally heated debate in a few years' time. If an ATP reform made today was liable to come under fire in the near future, then the credibility of the entire system would indeed be in danger.

(ii) The principle of the ATP ceiling (which is pegged to a consumer price index, not to a real wage index) is threatening to reduce the entire system to a new basic pension for employees within the next thirty years. If we do not allow flexibility in the ATP ceiling in order to accommodate real wage increases, ATP will no longer provide the income-related pensions that were so hotly fought for in the 1950s. Then the blue-collar workers will, if nothing is done, be left without an income loss guarantee, since their negotiated pensions (STP), unlike the negotiated pension schemes for salaried work (ITP), and for state and municipal workers, does not provide pensions on incomes above the ATP ceiling. Should we therefore raise the ATP ceiling? If the ceiling *is* raised, on the other hand, this will be at the expense of low-income earners and we will have a redistribution which is of advantage to high-income earners.

(iii) The 15-year rule, the 30-year rule and the ATP ceiling are all reasons why the pure taxation part of ATP contributions is growing and the actuarial (insurance) relationship in the correlation between benefits and contributions has become less over the years. Persons choosing more free time are subsidised by the system. Tax increases may reduce incentives to work, to save, to study etc. and may have negative effects on welfare. Bearing in mind that a more strict actuarial contribution/benefit linkage will at the same time neutralise redistributional effects, should we change the rules and strengthen the correlation between contributions and benefits? Leaving the ATP ceiling at an unchanged level, together with changes in the 15- and 30-year rules, will be primarily disadvantageous to the women in the workforce. The question is then whether other ways can be found in which to compensate them.

(iv) Saving is in general too low. One of the reasons for this is the ATP scheme's construction as a pay-as-you-go system. Should we instead try to boost saving by building up pension funds?

The answer I propose is that we ought not to change anything in the present construction of the ATP scheme. *No change to the form of indexation; no increase in the ceiling; no change to the 15- and 30-year rules.* If we allow ATP to remain the way it is, what will happen is that it will in time become a basic pension for employees. The matter of earnings-related pensions will then be an issue for trade union bargaining. *Let us then allow* negotiated pension insurance schemes to compensate for loss of income above the ATP ceiling. *That would encourage a stricter connection between contributions and benefits and it would also result in increased saving, since the premiums are funded.* Pension insurance supplied by insurance companies and banks might be an alternative. The advantages of scale in terms of administration and low costs of individual decisions, on the other hand, would make collective insurance more advantageous than individual schemes.

These systemic changes would only put the brake on cost increases in the long run. One should be able to meet contribution increases in the coming years by means of other reforms – for example changed investment rules for the National Pension Insurance Fund, so far limited to government bonds and other low-interest 'safe' stocks, which would allow for higher dividends; reduced marginal rates of income tax which would encourage a greater labour supply, and reforms which would limit early retirement and make it possible and attractive to work beyond the official retirement age. If these measures prove insufficient, it may be necessary to reduce pension levels.

NOTES

This study has been made possible by the financial support of the Swedish Commission for Social Research.
1. Premiums for individual firms vary considerably.
2. This subsidy has been deliberate with regard to women. Other possibly more effective means might be found, however, by which to compensate them. See also Ståhlberg (1990c).

REFERENCES

Auerbach A *et al* (1988) *The Dynamics of an Ageing Population: the Case of Four OECD Countries*, OECD Economic Studies, no 12, Paris, France.

Erikson R and Åberg R (eds) (1987) *Welfare in Transition*, Oxford University Press, Oxford.

National Social Insurance Board (RFV) (1987) *ATP och dess finansiering i det medel- och långsiktiga perspektivet* (The Financing of ATP in the Medium and Long Term), RFV anser 1987:9, Stockholm, Sweden.

Ståhlberg A (1990a) Life cycle Income. Redistribution of the Public Sector: Inter- and Intragenerational Effects, *The Study of Power and Democracy in Sweden*, English Series, Report No. 42, Uppsala, Sweden.

Ståhlberg A (1990b) Life-cycle Income Redistribution of the Public Sector: Inter- and Intragenerational Effects, in Persson I (ed) *Generating Equality in the Welfare State*, 97-121, Oslo, Norwegian University Press.

Ståhlberg A (1990c) Non-wage Labour Costs. A calculation of Pension Rights and Sickness Insurance Rights in Sweden in *Rencontre européenne sur les salaires, – Paris 22-24 Mars 1990. Actes du colloque*, Vol 3, 283-302. Paris: Ministère du Travail, d l'Emploi et de la Formation Professionnelle.

Swedish Statistical Yearbook (1989), Central Bureau of Statistics, Stockholm, Sweden.

Part Five

Shaping the Course of Policy

12   Principle, Process and Policy
Albert Weale

Begin with a truism. Objectives conflict in public policy. This is so not only in the obvious sense that there are distinct partisan preferences over public policy choices, but also in the stronger sense that competing considerations will lay claim to some plausibility. Thus in devising a pensions policy it is desirable both to achieve high minimum standards and to preserve established expectations. In constructing a scheme of income support it is desirable to secure an anti-poverty objective and to avoid high marginal rates of taxation. In health policy we want both freedom of choice and equity of provision, or both comprehensiveness of care and control of costs. And in economic policy we find the familiar quartet of conflicting objectives running from full employment, through stable prices and economic growth, to balance of payments equilibrium. Such examples can be multiplied. The obvious point is that a conflict of objectives cannot be avoided.

In resolving these conflicts reasonable people are likely to disagree. They will do so for all sorts of reasons. Sometimes the disagreements will arise from differences of value commitment. Sometimes they will arise because of differences in belief systems about the cause and effect relations that operate in the relevant portion of the social system. And sometimes disagreement will arise because of differences in assessments springing from the pervasive uncertainty that surrounds public decision making. I want to stress that there is always a core of reasonable disagreement in any important area of public policy. Once we have filtered out the prejudice and the partisan bias, after we have assembled the best evidence available and granted that we have laid out as full a list of the feasible options as we can manage, there will still be wide areas left for the exercise of judgement and of choice.

The principal thesis of this chapter can now be simply stated: the British process of policy making is ill-equipped to make these choices of policy on a principled basis. The British style of public administration is a process that precludes a principled style of policy making. To sustain my thesis I shall have both to assert a characterisation of the British style of public administration and to discuss the implications of this style as they affect the making of public policy.

12.1 THE STYLE OF BRITISH PUBLIC ADMINISTRATION

British public administration is typically flexible and informal, and its usual method is to make choices implicitly rather than explicitly. Cases are to be judged on their merits. General norms are to be avoided if the decision can be left to the continuous exercise of administrative discretion. There is a tendency to avoid programmatic statements or expositions of general principle governing particular areas of policy. The preference is for the particular over the general, the concrete over the abstract, the commonsensical over the principled.

In the field of economic policy there are many examples. When regional economic policy was strong under Labour governments, decisions on industrial developments tended to be made on the merits of particular cases, rather than in terms of established criteria and general rules. The City of London operates under a 'voluntary' system by which the Bank of England has determined credit and other policy by a series of nods and winks. The CBI has at times accepted voluntary price restraint as part of a notional exchange for reflationary measures. As Samuel Brittan, from whom these examples are taken, says, 'It is an explanation, but not an excuse to say that those concerned have transferred methods and procedures which might be appropriate for a private club to the sphere of public policy.'[1]

In environmental policy flexibility and informality are lauded as part of the distinctively British style of pollution control. The features are well illustrated by the use of air pollution control, which has historically been the most important and well-developed form of pollution control in Britain. Since the nineteenth century air pollution control for complex processes ('scheduled works') has operated under the principle of best practicable means. The Chief Inspector for air pollution has stated 'presumptive limits', which are emission standards that scheduled processes are supposed to meet, and the air pollution inspectorate has been able to require firms to use the technology that would enable them to meet these limits. However, built into the application and interpretation of the best practicable means proposal is a considerable degree of flexibility and administrative discretion. In addition to a judgement on emission limits, air inspectors have also been able to take into account other factors when deciding on an operating licence for a scheduled works process. The two most important considerations have been the local conditions within which a factory is operating and the financial consequences for the company of meeting the relevant technological requirements. Flexible and informal trade-offs are customarily made in relation to these three elements of presumed emission limits, local circumstance and financial viability.[2]

Health policy too has some similar features. Despite the oft-repeated characterisation of the National Health Service as being based upon the principle of 'need' rather than 'ability to pay', the operation and performance of the NHS instance the same features of flexibility and informality that we have seen in the other policy sectors. There are variations in standards of patient care from health authority to health authority. There is no statement of the range and quality of treatment that patients have a right to expect under the NHS. The courts have consistently refused to impose an obligation on health authorities to treat particular conditions, despite the pretence that the NHS offers comprehensive care. There is nowhere an obligation upon the government to make clear the service implications of the financial allocations that are provided for the service. In short, the NHS is characterised by fluid processes of resource allocation, the effect of their operation being to make choices about the volume and quality of care implicitly rather than explicitly.

The exception to the generalisations I have been advancing would appear to be the social security system. The UK is rare in an international context in having national scale rates for its social assistance programmes – that is for residual means-tested assistance as well as for social insurance. These are explicit benefit levels that are related clearly to conditions of entitlement. Of course there are issues of administrative discretion that arise in relation to payments from the Social Fund (see the Appendix at the end of the book), but the core of the system, by which I mean benefit entitlement under the scale rates, is both explicit and free of discretionary elements. Since social security spending currently absorbs about one-third of the public budget, it may seem strange to argue that the British style of public administration has the features of informality and flexibility that I have been claiming.

Appearances here are deceptive, however. As Atkinson shows so clearly in Chapter 7, there has always been a reluctance in the British system of social security to relate benefit levels to publicly identifiable measures of the standard of living. In one sense it is literally impossible to know whether social security scale rates are adequate, since there is no public statement of what would constitute an adequate minimum standard of living. Thus, whatever the appearances of objectivity in the social security scale rates, their origin is to be found in political choice rather than in research into minimally adequate living standards.

It is tempting to speculate on what might be the origins of this dominant ideology of administration. Part of it must be due to that Hobbesian strain in British political thought which is so fearful of disorder and which concentrates decision-making power in a sovereign authority to avoid a war of all against all. Perhaps this fear of anarchy is augmented by scepticism about the rational basis of social and political judgements, which is an obstacle to subjecting political authority to the test of rational scrutiny. However, it is important not to see this dominant style as simply reflecting the character of national institutions and culture. When we observe a dominant ideology of administration, we should treat it just as we would treat any other dominant ideology, namely as the product of an historical contest between conflicting ideas. In British political thought there have been at least two traditions that have sought to challenge the informality and flexibility of British administrative traditions. Utilitarian reformers in the nineteenth century and progressive liberals under the impact of ethical idealism at the beginning of the twentieth century sought to foster a greater degree of concern with the principled basis for public choice. The historical process by which both these challenges were fended off deserves closer scrutiny.

A further source of explanation is to be found in the general political and constitutional features of the United Kingdom. The absence of a nineteenth-century bourgeois political revolution meant that political and constitutional reform has taken place in a piecemeal and incremental way. There is no constitutional document enshrining general principles of public action, and the absence of judicial review for the constitutionality of statutes has meant that there is no tradition of judicial discussion of the basis of public action. There is then little institutional pressure within the political system to constrain its dominant informality and flexibility. Critics, such as Dicey, who was sceptical of the growth of collectivism during the nineteenth century, shunned the idea that one solution to the problems was to develop a body of administrative law.

In order to bring out the distinctive features of the British style of administration, it is useful to contrast it with its European polar opposite, namely the Federal Republic of Germany. Under the long-standing tradition of the idea of the *Rechtsstaat*, and by way of reaction from the totalitarian excesses of the Third Reich, the Federal Republic has developed a style of public administration that is both highly formal and concerned to articulate explicit principles of public action. Public policy must be made in accordance with a highly elaborate constitutional document (the *Grundgesetz*) and there is a marked tendency for the federal government to issue programmatic statements of policy in which general principles are laid down at a high level of abstraction. Constitutional and administrative courts are capable of overturning the elected government's public policy, and the federal bureaucracy is highly staffed with lawyers, rather than general administrators, in order to ensure that the constitutional proprieties are observed. A point not without relevance for the United Kingdom is that the German style of federal government closely resembles in many of its features the structure and style of policy making within the European Community.[3]

12.2   IMPLICATIONS

If the British style of public administration is as described, what are the implications for the manner in which conflicts between policy objectives are handled?

One implication is that these conflicts are unlikely to be raised in an explicit form, so that their resolution will typically take place through the operating procedures of the bureaucratic machine. Indeed, because the British system of public administration is poor at raising issues at the level of principle, we should expect these procedures to achieve certain outcomes despite formal declarations of policy. Examples can be seen in the way that many saw vestiges of former Poor Law practices retained in the post-war system of social security, or in the failure of the NHS to develop explicit principles of resource allocation to regional health authorities for the first thirty years of its existence. The rhetoric of policy, be it one of abolishing the Poor Law or moving towards a rational system of resource allocation, was at odds with its practice. Since the processes of policy find it difficult to raise policy problems at the level of principle, we should expect the routines of standard operating procedure to be decisive.

Moreover, the processes of policy making have to be understood within the specific institutional configuration of British government, and in particular within the structure of Treasury dominance. The role of the Treasury is most clearly seen in the negotiations with individual spending ministries over the annual public expenditure round when it is able to put the spending claims of one department against those of another in order to secure an overall expenditure limit. We should then expect cost control to be given more prominence than benefit measurement. The imposition of cost-improvement programmes upon health authorities as part of the system for controlling expenditure within the NHS reveals these tendencies at work. Adherence to the formal budget limits has been high among most health authorities, but research has shown that cost improvements in some authorities were only obtained at the price of service provision, contrary to the formal declarations of the policy. In effect a new balance was struck between cost control on the one hand and the volume and quality of care on the other, not by an explicit choice, but by an implicit determination arising from the process of public-expenditure control.

Given that the outcome from a conflict of objectives is not arrived at explicitly, a further consequence is that the scope for public participation in debating standards is limited. If the quality of health care falls because of the imposition of cost-control measures, there are no mechanisms, short of familiar political lobbying, for concerned citizens to express their grievances or sense of dissatisfaction. The courts will be cautious about judicial review. No explicit decision has been taken to be challenged. There is no public commitment to a specific level and quality of health care. And there are few economic mechanisms with which to express discontent, unless one is prepared to resort to the private system, which many people on grounds of conscience are not. Moreover, in the absence of a system of proportional representation, political protest has to be channelled through one of the two major parties. Within these organisations too many other topics compete for attention to allow service standards to be properly understood and discussed.

Before concluding this section, I should like to note one other implication of the British administrative style as I have characterised it. Conflicts over British social policy are often presented in terms of a clash between individualism on the one hand and collectivism on the other. No doubt this is, as Alan Peacock shows in Chapter 2, an illuminating way of presenting conflicts over objectives. However, properly to understand the workings of social policy we cannot divorce policy objectives from the institutions that will be used to implement them. It is meaningless to assert as an ideological objective a universal right to health care in the absence of any statement about the institutional mechanisms to implement that right. In practice, the NHS does not provide a strict claim right to health care; in Hohfeld's terminology it provides a 'liberty', or a right to compete with others for the attention of the health care system without any guarantee that one's claims will be acknowledged.[4] Thus, in the absence of any institutional specification of the means by which a right to health care is to be protected, a collectivist policy may leave some vulnerable groups as unprovided for as they would be under individualist arrangements. Conflicts over social policy objectives inevitably become conflicts over the means by which those objectives are to be achieved.

12.3 REMEDIES?

The argument I have been seeking to develop so far is that the British policy style is poor at handling conflicts of objectives and of principle. Such issues are difficult to raise because there are few processes that involve the statement of principle and in consequence choices are made implicitly through the standard operating procedures of the relevant government organisations. If we are seriously to examine the objectives of the welfare state, therefore, we need to examine the processes that select policies within it. Improving the performance of the welfare state is as much about reforming the machinery and operations of government as it is about selecting the 'right' policy in any particular field of public activity.

One starting point for thinking through such improvements is to note the paradox that in some ways there are too few constraints in the processes of policy making rather than too many. Of course other constraints imposed by public opinion and shortage of resources limit the freedom of action of government, and it may seem unhelpful here to suggest imposing additional constraints. Yet I want to suggest that there is a powerful argument for doing so. Indeed, I shall try to show that seeking to impose extra constraints that force governments to explain the principled basis for their decisions will contribute towards easing the other constraints of public opinion and resources. Public opinion is not fixed and immutable. One of the problems of securing adequate change is that there are too few processes for the public debate of principles. The same is even true of resource constraints. These may seem absolute, given by the material conditions of a society at any one time, but in practice there is always a psychological component to them, for the resources available to government are given by the citizens' willingness to pay, and this willingness will in turn be affected by an understanding of the principles and objectives that underlie public policy developments. By making it harder for governments to make policy choices in informal, flexible ways that leave much to implicit decision, we shall provide the conditions for a public understanding of the objectives of policy and the balance that must be struck between objectives when they compete.

The analogy that I shall appeal to here is that of 'policy-as-theory'.[5] This is a shorthand, and perhaps somewhat gnomic, way of underscoring the idea that the *processes* of public policy have an intellectual and argumentative component, and that we should not seek to understand those processes purely as the resultant of pressure-group and other political forces or bureaucratic structures. Policies are theories in at least two senses. In the first place, public policies presuppose theories in that they typically rest upon both value commitments and assumptions about cause and effect relationships in society. In understanding a policy, therefore, you cannot detach it from the web of assumptions that provides its rationale. These assumptions may pertain to the relationship between economic incentives, tax rates and work effort or they may involve judgements about the most efficient payment schemes for general practitioners (to take two random, but topical examples). Whether we like it or not, however, public policies will presuppose certain assumptions, and their implementation involves a commitment to the truth of certain beliefs. Since the beliefs typically go beyond experience, even when they are grounded in experience, they meet the requirements for being a theory and therefore we may say that the policies to which they are connected involve theoretical commitments.

The second sense in which policies may be taken as theories develops the idea more by way of metaphor. Consider what we understand about the process of theory formation in the natural sciences. Theory formation and development work well when a conventional set of disciplines operates on the practice of science. These disciplines involve the publication of evidence, the articulation of assumptions, the scrutiny of purported evidence and proposed assumptions by peer review, a commitment to the replicability of findings, a tolerance of cognitive dissonance, a willingness to entertain unorthodox opinions, and a willingness to be judged by the strength of one's arguments rather than the authority of one's position. I am not claiming that these disciplines constitute the standard operating procedures of all science as practised or even of normal science under routine conditions. But they do comprise a regulative ideal for science, and successful theory formulation and development is more likely to arise where these disciplines are practised than where they are not. To speak of policy-as-theory is to make a claim about the conditions under which successful policies are likely to be developed. Just as successful theory construction imposes procedural disciplines on intellectual hypothesis, conjecture and speculation, so successful policy formation and development requires procedural disciplines of a kind analogous to the ones that comprise the regulative ideals of science. On this understanding of policy-as-theory, the task for the analyst of public administration is to identify what procedures and processes might be functional equivalents in the policy process for the disciplines that institutionalise debate in the sciences.

In the remainder of this chapter, I cannot even begin to present a well-developed analysis of such a task. All I can do is offer some examples of how, by taking seriously the idea of policy-as-theory, we might see how the British style of public administration might be reformed so as to enable a more satisfactory treatment of conflicts of objectives. I shall consider in particular three functions: the articulation of assumptions (12.3.1), the rendering explicit of choices (12.3.2) and the spelling out of impacts (12.3.3).

12.3.1 THE ARTICULATION OF ASSUMPTIONS:

In order to be able to examine objectives and assess the ways in which they might conflict, it is necessary to have policy principles spelt out in a detailed, but general way. A programmatic statement will present the principles relevant to any particular field of policy and draw out their implications for some of the choices to be made.

Examples are provided by policy documents within the European Community which build upon a practice to be found in some member states such as the Federal Republic of Germany. A most striking set of such documents occurs in the field of environmental protection. Since this is a new field of policy activity it is possible to see policy principles being fashioned before one's eyes, so to speak. In particular, the principle of precaution, in German the *Vorsorgeprinzip*, has received most attention, since it has been directed towards a fundamental and pervasive problem in the field of environmental protection, namely how far one is justified in acting *in advance* of clearly established scientific accounts of damage and degradation. What the policy documents have sought to do is to stipulate the conditions under which public intervention is appropriate.[6] One criterion is that precautionary action, say the banning of certain chemical uses, is appropriate when the environmental degradation that is being risked is likely to be irreversible. Hence we may not know for certain that CFCs are causing ozone depletion, but there is some evidence to implicate them and hence we should ban their use to prevent the irreversible damage that might otherwise arise.

It is difficult to find parallel programmatic statements of policy principle within British public administration. White Papers are probably the device that come closest to such programmatic statements, but although they do contain discussions of objectives, they are usually too concerned with providing details of specific proposals to give more than cursory attention to discussions of principle. If we are looking for processes that do seek to articulate general principles, we should probably look at institutions that are marginal to the standard operating procedures of British government, for example the Beveridge Report, Royal Commission reports and statements by inter-departmental committees of enquiry and advisory committees. This process by which a statement of principles is fashioned outside the conventional departmental framework can be seen at work currently in discussions about a public philosophy of radiation protection. The debate about risk regulation in society was originally started by the Royal Society, it was taken up by the Health and Safety Executive in its discussion of the tolerability of risk from nuclear power stations and it is currently being pursued by the National Radiological Protection Board.[7] None of these institutions is central to the departmental structure of Whitehall. The high quality of the discussions they develop show how principles might be set out systematically and their implications developed.

One reason why the tradition of British public administration has not been enamoured of programmatic statements is that it distrusts vague commitments and ideas. Much of this distrust can be attributed to a failure sufficiently to distinguish between vagueness on the one hand and 'open texture' on the other. Concepts are vague when the conditions for their application cannot be stated; they are open-textured when it is impossible to state the *full* conditions for their application. The distinction is important. Vague concepts or principles are likely to be unhelpful. Open-textured concepts have the possibility of leading to creative policy developments. To say that government should prevent risks to health is a vague notion. To say that a government should regulate risks that are above a threshold of acceptability is to state something that is open-textured, but important. It generates a set of questions and an associated research programme. We begin to ask 'acceptable to whom?' and 'by what standards?'. We are led to enquire whether the standards should be common across a variety of risks. We can see that the concept implies a limit, as well as an impulse, to public action. In short, the idea is capable both of guiding action and of structuring the search for policy-relevant information, data and evidence.

It is important to understand that concepts and principles can only play this creative role in policy development if they are to some degree open-textured in the sense that I have defined. When we can state the conditions under which a concept applies, we have no further work to do. If we have to consider whether or not a concept or principle applies to a particular set of conditions, then we must engage in a process of refining both our principles and our understanding of policy dilemmas. One typical intellectual procedure by which this is done in public policy is by way of the notion of analogy. We see this process at work, for example, in debates about policy towards lone-parent families. One side to the debate seeks to develop the analogy between widowhood and other forms of lone parenting, whereas others resist the analogy. The point here is not to decide which party to any particular dispute is right. It is rather that the acceptance of a general principle about the need for social protection in the face of widowhood can give rise to a potential for new forms of policy understanding. General principles can play this creative role precisely because the full range of their application cannot be stated in advance.

It should go without saying that the attempt to develop programmatic statements for a particular policy area is not something that should be confined to government ministries. As I have noted, other institutions both within and outside government have played an important role in some debates about risk regulation, and I think it could be argued that Parliamentary select committees are playing an increasingly significant role in this regard. Nevertheless, although the development of programmatic statements should not be restricted to ministries, it should be required of them. The commitment of departments to particular forms of policy analysis and preferred policy solutions is something that needs to be expressed more openly and clearly. As Dunleavy and Rhodes have noted, civil servants will favour stable policies supporting their department's key role or 'mission' and will cultivate the political backing for their stance.[8] One way of seeking to establish departmental policy commitments on a more substantial footing is to require departments to lay out their objectives and policy principles. One thing that would rapidly become apparent through such an exercise is the fact that in regard to certain major policy problems we have no policy as such, merely a set of operating programmes. I doubt for example that anyone could state what government policy was towards the control of any major health problem, for example cancer, as distinct from simply listing the currently operative preventive and other programmes such as breast screening, cervical cytology and post-diagnosis surgery.

12.3.2 RENDERING CHOICES EXPLICIT

The statement of principles is a necessary condition for rendering choices explicit. Only by a formal statement of objectives is it possible to identify where conflicts of value are likely to arise. However, although essential to an understanding of where conflicts arise, the process of merely stating the principles is insufficient to render explicit the process of choice. To accomplish that task we shall need other procedures.

One of the more useful devices for seeing what choices are involved in a policy area was the former practice of planning public expenditure in volume terms rather than in terms of current money values. Despite its obvious dangers as an engine of inflation, volume planning did at least have the merit of focusing the attention of policy makers on the service implications of their financial and expenditure decisions. Under the present system of cash limits, the service implications are disguised. For example, there is no responsibility upon the government of the day to state the level and quality of service that an averagely efficient health authority might be expected reasonably to supply to its local population. Moreover, many of the political incentives in the planning process are simply perverse from the viewpoint of obtaining high-quality health services. For example, there are very strong temptations to allow for less than the going rate for inflation in any pay awards, thus passing financial dilemmas down the line to health authorities instead of seeking to resolve the tension between the cost and the quality of care at the level of central government. In the absence of proper volume measures, these conflicts are solved incrementally and implicitly by local management implementing 'cuts'. Planning in volume terms makes these choices explicit and therefore open to public debate.

It would be valuable if it were possible to go beyond volume planning and in those areas of policy where the government was responsible for service delivery for there to be a public statement about the range of citizens' entitlements under the various public programmes. To be sure such a statement would be difficult to formulate for many areas of public policy, but there are precedents to build upon. For example, if we have, as we now do, in education a core curriculum with specific targets for achievement at particular ages, parents and schools are at least being given a benchmark against which to measure the standard of service being provided. No doubt it would be more difficult to devise a similar statement in the field of health care because of the variety and complexity of clinical procedures. Nonetheless, there is surely a case for making expected service standards much more explicit. It is probably a long way off before we see a statement of the 'citizen's health care entitlements' which would provide some indication of the range and quality of services that might be expected from the National Health Service, but the effort of constructing such a package, and thereby delineating what was *not* to be included would greatly help to render explicit many of the inevitably difficult choices intrinsic to a modern medical care system.

Consider the case of accounting for the environment. At present there are two possible ways of drawing up the accounts.[9] The first approach is in terms of physical balances in which the units of account comprise items such as the type of environment (for example, areas of inland water or soil), living organisms, land resources and underground resources. These items can be provided with a measure of their stock at any one time and over time changes in the balance of stock can be recorded and adjustments made to the account. The second approach is to seek to convert these statements of physical stock into a monetary measure which can then be used to make adjustments to conventional national income accounts in order to provide measures of net national welfare. When considering the need to maintain explicitness of choice, there is much to be said for sticking close to the first approach with physical accounts. The second approach – the attribution of monetary values – inevitably involves making a whole battery of assumptions which it is difficult to make explicit. Shadow prices, defensive expenditures and rates of capital depreciation will need to be defined and given some numerical value. Of course, in principle the assumptions underlying these procedures could be made explicit and the proposed monetary valuations tested for their robustness relative to a specified set of assumptions. But policy choices have to be made in real terms and selective attention is a powerful constraint on policy choice. The case for ensuring that physical measures are given adequate weight in the policy process is therefore a strong one.

To advocate making choices more explicit is not simply to propose a change in the policy process. Any such change in the process is likely to have effects on the characteristic *outcomes* that we can expect. Choices are not kept implicit merely by accident or historical inertia – though no doubt these factors play an inevitable part. Choices are also kept implicit by characteristic constellations of interests operating in the policy process. Both those responsible for cost control, who fear the political unpopularity of benefits foregone by expenditure limits, and certain professional groups, who fear the challenge to their autonomy from a greater level of accountability, have an interest in the closed and unexamined nature of certain policy decisions. Equally, however, it is easy for members of these groups to overestimate the stability of a policy process that is dependent for its continuation on systematically concealing from service beneficiaries and the general body of citizens what choices are in fact being made on their behalf.

12.3.3 SPELLING OUT IMPACTS

Most public policies have a wide set of effects. Energy pricing affects the distribution of income. Transport planning affects the quality of the environment. Social security affects rates of household formation. Health care affects industrial productivity. And so on. To note these effects is another truism on a par with the claim that objectives conflict. The challenging task is to know how policy processes can be adapted to move away from their inherent departmentalism and towards an internalisation of these broader effects.

In this context the most fertile administrative invention has been the 'impact assessment'. Environmental impact assessments were first developed in the US as part of the National Environmental Policy Act in 1969. Taylor notes how quickly their use spread around the world.[10] The idea has also been developed for other public policy concerns, and at various times governments have used or contemplated 'family impact statements', 'health impact assessments', 'income distribution assessments' and so on.

The basic idea behind the impact assessment technique is that for major developments, either of capital projects or of policy initiatives, those responsible for the development should trace out, as formally and explicitly as possible, the effects that can be anticipated as they affect some particular area of social concern. By identifying these effects, the impact assessment provides both information relevant to the decision as to whether the project is worth going ahead with or not, and baseline data against which it is possible to measure the effects of the project as it is undertaken.

Part of the significance of the impact assessment technique rests with the changes that it induces in the organisation responsible for the policy. In the case of environmental impact assessments in the US federal administration, for example, the organisations subject to the requirement to conduct assessments found that they lacked the technical expertise to conduct them properly. Hence new professionals had to be recruited into the organisation. Their recruitment not only served to accomplish the technical tasks of conducting the impact assessment, but also changed the organisation's culture and outlook. There was now a group of people in the organisation responsible for thinking about the environment. These changes took some ten to fifteen years to accomplish, but they were real enough.

In terms of British administrative practice we are only beginning to develop the technique of impact assessment. The Central Policy Review Staff in the late seventies put pressure on Whitehall to develop impact assessments on income distribution from various public policies, and under a recent EC directive environmental impact assessments are required for major projects. Of course there are dangers with the use of this technique. There are so many good causes for which it is possible to require an assessment that any large-scale organisation, whether in the public or private sector, could quickly become overloaded if all consequences of possible social concern had to be spelt out. None the less, it is a proven technique which would undoubtedly be refined and improved by more extensive use.

12.4 CONCLUSION

My argument has been that the traditional style of British public administration means that our policy institutions are not well disposed for the making of difficult choices where objectives conflict. In conclusion, I wish to make two points.

The first is that in seeking to point to the existence of alternative procedures to those currently adopted in the policy process, I am not trying to impose a model of technical rationality upon public choice. My aim has been not to substitute the logic of technical rationality for the democratic preference for discursive rationality, but to strengthen public discourse by opening out to wider scrutiny the policy assumptions and principles. Perhaps, in any case, the distinction between technical and discursive rationality is over-sharp. In a modern economy there are many people whose jobs demand that they have the skills of data analysis, modelling and impact assessment that even highly technical policy areas require. Thus, one of the most striking changes that has taken place among environmental pressure groups in recent years is their increasing technical sophistication. If any gap now exists between the demands of expertise and the demands of democracy, it is not a gap between experts and the vast body of citizens. It is instead a gap between well-educated and articulate citizens on the one hand, and under-educated (and therefore vulnerable) citizens on the other. No doubt that is a problem that will need to be addressed, but it is hopelessly optimistic to believe that it can be dealt with by seeking to eliminate entirely the technical component from public decision making. Instead the need is to make that technical component more open and transparent.

The second is that a concern with improving policy processes is really implicit in any account of public policy that stresses its pluralistic basis, whether this be a pluralism of interests or a pluralism of values. If we cannot secure consensus about the outcomes that we value, then the *processes* by which we reconcile our differences of viewpoint assume that much more importance, for those processes become our reference points of assessment. To ensure that the principles of choice are adequately articulated in the process of policy making is therefore to do little more than to acknowledge the pluralistic values underlying the modern democratic state.

NOTES

1. Brittan (1988) p 88.
2. O'Riordan and Weale (1989) pp 277–94.
3. Scharpf (1988) pp 239–78.
4. See Hohfeld (1923).
5. See Majone (1989).
6. See, for example, *Leitlinien Umweltvorsorge* (1986).
7. See Royal Society (1983) and Health and Safety Executive (1988).
8. Dunleavy and Rhodes (1990) p 18.
9. See Pearce, Markandya and Barbier (1989).
10. See Taylor (1984).

REFERENCES

Brittan S (1988) *A Restatement of Economic Liberalism*, Macmillan, London.
Dunleavy P and Rhodes R A W (1990) Core Executive Studies in Britain, *Public Administration* **68** (1).
Health and Safety Executive (1988) *The Tolerability of Risk from Nuclear Power Stations*, HMSO, London.
Hohfeld W N (1923) *Fundamental Legal Conceptions*, Yale University Press, New Haven, USA.

Leitlinien Umweltvorsorge, Umweltbrief (1986) no 33, 17 December, Bonn.

Majone G (1989) *Evidence, Argument and Persuasion in the Policy Process*, Yale University Press, New Haven, USA and London.

O'Riordan T and Weale A (1989) Administrative Reorganisation and Policy Change: The Case of Her Majesty's Inspectorate of Pollution, *Public Administration* **67**(3).

Pearce D, Markandya A and Barbier E B (1989) *Blueprint for a Green Economy*, Earthscan, London.

Royal Society, The (1983) *Risk Assessment Report of a Royal Society Study Group*, London.

Scharpf F W (1988) The Joint-Decision Trap: Lessons from German Federalism and European Integration, *Public Administration*, **66**(3).

Taylor S (1984) *Making Bureaucracies Think*, Stanford University Press, Stanford, USA.

13 Is There Scope for Change?
Peter Barclay

Alan Peacock at the end of Chapter 2 poses the question as to why the ideas of classical libertarianism have resulted in so little fundamental change over the last ten years in the field of welfare policy. Part of the answer to that question (as was clear from the diaries of a former Cabinet Minister, Richard Crossman[1]) is that policy decisions in government tend to be taken on the hoof. They tend also to be almost wholly dominated by the immediate crisis, in which the underlying philosophy to be applied is instinctive, not rational. They are based on a list of options submitted by officials but only on rare occasions do they take consciously into account deeper political or social ideas. Much more important to hard-pressed Ministers are considerations of immediate expediency, pressures on their spending budgets and a consciousness of the baleful eye of the Treasury looking over their shoulders as they put pen to paper. They have to make an assessment of what can or cannot be pushed through Parliament, of what weight to give to stirrings on the government back-benches and how the results of the policy change can be decked out or dressed up as a positive sum game rather than zero or negative sum game (to use the public choice description).

However, in 1985 and 1986 Ministers did step back and take a sustained and detailed look at the social security system in the preparation of what came to be known as the Fowler Review. The depth of the analysis was greater than might have been supposed from the final outcome (although radical changes were made in the pensions field). This was because the operation was carried out subject to one overriding rule – that the new system must not cost any more than the old and preferably a good deal less. In the upshot, by robbing Peter to pay Paul, by taking from one group to give to another, it cost almost exactly the same (apart from Housing Benefit, where the initial cuts were subsequently and hurriedly modified in the wake of cries of pain from elderly voters whose thrift had built up nest-eggs such as to disentitle them under the new rules from any help with their housing costs).

The second reason for what in the upshot appears to have been a somewhat superficial post-review change is the almost blinding complexity of the system which has grown up in Britain over the post-war years; a complexity indicated in the summary account of welfare benefits given in the Appendix at the end of the book. A description which exemplifies this complexity and the haphazard and rickety benefit edifice to which it owes its existence is the following paragraph taken from the recent report[2] on disability benefits by the Social Security Advisory Committee:

> Some benefits are for income maintenance (for example Invalidity Benefit and Severe Disablement Allowance) while some are intended to help meet the extra costs resulting from disability (Attendance Allowance and Mobility Allowance). Some are contributory (IVB), some are not (SDA, AA and Mob A). While Invalid Care Allowance is taxable, other benefits (IVB, SDA, AA and Mob A) are not. IVB and SDA are taken into account for income support purposes. AA and Mob A are not (but AA is taken into account if the claimant is in private residential care). The roles of adjudication officers and doctors vary from benefit to benefit. For some, entitlement is based on how long the disability is expected to last (Mob A) but for others on how long it has already lasted (IVB and AA).

In fact the Fowler Review put disability benefits on one side to be tackled at a later date, and substantial improvements – but not necessarily simplification – are now promised by the government.[3] But the point about complexity and the muddle between contributory, non-contributory and means-tested benefits remains. The situation inhibits change – rather like that game of my childhood called Spillikins – if you move one little stick the whole thing is in danger of toppling.

So, bearing in mind the range of day-to-day pressures which bear upon Ministers in spending departments, the comparative rarity of any attempt to grapple with fundamentals (and the administrative upheaval in the life of officials involved in that process) and finally the inherent complexity of the system, what can be forecast for welfare benefits over the next decade?

Whatever government is in power it will find itself boxed in by both operational and financial constraints which in my view (and however dreary this may seem to the root and branch reformers) will prevent any *revolutionary* changes in the substance of the benefits themselves.

What are these constraints? First and foremost the operational constraint results from the fact that the whole method of *delivery* of benefits is in course of being totally and fundamentally reconstructed – and good-quality delivery of services is almost as important as the intrinsic value of the services themselves. Jack Wiseman (Chapter 3) has pointed to the importance of service delivery in policy formulation. The computerisation of the system currently in progress represents one of the largest, if not *the* largest, civilian computer project in Europe. It is gathering pace at the rate of six or seven offices a week and brings with it an ultimate reduction in personnel of over twenty thousand. On top of this, other organisational changes, such as the setting up of agencies, responsible to the Minister but headed by a Chief

Executive with a degree of autonomy in how the benefit service is to be delivered, the decentralisation of all but a core of ministerial policy advisers and the relocation of much of the work from inner cities to provincial centres are all understandably taking up so much of departmental energy and time that fundamental policy matters will be bound to take a back seat during the early years of the nineties.

If we then add the *financial* constraints on any change in the system we are left with the rather unexciting prospect of further miscellaneous tinkering to improve incentives and remove inequities, rather than anything more radical. Charles Carter (Chapter 6) has well described some of these constraints. Apart from the sheer size of the budget – over £1 billion of benefits paid out each week – resulting in constant reductive pressure from the Treasury, there are inherent areas of expenditure *increase* in real terms. Apart from unemployment payments these principally concern pensions and long-term incapacity benefits, the latter showing a rapid increase each year for reasons which are clear to no-one – and which the improvements in disability benefits announced in 1990 will do nothing to arrest. Single parents are the other claimant group which has shown a steady and constant increase, a problem which in turn cannot be adequately tackled other than by further public expenditure whether by increased disregards,[4] particularly to reflect child care expenses, or by tax allowances for child care, which could help to tackle the present disincentives in the system for the single parent who wishes to take up employment.

Therefore, while those who now hope for massive increases in social security resources will be disappointed, so will those who would welcome a reduction in benefit expenditure. For there seems to exist a correlation between total benefit expenditure and the percentage of GNP which this represents. Not only do we see the inexorable rise in real terms over the post-war years in benefit expenditure as a whole, but also the rise in the percentage of GNP represented by that expenditure. This increased from 5.37% in 1949 to 10.46% in 1979. During the Thatcher years it rose to a peak of 13.29% in 1982 and subsequently was reduced only slightly as unemployment fell.[5] Whatever government comes to power in the nineties it is difficult to see how that long-term trend can be reversed. It is after all of great political significance in capturing and maintaining the middle ground, for from these figures it may reasonably be claimed by some commentators that the fruits of prosperity are being shared across the board. Others would argue that one of the principal characteristics of income distribution in recent years has been the widening of the gap between the top incomes and the incomes of those on means-tested benefits. This has resulted from the basis adopted for uprating benefits each year in accordance with movements in the Retail Price Index rather than adjusting benefits to a greater or lesser extent in line with movements in indices of average earnings.

What other trends can be forecast for the future? One of the outstanding characteristics of any social security system is the existence of desirable lines of development which turn out to be irreconcilable, one with another. For example, it was a basic object of the Fowler Review to simplify the system and to target resources to those who need them most. The reforms which followed resulted in a much simplified system from an administrative point of view – and of course one that sits well with the computerised delivery machinery for which it was designed. But simplicity has been purchased at a price, namely the loss of a highly sensitive but necessarily complicated further benefit called 'additional requirements', which was able to provide extra weekly sums for those sick or elderly persons who had particular needs – such as extra heating or special diets. Single payments could also be made for expensive items for which people could not budget out of their weekly benefit – for example, a new bed, cooker, or shoes for the children. So we now have standard additions paid with basic income support. These premiums are based on assessment of average need and are then payable to all those in particular groups – pensioners, disabled people, families, single parents etc. – without regard for those individuals within the groups who most need extra help. Simplicity yes, but individual targeting on those most in need? No.

The tinkering to which I referred above, in so far as it seeks to remove inequities, is also inconsistent with the aim of simplification. Having worked as a tax lawyer over many years I can speak from experience, for precisely the same point applies to the tax system. Sir Edward Compton described the process well:

> Fairness more often than not is the downfall of the simple rule. Give way to fair play and back they come, those provisos and special conditions to complicate the rule and spoil the performance. This is particularly so where the government's dealings with the public consist of taking money from those who are thought to have it and paying money to those that are thought to need it.

Other policy irreconcilables concern the respective merits of means-tested and universal benefits and the perceived need to target (means test) on the one hand, and on the other to deliver the money to those on whom it is targeted but who may fail to take it up for one reason or another. Another example of irreconcilability is the failure to maintain the contributory principle in the face of perceived inequities between those with a contribution record and those who, through no fault of their own, are not able to work and pay contributions. For instance, a young student is severely disabled in an accident. He has never been in work and has therefore never paid National Insurance contributions. He is therefore unable to claim invalidity benefit, entitlement to which depends on being able to show a 'contribution record'. He therefore, for the rest of his life, has to depend on severe disablement allowance, which is worth only 60 per cent of invalidity benefit, and to make up the difference if he can through means-tested income support. Another young person of the same age who has been in work for a few years would be entitled to the higher benefit which he has 'paid for' through his contributions to the National Insurance Fund each week. To reduce his entitlement is seen to be an unacceptable breach of the contributory principle.

Yet there have been several cases over the last few years of contributory entitlements having been reduced. These arise from perceived abuse or from a desire to achieve savings in benefit expenditure. An example is contained in the Social Security (No.2) Act 1980. This included provisions to counter the 'abuse' of unemployment benefit (a contributory benefit) by persons retiring early with substantial occupational pensions who were not really in the employment field. Today claimants over 55 lose 10 pence unemployment benefit for every 10 pence by which their occupational pensions exceed £35 per week. Several other changes of a similar kind have resulted in the steady erosion of the contributory principle over the last few years – a process which I suspect will continue. A current example is the freezing of the additional pension in invalidity benefit proposed by the government in its disability benefit paper *The Way Ahead*. This component, like a similar amount paid with retirement pension, is related through contributions to previous earnings.

In short, the irreconcilables will continue to dominate attempts at improvement throughout the years ahead and changes for the better will generally make the system more complicated in the process.

Is part of the answer to adopt a wholly integrated tax/benefit system, which might also get over other inherent complexities and irreconcilables, mainly this time in the field of incentives? There are three problems here. First the *complexities* involved are formidable and there is not enough research going on to enable a workable system to be developed within the foreseeable future. I am not aware of any work that is currently proceeding inside the Department of Social Security on this proposal. This does not surprise me because, and this is the second problem, any such development would result in a further *complication of the tax system*, which it is still the unalterable and central intention of the Treasury to simplify, however unsuccessful its attempts may have been in the past. This is true of other countries – although a recent change in Australia might be a harbinger of good news. There, in the face of vigorous Treasury opposition, Social Security Ministers were nevertheless able to push through a system of attachment of earnings through the tax system whereby payment of maintenance by absent fathers to lone mothers is now successfully collected. (The tax network is the best intelligence system we have for tracing defaulters of any kind.)

But quite apart from Treasury opposition, there is a third problem with tax/benefit integration however attractive it may be in theory. This results from the *basis of assessment*. Benefit is dealt with on a daily or weekly basis responding to immediate need or changes in the circumstances of the claimant, while tax liability is calculated on an annual basis.

One of the other ways of simplifying the system is to reduce its coverage. So, since 1985 we have seen coverage reduced on a number of fronts – all have been areas where in effect social security officials have said 'it is no part of our job to deal with this – we are not trained to do so and others can do it better or it should not be done at all'. The list has lengthened remarkably since 1985: (a) hostels[7] – the charges are now met through housing benefit administered by local authorities; (b) sixteen- and seventeen-year-olds (who were in the main effectively removed from the benefit system in 1988);[8] (c) community care in general – and residential provision in particular – will be transferred to local authorities by 1993;[9] (d) students – since 1990 have mostly been disentitled to benefit during vacation periods even if they are available for work.[10]

Two of these cases have been concerned with the dismantling of the three-legged stool which propped up the board and lodging income support for those in lodgings, in hostels and in residential homes. The legs were, first, the personal allowance for incidental living expenses from income support, second housing benefit for accommodation costs paid through local authorities, and third the costs of care – i.e, support services provided by the establishment – paid by the Department of Social Security. It shortly will be for others (for example local authorities) to look after the costs of care. The benefit system will continue to pay out in addition and, whatever the context, standard benefits for living expenses under the income support and for rent under the housing benefit régimes. These changes were motivated by the desire to put those living in hostels and residential homes as far as is possible in the same position as regards benefits as those living in the community – leaving the costs of care to be borne in the main by local authorities. This creates a 'level playing field' and removes the 'perverse incentives' created by the benefit system in favour of residential care, where the costs are often high. The need for basic benefit is 'standard'; the cost of accommodation and care is not and can be better provided by a local authority and tailored to individual need.

In looking at *incentives* we run into poverty-trap problems. Here the combination of low wage rates and the high rate at which in-work social security (such as family credit and housing benefit) benefits fall off as income rises discourages claimants from taking work. This is a complex area. A step which would help but which would not universally be welcomed, particularly by the taxpayer, is to increase child benefit by substantial amounts. As a 10 pence increase in child benefit, or 1.4 per cent at rates prevailing in the early 1990s, would cost £50 million I cannot see any government in the nineties getting very far with this – although after several years of frozen rates, a £1 a week increase for the first child has been announced for April 1991. It is possible that a future government of whatever complexion may gradually have the resources and political will to make up the ground lost since the mid 1980s when the benefit began to decline in value in real terms. What remains to be done however is to persist in attempts to remove *disincentives* in the system. We need a sustained attack here and we need to monitor very carefully the sticks and carrots now influencing choices about taking employment or remaining on benefit. The voluntary unemployment penalty and the 'Actively Seeking Work Test' are among the sticks. Here under certain conditions claimants can suffer a 40 per cent reduction in their personal income support for a period of up to twenty-six weeks if they leave a job 'without good cause' or if, once unemployed, they fail actively to seek work. The new family credit is one of the carrots (soon to be extended to disabled people under a different name). Family credit provides a substantial additional income to those on low wages with children. It reduces in value as wages rise.

When you look at incentives from the claimants' point of view there are three points which together may influence the decision as to whether or not to seek work. First the costs of travel (particularly significant for the long-term unemployed, who often live in geographically isolated estates on the edge of large towns); secondly, for single mothers the costs and availability of child care; and thirdly, the problems of managing the perilous procedure of getting back into the benefit system if the job fails. Often claimants experience substantial delays as a result of administrative difficulties before their full benefits are re-established. The new computerised benefit system should substantially remove these difficulties as faster access to records will universally be achieved through the National Insurance number of the individual, which is centrally stored and easily accessed through a local terminal whether the claimant is in or out of work.

A fourth but little researched and important backdrop to the way in which claimants make decisons about returning to work is the fact that the social security system has failed to adapt to changes in the labour market. The growth of short-contract work, temporary work and other developments likely to reflect the results of advances in information technology have created a new situation for many seeking work. Minor changes in abstruse corners of the system, such as seasonal workers' benefits and certain rules affecting entitlement to unemployment benefit, such as what constitutes a normal working week, have signalled the existence of the problem and revealed the lack of a coherent attempt to cope with it. A review has been instigated by the Secretary of State for Social Security.[11]

I have mentioned continuing irreconcilabilities in the system and also the constraints which will, in my view, limit revolutionary changes in the foreseeable future. One other matter is relevant here and it is mentioned by Charles Carter (Chapter 6). This concerns *abuse of the system* and the political effect of abuse. The problem for an organisation spending such large sums of money as the Department of Social Security, delivered through some sixty thousand officials, is to be able satisfactorily to sort out the sheep from the goats – to ensure that those to whom the money is paid are entitled to it under the rules.

It was appropriate that a working party convened in 1986 by a voluntary organisation, the National Association for the Care and Resettlement of Offenders (NACRO), should have been chaired by a retired chairman of the Board of Inland Revenue.[12] There are obvious parallels between abuse and fraud in social security with avoidance and evasion in tax matters. But two significant differences stand out. First, to take full advantage of the social security system is to attract infinitely more odium than legitimately to avoid or reduce our tax burden which is the right of us all.

Secondly the resentment, which tends to be voiced loudest by those in work but on low wages, bears no relation to the facts. It is sometimes echoed by the government. Referring to the changes in Single Payments Regulations[13] in 1986 the NACRO Committee commented as follows:

> . . . it is impossible to judge how much abuse was occurring or how much of the money claimed represented genuine need among rising numbers of claimants (unemployed people in particular). Nor was evidence produced of amounts of benefit still unclaimed, although these are known to be substantial. The point of interest to us lies in the strength of Government feeling about possible abuse, compared with the relatively low level of expressed concern about exploitation of the tax system which involves much larger sums.[14]

These attitudes have been compounded by substantial failures to enforce payment of employers' contributions under the contributory benefit scheme due to staff shortages in the DSS and, some allege, to the moving of extra staff to work on cases of suspected fraud. Steps have recently been taken to attempt to meet these situations. I mention them only to point out that the delicate options available to any administration in this field will continue as an inherent problem in the system and as a limiting factor (together with possible increases in tax rates) to the winning of political support for substantially more generous benefits in the nineties at least so far as the 'undeserving' poor are concerned, as characterised by popular conception.

I must mention one recurring and intractable problem which will continue to cause trouble in the foreseeable future. This concerns the methods we have adopted over the years to deal with *exceptional needs* – in general the sums payable for what are regarded as essential domestic equipment, which the basic income support rates are not designed to cover. The pendulum has periodically swung from discretion to regulation and now it has swung back to discretion, this time in the Social Fund. Here there are two new characteristics both never before part of our benefit system – the introduction of loans and the introduction of cash limits to the annual sums made available to the Fund. In my opinion the design of the fund is flawed and the resources provided are inadequate but it is a very small corner of the system in expenditure terms although of great importance in the lives of those concerned. Controversy will continue to surround it but I venture to predict that by the end of the century we shall still be without an answer to the underlying problem of how to deal satisfactorily with exceptional needs.

Finally I should mention the question of the *adequacy* of the basic income support rates. However desirable it may be to improve, through research, ways of achieving an objective measurement of what the basic rates should cover, the problem is still largely a subjective one and the conclusion of the 1985 Green Paper was 'that it is doubtful whether an attempt to establish an objective standard of adequacy would be fruitful'.[15] This was an understandable device to avoid going down a road which might have led to huge public expenditure increases. But research will continue to be important in providing information about how people's living standards can be measured, however unwelcome the policy implications resulting from such research may turn out to be.

Neither the statistical monitoring of information by the Department of Social Security nor material derived from the Family Expenditure Survey can provide satisfactory information on the problems caused by life on a low income, or the strategies which people adopt to make ends meet or – perhaps the most neglected field – the ways in which many people manage to avoid dependence on benefits and get themselves back into work. The Social Security Advisory Committee concluded its Sixth Report in this way: 'We believe that research has a vital role to play in assisting those who make policy to make informed choices about expenditure on social security. And just as important, by examining and exposing the results of social security policies, research enables the rest of society to judge whether the right choices are being made.'[16]

This chapter has been devoted to a description and analysis of the changing shape of benefit policy in Britain. The reform of the Social Security System which took place in 1988 is part of that change. Reference has been made to the inherent complexity of the system as it has developed in a haphazard manner over the post-war years; this factor, together with financial and political restraints and inherent irreconcilabilities within the system, have combined to inhibit basic change. The overall result is twofold.

First, attempts during the last decade at fundamental reform of the structure of benefits have been less than radical in their outcome. (By contrast, changes in benefit delivery systems now in course of implementation are far-reaching and fundamental.)

Secondly, while it is difficult to predict changes over the next decade, it is doubtful whether we shall see any fundamental reforms in the benefit structure. What is more likely to occur is a steady stream of piecemeal changes. These will be designed to improve incentives and to iron out inequitable corners of the system and to concentrate help on those 'most in need'. At the same time savings will be achieved in some areas so as to obtain resources for the improvement of rates elsewhere. However, any substantial overall increase in resources for income maintenance will depend on the progress in the economy and the political will or complexion of administrations in power in the last decade of the century.

But those resources can only be devoted to shoring up a complex structure, rather than to the achievement of those far-reaching reforms for which many have argued. For those we must look to the twenty-first century when advances in technology and changes in social and political attitudes may lead towards the introduction of a system which is both simpler to administer and more discerning and generous to those in need. Whether this will happen, or indeed whether it is desirable that it should happen, will remain a staple social policy issue for very many years ahead.

NOTES

1. Crossman (1977).
2. HMSO (1988c) para 4.54.
3. HMSO (1990).
4. In the assessment of a claimant's entitlement to income support certain amounts of income from other sources (part-time earnings and savings) are not taken into account. In the case of single parents the amount of earnings thus disregarded is higher than in the case of other claimants.
5. HMSO (1989a).
6. Compton (1970), p 11.
7. HMSO (1988a).
8. HMSO (1988d), ch 2.
9. HMSO (1989b).
10. HMSO (1988b).
11. HMSO (1989c).
12. NACRO (1986).
13. Single payments were until 1988 made to claimants as of right if a defined exceptional need was shown to exist. The changes were introduced because of the need for the government to curb rapidly rising expenditure under those regulations as claimants came to intensify the use, or some would say abuse, of the system.
14. NACRO (1986) para 3.6.
15. HMSO (1985) vol 2, para 2.50.
16. HMSO (1988d) para 8.50.

REFERENCES

Compton E (1970) The Administrative Performance of Government, *Public Administration*, Spring 1970 pps 3-14.

Crossman R (1977) *Diaries of a Cabinet Minister*, Cape and Hamilton, London.

HMSO (1985) *Reform of Social Security*, Cmnd 9517, London.

HMSO (1988a) *Help with Hostel Charges – Proposals for Change*, Department of Health and Social Security, London.

HMSO (1988b) *Top-up Loans for Students*, Cm 520, London.

HMSO (1988c) Social Security Advisory Committee *Benefits for Disabled People: A Strategy for Change*, London.

HMSO (1988d) *Sixth Report of the Social Security Advisory Committee*, London.

HMSO (1989a) *Abstract of Statistics for Index of Retail Prices, Average Earnings, Social Security Benefits and Contributions*, London.

HMSO (1989b) *Caring for People: Community Care in the Next Decade and Beyond*, Cm 849, London.

HMSO (1989c) Response by the Secretary of State to the Social Security Advisory Committee's Report on the Social Security Benefit (Computation of Earnings) Amendment Regulations.

HMSO (1990) *The Way Ahead: Benefits for Disabled People*, Cm 917, London.

National Association for the Care and Resettlement of Offenders (1986) *Enforcement of the Law Relating to Social Security*, London.

14 Two Westminster Perspectives on Welfare Policies

14.1 THE FUTURE OF WELFARE POLICY: FRANK FIELD MP

There are three issues which form part of an agenda for the welfare state over the next two decades. The first centres on the emergence of an underclass. The second question is the disincentive effects of welfare for people on low income. The third item is the idea of an income that is derived not solely from work but also from wealth and from welfare.

The first item on the welfare agenda is the underclass. I now question the generally held assumption that everybody wants to be members of civil society. For the first time groups of unemployed and young single mothers don't think the offer of rejoining mainstream Britain is worth taking. They opt consciously to stay on the outside. Opting to remain separate from mainstream Great Britain is a characteristic of part of the underclass. Yet this separateness cannot be explained in terms of the 'culture of poverty'. The emergence of an underclass has little to do with inheriting 'bad habits' from previous generations. The American commentator Charles Murray explains the rise of the underclass in part by the overthrow of an established working-class culture based on hard work, self-respect and self-improvement.

There are a number of reasons why this change in attitudes has occurred. A lack of opportunities in the job market is certainly one. The work ethic is perhaps less deeply ingrained than mythology would have us believe. Once out of school with no prospect of employment the idea of existing without paid employment became a reality to very large numbers of young people. Some, perhaps many, have considerable ability and once on the outside of the labour market they use what entrepreneurial skills they possess to 'get by'. In areas of high unemployment, life on the outside with an income from welfare, working on the side, and possibly crime, offers a standard of living far in excess of what the labour market offers to unskilled workers. Indeed some of these outsiders express open hostility and contempt to those on the inside in low-paid jobs.[1] In addition there are those who, once unemployed, become totally demoralised and are not necessarily 'found' work once the job prospects improve.

Disillusioned young unemployed workers constitute a very difficult group for politicians and policy makers. In areas of near full employment some use the government's Employment Training programme simply to win time on welfare rather than as an entry into the labour market. Of this group many have criminal records, which makes the prospect of gaining employment a near impossibility. An availability-for-work test fairly applied is crucial so that people do take work when it is available. Without this structure many people's lives disintegrate. Just as employers are building up compacts with schools so too must similar arrangements be made for potential workers with criminal records. Some sort of amnesty on this front is needed. The criticism that some of the unemployed level against the pay and prospects of jobs which are available must be taken seriously. The low paid must be offered personalised training arrangements with generous job-counselling services. In this way the government can help the low paid to by-pass bad employers.

One of the fastest growing groups on welfare is young single mothers. No one has yet provided an adequate explanation of the rise in single parenthood. Lack of job prospects must have played some part in the conscious decisions of some young women to begin a family. Being wanted, and wanting somebody to love, is often a reported reason why some 14-, 15- or 16-year old girls become mothers. And once trends become established, previous forms of social control collapse quickly. One in four children are now born out of wedlock, as the traditional phrase puts it, although many of these are born to households that are stable unions. Spearheading a new strategy to incorporate those of the underclass who think they have a better deal on the outside will be difficult. Young girls must learn in school from other young single mothers that having a baby does result in jumping the housing queue, but only as far as the first available house in a down-at-heel council housing estate. The Young Mothers' Barton Hill group undertakes such work in schools around Bristol. The importance of the role of motherhood is stressed, but questions are posed as to whether it is necessary, or even desirable, to begin a family prior to the school leaving age, or very soon afterwards!

Linked to this must be a policy directed against young males who need to know that the state will hold them responsible for the maintenance of their children. In the early 1990s, debate on this topic changed in tempo thanks largely to the then Prime Minister's speech to the National Children's Home. What I myself have advocated is a twofold policy. First of all young males ought to be given an audit which gives them some idea of the cost, to them, of each of their children over that child's period of dependency. A maintenance order of £15 a week results over a sixteen-year period in costs amounting to £12,480. Similarly, potential young fathers must know that once a maintenance order is made against them, the mother will be given the option of requesting that the state take on the role of collecting such payments. Two issues are important here. If further disincentives are not to be built into the welfare system, the offer of state collection of maintenance must be made to mothers on welfare and mothers in work alike. If this offer is only made to the former group then many mothers will think twice before moving off benefit into all the uncertainties of work if, at the same time, she has to resume the task of pursuing the father for maintenance payments due to her. Similarly, a more effective system than the current attachment of earnings needs to be brought into operation. Many men slip the maintenance net by simply changing their jobs; the whole process of finding the new employer and then getting an attachment of earnings order from the court has to begin again. Maintenance orders attached to the man's National Insurance record would ensure that this dodge becomes pointless.

The second item on the agenda is the question of incentives. While this is now accepted as an issue amongst many politicians and commentators – in stark contrast to the position on the Left ten years ago – it is in no way given the weight I believe it should have. Incentives, or more accurately the disincentive effects for people on low incomes, arise largely because of the growing importance of the means tests in deciding who gets welfare provisions and to a lesser extent because of the rates levied in income tax and National Insurance. The Thatcher government appeared unaware of the inherent conflict in two of its major welfare objectives, namely, of concentrating help on the poorest, while at the same time reducing welfare dependency. The former policy was operated almost exclusively by extending the role of means-tested help and resulted inevitably in an increase in the numbers who became trapped in the welfare web. It is as easy to be caught in this web as it is difficult to regain financial freedom. A married couple, with two children, earning £60 a week have a net weekly income after claiming all the benefits to which they are entitled of £102.04. A new job, or a wage increase which takes the breadwinner to £170 a week, results in a net weekly income of only £118.53 because of means-tested benefits lost. In other words, a £110 a week increase on a wage of £60 leads to a net increase in weekly income of £16.49.[2]

The number of people dependent on means-tested welfare has increased significantly during the 1980s. The scheme of rent rebates run by local authorities and a national scheme for rates rebates were reformed and merged into the housing benefit scheme. The number covered for means-tested help on this front has almost doubled from 4.4 million claimants in 1979 to 8.6 million claimants in 1989. Family credit (see the Appendix at the end of the book) is the government's chief weapon to combat family poverty caused by low wages. It replaced family income supplement and although the numbers covered are very much smaller than in the case of housing benefit – a mere 315,000 – family credit gives substantial additional help and thereby creates a major disincentive for low-wage earners with children to improve their earnings. The other major means-tested benefit is income support (see Appendix) which replaced supplementary benefit in 1988. It too has seen a

large increase in dependency; a rise from 3 million claimants at the start of
the Thatcher stewardship in 1979 to 4.3 million at the end of the following
decade.

Two comments are worth making about these figures. First, they refer to
the numbers of heads of households claiming benefit, not to the number of
people whose living standards are at least partly determined by the benefit.
In considering the growth of dependency the latter figure is more relevant.
The 4,352,000 claims for income support in 1989, for example, covered
payments to 7,388,000 individuals. Second, it is not possible to add together
all the claims for means-tested help to arrive at a total figure of the numbers
dependent on means-tested welfare. There are a number of overlapping
claims where those who claim income support would also be claiming housing benefit. While no exact picture can be drawn the trend is clear. It points
in a markedly upwards direction.

Effective reform on this front will throw up howls of anguish. The only
strategy which offers the possibility of relegating means testing to a subsidiary welfare role is to break the link between the automatic increases in
means-tested eligibility when universal benefits are raised. In other words,
when the National Insurance old age pension or child benefit is increased
this strategy requires that equal increases should not be made in means-
tested assistance. An additional increase in old age pensions over and above
any inflationary increase, for example, would not be matched by an identical
increase in income support. The poorest pensioners, while getting the increase in National Insurance benefit if they were eligible, would lose out on
income support if that were their means of livelihood. This strategy would
also require that any major increase in child benefit would not be matched
by increases in the child additions to Income Support. In the short run this
would have the result of giving real increases in income to those above the
means-tested eligibility level. But without embarking on this policy, there is
no chance whatsoever of refashioning the welfare state as the provider of an
income floor on which people are free to make a whole range of decisions
as to how they behave.

Means-tested welfare benefits make up one side of the account. On the
other comes the imposition of the income tax. The poorest workers, once
into the tax system, pay 25 pence on each pound of earnings, together with
a National Insurance contribution of 9 per cent. Once a worker crosses the
tax threshold then a third of income is taken immediately in direct taxation.
Increasing incentives on this front cannot be achieved without a radical
reform of the income tax structure. In the early 1990s over half of all personal income is exempted from tax by one of a hundred or so tax allowances. These need to be phased out over a five-year period. The additional
revenue gained by the Exchequer should be used to reduce the standard rate
of tax. The phasing out of the main pension tax concessions together with
mortgage interest relief would in themselves allow the standard rate to be

cut to about 12 pence in the pound. For reasons of equity, incentives and personal choice such a tax reform should be advanced.

Now on to the third item on welfare's future agenda. A cry from the Left for many decades has centred on job security. This should be replaced by the idea of an income security, which for large parts of people's lives is guaranteed by their ability to work, but not exclusively so. An income security would also broaden the debate to take in both the desirability of, and the increasing number of people who are beginning to acquire, substantial wealth holdings.

Two debates need to be initiated here. It is important to enter into a dialogue with the voters on ways by which people's income from wealth, welfare and work can be maximised. This debate has hardly begun. One which is now at least under way centres on how is it possible to meet an individual's income needs, which now span between eight and nine decades, from not only work but also welfare and wealth. Both debates need to be run in parallel. One of the reasons for which I advocate a policy of tax neutrality as far as savings are concerned is that individuals have got to be almost at the point of insanity to invest in anything other than their own home, or an occupational pension, such are the tax advantages on these two forms of saving. Mortgage interest relief is granted on loans up to £30,000, and, moreover, when selling his or her home the individual is free from capital gains tax on the profits made.

Philip Chappell estimates the tax foregone in pension privileges to be in the region of £8-10 billion per year. Employer and employee contributions to occupational schemes are free of tax and totalled in 1989 a little short of £20 billion. In addition Chappell puts the contribution of the self-employed to such schemes at £1 billion a year. Further, he calculates the grant of rights in unfunded schemes at around £10 billion a year. As a 'ball-park' estimate therefore, tax relief for contributions to retirement schemes reduces the tax base by about £30 billion: with the present basic rate of 25 per cent and a higher rate of 40 per cent the total cost is therefore in the order of £8-10 billion.[3] These figures however exclude any additional cost for capital gains tax relief. Chappell notes that the Inland Revenue has consistently refused to give any estimate on this front. His own suggests that pension funds are currently making sales of securities which would generate taxable gains of about £15 billion per annum.

Pension fund tax privileges raise three policy considerations. First, one person's tax privileges is another person's tax increase. These tax privileges have also helped to ensure that the tax system is highly regressive. Philip Chappell gives three examples of a worker on £12,000 a year, £50,000 a year and £150,000 a year. Taking into account pension and Business Expenses Scheme contributions the average tax rate for each of these three workers is 21.5 per cent, 15.7 per cent and 12.1 per cent respectively. Second, these tax privileges distort the savings market. Those for home ownership and pension funds explain why the ownership of industrial wealth is much lower in this country than in America or in most European countries. Third, the vast majority of the population's savings are now tied up in these two forms of assets and over the next couple of decades the likelihood is that pension funds will become an even more important source of savings than they have been in the past. This itself raises a number of important issues. Thirty or fewer institutions control a majority stake in most list companies. These institutions, dominated by the pension funds, determine whether or not take-over bids are successful, and there is a growing belief that these funds increase the short-term attitude towards returns, which has such a debilitating effect on Britain's long-term competitiveness. Next, these huge assets of the pension funds are controlled by the pension fund managers and not by the members themselves. Democratisation of the pension fund industry so that individual 'shareholders' will have an increasing say in the actions of the company will be one of the big political economy questions of the coming decades.

Ownership in housing is bringing forth major social and economic changes. One aspect is seen in the effects which large-scale home ownership, and its subsequent inheritance, is having on the economy.[4] On an individual level the most important consequences can be seen in the financial and social freedoms resulting from inheritance and the ability to use one's existing house as a collateral for substantial loans. Nearly 70 per cent of the population are now home owners and for the first time many of them have inherited at least part of the equity in their parents' homes. These funds appear to be used at the current time to allow recipients to move themselves up the housing market or to enable their own children to acquire their first home by way of gaining a substantial down payment. But because many of today's inheritors are themselves already owner occupiers, substantial assets are being gained both for immediate consumption and for other forms of investment. Little work has so far been done on what this portfolio of investments is likely to be. What is clear from these changes is that for the first time a substantial group of the population not only has a significant wealth portfolio but, as with the rich through the centuries, these portfolios are allowing them both to raise large amounts of money in loans and also to convert some of these substantial wealth holdings into cash. The aim must be to extend the chances of acquiring such assets to the population in its entirety. Similarly, the political agenda should soon reflect the need to democratise pension funds, giving individual contributors the rights that would accrue to them if their savings were invested directly in industrial share portfolios.

One last point. Over the past couple of decades a number of right-wing economists have insisted that the value of future entitlements to National Insurance benefits should be counted as part of a person's wealth. Indeed the Royal Commission on the Distribution of Income and Wealth, before its demise, presented wealth data under different headings including one which took into account the computed value of the National Insurance old age pension. But as presently constituted, these entitlements are different from many other of the assets appearing in wealth portfolios; they cannot be transformed into liquid assets. One of the items which will, I hope, appear increasingly on the political agenda is the proposal to allow individuals to capitalise part of their entitlement to child benefit and the National Insurance pension. My guess is that many individuals would use the freedom resulting from this reform to buy into the housing market – and with the changes in the value of housing over the past few decades who can blame them? I have set out elsewhere how such a scheme should be run and the careful safeguards that would need to be built into it.[5]

I have concentrated on three items which are likely to appear in the debate about the reform of welfare over the next couple of decades. In the first place I have questioned a central underpinning assumption in the debate about welfare in this century. Reformers have assumed that the 'dispossessed' are anxious to rejoin mainstream society. The emergence of an underclass poses a question of incentives; while beginning to emerge on the agenda, it has not yet gained the significance it deserves. All too often the only option for claimants is to use their ingenuity to maximise their income within the welfare system. Far too little thought has gone into rewarding a claimant's entrepreneurial skill in leaving the welfare rolls. A third part of the new agenda must be to debate ways by which adequate income is assured for each member of civil society, while accepting that this income will be gained from work, welfare and wealth. Politicians and policy makers and voters need to consider not only ways of maximising income from the first and third of these sources. They must similarly be concerned with how income derived from work and wealth, together with welfare, can be made to match the needs of a lifetime which, for a growing proportion of us, now exceeds eighty years.

NOTES

1. See Ashby and Butters (1989).
2. HC Debates (1990), 18 April, cols 88–9, London.
3. See Chappell (1989).
4. Field (1990b).
5. Field (1990a), pp 176–8

REFERENCES

Ashby P and Butters T (1989) *Britain's New Underclass*, Full Employment UK, London.

Chappell P (1989) Are Pensions Unduly Privileged? Address to Confederation of
British Industry Annual Pensions Conference, 28 September.
Field F (1990a) *Losing Out: The Emergence of Britain's Underclass.*
Field F (1990b) Letter to *The Independent*, 27 March, and *The Guardian*, 16 April.
HC Debates (1990) 18 April, col 88-9, London.

14.2   FAMILY POLICY: TIMOTHY RAISON MP

SUMMARY
This section begins by referring very briefly to the main developments in
social policy since Mrs Thatcher came to office in 1979, and then turns to
its main theme, family policy. It seeks to define family policy, and argues
that the increasing breakdown of traditional family life and marriage is creating a mounting quantity of human hardship, which should be faced by
those concerned with social policy. Divorce, in particular, seems to create as
many problems as it solves.

What can be done about all this? Perhaps the trend towards making divorce 'easier' should be reversed. But ways should also be examined of how
the social security and tax systems might be made to give more support to
family life. The value of Child Benefit is stressed, and the possibility mooted
that it might be doubled. Enlarged Child Benefit looks a better approach to
the problem of child care than do special tax concessions. The need for
expansion of pre-school education is stressed, as is the need for adequate
rented housing for less well-off families.

SOCIAL POLICY IN THE 1980S
As the years of Mrs Thatcher's government passed by, so the pace of change in
social policy accelerated. In the first years after 1979, there was indeed a rather
cautious attitude towards change, for all the philosophising. The main concern
in those years was to try to bring public spending under tighter control – a task
not made easier by the high unemployment of that period. This in turn led to
a series of attempts to obtain a firmer grip on local government spending,
whether funded by central government or by the ratepayer. It also led to an
early decision to break the automatic linking of Retirement Pensions to earnings as well as to the cost of living. A start was made too with tightening up
the management of the National Health Service, and with increasing choice for
parents in the education system. Politically very significant, the very successful
policy of allowing tenants to buy their council houses got under way – and in
due course had to be accepted by the Labour Party.

But it was not, however, until the second half of the 1980s that the
major changes of direction took place. In 1986 came the Social Security
Act, which considerably changed the income-related benefits, truncated the

State Earnings Related Pension Scheme (SERPS), yet kept child benefit – perhaps overall a less radical reform than had been expected, but still significant. The 1983-7 Parliament also saw the abolition of the Metropolitan County Councils and the Greater London Council – both actually creations of the Conservatives. Then after the 1987 election came the major series of reforms embodied in the 1988 Education Reform Act, the 1988 Housing Act, the 1988 Local Government Finance Act and the 1990 National Health Service and Community Care Act. The National Curriculum, the abolition of the Inner London Education Authority, the reshaping of the funding of higher education, the further clipping of the local authorities' housing wings, the Community Charge and the Unified Business Rate and the creation of self-governing hospitals were but some of the major changes brought in.

So it was a hectic period; but it is not my purpose here to describe or analyse what happened – and indeed it is too early to make any comprehensive assessment of the results. Tables 14.1 and 14.2 may, however, help to indicate certain trends. The first shows the movement of certain benefit levels between 1978 and 1990. The picture revealed is not one of very dramatic change, though the breaking of the link between retirement pensions and earnings (as opposed to prices) has had an effect which is begin-

Table 14.1: Benefit levels, 1978-90 (at equivalent value of April 1990 prices for retirement pensions and child support, and April 1987 prices for supplementary benefit)

Year (month varies with benefit changes)	Standard rate retirement pension for man or woman on own insurance (under 80)	Supplementary benefit for single householder (short term) (exclusive of housing costs)	Levels of support for two-child family on average earnings (benefit and tax allowances)
	£	£	£
1978	47.52	28.94	14.89
1979	48.38	29.17	18.43
1980	48.88	29.94	17.10
1981	47.60	29.55	16.88
1982	49.72	30.66	17.71
1983	49.15	30.53	18.77
1984	49.24	30.77	18.84
1985	49.95	30.86	18.26
1986	49.65	30.73	18.22
1987	48.54	30.40	17.82
1988	48.66		17.15
1989	47.72		15.87
1990	46.90		14.50

(*Source*: DSS *Abstract of Statistics*, HMSO 1990)

Table 14.2: Real weekly earnings after income tax, National Insurance contributions and child benefit: by selected family type**, †*

	1971	1981	1985	1986	1987	1988	Percentage change 1971-81	1981-8
Single man								
Lowest decile pt	75.4	82.3	85.7	88.9	91.5	96.8	9.2	17
Median decile pt	111.5	122.2	131.8	138.4	145.0	154.8	9.6	26
Highest decile pt	176.4	199.0	219.1	233.0	250.7	273.2	12.8	37
Single woman								
Lowest decile pt	48.4	61.5	67.5	69.8	71.6	75.2	27.1	22
Median decile pt	67.5	84.9	92.6	97.0	101.5	108.4	25.8	27
Highest decile pt	105.3	137.7	143.2	155.0	164.9	182.8	30.8	32
Married man no children								
Lowest decile pt	80.9	88.7	93.8	96.9	98.9	104.0	9.6	17
Median decile pt	117.0	128.5	139.9	146.3	152.4	161.9	9.8	26
Highest decile pt	181.9	205.3	227.1	240.9	258.0	280.4	12.9	36
Married man‡ 2 children§								
Lowest decile pt	94.7	102.8	109.2	112.2	114.0	118.5	8.6	15
Median decile pt	130.8	142.6	155.3	161.7	167.5	176.4	9.0	23
Highest decile pt	195.7	219.4	242.5	256.3	273.1	294.9	12.1	34

(*Source*: Inland Revenue)
* At April 1988 prices
† Figures relate to April each year and to full-time employees on adult rates whose pay for the survey pay-period was not affected by absence
‡ Assuming no wife's earnings
§ Aged under eleven

ning to be revealed in these figures. The effect of the failure to uprate child benefit in line with price rises in the later 1980s can be clearly seen from the figures.

Table 14.2 shows what happened during the 1970s and 1980s to the earnings of certain groups in work after income tax, National Insurance contributions and child benefit have been taken into account. Between 1981 and 1988, net real earnings, after allowing for inflation, increased at the median point of distribution by at least 23 per cent. The prosperity of all groups, except the least well-off single women, increased by more in the 1980s than in the 1970s – in many cases substantially more; the better-off earners generally gained most. The Thatcher government's approach was never to claim that all would gain equally: it was to postulate that all would gain in real terms, if only the obsession with relative wealth and poverty could be forgotten.

FAMILY POLICY IN THE 1990S

But it is not primarily the 1980s that concern me. I want rather to consider a theme that seems to be creeping up on us in social policy in the 1990s – a theme that is somewhat different from the questions of the distribution of resources that normally dominate social policy, though they do come into it. I can best describe the theme as family policy.

What do we mean by 'family policy'? Is it simply a piece of rhetoric, useful to provide a phrase for a manifesto or a Party Conference speech? Is it something more – a pudding into which a ministerial Jack Horner can put his thumb and draw out a plum and say what a good boy is he? Or could it be the implementation of a coherent strategy of support for parents in their task of bringing up their children?

In my view, it is the third of these lines that we should follow; but first we have to say what we mean by a family. There is a modern tendency to say that where there are children there is a family, and that family policy simply means providing for children; but in reality it should mean more than that. It should entail backing for the family as the institution in which children are most likely to thrive, and support for marriage as the cement most likely to hold the traditional nuclear family together and provide the stability which most children need. Sadly, this institution is under great pressure today.

Let us start by summarising the statistics of family breakdown. There were 27,000 divorce decrees absolute granted in the United Kingdom in 1961 and 166,000 in 1988 (down from 175,000 in 1985). Divorce has escalated particularly in the lower socio-economic groups, who are least able to cope with its financial consequences. Live births outside marriage went up from 54,000 to 198,000 over the same period. They are now over one-quarter of births in England and Wales. The percentage of births registered in the joint names of the parents increased from 38 per cent to 70 per cent, but it seems very probable that such unions will not endure as long as marriages: indeed there is research evidence to that effect. In 1987 there were about 900,000 unmarried couples in Britain, with more than 400,000 dependent children. Between 1961 and 1985 the number of single-parent families rose from 474,000 to 940,000. Of the 940,000 single parents heading families, 370,000 were divorced women, 180,000 single women, 175,000 separated women, 120,000 widows, and 95,000 men. Between 1970 and 1986 the number of divorced couples with one or more children under sixteen rose from 35,876 to 86,286.

There has been some slowing down in certain aspects of family breakdown but overall the statistical picture is reasonably clear. So, too, is the fact that family breakdown or single parenthood tends to lead to impoverishment, housing problems and particular difficulties over child care. A report by the National Council for One-Parent Families[1] showed that the average household income for one-parent families was consistently below half that of two-parent families; that in 1986, 93.8 per cent of single mothers were dependent on supplementary benefit; and that the signs were that single-parent families were disproportionately represented among the homeless. The particular problems of single parents with young children who wish to work are obvious.

Of course, many single parents cannot in any sense help their plight and many bring up their children admirably, but there seems little doubt that crime is particularly prevalent among the children of single parents. It is said, for example, that something like 80 per cent of the inmates of the Aylesbury Young Offenders Institution, which takes the worst offenders in the 17-21 age group, are from broken homes.

The impact of the mounting divorce rates seems peculiarly sad. What should be done? Polly Toynbee has proposed that

> the State should do more to support the increasing numbers of one-parent families which result from the rising divorce rate ... Women and children will suffer needlessly until the State faces up to the reality of its inability to do anything about the revolution in national morals. What it can do is shape a society that makes a place for women and children in family units, self-sufficient and independent, protecting children as effectively as possible from the worst effects of divorce.[2]

In a sense, her argument is that the feminist revolution still has to be completed, but what was striking about the article was its bleak honesty about the unhappiness that divorce brings.

> Divorce is a financial catastrophe for most families. Women and children lose an average of half their income after divorce ... Remarriage is by far the best prospect for women ... But failure of second marriages is even greater, with two-thirds ending in divorce ... The blow falls doubly hard on children. A fifth of all children will see their parents divorce before they reach 16. Evidence is now mounting that shows quite how badly they suffer emotionally, educationally and financially. And the effects for most last right on until adult life. This is partly for emotional reasons and partly because they will have a childhood significantly poorer and in worse housing than children of the same class whose parents didn't divorce.

Research conducted by Gwynn Davis and Mervyn Murch at Bristol University[3] indicates that 51 per cent of men and 28 per cent of women regret having divorced, and that, even having remarried, 37 per cent of men and 21 per cent of women wish they were still married to their former spouse. And, in Polly Toynbee's view, even where divorce leaves the adults, or one adult, happier, the children almost certainly are not.

Yet in spite of all this, the conclusion is that all we can do is to accept the fact of marriage breakdown and try to offset its effects through state action. The damage that divorce can do to children above all is recognised, yet there is no willingness even to contemplate a reversal of the trend. A similar view has been expressed by Lady Ewart-Biggs.[4] She accepts that 'there is undoubted evidence that divorce is very bad for children', deplores the 'weakening or diminution of the traditional family', yet argues that 'it is important to accept the changing patterns of family life by recognising single parent and reconstituted families as a fact to be accommodated'.

The essence of this position is feminist; it comes down, in effect, to the conclusion that the interests of the child should be ultimately secondary to the right of the mother to be free (if usually miserable). The Law Commission5 too has stressed the interests of children, but their approach is essentially to try to contain the hardships involved in the divorce process, rather than to do anything more fundamental. And they stand by the principle of 'no-fault' divorce.

Perhaps the introduction of this principle – even more than easier divorce – has been the real error. I would not argue that fault *always* lies with one party, any more than I would argue that divorce should be abolished; but it may well be that, as the notion of fault of a guilty party has been ended, so the sense of responsibility has also diminished. For what comes through, time and again, in cases of family breakdown is the selfishness shown by those involved.

But, it will be said, this is mere moralising. What can be done about it? Obviously the first point is to decide that the family is worth taking active steps to support. This is partly a matter of moral support. It is partly a matter of the law: bluntly, divorce should be made harder – not easier – to obtain. It is also a matter of such practical measures as tax and benefit policies. Politicians should perhaps be chary of carrying too great a share of the moral burdens of society; but they do make the laws and determine tax and social security provisions.

The new tax arrangements which came into force in April 1990 provided a married couple's allowance, replacing the existing married man's allowance. This is in a way welcome, as it supports marriage, although there is comparable relief for unmarried couples *where there are no children*. Clearly it is where there are children that the greatest support is likely to be needed.

In some ways, the easiest method of giving that support is to extend tax allowances to cover children, as indeed used to be the case. It has the advantage that many people seem to accept the notion of tax allowances, even though they benefit the rich, while they will not accept the notion of nonselective benefits. However, child tax allowances have the drawback that they do not help those who do not pay tax – a substantial, and one might hope increasing, proportion of the population. The less well-off therefore can only be helped by targeted benefits, at present family credit and income support.

Until the late 1970s child tax allowances were combined with taxable family allowances. But the two were replaced by the much simpler untaxed child benefit, which involved no means testing or tax asssessment, as well as being paid to the mother as family allowances had been. Although the government has appeared to be intent on running down child benefit, its practical advantages – so long as there is any general policy of providing help with the upbringing of children – seem evident. The more generous it can be, the less are we forced to rely on selective benefits. The latter not only carry the burdens of means testing and low take-up, but also lead to the poverty trap and may in some degree encourage deliberate single parenthood. We are, of course, a long way from the point where child benefit does not need to be supplemented by some level of targeted benefit for those with special needs; but the nearer we get to that point the less the requirement for such special benefits as the single-parent allowance.

Obviously a policy of trying not to reinforce single parenthood by providing too much in the way of special cash benefits or housing leads straight into the argument that the children, who cannot be held responsible for their condition, will suffer; and of course public policy must see that they are provided for at an acceptable level. But in this provision it is reasonable that the cost of supporting the young single parent and her child should be shared where possible with her own family and voluntary agencies rather than be seen as the exclusive duty of the state.

But if the emphasis in policy should be on child benefit rather than either selective benefits or tax allowances, it clearly follows that child benefit has to be provided at a level which will enable it to do its job effectively. From April 1990, the weekly rate of benefit of £7.25 was received by 12,020,000 children in Great Britain. The cost of this was likely to be in the region of £4.5 billion. What would happen if there were a dramatic increase in the rate of child benefit – say, a doubling to £14.50 a week? Provided that there were corresponding savings in family credit and income support payments, the net increase would be £3.4 billion – a very large sum, which on the face of it would be out of the question. But there is another possibility if we are prepared to look at benefits and taxes together. If the married couple's tax allowance were to be dropped, that would make available an estimated £5 billion which could be spent on increased child benefit. If it were kept only for couples where either spouse was sixty-five or over, the saving would be £4.5 billion.

To do this would of course, in a way, run against the grain of what I have been arguing – that we should give specific support to marriage. But against this would be recognition that it is where there are children that the burden on married couples is greatest, and that a redistribution in their favour would be only just. On top of this there would also be some redistribution to the least well-off parents – those who are too poor to benefit from tax allowances (although they are entitled to varying levels of targeted benefits).

There are those who argue that to switch so large an amount from tax relief to benefits would be a tactical mistake, in that benefits seem more vulnerable to cuts. The benefit would, of course, have to be index-linked in line with other benefits. But it will also be held that so sudden a switch would be too hard on married couples without children. If that were accepted, it would be perfectly feasible to phase the change-over, say, between three and five years. It would also still be possible, at no cost to the Exchequer, to set aside over £1 billion for a reduced married couple's allowance. Above all, of course, there would be the cry that millions – perhaps even billions – of pounds were going to families that did not need them. But child benefit unquestionably does more for the less well-off than do tax allowances.

One of the most difficult areas of family policy is the effect of children on the ability of the parents to go out to work. The desire to get out of the house and the desire to earn money are both understandable. It would be wrong to penalise the working single parent by clawing back his or her earnings through a corresponding loss of benefit; but an enlarged child benefit could in due course do away with the need for the special single-parent benefit. It is also right not to load the odds against the parent (single or married) who stays at home to look after her child. Tax relief on child care costs means that the parent who stays at home is doubly disadvantaged: she or he receives neither earnings nor tax relief. Again the provision of higher child benefit points in a fairer, more neutral direction. It might also do something to help overcome the feeling of inferiority that is being induced among women who do not go out to work.

Having said this, however, I firmly believe that we need a major expansion of education for the under-fives, particularly in the three to five age range. Attendance should be voluntary and school places should be provided by both the public and the private sectors: the target should be that it should be available for all three- and four-year olds. The arguments for this were set out in the House of Commons Select Committee Report, *Educational Provision for the Under-Fives*, published in January 1989. They are rooted fundamentally in the educational and social needs of children rather than in the desirability of equal opportunities for women to work, which has sometimes been the key factor in the case for greater educational provision for pre-school age children.

Coupled with the right tax/benefit structure for the support of the family must be adequate housing provision. A true family obviously needs a home. The spread of home ownership seems very much in line with an effective family policy, but clearly there are those who cannot afford to buy. They have to be able to rent. Housing benefit has proved to be an important part of the answer: the January 1989 public expenditure White Paper estimated that in 1989-90 well over four million households would be in receipt of rent rebates and allowances. The stock of council housing has declined as more houses have been sold off, but there were still 4.32 million houses in 1987-88. The emphasis in new 'social' housing has, however, switched from council housing to housing association provision. Indeed, the 1989 White Paper says that in most cases local authorities should not need to build new houses themselves. In one or two cases, such as Chiltern District Council, local authorities have completely handed over the actual provision of housing to housing associations. This is welcome, so long as families are actually housed; but it is impossible not to feel concern about the position in some parts of the country. The emphasis is normally on those designated as homeless – a condition often caused by family breakdown or family disputes. However, this emphasis, understandable though it is, tends to overshadow conventional needs in areas of shortage where new council housing is disappearing and the voluntary sector is not strong enough to take on the job. The new approach is that local authorities should take on the role of 'enablers' – that is, that they should make sure that needs are met by somebody, but not necessarily by themselves. It is very important that the job should be done effectively. For the time being, at least, that may require continued local authority building, certainly in areas where the private rented sector and housing associations cannot cope with the load.

The hardest area of all in terms of family policy is the area that might loosely be described as morality. It is an error for politicians to take on themselves the main burden of prescribing sexual morality in particular – this is a task for the churches, other voluntary bodies and individuals themselves. But the politicians have to make the law and dispense resources: they have to decide what to do about divorce, family planning, Aids, and so on, whether through legislation, education or particular schemes. They know that it is a hard and unpredictable task. Thus the 1967 Abortion Act and the provision of family planning by the NHS were followed by more, rather than fewer, illegitimate births – though no one can be quite sure why. Similarly, the heavy promotion of the use of condoms may or may not lead to a reduction in Aids: its direct value to prevention *could* be offset by the further relaxation of sexual taboos and the further undermining of the monogamous basis of family life. In other words, even if Aids is reduced other evils may increase. This, of course, particularly applies to those anti-Aids advertisements which do not stress the dangers of promiscuity.

Difficult waters indeed – as is the whole question of the impact of the media on personal behaviour and on crime. Again, evidence on cause and effect is far from decisive, but there is surely enough violence, cruelty, theft, drug-taking, drunkenness and degradation generally to lead us to the view that, for all that may go wrong inside any family, it is folly to allow tax/benefit policy to undermine the family as the crucial institution in combating these evils. Maybe the condition of family life is stronger than the gloomier facts suggest. But if it is, it still needs the support of a family policy that is more than mere political platitudinising.

NOTES

Part of the second half of this chapter first appeared in *The Spectator*, 10 February 1990. The author is grateful for permission to reproduce it.

1. National Council for One-Parent Families (1988).
2. Toynbee (1989).
3. Davis and Murch (1988).
4. HL Debates, 29 November 1989.
5. Law Commission Report (1988).

REFERENCES

Davis G and Murch M (1988) *Grounds for Divorce*, Clarendon Press, Oxford.

HMSO (1989) *Educational Provision for the Under-Fives*, House of Commons Select Committee, London.

HMSO (1990) *Abstract of Statistics*, Department of Social Security, London.

HL Debates (1989) 29th November, London.

Law Commission Report (1988) *Facing the Future*, London.

National Council for One-Parent Families (1988) *Helping One-Parent Families to Work*, London.

Toynbee P (1989) The Worm Turned Syndrome, *The Observer*, 10 September.

15 On Rediscovering the Middle Way in Social Welfare
Robert Pinker

15.1 LIBERTY AND WELFARE

The title of this volume, *The State and Social Welfare*, acknowledges that the idea of welfare encompasses a variety of ends while leaving open the question as to how these ends are to be pursued. As Tom and Dorothy Wilson, among others, remind us, welfare is not the only concern of the state, and statutory social services are not – and need not be – the only providers of welfare (Chapter 1).

The case in favour of following a middle way in the pursuit of welfare objectives rests on an overriding commitment to the ideal of a free society and an acceptance that compromises have to be made between a number of equally desirable political objectives which cannot be reconciled to everyone's complete satisfaction by appeal to any particular guiding principle. As Isaiah Berlin observes, 'In a society dominated by a single goal there could in principle only be arguments about the best means to attain this end – and arguments about means are technical . . . they can, at least in principle, be reduced to positive sciences.'[1]

In free societies, however, there cannot be a 'total acceptance of any single end' and, given this inability to accept any objective as ultimate, it follows that in such a society: 'The reality of political questions presupposes a pluralism of values.' Only in totalitarian societies is this plurality subordinated to 'one absolutely specific, concrete, immediate end, binding on everyone.'[2]

This issue is explored by Raymond Plant in Chapter 4, where he reviews the debate between the advocates of negative and positive versions of liberty. Liberty itself becomes a contested concept as soon as it is applied to the substantive problems of economic and social policy. Neo-liberals who see negative liberty as sufficient in itself view almost all forms of statutory welfare as a threat to freedom, and dismiss the concept of social justice as lacking in specificity and moral authority. Collectivist advocates of positive liberty link freedom to act with ability to act and link this ability in turn with rights and access to certain basic social services.

Nevertheless we are all familiar with these arguments and counter-arguments and we know perfectly well that Raymond Plant's conclusion will no more settle the issue to everyone's satisfaction than will the counter-arguments of Hayek, Joseph, Murray and the other neo-liberals, and the reason why the dispute cannot be concluded is that there is cogency and substance on both sides of the argument.

The range of policy options in social welfare constitutes one of the several institutional dimensions of a more general and continuous debate about what the relationship should be between the state, civil society and the individual citizen. At this level there are plenty of descriptive and analytical models which categorise the policy options but the distinctions which Alan Peacock draws in Chapter 2 between libertarian, social market and collectivist positions are readily acceptable for most practical purposes. These distinctions can be applied to Nicholas Barr's discussion of pension schemes, where he explores the degree of voluntarism or compulsion consistent with various policy objectives in social security (Chapter 8). The models also have obvious conceptual links with the distinctions which Tom and Dorothy Wilson draw between the different 'poverty levels' used as policy objectives.

Alan Peacock reminds us of Muller-Armack's definition of the middle position – the 'social market economy' – as one in which the values and ends of the free market economy are reconciled with 'the demands of distributive justice' (Chapter 2). At the same time he draws attention to differences in emphasis and priority between the social market economists who want to preserve private ownership within the productive market and those who favour both competition within the productive market and more state intervention to enforce greater equality in the ownership of capital resources on the lines advocated by John Stuart Mill.

Whether we conceptualise the middle ground as a point of departure or arrival, or simply as the natural place to be, is a matter of personal biography; but there is an alternative and more starkly dichotomous model which explains the political survival of the middle ground in terms of unavoidable deadlock. I refer here to Michael Oakeshott's argument that 'Hidden in human character, there are two powerful and contrary dispositions, neither strong enough to defeat or put to flight the other'. The first of these dispositions, Oakeshott suggests, is 'to be "self-employed", in which a man recognises himself and all others in terms of self-determination', and the second is 'a disposition to identify oneself as a partner in a common enterprise ... the search for Truth, the pursuit of the Common Good ... It is a co-operative undertaking and therefore in terms of managerial decisions about performances; and there is a notional "one best way of conducting it" '.[3]

From these two dispositions follow conflicting views about the role of the state in political life. On the one hand the state is conceptualised as a civil association based solely on a system of rules, or a covenant, under which citizens go about their own business while recognising a common authority. In this kind of state there is no role for redistributive economic or social policies because the state has nothing to distribute. The alternative view is one in which the state becomes the agent of various common enterprises directed towards a number of collective and enlightened ends such as greater prosperity and more social justice. Over time this version of the modern state becomes synonymous with an idea of a welfare state which Oakeshott describes as 'an association of invalids, all victims of the same disease and incorporated in seeking relief from their common ailment, and the office of government as a remedial engagement'.[4] The most insidious feature of this process, once started, is that the state increasingly involves itself in the affairs of civil society and the private lives of its citizens. In an unremitting 'quest for community' the state becomes part of the community (and vice versa), and the distinctions between the formal and informal dimensions of welfare activity – so essential to personal liberty – are lost.

Western parliamentary democracies, with their mixed economies of welfare, are manifestly not dominated by either of Oakeshott's two contrary dispositions. They reflect a state of ideological deadlock, or compromise, in which neither disposition is 'strong enough to defeat or put to flight the other'.[5] Nevertheless, as Jack Wiseman illustrates in Chapter 3, the pressures exerted by the numerous social groups with vested interests in state welfare are always pushing in the collectivist direction and thereby stretching further and further the boundaries of coercive propriety. The outcome is a bewildering labyrinth of contradictions and compromises which annoy radical collectivists and liberal individualists in equal measure.

15.2   DEFINING THE MIDDLE WAY

Definitions of the middle way are as fraught with problems of relativity as are definitions of poverty and need. What is construed as the middle way is always subject to the contingencies of time and place, and historical comparisons yield little consistent guidance in this matter. Viewed from the perspective of A.V. Dicey's *Law and Opinion in the Nineteenth Century*, published nearly a century ago, Mrs Thatcher's Britain would have seemed like his nightmare vision of bureaucratic collectivism come true.[6] When Harold Macmillan wrote his 'classic statement of liberal collectivism', entitled *The Middle Way*, in 1938 he set out proposals for nationalisation and other forms of state intervention, which Mr Kinnock and his senior colleagues would probably find too radical for the Labour Party today.[7] In 1942 William Beveridge was looked on as a radical collectivist reformer but by 1976 Vic George and Paul Wilding were categorising him as a 'reluctant collectivist', and it is a moot point where Beveridge ranks today in the respective hierarchies of esteem in the British Conservative and Labour parties.[8] As for Keynes – another of George and Wilding's reluctant collectivists – there is no doubt as to where he stood in Mrs Thatcher's demonology but evidence of his continuing influence on contemporary Labour Party thinking is hard to come by.

Throughout the 1980s successive Conservative governments reaffirmed their determination to reshape British social policies on neo-liberal lines, with the eventual aim of reducing the role of the state and encouraging the growth of welfare pluralism – that is to say, the provision of services by a variety of agencies, official and private. So far the changes have been marginal rather than radical – much to the chagrin of the government's more libertarian supporters.

As for the Labour Party, the 1980s were years of frustration and disappointment after the loss of three general elections in a row between 1979 and 1987. Since then, in its policy reviews, the Labour Party seems to have undergone a late conversion to welfare pluralism, although its new policies are significantly more collectivist and egalitarian than those of the Conservatives. Although Frank Field takes care to describe his contribution in Chapter 14 as 'a personal perspective on welfare policies', the reader is left in doubt as to where the boundaries between the personal and the party-political should be drawn. In effect Field sets out a radically redistributive programme for the reform of the British systems of taxation and social security, without once mentioning socialism. At the end one is left speculating as to the kind of political party – other than a socialist one – that would implement such a programme or could do so successfully except within the framework of a broader socialist strategy.

Clearly the path towards welfare pluralism can be followed either from ideological conviction or from electoral necessity, and it is not therefore surprising that the term is identified with some significantly different social welfare objectives. There is one version in which the range and variety of service providers is increased but the statutory authorities of central and local government continue as the main source of funding, through transfer payments of one kind or another. There is also a second version, in which a new plurality of service providers is developed as an *alternative* to statutory funding, with the ultimate goal of privatising the finance of social welfare itself. John Gray, for example, offers 'a pluralist solution for welfare', in which 'Policy ought to aim to return provision to private hands under a regime of lower taxation and targeted voucher schemes'. Gray argues that 'There will always be a need for some means-tested benefits, that a voluntarist version of Bismarckian self-insurance has considerable promise and that (partly because of the costs of targeting) there is no reason why some benefits should not be universal.'[9]

Welfare pluralism is clearly becoming such a diffuse concept that it can be fitted with equal facility into both institutional and residual models of welfare. Pluralism is intrinsic to Jack Wiseman's 'public choice perspective' (Chapter 3) and Alan Peacock's review of welfare payments (Chapter 2). It is a central element in the descriptive and analytical content of Nick Barr's discussion of pension schemes (Chapter 8) and in Charles Carter's review of the changes in public opinion which have supported the government's retreat from unqualified universality in welfare (Chapter 6). Alan Ryan's emphasis on the role of 'enablement' as a possible justification of the welfare state rests on the premise that we should try to minimise interference in people's choices while guaranteeing a basic range of services (Chapter 5). Alastair McAuley describes the accelerating trend towards pluralism in the Soviet welfare system (Chapter 10).

15.3   CONFLICTS WITHIN PLURALISM

Nevertheless, as we have noted, within the broad framework of this seeming consensus on welfare pluralism, there are still some clear ideological differences regarding what the objectives of the welfare state and the scope of its responsibilities ought to be. As the Wilsons observe, there are disagreements about what the minimum level of guaranteed support should be and whether the state should be responsible for any provision above a safety-net level (Chapter 1). Linked to this issue is the vexatious subject of defining poverty, whether it is definable and whether absolute and relative criteria of need can ever be reconciled.

Secondly, there are differences of view about the extent to which social policies should be used as agents of horizontal and vertical redistribution. Central to this area of the debate are the conflicting explanations of the causal relationship between poverty and inequality and the importance which should be attached to the relative dimension of need. It follows that if poverty is *defined* as both a relative and an undesirable state, it can only be eliminated by ending inequality.

Thirdly, there are disagreements about the extent to which statutory social policies can and ought to serve as agents of solidarity and as moral exemplars for other forms of political and economic behaviour. The belief that this should be the overarching strategic objective of the welfare state pervades all the work of Richard Titmuss, in sharp contrast to F.A. Hayek's view that the notions of social solidarity and social justice are respectively indefinable and misleadingly tendentious. The normative core of Titmuss's approach rests on the premise that only statutory social services provided universally on the basis of need can guarantee the growth of a positive association between citizenship, service usage and self-respect. Conversely Hayek asserts that comprehensive welfare provision by the state destroys the disposition towards self-help and undermines the constitution of liberty. Self-respect and dependency on the state, he argues, are incompatible conditions.

Fourthly, there are conflicts between pluralists concerning the extent to which freedom of choice should be extended at the expense of uniformity of provision with regard to the division of welfare responsibilities between the statutory, voluntary and private sectors. There are several possible dimensions to the pluralist division of welfare. In pension schemes the role of the state can be limited to a compulsory basic flat-rate benefit, to be topped up on a voluntary basis by private schemes. In principle at least this approach can be applied to health and other social services with the state supplying basic services and the individual supplementing these services, or even substituting for them, by private purchase. Alternatively the state could limit its role to the provision of cash payments or vouchers for specific services which recipients could spend as they chose in the statutory, voluntary or private sectors. The proposals presented in a report to the British government for the reform of the personal social services are yet another variation.[10] Cash payments would be made not to the individual concerned but to local authorities, which would be responsible either for supplying themselves, or for buying in, the services required. British housing policy has always been pluralist; but in the 1980s the role of government in subsidising the provision of public housing has been sharply curtailed while at the same time expenditure on means-tested housing benefits has gone up. Perhaps the most radically individualist form of pluralism within an institutional model of welfare would be one which maximised both choice and potential access to services, by relying mainly on generous transfer payments.

In their introductory essay Tom and Dorothy Wilson touch on all these issues of conflict and value choice in reviewing what they see as the main options in income maintenance policy – to limit state provision to a static poverty level, to aim for a fully relative poverty level rising in line with average earnings or to settle for a qualified relative poverty level which 'rises less than current earnings but permits some adjustment to increasing affluence' (see above, p 18). Each of these three options has different redistributional implications and, as the Wilsons point out, there comes a point in compulsory pension schemes at which people begin to resent 'official arrangements that will prevent them from determining their own chosen patterns of lifetime expenditure' (see above p 20).

The provision of benefits in kind imposes further restriction on freedom of choice, which, for particular benefits, may nevertheless be thought acceptable. The Wilsons describe and analyse these cases – in particular the health service – and draw attention to the conflict between different objectives which then emerges. A further conflict between various objectives would be encountered, as they suggest, if it were proposed to substitute a negative income tax for cash benefits.

None of the contributions in this volume offers a welfare panacea, and all of them accept the need to reconcile welfare objectives with economic realities and with the right of individual choice implicit in the institutions of pluralist democracies. Some measure of the changes in expert and lay opinion which have occurred during the last thirty years can be gauged from reading, or re-reading, Titmuss's two essays, 'The Irresponsible Society' and 'The Social Division of Welfare', both published in the second half of the 1950s.[11] The message in both essays was uncompromising: a significant expansion in the role of the private and voluntary sectors at the expense of statutory services would – by generating new social divisions relating to access and entitlement – undermine the quest for equity, add to inequalities and weaken social solidarity. The tenacity with which the principle of a unitary and institutionally dominant statutory welfare system has been defended owes much to the influence of Titmuss. In the West this rearguard action has been a uniquely British phenomenon, as has been the growth of a separate discipline of social administration within the social sciences.

This process of subject specialisation, which coincided with the creation and development of the post-war British welfare state, brought together what Alan Peacock describes as 'a wide range of influential writers on welfare state problems' who viewed the statutory social services as a permanent and pre-eminent feature of modern industrial society (Chapter 2). The Titmuss school went further than this, however, in so far as they saw these services as potential agents of radical social change and redistribution which would transform Britain into a more egalitarian, altruistic and socially unified nation.

For an academic discipline so preoccupied with the goal of solidarity, it is ironic that the relations of the discipline of social administration with the other social sciences throughout the 1950s and 1960s were so fraught with conflict and suspicion. During the years of the Titmuss ascendancy the discipline increasingly took on the character of a collectivist enclave of scholars besieged by amoral economists, predatory lawyers and untrustworthy sociologists. Entrepreneurial values were deemed to be intrinsically antipathetic to social welfare values. The new discipline became synonymous with a collectivist ideology in which the concepts of social need, social justice and equity as equality were virtually sanctified as self-evidently first-order principles. The economic study of welfare problems also suffered from this artificial division of labour as it became more theoretically polarised and isolated from substantive, first-hand understanding of social policy institutions.

It was not until the economic recession caused by the international oil crisis of the mid 1970s that these barricades of mistrust between the social sciences began to break down in the field of British social welfare studies. Up to that time the concept of need and the imperative of meeting need had dominated social policy literature. The extra resources were to be found by raising levels of taxation both absolutely and in relation to rising economic growth. Belief in the virtues of monopolistic state provision was reinforced by this complacent assumption that the harder wealth producers worked the more they could be taxed. After the first checks in welfare expenditure between 1974 and 1976 there was a quickening of interest in resources, incentives, efficiency and effectiveness. Pluralism and the expansion of consumer choice in a more mixed economy of welfare came to be seen as acceptable policy objectives within the discipline of social administration.

Certainly there had been some major advances in knowledge within this tradition, notably in the field of empirical investigation into the extent and nature of social injustice. Nevertheless, as I argued at the time in *Social Theory and Social Policy*, this evidence had been generally 'related to both claims and counter-claims of a moral kind, and their translation into political programmes of action and ideology'.[12] The arguments were directed more towards moral and political ends than academic ones.

Tony Atkinson, in his chapter on the determination of benefit scales in Britain, properly draws a distinction between the 'presentation of political argument' and the 'scientific analysis of social policy' (Chapter 7). Political arguments are bound to arise in a subject field such as social welfare but in the post-war history of British social policy studies the political disagreements became so embedded in the academic debate that they often impeded the process of scientific enquiry itself. For example, the academic debate about the determination of benefit scales and a national minimum was too often subordinated to a wider dispute about the strategic objectives of social policy.

Many collectivists objected strongly on moral and political grounds to the idea of the state limiting its income support services to a static minimum level. On the other hand some neo-liberal individualists objected with equal vigour to the idea of the state becoming so deeply and *unconditionally* involved in providing support beyond a minimum level. Consequently the significant definitional advances which have been made in this highly complex field of enquiry have not received the recognition they deserve, simply from dislike of their normative and political implications.

If pluralism as a model of social welfare and inter-disciplinary pluralism as a mode of social enquiry go together, the post-war history of British social policy studies casts some light on the reasons why both enterprises developed so belatedly in this country – at least within the subject field of social policy itself. If welfare pluralism is synonymous with the normative middle ground in social policy studies, it is because no single political, social or economic welfare objective should be treated as being more important than the others and no single social science can be accorded a more central academic role than the others. Social administration becomes – with economics, social philosophy, political science, sociology and so on – part of a broader inter-disciplinary undertaking, and if this is too ambitious an enterprise, it will be sufficient to describe it as a step in the direction of reconstituting a modern discipline of political economy.

The normative character of a pluralist welfare position based on this degree of inter-disciplinarity accommodates a range of value positions reflecting the diverse ideologies of democratic welfare-capitalism. Its normative membership is equally diverse, including natural conservatives who are content to defend the status quo, whatever that happens to be, and those who wish to move policies a little towards the collectivist left or the individualist right.

The pluralist approach to welfare accepts the obligation to guarantee certain standards of security from poverty and need, while acknowledging that there can be no absolute normative consensus as to what these standards should be. It recognises the importance of permitting diversity of choice within a mixed economy of social services as far as this is practically possible. It does not see the relief and elimination of poverty as an objective which is inconsistent with inequality.

Albert Weale argues that because objectives inevitably conflict in public policy it is all the more desirable that policy choices should be made – and be seen to be made – on a principled basis (Chapter 12). He goes on to suggest three functional procedures of central importance in the appraisal of policies. These consist of programmatic statements of the principles involved, explicit statements of the conflicts which arise in the selection and ordering of policy objectives and the systematic and continuous assessment of the effects of policies on public welfare. Any attempt to improve the quality of the services provided in a pluralist society is bound to generate conflicts of interest and value, and Weale considers that these functional procedures are a precondition of informed public debate on issues of public policy. As he remarks at the end of his essay: 'If we cannot secure consensus about the outcomes that we value, then the *processes* by which we reconcile our differences of viewpoint assume that much more importance, for those processes become our reference points of assessment.' (See above, p 250.)

The pluralist approach to welfare is essentially sceptical and pragmatic and, while accepting the need to define objectives, never for a moment assumes that the pursuit of these objectives will produce entirely satisfactory solutions. It therefore follows that all pluralists, libertarian or otherwise, will accept Jack Wiseman's general rule of a libertarian society 'that *there should be no rule which does not embody a rule/procedure for its own peaceful change*'. (See above, p 65.)

Pluralists also recognise that the enhancement of welfare is conditional on the creation of wealth but at the same time accept that conflicts between economic and social policy objectives are bound to occur and that they can never be more than provisionally or partially reconciled.

15.4   PLURALISM AND DEMOCRACY

These conflicts are unavoidable because, as T.H. Marshall points out,

> The trouble is that no way has been found of equating a man's value in the market (capitalist value), his value as a citizen (democratic value) and

his value for himself (welfare value). But that is not all. The democratic and welfare components have each its own internal, unsolved problem – how to find a balance, so perfect as to silence all discontent, between equality of persons and their circumstances on the one hand and equality of opportunity, that great architect of inequality on the other . . . The problem is structural in origin, but there is no purely structural solution to it.'[13]

Marshall goes on to claim that the institutional contradictions of democratic welfare-capitalism should be seen as evidence of its social resilience and strength rather than as a weakness. In any event 'The task of banishing poverty from our "ideal type" society must be undertaken jointly by welfare and capitalism. There is no other way – . . . [apart from] . . . something more totalitarian and bureaucratic, and that is not at all what the more novel and significant elements in the movements of protest are seeking.'[14]

Democracy allows free play to the welfare interest groups which preoccupy public choice theorists, as markets provide for the expression of consumer preferences and the determination of prices, but the respective criteria by which the democratic system and the market system work often come into conflict with each other. Western critics of Russian and Chinese experiments in liberalising their socialist economies have been quick to point out that you cannot have freely competitive markets without freely democratic political institutions. They are less willing to recognise that the institutional processes of representative democracy inevitably create market imperfections in the furtherance of social welfare objectives. Undue reliance on the 'trickle-down effect' under conditions of minimal statutory welfare provision is as likely to destroy the basis of political stability in democracies as is an excess of dirigiste social planning. The genius of the market economy lies not in its capacity to function well under conditions of near perfect competition but in the fact that it functions with reasonable efficiency under conditions of imperfect competition, and it still remains to be seen whether a form of democratic socialism can be devised which allows the market economy to work as efficiently as it does in non-socialist societies.

How, then, are we to construct a set of welfare objectives which take account of Marshall's three competing criteria, the market values of capitalism, the democratic values of citizenship, and the welfare values of social policy? From a pluralist perspective we start by recognising that each of these values merits respect and consideration but that none of them can claim a status of absolute superiority over the others. Furthermore there is ample historical evidence to suggest that market values and welfare values are both subject to a political equivalent of the law of diminishing marginal utility and that the democratic process works reasonably well, despite its imperfections, as the mechanism through which these shifts in marginal preferences are expressed. Advocates of proportional representation argue that the process would work even better if political parties had to be more immediately and continuously responsive to the plurality of changes in public opinion. As Albert Weale observes, 'in the absence of proportional representation, political protest has to be channelled through one of the two major parties.' (See above, p 241.) In this respect democracy is itself a contested concept.

What we know about public attitudes to social welfare at the beginning of the 1990s suggests that there is a substantial basis of electoral support for middle-of-the-road pluralist policies and that the groundswell of support in Britain for the Thatcher administration's more radical neo-liberal policies was never, in fact, as strong as it has been commonly supposed. There is also the evidence of public opinion surveys in the election year 1987 – and later – that the main trends in public attitudes to welfare ran counter to the social policies of the Conservative government, which had won its third successive election victory. Although the Conservatives favoured tax cuts at the expense of greater welfare spending, increased private provision in place of state welfare and increased reliance on selectivity, the majority of voters expressed general support for adequate levels of statutory provision. Only a very small minority wanted tax cuts at the expense of welfare.[15] At the same time there was not much electoral support across the parties (including Labour) for greater equality or more redistribution, even if these policies meant higher taxes. The Conservatives won in 1987 despite a widespread lack of sympathy with their social ideology because voters placed greater importance on economic considerations. Labour lost because of widespread doubts about its ability to manage the economy, because it seemed to be less united as a party than the Conservatives and because it was still expected to introduce radical socialist policies if it was elected.

The key findings of the British Social Attitudes research and other surveys suggest that the biggest single group of voters – ranging from just over 40 per cent to over 50 per cent, depending on the surveys used – support an institutional version of welfare pluralism. They want to keep the existing welfare state system, with more scope for the private and voluntary sectors. The great majority, however, oppose any further run-down in state services, and want more services rather than tax cuts and privatisation. The clear message is that 'Neither socialist planning nor free enterprise enjoys majority support' among British voters.[16] The largest single group of voters seems to favour a pluralist model of welfare in which the state continues to play a major role.

This is not, however, to argue that both the institutional and residualist models of welfare no longer have political relevance. Beneath the middle ground of pluralist consensus there are still some fundamental disagreements about the role of the state as the main source of social service funding. In continental Europe too there are still some fundamental, ideological differences of view with regard to the sovereignty of nation states as such and the kind of community in which authentic sovereignty can coexist with common membership.

15.5 COMPARATIVE PERSPECTIVES

This leads to the comparative and more specifically European dimension, which has profoundly changed the ideological frames of reference within which we were once accustomed to think about social welfare. Almost up to the time that we joined the Common Market it was a central tenet of conventional wisdom that Britain pioneered the creation of the first major post-war welfare state and that the post-war reforms of 1945–50 set the altruistic standards which other, less enlightened, European nations have been striving to reach ever since. The main anxiety of British collectivists and socialists in the 1960s was that the broad universalist structure of the British welfare state would be subverted by contact with the social market economies of Western Europe.

However the comparative welfare league tables looked a quarter of a century ago, it is ironic – and a revealing index of social and political change – that Mrs Thatcher's anxieties about the provisions of the Social Charter stemmed from the conviction that its provisions were too collectivist and too egalitarian. The fact of the matter is that collectivist and competitive market values seem to coexist quite happily with the versions of welfare pluralism which have developed elsewhere within the European community. British collectivists mistook the absence of universalist forms of social service provision for a lack of commitment to the ideals of collectivist welfare.

As Mangen makes clear, however, Britain has always been much more concerned with the relief of poverty in absolute terms than have our continental neighbours, to whom the idea of solidarity is more closely linked with preserving social status over the individual lifespan by means of earnings-related benefits (Chapter 9). Under Mrs Thatcher the British government curtailed the scope of the State Earnings Related Pension Scheme (SERPS) in 1988. At the same time it was probably less preoccupied than previous British governments with the relief of poverty – which largely accounts for its reservations about the more egalitarian provisions of the Charter.

Other recent political events, I suggest, have broadened our comparative knowledge and interest beyond the boundaries of the European community. Mr Gorbachev's dramatic opening up of the Soviet Union and, by association, other Eastern European socialist countries has fundamentally changed the terms of the debate between neo-liberals, middle-of-the-road collectivists and socialists. The adoption of policies of *glasnost* and *perestroika* have shown unequivocally that highly planned economies do not work (Chapter 10).

When we put together the evidence from Western and Eastern Europe, two things stand out: in the European community, welfare pluralism is the norm rather than the exception but, within these mixed economies of welfare, the state – through the various institutions of central, regional and local government – still plays a vitally important role in the financing and general direction of social policies. In Eastern Europe the tides of government policy and public opinion would appear to be moving away from centralised state planning towards more competition, free enterprise and welfare pluralism.

15.6   THE TRIUMPH OF CONVERGENCE THEORIES AND THE END OF IDEOLOGY?

What then do all these momentous changes signify with regard to the future of European social welfare policies? Do the developing trend towards welfare pluralism, the growing membership of the European Community, the impending implementation of the European Community Single Market Act in 1992 and – most remarkably of all – the recent revolutionary events in the Soviet Union and Eastern Europe signify the end of radical welfare ideology and a vindication of the various convergence theories which were so confidently advanced and so widely rejected by radicals of the left and the right in the 1960s?

Convergence theory was developed and espoused by a number of leading sociologists at that time, notably S.M. Lipset, Daniel Bell and Raymond Aron.[17] These theorists began by contrasting 'traditional' and industrial societies in terms of their respective scale, their institutional differentiation and the complexity of their divisions of labour. They went on to emphasise the common economic and technological characteristics of industrial societies. While recognising the marked political and ideological differences between capitalist and socialist societies, they categorised them as two distinct subtypes of industrial society which were becoming more similar over time.

Another widely influential book at this time was *Industrialism and Industrial Man* (1962) by Kerr, Dunlop, Harbeson and Myers.[18] These writers advanced a thesis called 'the logic of industrialism', which rested on the premise that, as industrial societies develop, they become increasingly responsive to the same kinds of economic and technological imperatives. The phenomenon of class conflict which characterised these societies in their early stages loses its appeal and potential as an agent of social change. The growth of representative democracy, the diffusion of economic prosperity and the development of statutory social services all contribute to the reduction of extreme social inequalities and the mitigation of class conflict.

As long as economic growth is maintained and welfare expectations are largely met, capitalist societies will be characterised by normative consensus rather than ideological conflict. Piecemeal social engineering rather than radical change will be the order of the day. As Lipset wrote at the time in *Political Man*, some ideologically motivated intellectuals have a tendency to imagine that members of the general public might become dangerously apathetic unless they find themselves confronted with political extremes.[19] This complementary thesis was developed in greater detail by Daniel Bell in his major work, *The End of Ideology*. His argument and analysis were supported by other theories predicting the convergence of social classes and a gradual change in the profile of class structure in advanced industrial societies from a pyramid with a broad base of poor and low-income workers and a small apex of very wealthy people to a lozenge shape with a narrow apex and base and a broad band of prosperity containing the majority of citizens. This was, of course, the embourgeoisement thesis – the middle-range theory of social stratification, which complemented the macro-theories of convergence and the end of ideology.[20]

The comparative scope of these theories included both capitalist and socialist societies. As capitalist societies adopted some of the collectivist features of socialist societies, so would socialist societies adopt some of the free-market and pluralist features of capitalism. In short, the argument went, we were witnessing the end of ideological extremism and, as capitalist and socialist societies became more alike, we would witness the end of ideology itself.

Ten years later, in the mid 1970s, Harold Wilensky was arguing in *The Welfare State and Equality* that ideology was far less important a determinant of social policies than intellectuals imagined.[21] There *was*, he claimed, a general trend towards convergence in social policies but they did not always move in the same direction. He identified two general and countervailing trends – governments which come to power supporting policies of welfare cutback become more disposed towards welfare spending as their terms of office extend, and governments which start out supporting high welfare spending end up cutting back on welfare budgets. Perhaps the most influential model of social welfare to emerge from this period of debate was Marshall's model of democratic welfare-capitalism.

Social scientists at the time and since then have disagreed sharply about the credibility of these theories. It was argued that convergence theory was premised on a very short timespan of thirty or forty years, that trends in the embourgeoisement of class structure oversimplified highly complex processes of normative change and that the persistence of extreme poverty among a minority of people in capitalist societies, along with the mounting evidence of racial and sexual inequalities, meant that significant differences still persisted within and between capitalist societies, giving rise to new forms of ideological conflict. Finally it was argued that theories positing the end of ideology were themselves highly ideological in their tacit acceptance of the status quo and the apparent trends towards pluralist political systems.

Looking back on these debates and the political events which have followed them, it seems that the evidence throughout Western Europe of a general trend towards embourgoisement is clear-cut despite the persistence of poverty in a much diminished residuum of relatively deprived people. It is when we look at the socialist societies of Eastern Europe with the benefit of all the new evidence emerging from *glasnost* and *perestroika* that we are confronted with industrial nations riven with extremes of social and ethnic inequality, grossly inadequate social services and standards of living which are strikingly low outside the worlds of their privileged political elites.

The evidence of convergence is limited to the wealthier mixed capitalist societies of Western Europe. In economic, social and political terms the Eastern socialist societies are far more remarkable for their differences than for their similarities. Only in terms of their rising aspirations and expectations are they beginning to move in the same direction. We must also question whether economic and technological imperatives have been of such overriding causal significance in the dynamics of social and political change as Clark Kerr and his associates argued in the early 1960s. As Raymond Aron observed with more subtlety at the time, 'Even if, as optimists suppose, industrial societies do tend to resemble each other, it does not follow that they will arrive at the same moral outlook . . . Something more than affluence is needed for the spread of political democracy.'[22]

Rather than talking about the end of ideology it would be more accurate to talk about a growing disenchantment and scepticism regarding the two great ideologies which have dominated political life since the industrial revolution – the theories of classical political economy in their purest, competitive liberal, form which provided the rationale for that revolution, and the Marxist tradition of theory which provided the counter-critique and offered an alternative path to social development.

15.7   PLURALISM, CONVERGENCE AND THE EUROPEAN COMMUNITY

In the West it is equally unclear how far the movement towards ideological convergence will go and what varieties of pluralism will be accommodated within the Community. How far convergence will be permitted to go remains to be seen but the success of the Community will depend on our ability to reconcile the goals of economic and social policies, to achieve compromises between the different national interests and political ideologies which specify these goals and to secure a state of mutual tolerance for differences which cannot be reconciled. The idea of the *internal market*, with a European currency and exchange rate mechanism provides for a high degree of economic interdependence and depends on a great deal of ideological forbearance on the part of member states. The same can be said about the provisions of the Social Charter. These new institutional arrangements will apply to nations with very different traditions of social welfare and economic development.

A comparison of recent trends in the social policies of Britain and the original six founder-member states reveals some interesting differences as well as similarities. If there is an overall trend towards convergence it is neither unilinear nor consistent in direction. The original six member states are and always have been, from the 1950s onwards, pluralist or mixed economies of welfare. Steen Mangen examines the social security systems of two of the founder-member states, West Germany and France, along with Spain (Chapter 9). His analysis shows very clearly the diverse nature of welfare pluralism and the distinctive institutional arrangements deriving from the different political traditions which characterise these three countries.

By contrast the British welfare state from 1945 to 1979 functioned as a set of protective institutions dominated by the statutory services and resources of central and local government. Although the occupational welfare sector grew steadily throughout this period, successive governments were largely content to work within the broad statutory framework set up between 1945 and 1948. Since 1979, however, British social policies have been moving closer to the pluralist models of continental Europe, as the Conservative government has actively encouraged the growth of the occupational, private and voluntary sectors as potential *alternatives* to statutory provision. Once again, however, judgements about the relative significance of these trends towards convergence depend upon which continental country is chosen as the point of reference.

Secondly, for the past fifteen years, Britain, in common with all the countries of Western Europe, has been struggling to contain or cut levels of welfare expenditure in response to a series of economic crises and against a background of mounting demand and rising levels of expectation. Mangen illustrates the diversity of the initial responses to these crises on the part of his three chosen countries – and also the similarity of the eventual outcomes. In the early 1980s the whole ideological thrust of the German government's *Wendepolitik* was towards cutting back on state welfare expenditure but these policies had to be pursued within a tradition of cross-party consensus and corporatism. By the mid 1980s retrenchment was giving way to 'stabilising strategies' and modest expansion in some welfare provisions. To date, at least, the neo-liberal transformation of the German welfare state has not taken place. In the cases of France and Spain, newly elected socialist governments launched major expansionary reform programmes in the early 1980s, but these were gradually cut back in response to rising unemployment and budgetary deficits.

If any common trend emerges from the recent history of social policies in these three countries, it is that such convergence as has occurred has been the outcome of economic necessity rather than ideological preference. Even within the broad tradition of continental pluralism there is considerable diversity in the sources and methods of welfare funding and in the forms of service delivery.

Thirdly, however, Britain has been moving in the direction of increasing central government control, while the rest of Western Europe has been moving towards increasing decentralisation. This was the great contemporary paradox of British social policy during the Thatcher years – a radical government determined to roll back the frontiers of the state at one and the same time delegated more welfare responsibilities to non-statutory authorities as well as to the market, while exercising stricter control than ever before over the statutory services which it had retained. This is explained by the central government's deep mistrust of local government, which left it without an alternative authority to which services could be delegated within the statutory sector. Consequently central government departments were much more directly involved in the regulation, monitoring and sanctioning of local government activity.

Mrs Thatcher was caught in that iron law of political change which states that the more radical are the changes intended, the more power must be concentrated in the hands of the central government, even if the overriding objective is to reduce the responsibilities of the central government. Mangen shows how much more powerful and authentic is the tradition of decentralisation to regions and localities in Germany, France and Spain than is the case in Britain. Even in France a process of transferring responsibilities from central to regional and departmental authorities belatedly took place after 1982.

The views which Mrs Thatcher expressed in 1988–9 at Bruges and Madrid are indications that ideological divergence is still alive in Western Europe. At Bruges she remarked that 'We have successfully rolled back the frontiers of the state in Britain only to see them re-imposed at a European level . . . The Treaty of Rome was intended as a charter for economic liberty – our aim should not be more and more detailed regulation from the centre. It should be to de-regulate, to remove the constraints on trade and to open up . . .'

In Madrid Mrs Thatcher focused her attention on the then draft proposals for a European Charter, equating their provisions with bureaucratic control and socialism, notably those relating to a guaranteed minimum wage, schemes for job creation and for tackling unemployment, continuous job development and training and increased worker participation. Other proposals concerning health and safety, the encouragement of cross-national labour mobility and transferability of pension rights, social security rights for migrant workers and the mutual recognition of technical qualifications were more sympathetically received.

In this debate Mrs Thatcher was marked out as the major dissident, in conflict with her European partners. Closer analysis of the social and economic policies of some of these partners suggests, however, that differences of political tradition and ideology persist in continental as well as insular forms. A general convergence towards welfare pluralism is taking place but its institutional character still differs markedly across the member states. There were certainly inconsistencies in Mrs Thatcher's appeal for increased economic deregulation in Europe and her dirigiste control of social policies within Britain. At the same time this dirigisme was directed towards libertarian welfare ends, and it was entirely consistent with her objection to some of the European Charter proposals, notably with regard to wage regulation, employment guarantees and worker participation. Indeed it is difficult to see how these provisions, if implemented, would be consistent with the requirements and objectives of the European Monetary Union.

The rest of Western Europe has always followed pluralist policies in social welfare, and Britain is now moving in that direction with the growth of occupational pensions, the sale of council houses and the encouragement of private and voluntary initiatives in health care, education and the personal social services. We may then ask whether, in the long run, a process of convergence will ensure the achievement of compromise and coexistence within the same Social Charter. In my view the disagreements over the Social Charter turn not so much on the momentary dissimilarities in the directions of social policy as on divergent visions of the future of social policy. The rest of Europe seems to have settled for a middle-ground version of pluralism in which the state continues to play a major role either directly or indirectly. It remains to be seen whether British social policy continues to move towards a more radical model of pluralism in which privatisation programmes will reduce the role of the government to a residual status, despite the evidence of electoral resistance to these objectives.

Unlike the other European Community member states, Britain has a first-past-the-post electoral system, which inhibits the growth of new centre parties. Middle-ground pluralist policies in Britain are the order of the day when *both* of the two big parties are strong and neither can win a substantial majority over the other in Parliament. Over the 1980s the British Conservative governments grew more radical and more openly ideological as their majorities increased. We have to go back to 1945–50 to find a period when Labour held a comparable majority and the Conservative opposition was in relative eclipse. Even then the radical collectivist policies which led to the creation of our post-war welfare state were only possible because of massive US Marshall Aid. Unlike the other Western European beneficiaries of Marshall Aid, Britain gave the implementation of new social policies priority over the restructuring of the economy. The economic facts of life did not catch up with Britain until the late 1960s. In the meantime the rest of Western Europe was following more cautious pluralist policies giving priority to economic regeneration and developing social policies at a more gradual pace as they could afford to do so.

The Soviet Union and the eastern bloc nations rejected the offer of Marshall Aid and failed not only to modernise their economies but also to create the wealth needed for social reform. Now they are in a similar position to that of Britain in 1945 – whether they wish to democratise their socialism or create open, competitive market economies, their chances of success without massive aid from the mixed capitalist economies of the West look quite remote. This is hardly a scenario for the end of ideology and a relatively trouble-free transition to some form of welfare pluralism, since the peoples of Eastern Europe have yet to discover and articulate in a climate of greater freedom their own singular visions of a better future.

15.8   CONCLUSION

Firstly, the processes of social change in occupational structure, the distribution of wealth and income and the growth of powerful vested interests in statutory social services which cut across the social classes suggest that, in representative democracies, the majority of voters will reject the ideological extremes of both neo-liberalism and collectivist or socialist planning.

Secondly, democratic welfare-capitalist societies have so far been manifestly more successful than any other kind of society in raising general living standards and reducing the incidence and scope of extreme poverty. There is as yet no convincing evidence that the workings of competitive capitalist markets have been seriously compromised by the costs of statutory social welfare or that the limitations which statutory social welfare imposes on personal liberty are more politically significant than the extensions of personal liberty which it provides to poorer citizens. At least it can be said that after decades of scholarly argument we are no nearer than we were to agreeing on a felicific calculus which will settle these questions once and for all.

Thirdly, despite the conflicts which arise between the objectives of economic and social policy in democratic welfare-capitalist societies, the evidence suggests that socialist societies which lack competitive market economies have been much less successful in maintaining general living standards and the quality of social services.

Fourthly, membership of the European Community will in time make pluralists of us all, although, as I have argued, there will be great diversity in the models of pluralism among the member states beyond the minimalist requirements of whatever kind of social charter is eventually implemented.

Neither the European Community nor the impending implementation of the Single Market Act in 1992 is likely to mean the end of ideological conflict within and between member states but they will continue to impose institutional limitations on radicals of all persuasions. Nevertheless it can be argued that it was the vagaries of the international economy rather than the requirements of the Community which had the most inhibiting effect on the freedom of member states to implement radical changes in their social policies throughout the 1980s. Each member state had to reach a compromise between its welfare aspirations and economic realities, and these compromises rather than any clear-cut realisation of policy objectives account for the diverse forms of welfare pluralism which have prevailed throughout the Community. If, however, member states eventually press on to full monetary union, social policy options are bound to be more closely circumscribed by the terms of this union and those of the European Charter. It remains to be seen what kind of Community will emerge. In the aftermath of Mrs Thatcher's resignation it was possible that the case for diversity would win more supporters as it ceases to be exclusively identified with the interests of the United Kingdom.

NOTES

1. Berlin (1980) p 149.
2. *Ibid* pp 150–2.
3. Oakeshott (1975) pp 323–4.
4. *Ibid* p 308.
5. *Ibid* p 323.
6. See Dicey (1905).
7. See Cutler *et al* (1986) p 27; Macmillan (1966).
8. George and Wilding (1976) pp 42–61.
9. Gray (1989) p 62.
10. See HMSO (1988).
11. Both essays are now available in Abel-Smith and Titmuss (1987).
12. Pinker (1971) pp 105–6.
13. Marshall (1981) p 119.
14. *Ibid* p 121.
15. Taylor-Gooby (1987) p 4; Heath and Evans (1988) p 55.
16. Lipsey, Shaw and Willman (1989) pp 7–8.
17. See Lipset (1960); Lipset (1964); Bell (1960); Aron (1967).
18. See Kerr *et al* (1962).
19. See Lipset (1960) chs 10, 13.
20. The embourgeoisement thesis is critically discussed in Goldthorpe and Lockwood (1963) and Runciman (1964).
21. See Wilensky (1975).
22. Aron (1967) p 242.

REFERENCES

Abel-Smith B and Titmuss K (eds) (1987) *The Philosophy of Welfare: Selected Writings of Richard Titmuss*, Allen and Unwin, London.
Aron R (1967) *Eighteen Lectures on Industrial Society*, Weidenfeld and Nicolson, London.

Bell D (1960) *The End of Ideology*, Free Press, Glencoe, USA.

Berlin I (1980) Does Political Theory Still Exist? in Berlin I *Concepts and Categories: Philosophical Essays*, Oxford University Press, Oxford.

Cutler J, Williams K and Williams J (1986) *Keynes, Beveridge and Beyond*, Routledge and Kegan Paul, London.

Dicey A V (1905) *Lectures on the Relations between Law and Public Opinion in England in the Nineteenth Century*, Macmillan, London.

George V and Wilding P (1976) *Ideology and Social Welfare*, Routledge and Kegan Paul, London.

Goldthorpe J and Lockwood D (1963) Affluence and the British Class Structure, *Sociological Review*, July.

Gray J (1989) *Limited Government: A Positive Agenda*, Institute of Economic Affairs, London.

Heath A and Evans G (1988) Working-class Conservatives and Working-class Socialists, in Jowell R, Witherspoon S and Brook L (eds) *British Social Attitudes: The Fifth Report*, SCPR, Gower, Aldershot.

HMSO (1988) *Community Care: Agenda for Action: A Report to the Secretary of State for Social Services* (Griffiths Report), London.

Kerr C, Dunlop J, Harbeson F and Myers C (1962) *Industrialism and Industrial Man*, Heinemann, London.

Lipset S (1960) *Political Man*, Heinemann, London.

Lipset S (1964) *The First New Nation*, Heinemann, London.

Lipsey D, Shaw A and Willman J (1989) *Labour's Electoral Challenge*, Fabian Research Series 352, Fabian Society.

Macmillan H (1966) *The Middle Way*, St Martins Press, London.

Marshall T H (1981) *The Right to Welfare and Other Essays*, Heinemann Educational Books, London.

Oakeshott M (1975) *On Human Conduct*, Oxford University Press, Oxford.

Pinker R (1971) *Social Theory and Social Policy*, Heinemann Educational Books, London.

Runciman W (1964) Embourgeoisement: Self-rated Class and Party Preference, *Sociological Review*, July.

Taylor-Gooby P (1987) Citizenship and Social Welfare, in Jowell R, Witherspoon S and Brook L (eds) *British Social Attitudes: The 1987 Report*, SCPR, Gower, Aldershot.

Wilensky H (1975) *The Welfare State and Equality*, University of California Press, California, USA.

APPENDIX
Social Security in the UK

The National Insurance arrangements in the UK are somewhat unusual in that one unitary system covers the whole employed population for all insured risks. One earnings-related contribution paid jointly, but not in equal shares, by all employees and employers gives entitlement in general to all insurance benefits. These benefits are flat-rate in the sense that they are unrelated to previous earnings, but are paid at higher rates in the case of long-term risks such as retirement, invalidity or widowhood and at lower rates for short-term interruption of earnings by unemployment or sickness. In the case of pensions there are state earnings-related supplements (SERPS) to the flat-rate benefits unless the employees have been covered by alternative occupational or private pension arrangements.

The insurance arrangements are complemented, to an unusual degree, by state financed non-contributory benefits, available on a national basis at the same rates and on the same conditions of eligibility. Some of these are not means-tested, as in the case of child benefit and special allowances for the disabled. Others are subject to a test of means, such as the income support benefits for non-employed persons, family credits for low-income employed persons with children, and housing allowances for any people with low incomes, whether from earnings, state benefits or private sources.

Unless otherwise stated benefits are taxable and adjusted annually in line with the Retail Price Index. The apparent simplicity of this comprehensive system is deceptive as even the following simplified account shows!

1 NATIONAL INSURANCE BENEFITS

These are financed out of contributions on a pay-as-you-go basis.

CONTRIBUTIONS

Employees earning above a (low) minimum are in general required to pay contributions from age 16 to 65 (men) or 60 (women) (or up to retirement) on all earnings up to a maximum. (This shows that the National Insurance and taxation systems are not fully integrated.) The minimum and maximum are roughly equivalent to 25 and 150 per cent of average male earnings.

The rates of contribution are higher for employees covered by SERPS.

Employers pay contributions on all earnings above the minimum without any ceiling. The rates of contribution vary according as to whether or not the employee is covered by SERPS and are also higher for the upper bands of earnings. This is in effect a tax on employment, and may discourage the use of labour-intensive methods of production. There are substantially higher payroll taxes in many other countries.

BENEFITS
Long-term
Retirement pensions: to qualify for a full pension at age 65/60 contributions must normally have been paid for 90 per cent of working life. Pensions are reduced for 'missing' years of contributions and increased for additional years, up to a maximum of five, worked beyond the retirement age. Married women who have not earned a pension on their own contributions may receive a pension on their husband's contributions, which is equal to about 60 per cent of a full pension.

Widow's benefits: an unusual British feature is the lump-sum payment made to most widows on the death of their husbands if the latter had had an adequate contribution record. They may also be entitled to weekly benefits if they have dependent children or if they are over age 45 at the time of their husband's death.

Widowed Mother's Allowance may be paid to any widow who has at least one child for whom she is receiving child benefit, together with an additional tax-free allowance for each child.

Widow's pension varies with the woman's age at time of bereavement up to age 60 when a full retirement pension is payable. Widows also inherit any SERPS pension which their husbands had earned (but see below).

Invalidity pensions are normally payable after 28 weeks on sickness benefit if the insured person is still incapable of work. The amount paid up to the maximum pension depends on contribution records and there are allowances for dependent adults and children.

State Earnings Related Pensions (SERPS) are payable on top of the flat-rate pensions in respect of contributions paid after 1978 (unless the insured person is covered by an occupational or private pension). If SERPS is already in payment or will be drawn before 1998 the amount is calculated on the basis of 25 per cent of earnings in the *20 'best'* earnings years. This unusually generous formula will be changed by annual stages between 1998 and 2008 to 20 per cent of *average lifetime* earnings, adjusted for inflation. Likewise the widow's entitlement to 100 per cent of her late husband's SERPS will be reduced over the same period to the more usual 50 per cent.

Short-term

Unemployment benefit is paid from the fourth day of unemployment for a maximum of 52 weeks. To qualify the unemployed person must have a prescribed contribution record, must be capable of, available for and actively seeking work. When unemployment benefit is exhausted (or for some reason not payable) the unemployed person can claim income support (see below) for an indefinite period.

Statutory Sickness Pay (SSP): most employees receive SSP from their employers after 4 days of sickness for up to 28 weeks. This is payable at one of two rates according to earnings and is paid together with any occupational sick pay to which the employee may be entitled. SSP is recoverable by the employer from the state.

Sickness benefit (tax free) is payable to employees without rights to SSP, after 4 days of sickness for up to 28 weeks.

2 NON-CONTRIBUTORY, NON-MEANS-TESTED BENEFITS

These are financed out of general tax revenues.

BENEFITS FOR CHILDREN

Child benefit: a tax-free flat-rate benefit paid in respect of children up to age 16, or 19 if disabled or if in full-time education. Unlike other benefits, it has not been regularly indexed for inflation, a controversial issue.

One-parent benefit: tax-free benefit payable in addition to child benefit for the first child of any single parent (divorced, separated or unmarried).

BENEFITS FOR THE DISABLED

These are awarded on the basis of independent medical assessment.

Severe disablement benefit: a tax-free benefit for people of working age who have not been able to work for 28 weeks but have not paid enough contributions to entitle them to National Insurance benefit.

Attendance allowance: a tax-free benefit paid to people needing frequent attendance because of severe mental or physical disability. Paid at a higher or lower rate according to whether attendance is needed by day *and* night or day *or* night.

Mobility allowance: a tax-free allowance for people between ages of 5 and 80 who are unable or virtually unable to walk because of physical disability.

Invalid care allowance: for people of working age who provide at least 35 hours' care per week for a person receiving attendance allowance.

3   MEANS-TESTED BENEFITS

These are financed out of general tax revenues.

Income support is the most important and plays an unusually large part in providing, in whole or in part, an income for people without adequate other means of support, whether from the benefits above, or other sources. It is available to persons of 18 years and over whose resources are below a certain level fixed annually by Parliament. It is not paid to persons in full-time employment and persons under 60 must normally register for work. In assessing entitlement certain amounts of income from other sources may be disregarded and also savings up to certain limits and the value (however large) of an owner-occupied house. The benefits consist of three parts:

(i)   Personal allowances for subsistence which vary with the age, marital status and the number and ages of the children of the applicant.

(ii) Premiums are paid in addition to the above in the case of families, elderly or disabled people and single parents to cover the average expenditure required to meet their special needs.

(iii) Housing allowance (see below).

Family credit: a tax-free benefit for low-income working families who have at least one child under 18. This is in fact a state subsidy for low wages and as such defended as a cheaper way of helping the working poor than increases in universal child benefit.

The amount payable, up to a maximum, depends on the earnings and savings of the parents and the numbers and ages of the children. The maximum rates are payable when the resources of the family are at about income support level and rates are scaled down by 70 pence for each pound earned above this level.

Housing benefit may be paid to low-income persons, whether at work, drawing National Insurance or other state benefits or living on other means. Eligibility for benefit, and the amount paid, is assessed on the basis of income, savings, the numbers and ages of children and the amount paid in rent and Community Charge (the poll tax to cover local authority services). The maximum is actual rent plus 80 per cent of the Community Charge, for which recipients of income support are eligible.

The **Social Fund** is another unusual, and controversial, feature of the British arrangements. The Fund has a budget which is a fixed sum voted annually by Parliament. Out of this grants may be made to low-income families to help them with items such as the costs of a funeral, the equipment needed for a new baby, adaptations to the houses of elderly or disabled persons. Low-interest, repayable budgeting loans may also be made to help people on income support spread the cost of heavy items of expenditure.

4   EXEMPTION FROM NATIONAL HEALTH SERVICE CHARGES

All people of pension age, children under 16, persons receiving income support or family credit are automatically exempt from prescription charges for drugs. (In fact charges are paid for only a relatively small proportion of prescriptions.) People on income support or family credit and all children under 16 also receive free dental treatment and vouchers for NHS spectacles and other benefits such as free school meals. Other people with low incomes may be eligible for some of these benefits free or at low cost on a test of means.

Dorothy Wilson

Index